A MAGNIFICENT FAITH

A Magnificent Faith

Art and Identity in Lutheran Germany

BRIDGET HEAL

OXFORD
UNIVERSITY PRESS

Great Clarendon Street, Oxford, OX2 6DP,
United Kingdom

Oxford University Press is a department of the University of Oxford.
It furthers the University's objective of excellence in research, scholarship,
and education by publishing worldwide. Oxford is a registered trade mark of
Oxford University Press in the UK and in certain other countries

Published in the United States of America by Oxford University Press
198 Madison Avenue, New York, NY 10016, United States of America

British Library Cataloguing in Publication Data
Data available

Library of Congress Control Number: 2017932098

ISBN 978–0–19–873757–5

Printed and bound by
CPI Group (UK) Ltd, Croydon, CR0 4YY

For Guy and Tom

Acknowledgements

The majority of the research for this project was undertaken during a two-year stay in Berlin. I am grateful to the Alexander von Humboldt Stiftung for helping to finance that stay, to Claudia Ulbrich and the staff of the Friedrich-Meinecke-Institut at the Freie Universität for providing me with a home, and to the School of History in St Andrews for making it possible for me to be there for so long. The Herzog August Bibliothek in Wolfenbüttel provided financial support and a welcoming base for two summers. The writing was undertaken with the help of a fellowship from the British Academy. The Carnegie Trust for the Universities of Scotland helped to finance the illustrations. During my time in Berlin, I benefited from many conversations with wonderful colleagues, in particular, Ruth Slenczka, Claudia Jarzebowski, Vera Isaiasz, Nadine Jaser, and Jonathan Strom. Thank you also to the archivists and librarians, in particular Uwe Kahl at the CWB in Zittau for his generous help at the start of the project, and to all the pastors who let me into locked churches. Parts of this research were presented at conferences and seminars in the United Kingdom, United States, and Germany. Thank you to Renate Dürr and Philip Hahn in Tübingen, to Mary Frandsen and to many others for thought-provoking discussions.

Thank you to Bruce Gordon, especially for the time spent in Wolfenbüttel in the summer of 2013 discussing this project, and for reading and providing incisive and supportive comments on the final manuscript. Thank you, as ever, to my *Doktormutter* Lyndal Roper for stimulating questions and encouraging conversations. Thank you to Neil Gregor, my *German History* co-editor for three years, for the intellectual generosity and friendship that have made me think about my material in new ways. Bob Kolb read the whole manuscript in draft—I am hugely grateful for his help and advice on the finer points of Lutheran theology. Clive Holmes did the same and polished the final product skilfully. In St Andrews, thank you to my Reformation Studies Institute colleagues and to all our students—as a Reformation scholar, I feel incredibly fortunate to have ended up here. At OUP, I would like to thank Stephanie Ireland and Cathryn Steele for their enthusiasm, efficiency and patience, and the anonymous readers who commented on the proposal and manuscript. Ben Pope did a fantastic job with the footnotes and bibliography—without him, this would have sat on my desk for many more months. Thank you to my parents, especially my mum, for help and support, both intellectual and practical. The research for this book was carried out with a small child in tow, so thank you Tom for being so wonderfully adaptable, for enjoying Berlin and Wolfenbüttel, and for saying, when confronted with one final Lutheran church (Bückeburg) in the summer of 2014, 'this one is epic'. Finally, thank you to my husband, Guy Rowlands, for making the whole thing possible, both logistically and emotionally.

Contents

List of Figures

List of Plates

List of Abbreviations

BLHA	Brandenburgisches Landeshauptarchiv (Potsdam)
CWB Zittau	Christian-Weise-Bibliothek Zittau
EKLAB	Evangelisches Landeskirchenarchiv in Berlin
GStPK	Geheimes Staatsarchiv Preußischer Kulturbesitz (Berlin)
LW	*Luther's Works*, edited by J. Pelikan, H. T. Lehmann, et al. (St Louis and Philadelphia, 1955–)
StadtAD	Stadtarchiv Dresden
RatsAG	Ratsarchiv/Stadtarchiv Görlitz
Sehling EKO	*Evangelische Kirchenordnungen des 16. Jahrhunderts*, edited by Emil Sehling, Institut für evangelisches Kirchenrecht der EKD, Heidelberger Akademie der Wissenschaften (Tübingen, 1902–)
SHStAD	Sächsisches Haupstaatsarchiv Dresden
SLUB Dresden	Sächsische Landesbibliothek—Staats-und Universitätsbibliothek Dresden
SStAC	Sächsisches Staatsarchiv Chemnitz
SStAL	Sächsisches Staatsarchiv Leipzig
StadtAFr	Stadtarchiv Freiberg (Sachsen)
StadtAZw	Stadtarchiv Zwickau
Thür HStA Weimar	Thüringisches Hauptstaatsarchiv Weimar
WA	*D. Martin Luthers Werke: Kritische Gesamtausgabe* (Weimar, 1883–)

Introduction

In the mid-eighteenth century, the Italian artist Bernardo Bellotto, pupil and nephew of Canaletto and court painter to the Saxon Elector, produced seventeen idealized images of Dresden's cityscape.[1] One, painted between 1751 and 1753, shows the view from the right bank of the Elbe towards the Augustusbrücke and Altstadt (Fig. 0.1). In the foreground are scenes of everyday life on the river; in the background two churches dominate the city's skyline. On the left, rising above the central arches of the bridge, is the Frauenkirche, with its distinctive cupola. On the right, situated between the Augustusbrücke and the Saxon Elector's residential palace, is the *Hofkirche* (court church), its tower still swathed in scaffolding. These two splendid ecclesiastical structures stood as witnesses to Dresden's confessional bifurcation. The Frauenkirche was Lutheran, and its foundation stone, laid on 26 August 1726 in a solemn ceremony that took place before an audience of 10,000, contained a copy of the Augsburg Confession, the 1530 statement of faith that defined Lutheranism. The *Hofkirche* was Catholic, begun in 1739 at the behest and expense of Elector Friedrich August II and his wife Maria Josepha, daughter of Emperor Joseph I. Yet, both churches deployed, in their construction and in their furnishing, the visual idioms of the baroque. The Frauenkirche, designed by George Bähr, accommodated 3,500 worshippers. Its cupola led eighteenth-century travellers to compare it to St Peter's Basilica in Rome, and it was adorned inside with frescoes, stucco work and a massive carved stone altarpiece depicting Christ in the Garden of Gethsemane (Fig. 0.2). The *Hofkirche*, dedicated to the Trinity, was designed by an Italian architect, Gaetano Charivari. The *Hofkirche*'s Catholicism was clearly legible in its multiple side altars and in its paintings and sculptures of saints. Yet, in terms of theatricality and visual splendour, neither church outdid the other.[2]

The aim of this book is to explain how and why Lutheranism—a confession that insisted upon the pre-eminence of God's Word—became, in some parts of the Holy Roman Empire, a visually magnificent faith, a faith whose adherents sought

---

[1] Dirk Syndram, 'Princely Splendour: An Introduction', in Dirk Syndram and Antje Scherner (eds), *Princely Splendour: The Dresden Court 1580–1620* (Dresden, 2004), 17–21, esp. 17.

[2] Amongst the numerous recent publications on the Frauenkirche see in particular Heinrich Magirius, *Die Dresdner Frauenkirche von George Bähr: Entstehung und Bedeutung* (Berlin, 2005). On the *Hofkirche* see Klemans Ullmann, *Katholische Hofkirche Dresden* (Dresden, n.d.); Joachim Menzhausen (ed.), *Ecclesia Triumphans Dresdensis*, exh. cat., Künstlerhaus Wien (Vienna, 1988), especially Siegfried Seifert, 'Das Bildprogramm der katholischen Hofkiche in Dresden, Kathedrale des Bistums Dresden-Meissen', 9–20.

Fig. 0.1. Bernardo Bellotto, view of Dresden from the right bank of the Elbe, 1751–3.
Credit: © bpk | Staatliche Kunstsammlungen Dresden | Jürgen Karpinski.

to captivate Christians' hearts and minds through their eyes as well as through their ears. This is not a history of Lutheran art.[3] Nor is it primarily a history of Lutheran theologians' teaching on images, for that history has been recounted in detail elsewhere.[4] Rather, it is an attempt to incorporate visual evidence, 'the evidence of the arts', into the broader frameworks of Reformation history.[5] It seeks to use images—and textual accounts of their creation and use—to illuminate current debates about confessional culture and identity. Reformation scholarship has long since abandoned its sole focus on doctrine and devotion, on religious leaders and institutions and on the beliefs and practices that they disseminated. It also no longer dwells, in a German context, on confessionalization, on the role that religious confessions—Lutheranism, Calvinism, and Catholicism—played in state-building. This particular paradigm served an important purpose: it confirmed religion's place in the transformations of political and social life that took place during the early modern period.[6] Reformation histories now, however, tend to

---

[3] For a sophisticated elucidation of the Reformation's impact on art see Joseph Koerner, *The Reformation of the Image* (London, 2004).

[4] H. von Campenhausen, 'Die Bilderfrage in der Reformation', *Zeitschrift für Kirchengeschichte*, 68 (1957), 96–128; Margarete Stirm, *Die Bilderfrage in der Reformation* (Gütersloh, 1977); and Sergiusz Michalski, *The Reformation and the Visual Arts. The Protestant Image Question in Western and Eastern Europe* (London, 1993) remain useful works. See also Gabriele Wimböck, Karin Leonhard, and Markus Friedrich (eds), *Evidentia. Reichweiten visueller Wahrnehmung in der Frühen Neuzeit* (Berlin, 2007), especially the essays by Wimböck and Friedrich; Thomas Lentes, 'Zwischen Adiaphora und Artefakt. Bildbestreitung in der Reformation', in R. Hoeps (ed.), *Handbuch der Bildtheologie. Band I. Bild-Konflikte* (Paderborn, 2007), 213–40.

[5] For a stimulating discussion of the use of visual evidence see Francis Haskell, 'Visual Sources and *The Embarrassment of Riches*', *Past and Present*, 120 (1) (1988), 216–26, here 226.

[6] For a recent overview see 'Forum: Religious History beyond Confessionalization', *German History*, 32 (4) (2014), 579–98.

Fig. 0.2. Dresden, interior of the Frauenkirche (pre-1945 photo).

Source: From K. Ellwardt, *Evangelischer Kirchenbau in Deutschland* (Petersburg, 2008), p. 86.
Credit: © Michael Imhof Verlag GmbH and Co.

look more broadly, placing alongside these established scholarly discourses the concepts of confessional culture and identity. They examine mental worlds shaped—at the level of the individual Christian, the family, and the wider community—by a sense of religious belonging.[7] Confessionalization can now be seen not simply as a religious or political policy, but rather as 'a cultural process of identification and self-fashioning'.[8]

The concepts of confessional culture and identity promise much: the recognition of the importance of religion in determining the thoughts, feelings, and actions not only of the educated elite but also of the 'common' man and woman; and the incorporation of a wide variety of sources and approaches—from political and gender history to the history of the senses and emotions—into the writing of Reformation history. Ultimately, these concepts perhaps have the potential to bridge the conceptual gap between church history, often still too narrowly focused on individual reformers, on institutions and on doctrine, and social or cultural history, which in its comprehensiveness may, on occasion, lose sight of the theological ideas that lay at the heart of movements for religious reform. They also, however, bring with them problems common to all such discussions: the danger, for example, of reifying abstract terms, of implying that culture and identity exist outside of the individuals or groups that articulate them, and descend, as the dove of the Holy Spirit descends in so many early modern images, to bestow a uniform religious consciousness upon passive recipients.[9] In fact, as recent scholarship has emphasized, the construction of confessional cultures and identities was a complex and contingent process. There was no static 'Catholic', 'Lutheran', or 'Calvinist' consciousness that could be invoked and imposed from above; rather, each was negotiated within a particular historical setting through a process in which the populace and religious and political elites all played their parts.[10]

Theologians were, as Thomas Kaufmann suggests, the key designers of Lutheran confessional culture; they were its architects and its engineers.[11] Yet, their designs were developed not through the straightforward implementation of Luther's theology, but rather through a process of conflict with fellow Lutherans as well as with Catholics, Calvinists, and others. Even during the era of 'Orthodoxy', after the 1577 Formula of Concord and before the rise of Pietism in the late seventeenth century, Lutheran teaching was far from uniform. Johann Arndt (1555–1621), for

---

[7] See, for example, Thomas Kaufmann, *Der dreißigjähriger Krieg und Westfälischer Frieden: Kirchengeschichtliche zur lutherischen Konfessionskultur* (Tübingen, 1998); Thomas Kaufmann, *Konfession und Kultur: Lutherischer Protestantismus in der zweiten Hälfte des Reformationsjahrhunderts* (Tübingen, 2006); Joachim Eibach and Marcus Sandl, *Protestantische Identität und Erinnerung: von der Reformation bis zur Bürgerrechtsbewegung in der DDR* (Göttingen, 2003); Volker Leppin and Ulrich A. Wien (eds), *Konfessionsbildung und Konfessionskultur in Siebenbürgen in der frühen Neuzeit* (Stuttgart, 2005); Robert Kolb (ed.), *Lutheran Ecclesiastical Culture, 1550–1675* (Leiden and Boston, 2008).

[8] Nicholas Terpstra, *Religious Refugees in the Early Modern World: An Alternative History of the Reformation* (Cambridge, 2015), 307.

[9] Rogers Brubaker and Frederick Cooper, 'Beyond Identity', *Theory and Society*, 29 (1) (Feb. 2000), 1–47.

[10] See, for example, Marc Forster, *Catholic Revival in the Age of the Baroque: Religious Identity in Southwest Germany, 1550–1750* (Cambridge, 2001).

[11] Kaufmann, *Konfession und Kultur*, 25.

example, shaped post-Reformation Protestantism in profound ways. He is a key figure for this study, and his devotional writings, in particular his *Vier Bücher vom wahren Christentum* (*True Christianity*) of 1605–10 and his *Paradiesgärtlein* (*Little Garden of Paradise*) of 1612, were best-sellers. Yet, Arndt was a problematic figure for the Lutheran church, because true evangelical teaching on justification seemed, to some, to have disappeared beneath his extensive discussions of internal spirituality and renewal.[12] Even at the level of theological discourse, defining 'Lutheran' was no easy task. More importantly, perhaps, the *reception* of theologians' and pastors' designs, the process by which they were turned from normative plans into lived religious practices, was far from straightforward. Confessional culture and identity were shaped, this study will suggest, by all members of the community: theologians and pastors; princes and nobles; and the 'common' man and woman. If we imagine early modern Lutheran confessional culture as a church under construction (Dresden's Frauenkirche, for example), then its final form certainly owed as much to its financial patrons, to its craftsmen and artists, and to the members of its congregation as to its original designers.

As analytical tools, both 'culture' and 'identity' lack conceptual clarity. Used without due caution, they may obscure the intricate realities of religious, political and social interaction, and imply a spatial or temporal homogeneity that never in fact existed. Even during Germany's so-called 'confessional age'—the period between 1555, when the Religious Peace of Augsburg guaranteed Lutheranism's legal status, and 1648, when the Treaty of Osnabrück imposed a lasting religious settlement on the Empire—Lutheran confessional consciousness was certainly not uniform or general. Our understanding of Lutheranism has been enriched immeasurably by recognition of the importance of a dynamic of theological conflict during the second half of the sixteenth century; of long-lasting diversity within Lutheran theology and piety; and of the processes not only of confessional demarcation but also of cross-confessional borrowing that took place during the 'confessional age'.[13] Beyond the level of the theological elite, Lutheran identity was understood and invoked by both individuals and groups in ways that were heavily dependent upon immediate socio-political context. The experience of being Lutheran in seventeenth-century Berlin, under the rule of a Calvinist Elector, was, for example, very different to the experience of being Lutheran in seventeenth-century Dresden, at the court of Germany's leading Lutheran prince. Moreover we must, of course, locate religious belonging within complex patterns of allegiance and identification that were shaped not only by high politics but also by social status and gender. At the level of both the individual and the community, confessional identity never

[12] Ibid., 11–12.
[13] See in particular the ongoing Mainz project 'Controversia et Confessio', *http://www.controversia-et-confessio.de/* (accessed 18/02/2016). For a useful summary see Irene Dingel, 'The Culture of Conflict in the Controversies Leading to the Formula of Concord (1548–1580)', in Kolb (ed.), *Lutheran Ecclesiastical Culture*, 15–64. See also Kaspar von Greyerz, Manfred Jakubowski-Tiessen, Thomas Kaufmann, and Hartmut Lehmann (eds), *Interkonfessionalität—Transkonfessionalität—binnenkonferrionelle Pluralität* (Gütersloh, 2003).

existed in isolation: early modern Lutherans, just like everyone else, had multiple levels of self-understanding.

Yet, this knowledge—this awareness of the complex nature of religious identity—must co-exist with recognition of the fact that by the mid-seventeenth century distinct confessional cultures *did* exist across Europe. In the Holy Roman Empire, Lutheran, Calvinist, and Roman Catholic were identifiable to contemporaries not only because of their doctrinal teachings, ecclesiastical structures, and liturgical rituals but also because of their particular social and cultural practices. Without denying chronological and geographical diversity, we can (and must) acknowledge underlying unities. Lutherans adhered, broadly speaking, to the doctrinal tenets of the Augsburg Confession and celebrated communion in particular ways. They also set themselves apart through particular readings of history, through particular commemorative practices, through particular attitudes towards women and family life, and through the uses that they made of music and images.[14] All of these genres—history writing, the commemoration of the dead, domestic advice litera-ture, music and art—were, of course, permeable; none existed, during the early modern period, in a uniquely and exclusively Lutheran form. But all were inflected to some extent by Luther's Reformation. We should ask, therefore, not *whether* there was a Lutheran confessional culture and identity, but rather *why* it was expressed in particular ways at particular times and in particular places, *why* it was felt and articulated more intensely by some individuals and groups than others, and *how far* it extended beyond the sphere of doctrine and devotion.

This study uses images, and attitudes towards the visual, as a lens through which to examine what it meant to be a Lutheran at different times and in different places, and as a yardstick to measure the development of Lutheran confessional culture. The construction of Dresden's Frauenkirche was, as we shall see, impelled by religious conflict within a bi-confessional city. The church was built, literally, upon a copy of the Augsburg Confession, and its interior was designed for Lutheran ritual, for the hearing of sermons and the receiving of communion in both kinds. In all of these ways, it was a monument to Lutheran confessional consciousness. And yet, as an ensemble, it challenges many of our preconceptions about the nature of Protestant visual culture. We know, of course, that Lutheranism, unlike other forms of Protestantism, was rarely iconoclastic. There was some targeted removal of idolatrous images during the early decades of the Lutheran Reformation, and plenty of subsequent neglect of superfluous paintings and sculptures. But many medieval images survived intact and *in situ* in Lutheran churches, and Lutheranism developed its own traditions of printed, painted, and sculpted religious art, most famously in the Wittenberg workshop of Lucas Cranach the Elder (*c.*1472–1553) and his son, Lucas Cranach the Younger (1515–86).[15]

---

[14] Kaufmann, *Konfession und Kultur*, esp. 12–13, 25.
[15] On the survival of images in Lutheran churches see Johann Michael Fritz (ed.), *Die bewahrende Kraft des Luthertums* (Regensburg, 1997). For a recent response, which challenges the notion of straightforward preservation, see Caroline Walker Bynum, 'Are Things "Indifferent"? How Objects Change Our Understanding of Religious History', *German History*, 34 (1) (2016), 88–112.

Cranach the Elder, a close friend and ally of Luther, devised new iconographies for woodcut propaganda and book illustration, produced portraits of the Reformation's leading protagonists and initiated a tradition of evangelical altarpieces with the Schneeberg Altar (1539), Torgau Altar (1545), and Wittenberg Altar (1547), the latter a post-iconoclastic icon that has come to epitomize Lutheran visual culture.[16] It was under his son, however, in the context of the Empire's post-1555 religious settlement, that the production of Lutheran art gained momentum.[17] The funeral sermon preached for Cranach the Younger by Georg Mylius, doctor of theology and chancellor of the University of Wittenberg, stated that his works could be seen, at that time (1586), 'in churches and schools, in castles and houses'.[18] Like his father, Cranach the Younger ran a highly successful business. He worked for Saxony's electoral and ducal courts, for other princes and nobles, and for the burghers of the region's prosperous territorial cities. Throughout the second half of the sixteenth century his Wittenberg workshop produced, alongside many secular works, portraits of the Lutheran reformers, visualizations of Lutheran doctrine, statements of faith on behalf of Lutheranism's political patrons, and furnishings for Lutheran churches. Both in the territories that constituted the heartland of the Reformation and further afield the production of the Cranach workshop was highly influential during the sixteenth century, establishing a number of confessionally specific visual traditions.[19]

For many of the Empire's Lutherans, images—both those produced by the Cranach workshop and others—shaped both private devotion and public worship. But the art that was produced for these Lutheran audiences is often characterized as primarily polemical or pedagogical, as deliberately eschewing the aesthetic pleasures and affective powers of Catholic visual culture. Lutheran images, we tend to believe, were devised primarily 'for the sake of simple folk', to spread and consolidate Reformation teaching in an age of limited literacy. This was, of course, the powerful message of Bob Scribner's seminal work on popular Reformation propaganda.[20] Art historians have adopted different approaches and examined different bodies of evidence, but still tend to emphasize the instructional imperatives that lay behind Lutheran art. Joseph Koerner suggests, for example, in his subtle analysis of the relationship between religious reform and artistic production, that the didacticism required of Lutheran images detracted from their artistic value, making them 'less visually seductive, less emotionally charged, [and] less semantically rich'.[21] From the perspective of church history, Kaufmann asks whether Reformation art can possibly be attributed with a 'sensuous and aesthetic religious

---

[16] See in particular Koerner, *The Reformation of the Image*, 177–85.

[17] Ruth Slenczka, 'Cranach der Jüngere im Dienst der Reformation', in Roland Enke, Katja Schneider and Jutta Strehe (eds), *Lucas Cranach der Jüngere—Entdeckung eines Meisters* (Munich, 2015), 124–37.

[18] Quoted in Enke et al. (eds), *Lucas Cranach der Jüngere*, 91.

[19] Slenczka, 'Cranach der Jüngere', 134.

[20] R. W. Scibner, *For the Sake of Simple Folk: Popular Propaganda for the German Reformation*, 2nd ed. (Oxford, 1994).

[21] Koerner, *The Reformation of the Image*, 28 and 226 ff.

quality' over and above its didactic and commemorative cultural aims.[22] And Meinrad von Engelberg's monumental study of early modern restorations of medieval churches argues that evangelical orientation towards the Word made Protestant *Barockiserung* campaigns 'unnecessary and incidental'. Electoral Saxony developed, he acknowledges, its own baroque style, but he sees this as primarily a secular rather than a sacred phenomenon. It met, he argues, the 'profane representation needs' of its courtly or bourgeois patrons, rather than the spiritual needs of its Lutheran audiences.[23]

At the level of theology, of normative texts, the reasons for such characterizations are not hard to find: the Lutheran rhetoric of images as adiaphora, as matters of indifference to salvation; the absence, in comparison to post-Tridentine Catholicism, of a proper Lutheran theology of images to underpin their use in public liturgy and private devotion; an ongoing concern about the dangers of idolatry; and, on occasion, for example during the 1520s and again during the era of Pietism, a strong condemnation of the financial cost of art.[24] At the level of visual culture, the artistic production of the Cranach workshop still dominates both scholarly discussions and public perceptions of Reformation art. The propaganda, book illustration, portraiture, and church furnishings that emanated from the Wittenberg workshop of Cranach the Elder and his son tend to be characterized as simple in style and as lacking in expressive power. In art-historical studies, Cranach the Elder's early work in Vienna, which is seen as innovative and dramatic, is contrasted with his later work in Wittenberg, which described as formulaic and restrained and is compared unfavourably with that of his contemporaries Albrecht Dürer and Matthias Grünewald. This stylistic shift, perpetuated in the works produced under Cranach the Younger's supervision, may be attributed in part to the pressures of mass production for both court and town in the busy Wittenberg workshop.[25] It may also be attributed, as in Koerner's study of the Wittenberg Altar, to Cranach the Elder's formulation of a Protestant visual aesthetic, an aesthetic that made deliberate use of a simple style, of allegorical iconographies, and of inscriptions in order to reduce the verisimilitude of the image, to protect it and its viewers against the dangers of idolatry.[26] The Cranach style should be understood, recent scholarship suggests, not as a decline in artistic quality, but

---

[22] Thomas Kaufmann 'Die Sinn- und Leiblichkeit der Heilsaneignung im späten Mittelalter und in der Reformation', in Johanna Harberer and Berndt Hamm (eds), *Medialität, Unmittelbarkeit, Präsenz. Die Nähe des Heils im Verständis der Reformation* (Tübingen, 2012), 11–44, here 25.

[23] Meinrad von Engelberg, *Renovatio Ecclesiae: Die 'Barockiserung' mittelalterlicher Kirchen* (Petersberg, 2005), esp. 39, 190, 214.

[24] On images in Counter-Reformation theology see Christian Hecht, *Katholische Bildertheologie in der frühen Neuzeit: Studien zu Traktaten von Johannes Molanus, Gabriele Paleotti und anderen Autoren*, 2nd ed. (Berlin, 2012).

[25] For an overview see Bodo Brinkmann, 'The Smile of the Madonna: Lucas Cranach, a Serial Painter' in Bodo Brinkmann (ed.), *Cranach*, (London, 2007), 17–27; Dieter Koepplin and Tilman Falk, *Lukas Cranach: Gemälde, Zeichnungen, Druckgraphik*, 2 vols. (Basel and Stuttgart, 1974), vol. 1, 12–15; Enke et al. (eds), *Lucas Cranach der Jüngere*, 20–1.

[26] Koerner, *Reformation of the Image*, esp. 221–3, 226.

rather as the result of a deliberate decision, as a method intended to fit art to a new doctrinal context and to create new type of Christian image.[27]

Unlike Cranach's paintings, Dresden's Frauenkirche does not fit easily within our preconceptions of Lutheran art as primarily didactic and commemorative, and as aesthetically restrained. In order to explain how a confession that was rarely iconoclastic, but that did not, initially, grant images a prominent role in religious devotion, became a magnificent faith capable of producing monuments such as the Frauenkirche, this book adopts a broad chronological span. It moves from Luther's response to the iconoclasm of the 1520s, through the confessional disputes and crises generated by the reformer's death, by Charles V's 1548 attempt to re-impose Catholicism throughout the Empire, and by Germany's 'Second' Calvinist Reformation, to the flourishing of baroque court culture during the later seventeenth and early eighteenth centuries. Throughout, the book also moves, as far as possible, between the elite cultures of the princes, nobles, and educated theologians and the popular cultures of the 'simple folk', asking when, where, and why images became part of a broader Lutheran confessional identity. Lutheran culture and identity were, of course, profoundly shaped by the Empire's fragmented political structures, by intense regional diversity. The book also seeks to balance, therefore, the investigation of texts and printed images that had Empire-wide audiences with the investigation of local case studies.

Texts such as Luther's Bible translation and his *Small Catechism* (both of which were frequently illustrated) helped to create a supra-regional sense of confessional identity. So, of course, did events that affected the whole Empire, such as the Thirty Years' War. But confessional culture was also constructed in response to local circumstances. The case studies presented here are drawn, in the main, from Electoral Saxony and Brandenburg, two of the Empire's most important Protestant territories. Each had a very different confessional and political history. Electoral Saxony, the heartland of the Reformation, was ruled by the Albertine branch of the Wettin dynasty from 1547. After the 1577 Formula of Concord it stood, apart from a brief flirtation with Calvinism under Christian I (r. 1586–91), as a bastion of Lutheran Orthodoxy until Elector Friedrich August I converted to Catholicism in 1697 in order to win election to the Polish throne. Although Saxony's electors led the *Corpus Evangelicorum*, the grouping of Protestant Imperial Estates established in the wake of the Peace of Westphalia, they failed to exploit this political capital, and leadership of the evangelical cause effectively passed to Brandenburg and, in the eighteenth century, Hanover.[28] In Brandenburg the Hohenzollern Elector, Joachim II, had introduced a late and moderate Lutheran Reformation in 1539, but in 1613 Elector Johann Sigismund converted to Calvinism. Thereafter Brandenburg's

---

[27] Norbert Michels (ed.), *Cranach in Anhalt: vom alten zum neuen Glauben* (Petersberg, 2015), esp. 13–6.

[28] Herbert Smolinsky, 'Albertinisches Sachsen', in Anton Schindling and Walter Ziegler (eds), *Die Territorien des Reichs im Zeitalter der Reformation und Konfessionalisierung, ii: Der Nordosten,* (Münster, 1991), 8–32; Joachim Whaley, *Germany and the Holy Roman Empire. Volume II: The Peace of Westphalia to the Dissolution of the Reich 1648–1806* (Oxford, 2013), esp. 151; Jochen Vötsch, *Kursachsen, das Reich und der mitteldeutsche Raum zu Beginn des 18. Jahrhunderts* (Frankfurt am Main, 2003).

Lutheran and Reformed Protestants lived in uneasy co-existence: most of the territory's inhabitants remained loyal to the Wittenberg Reformation, but they were ruled over by a Calvinist court. Friedrich Wilhelm, the Great Elector (r. 1640–88), laid the foundations for Brandenburg's rise to power through his military and administrative reforms, and in 1701 Elector Friedrich III was crowned 'King in Prussia' in Königsberg. During the late seventeenth and early eighteenth centuries the territory's religious and cultural life was profoundly shaped by the arrival of religious refugees from France and the Netherlands, and by the growth of Pietism.[29]

What emerges from this broad chronological and geographical sweep is not one coherent narrative, not one detailed map of a path that led ineluctably from Wittenberg in the 1520s to Dresden's Frauenkirche in the eighteenth century. Rather, it is an account of a series of turning points, of particular events and processes that, over the course of 200 years, shaped Lutheran attitudes towards images in two key parts of the Empire. Lutheran confessional culture drew, to a much greater extent than either Catholic or Calvinist, on the authority and memory of one individual figure: Luther himself.[30] The book opens, therefore, with a discussion of the Reformation's legacy, with an account of the developments in Wittenberg during Luther's lifetime that considers both theological discourse and visual culture. Luther's own thoughts on images, which were frequently cited by later authors, were shaped in the crucible of the fiery 1520s, in response above all to the radicalism of Andreas Bodenstein von Karlstadt. Lutheran confessional identity may have developed only gradually, over the course of decades, but here already, in the bitter conflicts of the Reformation's early years, moderation with regard to images distinguished Luther and his followers from those he scathingly labelled as 'Schwärmer' or fanatics. Yet, images were clearly already also much more than just religious markers: incorporated into many of Luther's Bibles and catechisms, they played an important part in disseminating the Gospel. The care with which Philip Melanchthon oversaw the illustration of his early catechetical works, and Luther the illustration of his 1534 complete Bible, suggests that images, even at this early stage, were far from unnecessary and incidental to evangelical devotion.

It was in part at least in dialogue with its early Wittenberg origins that Lutheran visual culture developed during the later sixteenth and seventeenth centuries, the era of the 'confessional image' that forms the focus of Part I of this book. By the time of Luther's death (1546), his followers had found no satisfactory solution to the image question. Although the reformer's writings provided theoretical justifications for the retention and use of religious images, in practice the visual environment in which adherents of the Wittenberg Reformation worshipped varied considerably from place to place: some churches had been thoroughly stripped; others retained almost all of their pre-Reformation furnishings; a few had acquired new, evangelical images. Subsequent developments—the era of crisis that followed the Augsburg

---

[29] Bodo Nischan, *Prince, People, and Confession: The Second Reformation in Brandenburg* (Philadelphia, 1994); M. Rudersdorf and Anton Schindling, 'Kurbrandenburg' in Schindling and Ziegler (eds), *Die Territorien des Reichs, ii*, 34–66; Karin Friedrich, *Brandenburg-Prussia, 1466–1806: The Rise of a Composite State* (Basingstoke, 2012).

[30] Kaufmann, *Konfession und Kultur*, 18 ff.

Interim (1548), followed by the gradual spread of Calvinism in the Empire—embedded images more firmly in Lutheran confessional consciousness. This was, as ever, a complex and contingent process: in Ernestine Saxony, for example, the removal of altars and altarpieces served, briefly, as a way of demonstrating loyalty to the Gnesio-Lutheran cause, of distinguishing the territory from its Albertine neighbour where Philip Melanchthon advocated compromise with the Catholics on ritual and images.[31] From the 1560s onwards, however, Germany's Lutherans were confronted on the one hand by a resurgent Catholic church and on the other by Calvinism, with its determined attacks on what it regarded as left-over papal superstitions. Encounters with Calvinism served, as recent scholarship has emphasized, to strengthen Lutheran confessional consciousness.[32] Images, and accounts of behaviour towards them, show the extent to which this was a constitutive moment not only for Lutheran theologians but also for the Lutheran laity. For pastors and preachers who engaged in polemical battles with the Calvinist iconoclasts; for members of the Saxon nobility who commissioned epitaphs and altars that demonstrated their Lutheran orthodoxy; and for the inhabitants of Berlin who, in 1615, rioted in protest against their Calvinist rulers' iconoclasm, images served as public expressions of confessional identity.

We cannot, however, see the visual magnificence of the Frauenkirche as merely the product of decades of confessional delineation, as a Lutheran statement of belief (*Glaubensbekenntnis*).[33] If the disputes of the later sixteenth and early seventeenth centuries created a 'confessional image', then the changing religious climate of the seventeenth century and the political and social traumas of the Thirty Years' War created a 'devotional image', an image that played an increasingly important part in Lutheran piety. This devotional image is the focus of Part II of the book. The seventeenth century was the era of the *Frömmigkeitsbewegung*, a movement for the renewal of spiritual life that had Johann Arndt as its greatest exponent. In this movement, and in the devotional texts that it generated, images were assigned a new spiritual significance, and their ability to move the heart and soul was articulated with new vigour. Images retained their didactic importance; indeed, the period witnessed some remarkable experiments in visual pedagogy, from Sigismund Evenius's *Christliche Gottselige Bilder Schule* (1636) to Melchior Mattsperger's *Geistliche Herzens-Einbildungen* (1684–92), the earliest hieroglyphic Bible. But images were also used, as changes in Passion iconography demonstrate, to stimulate piety and provoke compassion in much more explicit ways than before. Traditional iconographies such as the *Ecce Homo* and Christ in Prayer in the Garden of Gethsemane, which had been largely absent from early Lutheran art, enjoyed new popularity.

[31] The Gnesio-Lutherans, with Matthias Flacius Illyricus and Nikolaus von Amsdorf as their most important representatives, defended against Melanchthon's compromises a theology and church practice that they considered true to the original form of Lutheranism.
[32] Kaufmann, *Konfession und Kultur*, 21. See also Bodo Nischan, *Lutherans and Calvinists in the Age of Confessionalism* (Aldershot, 1999); Bridget Heal, '"Better Papist than Calvinist": Art and Identity in Later Lutheran Germany', *German History*, 29 (4) (2011), 584–609.
[33] Jan Harasimowicz, *Kunst als Glaubensbekenntnis: Beiträge zur Kunst- und Kulturgeschichte der Reformationszeit* (Baden-Baden, 1996).

The crucifix, which during the era of Lutheran–Calvinist conflict had served as a confessional marker, now became the most important Lutheran devotional image (*Andachtsbild*). These devotional changes can also be seen in practices of visual commemoration, in the epitaphs and memorials of the period that not only fulfilled social and political needs but also chronicled emotional loss and offered individual and communal consolation.

Ultimately, however, a monument as spectacular as Dresden's Frauenkirche would have been unthinkable without the political and economic changes that shifted power and cultural patronage firmly towards Germany's courts and princely residential cities in the aftermath of the 1648 Peace of Westphalia. This was the era of princely consolidation within the Empire, of the baroque, and of the 'magnificent image' addressed in Part III of this book. In Saxony, many elements of baroque court culture were already present under Elector Johann Georg II (r. 1656–80), who used art and music for both pious and political purposes. He created in Dresden's castle chapel an astonishingly rich environment of worship, with Italianate music, paintings, sculptures, tapestries, elaborately decorated vestments and jewel-encrusted liturgical vessels. In Electoral Saxony, the Lutheran baroque was certainly not confined to the environment of the court: wherever there was money, churches were rebuilt or at least refurbished in baroque style, from Görlitz in the east to the silver-mining towns of the Erzgebirge in the south. But while Saxony's Lutherans revelled in the baroque, in a visual culture that was sensuous and aesthetic, shaped by cultural contact with Catholic Italy, Brandenburg's did not. The comparison between the two territories, pursued throughout this book, highlights the extent to which the development of a rich Lutheran visual culture was not pre-determined by the events and ideas of the Reformation itself, but was instead the result of long-term changes and particular local circumstances. In some of Brandenburg's Lutheran churches, there were, to be sure, baroque furnishings: Andreas Schlüter's 1703 pulpit for Berlin's Marienkirche was perhaps the most spectacular example (Plate 1). But in Brandenburg-Prussia the religious context—the dominance of Calvinism, the climate of co-existence, the importance of Pietism—was not conducive to the flourishing of a Lutheran baroque.

By positing a series of shifts from the confessional to the devotional to the magnificent image I do not intend to imply a clear-cut succession of either functions or types of Lutheran art. Images were confessional throughout: as the final chapter of the book will show, they served to define religious boundaries even during the first half of the eighteenth century, well after the so-called 'confessional age'. Images were devotional throughout: Cranach's Crucifixions may have been less obviously gruesome than their pre-Reformation predecessors, but the contemplation of Christ's Passion was never a pedagogical rather than a devotional process, or an intellectual rather than an emotional exercise. And images were magnificent throughout, from the simple but beautiful aesthetic of the chapel at Schloß Hartenfels in Torgau, which had been consecrated by Luther himself in 1544, to the gilded splendour of Dresden's Frauenkirche. The tripartite division is intended, rather, as a way of imposing thematic structure on a broadly chronological study, of focusing the reader's attention on decisive turning points in the development of Lutheran visual culture.

Moreover, by beginning and ending this book with Dresden's Frauenkirche, I do not intend to suggest that this church was in any sense typical, and that it should be read as a representative example of Lutheran confessional culture. Rather, the Frauenkirche is important precisely because it is exceptional (though by no means, as we shall see, unique). It is important because it challenges us to rethink our broad assumptions about the relationship between Protestantism and the arts. We know that rich and diverse visual cultures developed across Protestant Europe during the sixteenth and seventeenth centuries; we know that even in its more radical forms the Reformation redirected rather than eliminated religious art.[34] And yet, beyond the level of the specialist study, the dominant narrative remains one of iconoclasm and whitewashing. When Nicholas Terpstra writes, for example, that because of Protestantism's ambivalence about sacred space and its ongoing orientation towards iconoclasm 'any physical icon like a towering church would be a paradox and contradiction', he echoes decades—centuries even—of scholarship that has equated and continues to equate bare, simple churches with evangelical faith.[35] In explaining the 'paradox and contradiction' that was Dresden's Frauenkirche, this book invokes some very familiar stories—Luther's moderation with regard to images, for example—as well as examining many whose relevance is perhaps less immediately apparent: the importance of Calvinism as a constitutive other; the changing devotional climate of the post-Reformation era; the crucial importance of cross-confessional and cross-cultural transfer; the new socio-political context of the age of princely consolidations. In doing so, it invites the reader to understand the monument not only in the immediate context of eighteenth-century Dresden but also to place it in a broader temporal frame, seeing it as a manifestation of the long-term developments that turned Lutheranism into a magnificent faith.

---

[34] See, for example: Paul Corby Finney (ed.), *Seeing Beyond the Word: Visual Arts and the Calvinist Tradition* (Grand Rapids, 1999); Kenneth Fincham and Nicholas Tyacke, *Altars Restored: The Changing Face of English Religious Worship, 1547–c.1700* (Oxford, 2007); Tara Hamling, *Decorating the 'Godly' Household: Religious Art in Post-Reformation Britain* (New Haven and London, 2010); Mia Mochizuki, *The Netherlandish Image after Iconoclasm, 1566–1672: Material Religion in the Dutch Golden Age* (Aldershot, 2008); Andrew Spicer (ed.), *Lutheran Churches in Early Modern Europe* (Farnham, 2012).

[35] Terpstra, *Religious Refugees*, 284.

1

The Reformation Legacy
Images in Luther's Wittenberg

In 1529, Luther produced an illustrated version of the prayer book (*Betbüchlein*) that he had written in 1522. In its preface, he stated that he had included images in this new version especially for the sake of 'children and simple folk who are better moved to retain the divine stories through images and parables than through mere words or teaching'.[1] There was nothing unusual in the argument that he presented here: similar justifications for the use of religious images had been articulated by Christian theologians since the time of Pope Gregory the Great.[2] They continued to echo through Lutheran defences of images into the eighteenth century, even though some commentators took care to qualify the idea of images as the 'Bibles of the illiterate' with reminders of the primacy of Scripture.[3] The conviction that the main purpose of Protestant art was to teach has proved remarkably tenacious. Lutheran visual culture is described as having sacrificed both aesthetic pleasure and affective power to the demands of pedagogy.[4] In a confession that was ambivalent in its attitude towards images, their role in religious instruction—in pastoral practice—was, it seems, one of the key reasons for their survival.

Protestant piety was, of course, oriented towards the Word. But images continued to play a significant role in impressing God's Word on Christians' minds and hearts. Their real significance for 'children and simple folk' is perhaps best encapsulated not in the prescriptive writings of theologians, but in a vignette from Johann Grimmelshausen's picaresque novel *Simplicissimus*, set during the turmoil of the Thirty Years' War and first published in 1668. Grimmelshausen's eponymous hero is the son of a Spessart peasant, who has been raised in isolation on a farm. In the opening chapters of the book, his home is destroyed by soldiers and his family and servants are tortured and raped. Simplicissimus runs away to the forest, where he finds refuge with a former soldier who has become a Protestant hermit. The boy was 'by name a Christian' but knew nothing of religion and could not read or write. Grimmelshausen's description of the encounter of this most simple of simple

---

[1] WA 10/2, 'Betbüchlein', 331–495, here 458. LW 43, 'Personal Prayer Book', 5–45.

[2] Celia Chazelle, 'Pictures, Books, and the Illiterate: Pope Gregory I's Letters to Serenus of Marseille', *Word and Image*, 6 (1990), 138–53; Eugène Honée, 'Image and Imagination in the Medieval Culture of Prayer: A Historical Perspective', in H. van Os (ed.), *The Art of Devotion in the Late Middle Ages in Europe, 1300–1500* (Princeton, 1994), 157–74.

[3] See, for example, Martin Chemnitz, *Examination of the Council of Trent Part IV*, tr. Fred Kramer (St Louis, 1986), 103.

[4] Koerner, *Reformation of the Image*, 28 and 226 ff.

folk with an illustrated Bible provides a wonderful glimpse of the role that images might play in religious communication.

Simplicissimus, living in a hut in the forest, one day saw the hermit reading. His curiosity was aroused by the book that engaged his mentor's attention so deeply. As soon as the hermit laid it aside, Simplicissimus picked it up:

> The first thing my eye lit upon was the opening chapter of the Book of Job with a fine woodcut, beautifully coloured in, at the head. I asked the figures in it strange questions and when I received no answer I said … 'You little wretches, have you lost your tongues? Haven't you just been chatting to my father (for that was what I called the hermit) for long enough? I can see you're driving off that poor Da's sheep and have set fire to his house. Stop, stop! I'll put out the fire,' and I stood up to go and fetch some water, for I thought it was needed.[5]

In the image of the suffering Job, beloved of Lutheran commentators and illustrators, Simplicissimus finds an echo of his own traumatic experiences. After his animated questioning of the figures, the hermit, his protector and adopted father, reassures him: 'these pictures are not alive. They have been made to show us things that happened a long time ago.' The coloured woodcut in the hermit's Bible captures Simplicissimus's attention, draws him in, and leads him to seek instruction. He learns to read and to write, and through his life with the hermit 'to know God and to serve him honestly', though his innocence and piety are soon destroyed by his encounters with the vulgarities and vices of the wider world.[6] Of course, Grimmelshausen's story is, in part, a literary device intended to demonstrate Simplicissimus's naivety. The anecdote does, however, remind us of the power of images and of the visceral responses that they might provoke—of the very reasons why their roles in religious education and devotion were so fiercely contested during the sixteenth century.

This chapter focuses on Luther's own writings and on the tradition of illustrated Bibles and catechisms that developed in Wittenberg during his lifetime, the tradition to which the Bible owned by Grimmelhausen's hermit was an heir. Luther's teachings must stand at the start of any discussion of the development of confessional culture, for Lutheranism always drew extensively on the memory and authority of the reformer himself. Rather than providing a comprehensive survey of Luther's pronouncements on images, the chapter highlights two key themes: the role that images played in defining religious boundaries during the early decades of the Reformation; and the continued importance of the visual in his theology.[7] Luther's mature position on images emerged from the turmoil of the 1520s. His rejection of radicalism—in particular his conflict with Andreas Bodenstein von Karlstadt—ensured that from an early stage, images' presence constituted, for him

---

[5] Johann Jakob Christoffel von Grimmelshausen, *The Adventures of Simplicissimus*, tr. Mike Mitchell (1999), 39.

[6] Ibid., 42.

[7] For useful discussions of Luther's position on images, see Stirm, *Die Bilderfrage*; Gudrun Litz, *Die reformatorische Bilderfrage in den schwäbischen Reichsstädten* (Tübingen, 2007), 20–7; Markus Friedrich, 'Das Hör-Reich und das Sehe-Reich. Zur Bewertung des Sehens bei Luther und im frühneuzeitlichen Protestantismus', in Wimböck et al. (eds), *Evidentia*, 453–82.

and his followers, a sign of moderation. As Johannes Bugenhagen put it in his 1529 church ordinance for Hamburg, 'we may not be iconoclasts', a sentiment that persisted into the later sixteenth and seventeenth centuries when Germany's Lutherans were confronted by a second, Calvinist Reformation.[8]

Physical images were confessional markers, symbols of allegiance to the Wittenberg movement. Mental images, for example of Christ on the Cross, were much more than that. For Luther they were inevitable parts of religious devotion: the Christian could not think or understand without them. Moreover, although hearing was now granted pride of place amongst the senses, Luther still acknowledged the importance of sight. For Luther the divine was unknowable—he wrote often of the *Deus Absconditus* (Hidden God). Christians, in their sinful state, could become acquainted with this Hidden God only when he revealed himself through the Word (in oral, written, and sacramental forms) and through responding faith.[9] Images and visible signs could, however, play a part in making Him accessible to frail human understanding. Both physical and mental images were part of the process through which the Christian understood and experienced Scripture, while external signs such as the Eucharist made the Word palpable ('greifflich und empfind- lich') to the hearts, eyes, and hands of the faithful.[10]

The second part of the chapter turns to the images themselves, focusing not on the ephemeral propaganda of the early Reformation but on the illustrations to the texts that defined Lutheran piety and identity throughout the early modern period: Luther's Bible translation and his *Small Catechism*. These illustrations demonstrate the sophistication with which Luther and his followers—in particular Philip Melanchthon and Lucas Cranach the Elder—used visual means of communication. The illustrations did not simply, as Grimmelshausen's hermit suggested, show 'things that happened a long time ago'; rather they explained and interpreted the texts that they accompanied. They guided, in this word-orientated devotional culture, the reader's engagement with Scripture and the catechumen's learning and understanding of the key tenets of the Lutheran faith.

LUTHER ON IMAGES

Martin Luther's early writings contain rejections of false, Catholic teaching on images. These were, however, merely passing references, made by the reformer in the course of his discussions of the dangers of false worship and works righteous- ness.[11] It was not until 1522 that the image question gained real prominence. At Christmastime 1521, while Luther was being held in protective custody at the Wartburg in the aftermath of his condemnation at Worms, Andreas Bodenstein von Karlstadt celebrated the first public evangelical Mass in Wittenberg, adminis- tering communion in both kinds in the castle chapel. On 24 January 1522, the

---

[8] Sehling EKO 5, 513.
[9] See, for example, Koerner, *The Reformation of the Image*, 201–11.   [10] WA 47, 139.
[11] Stirm, *Die Bilderfrage*, 30–7.

town council issued an ordinance that reformed Wittenberg's liturgy and stated that all but three altars should be removed from the parish church 'in order to avoid idolatry'.[12] It seems that there was little actual destruction: Wittenberg's Augustinian friars had already burned their images and altars, but later reports of extensive popular iconoclasm in the parish church find no corroboration in contemporary sources.[13] This urban Reformation did, however, prompt the first of the sixteenth century's polemical exchanges over images: on 26 January, Karlstadt published a pamphlet that offered a full theological defence of iconoclasm, *Von der Abthuung der Bilder* (*On the Removal of Images*). He argued that images were prohibited in the Old Testament because men were, by nature, frivolous and inclined to worship them. They could not, as Pope Gregory the Great and numerous other medieval commentators had suggested, serve as books for the illiterate, for the laity could 'learn nothing of salvation from them'.[14] Karlstadt's position was refuted by Luther in the third of his *Invocavit* sermons, preached immediately after his return, and also provoked a quick response from Hieronymous Emser, Catholic court preacher in Dresden. Emser justified religious images by invoking Scripture and the traditions of the early church, arguing that they served to teach and to remind, to stimulate 'virtue and devotion', and to mark out sacred space.[15]

Luther's theological position on images may have been fully formed before his return from the Wartburg.[16] But it was Karlstadt's activities during the so-called 'Wittenberg disturbances' that forced him to confront the image question head on. Subsequent perceptions of these 'disturbances' were decisively shaped by the account given in Luther's *Invocavit* sermons preached in March 1522 and first printed as a group in Straßburg a year later. These sermons testify to Luther's desire to vilify Karlstadt and to re-establish his own authority at the head of the Wittenberg congregation. The third sermon, on images and monastic vows, was printed earlier than the others in Augsburg and rapidly went through a number of editions.[17] Although Luther's original preached sermon probably said less on images than its written redaction, the widely received printed version ensured that from a very early stage in the Reformation the removal of images was synonymous with radicalism.[18] Images were, Luther argued, in a statement that reappeared in all subsequent debates, amongst 'the things that are not necessary but that are left free by God, which we may keep or not'. These 'things', later referred to as adiaphora, 'must not be forbidden by anyone, and if they are forbidden this is wrong because it is against God's ordinance'.[19] Yet, Luther was not ready, at this stage, to offer a positive

---

[12] Sehling EKO 1, 697 f.; see Volker Leppin, 'Kirchenausstattungen in territorialen Kirchenordnungen bis 1548' in Sabine Arend and Gerald Dörner (eds), *Ordnungen für die Kirche— Wirkungen auf die Welt. Evangelische Kirchenordnungen des 16. Jahrhunderts* (Tübingen, 2015), 137–55, here 138–43.

[13] Natalie Krentz, *Ritualwandel und Deutungshoheit: Die Frühe Reformation in der Residenzstadt Wittenberg (1500–1533)*, 200–10, 232.

[14] Bryan Mangrum and Giuseppe Scavizzi (eds), *A Reformation Debate: Karlstadt, Emser, and Eck on Sacred Images. Three Treatises in Translation* (Ottawa, 1991), 23, 25.

[15] Ibid., 51. See also Krentz, *Ritualwandel*, 236.   [16] Stirm, *Die Bilderfrage*, 30.

[17] Krentz, *Ritualwandel*, 221, 232–4.   [18] Ibid., 235–6, 241–2.

[19] WA 10/3, 'Ein ander Sermon D. M. Luthers Am dinstag nach Invocavit', 21–30, here 21–2; LW 51, 79–83, here 79.

defence of images: 'we may have them or not have them, although it would be better if we did not have them at all. I am not partial to them.'[20] He emphasized above all the importance of preaching and the Word: 'it should have been preached that images are nothing and that no service is done to God by erecting them; then they would have passed away by themselves.'[21]

Luther's desire to create distance between those who had, in his view, redis-covered Christian truth and the radicals—the *Schwärmer*, as he described them—was only increased by the events of 1523–5.[22] Karlstadt left for the town of Orlamünde in May 1523, where he preached an increasingly mystical-spiritualist message, abolished infant baptism, and removed images.[23] Elsewhere there was further violence against images: in March 1522 Zwickau's inhabitants had stormed the Cistercians' Grünhain Cloister; two years later at Mallerbach outside Allstedt peasants destroyed a Marian chapel at Thomas Müntzer's behest.[24] Such incidents increased markedly with the outbreak of the Peasants' War in the summer of 1524. Further afield in Zürich isolated attacks on religious images provoked the council to decree an orderly stripping of the city's churches in June 1524: Luther's other Sacramentarian opponents, above all Huldrych Zwingli, were also now encour-aging the rejection of religious images.[25] Luther's meetings with Karlstadt in Jena and in Orlamünde in August 1524 led to a further hardening of positions. On his way to Orlamünde, Luther preached at Kahla, where the pastor was a supporter of Karlstadt. There Luther's access to the pulpit was blocked by a symbol of the local community's rejection of images: a broken crucifix, over which he had to climb.[26] According to an account of events provided by pastor Martin Reinhart, Karlstadt's disciple in Jena, at Orlamünde Luther then confronted a congregation of self-assured peasants who defended their right to choose their own pastor, their mystical understanding of divine truth, and above all their rejection of religious images. When asked by a member of Orlamünde's council whether religious images were not forbidden in the Decalogue, Luther argued, as he had already done in 1522, that the first commandment prohibited only 'idolatrous images', images that were worshipped. 'What harm does a crucifix on the wall that I do not pray to do to me?,' he asked.[27] But Luther failed, during this confrontation, to

---

[20] WA 10/3, 26; LW 51, 81.   [21] WA 10/3, 28–9; LW 51, 83.

[22] On this tumultuous period, and Luther's relationship with Karlstadt, see above all Lyndal Roper, *Martin Luther: Renegade and Prophet* (London, 2016).

[23] Martin Brecht, *Martin Luther. Shaping and Defining the Reformation, 1521–1532*, tr. James Schaaf (Minneapolis, 1990), 158.

[24] Serguisz Michalski, 'Die Ausbreitung des reformatorischen Bildersturms 1521–1537' in Cécile Dupeaux, Peter Jezler, and Jean Wirth (eds), *Bildersturm. Wahnsinn oder Gottes Wille?* (Bern, 2000), 46–51, here 47. On Zwickau see also Susan Karant-Nunn, *Zwickau in Transition, 1500–1547: The Reformation as an Agent of Change* (Columbus, 1987), 125 ff.

[25] Dupeaux et al. (eds), *Bildersturm*, 299; see also Lee Palmer Wandel, *Voracious Idols and Violent Hands: Iconoclasm in Reformation Zurich, Strasbourg, and Basel* (Cambridge, 1995).

[26] WA 15, 'Ein Bericht der handlung zwischen Doctor Martino Luthero und Doctor Andreas Bodenstein von Karlstadt, zu Jen geschehen', 334–41; Brecht, *Martin Luther: Shaping and Defining the Reformation*, 159–61; Roper, *Martin Luther*, 253–5.

[27] WA 15, 'Die Handlung Doctor Martini Luthers mitt dem Raht unnd gemein der Stat Orlamünd', 341–7, esp. 345–6. On Reinhart see Amy Nelson Burnett, *Karlstadt and the Origins of the Eucharistic Controversy: A Study in the Circulation of Ideas* (New York and Oxford, 2011). See also

provide any positive reason for the peasants to retain their images. He departed from Karlstadt and his congregation in absolute enmity, and later referred to the events as the 'Orlamünde tragedy'.[28]

Whatever Luther's earlier reservations about images, by now their destruction was irrevocably associated with radicalism in his mind. In a letter of December 1524, he warned Straßburg's Christians against Karlstadt, in particular against his iconoclasm. He, Luther, had done more through his writings against images than Karlstadt would ever do with his fanaticism. Karlstadt's iconoclasm would, he emphasized again, 'trap Christian freedom with law and conscience'.[29] A sense of deep personal animosity pervaded the letter. This reached a broad public audience in Luther's tract *Wider die himmlischen Propheten, von dem Bildern und Sacramenten* (*Against the Heavenly Prophets in the Matter of Images and Sacraments*), published in two parts at the end of 1524 and beginning of 1525.[30] This lengthy tract contains his fullest discussion of the image question.[31] To a much greater extent than the third *Invocavit* sermon of 1522, it is framed as a vituperative attack on Karlstadt himself: 'Doctor Andreas Karlstadt has deserted us, and on top of that has become our most offensive enemy', Luther states in its opening paragraphs. Luther describes his former colleague as 'Satan, who here pretends to vindicate the sacrament, but has much else in mind'. He attacks Karlstadt's focus on external works such as iconoclasm, and his concomitant failure to teach about faith and love:

> Even rascals are able to do and teach what he urges. Therefore something higher must be there to absolve and comfort the conscience. That is the Holy Spirit, who is not acquired through breaking images or any work, but only through the Gospel and faith.[32]

In making a must out of that which should be free, in compelling Christian consciences with regard to images, Karlstadt was doing as much damage as the Catholics:

> For although the matter of images is a minor, external thing, when one seeks to burden the conscience with sin through it, as through the law of God, it becomes the most important of all. For it destroys faith, profanes the blood of Christ, blasphemes the Gospel, and sets all that Christ has won for us at nought, so that this Karlstadtian abomination is no less effective in destroying the kingdom of Christ and a good conscience than the papacy has become with its prohibitions regarding food and marriage, and all else that was free and without sin.[33]

Moreover, in Luther's eyes iconoclasm in the manner promoted by Karlstadt endangered not only individual souls but also proper social and political order. Luther's deep-seated hatred and fear of disorder and revolt emerges clearly in his

Karl-Heinz zur Mühlen, *Reformatorische Prägungen: Studien zur Theologie Martin Luthers und zur Reformationszeit* (Göttingen, 2011), 188.

[28] Quoted in Brecht, *Martin Luther: Shaping and Defining the Reformation*, 161.
[29] WA 15, 'Eyn brieff an die Christen zu Straspurg widder den schwermer geyst', 391–7, here 395.
[30] Brecht, *Martin Luther: Shaping and Defining the Reformation*, 164 ff.
[31] WA 18, 37–125; on images see 67–84. On the subsequent significance of this tract see Kaufmann, *Konfession und Kultur*, 165. For an English translation see LW 40, 79–101.
[32] WA 18, 62, 64–5; LW 40, 79–82.   [33] WA 18, 73; LW 40, 90–1.

discussion of what he sees as Karlstadt's rabble rousing. The breaking of images was proceeding in a disorderly way and without proper authority:

> Their prophets stand, crying and arousing the masses, saying: heigh, hew, rip, rend, smash, dash, stab, strike, run, throw, hit the idols in the mouth. If you see a crucifix, spit in its face. This is to do away with images in a Karlstadtian manner, to make the masses mad and foolish, and secretly to accustom them to insurrection.[34]

In *Wider die himmlischen Propheten*, as elsewhere in his writings, Luther took care, however, to distance himself not only from the iconoclasm of the detested *Schwärmer* but also from Catholic image practice. Luther argued that he was not, as Karlstadt had suggested, a 'protector of images', for he had permitted the removal of images provided that it was done in an orderly fashion, without fanaticism and violent destruction. As in 1522, he emphasized above all the importance of the Word: 'I approached the task of destroying images by first tearing them out of the heart through God's word and making them worthless and despised…For when they are no longer in the heart, they can do no harm when seen with the eyes.' Here again Luther's own attitude towards images is hardly enthusiastic: when God's Word is properly preached, 'the people themselves willingly drop [the matter of images], despise them, and have none made'.[35] But faced with Karlstadt's radicalism he nonetheless constructed a full defence of them according to both the Law of Moses and the Gospel, arguing that provided images are not worshipped they can usefully be kept for remembrance and as witnesses, just like the stones erected by Joshua and Samuel as reminders of God's intervention.[36]

In the conflicts with Karlstadt and the other *Schwärmer* that so decisively shaped his public position on images, Luther presented himself as the rational reformer, the reformer who rejected the dreams and visions of his radical opponents in favour of the authority of the written Word. Yet, he was also a deeply emotional theologian, and one who constantly emphasized the importance of experience.[37] Ultimately, his anthropology, his understanding of man's fallen nature, was as important as his hatred of radicalism in determining his attitude to images. It led him to believe that mankind lives not primarily through abstract thoughts but through images in the soul, and that those images are essential to perception and understanding.[38] In *Wider die himmlischen Propheten*, Luther recounted his own experience of contemplating Christ's Passion:

> I know for certain that God desires that one should hear and read his work, and especially the Passion of Christ. But if I am to hear or think, then it is impossible for me not to make images of this within my heart, for whether I want to or not, when I hear the word Christ, there delineates itself in my heart a picture of a man who hangs on the cross, just as my face naturally delineates itself on the water, when I look into it. If

---

[34] WA 18, 71; LW 40, 88–9.   [35] WA 18, 67–8; LW 40, 84–5.

[36] WA 18, esp. 70–8. See Joshua 24:26; I Samuel 7:12.

[37] Mühlen, *Reformatorische Prägungen*; Kaufmann, 'Die Sinn- und Leiblichkeit der Heilsaneignung', 26–7.

[38] Stirm, *Die Bilderfrage*, 91.

it is not a sin, but a good thing, that I have Christ's image in my heart, why then should it be sinful to have it before my eyes?[39]

The heart, in which Christ's image appeared, encompassed, for Luther the soul (*anima*), the mind (*intellectus*), the will (*voluntas*), and emotion (*affectus*). It was the seat of faith, and it was the place where the Word of God must operate.[40] In describing the presence of an image of Christ in the heart, and in using that presence as a justification for physical images, Luther therefore acknowledged the importance of the visual for understanding Scripture and experiencing faith.

During the later sixteenth and seventeenth centuries, Lutheran commentators—in particular Johann Arndt—produced more detailed accounts of the relationship between outer (physical) and inner (spiritual) images, and suggested that the former could create the latter, either spontaneously or through the mediation of the Holy Spirit.[41] Luther never went so far. He did, however, reiterate on a number of occasions the conviction that images aided memory. In the 1529 edition of his prayer book, Luther wrote that he had added woodcuts—a cycle of 50 full-page images, depicting scenes from the Creation to the Sending out of the Apostles—to his original text for the sake of children and simple folk who were better moved to retain divine stories through them than through mere words. He advocated a 'layman's Bible' that illustrated all the important scriptural stories in order, for:

One cannot present God's words and works to the common man too much or too often. Even if one sings and speaks, proclaims and preaches, writes and reads, paints and draws, Satan and his cohorts are always strong and alert for hindering and suppressing them.[42]

Again in a sermon preached on Easter day 1533 in the castle chapel in Torgau, Luther emphasized the importance of images, both physical and mental, and advocated the multiplication of media for communicating the Gospel message. As part of a series of sermons on the articles of the creed, Luther addressed the belief that Christ descended into hell and on the third day rose again from the dead. He was pleased, he said, when this story was painted, performed, sung, or said 'for the simple folk'. It was such stories, rather than the reasoned and subtle theological disputation of detail, that were necessary to faith. We always, Luther emphasized, create thoughts and mental pictures of whatever is presented to us in words, for we 'cannot think or understand anything without images'. Paintings of the Descent into Hell therefore showed, in a straightforward manner, the 'power and usefulness' of this article of the creed.[43]

[39] Translation from Koerner, *The Reformation of the Image*, 160.
[40] Miikka Anttila, *Luther's Theology of Music: Spiritual Beauty and Pleasure* (Berlin, 2013), 109. Birgit Stolt, *Martin Luthers Rhetorik des Herzens* (Tübingen, 2014).
[41] See Chapter 4.
[42] WA 10/2, 'Betbüchlein, 1522', 331–501, here 458. Pages 341–3 discuss the various editions. LW 43, 5–45, here 43. On the *Passionalbüchlein* see also Gerhard Ringshausen, *Von der Buchillustration zum Unterrichtsmedium: Der Weg des Bildes in die Schule dargestellt am Beispiel des Religionsunterrichtes* (Weinheim and Basel, 1976), 33 ff.
[43] WA 37, 63. Ringshausen, *Von der Buchillustration zum Unterrichtsmedium*, 34. On this sermon see also Joseph Koerner, *The Moment of Self-Portraiture in German Renaissance Art* (Chicago, 1993), 382.

Beyond such discussions of physical and mental images, Luther also spoke more broadly of the relationship between the material and spiritual. He emphasized the importance of external signs of God's promise, both in the Old Testament (e.g. Noah's Ark and the Brazen Serpent) and in the New (above all baptism and the Eucharist).[44] One of his fullest discussions of such signs was given in a 1539 sermon on John 3:22, which describes Jesus and the disciples baptizing in the Judean countryside. Luther spoke of John the Baptist's baptism of Christ as a sign of his status as the Messiah, and also cited various Old Testament examples, arguing that 'from the beginning of the world God appointed signs in addition to His Word, so that people had an opportunity to behold with their physical eye that God loved his people and the church and was disposed to be their benefactor'. Alongside the 'outward ministry' God has also given us, he argued, visible signs, 'so that we do not complain that we cannot find him'. These were baptism, absolution, and most importantly the Eucharist, 'so that we have Christ closest to us, not only in our hearts, but also on our tongue, so that we can feel Him, grasp Him, and touch Him'.[45] The significance of Luther's teaching on the Eucharist, of his belief in the real presence of Christ, for the question of images will be explored more fully in Chapter 2, in the context of the debates that arose during Germany's Second Reformation.[46] Here we need only note the prominence accorded to the senses in Luther's account of the Christian's encounter with Christ: not merely, as we might expect, hearing, but also sight and touch: 'He gives Himself to us not only in the heart, but also in the eyes and in the hands,' through signs that are 'graspable and perceptible.'[47]

The Reformation has long been associated with a reprioritization of the senses, with a shift from visual to verbal piety.[48] In an oft-cited passage from his interpretation of Psalm 8, presented in a sermon preached in Merseburg in 1545 towards the end of his life, Luther stated that 'Christ's kingdom is a hearing-kingdom, not a seeing-kingdom; for the eyes do not lead and guide us to where we know and find Christ, but rather the ears must do this'.[49] This statement seems, indeed, to suggest the subordination of the image to the Word. We should not, however, read even

[44] Carlos Eire, *War Against the Idols: The Reformation of Worship from Erasmus to Calvin* (Cambridge, 1986), 72; Stirm, *Die Bilderfrage*, 96 ff.

[45] WA 47, 138–9; LW 22, 420.

[46] Michalski points out that almost all opponents of images are opponents of real presence: Sergiusz Michalski, 'Bild, Spiegelbild, Figura, Repraesentatio: Ikonitätsbegriffe im Spannungsfeld zwischen Bilderfrage und Abendmahlskontroverse', *Annuarium historiae conciliorum,* 20 (1988), 458–88, here 460–3.

[47] WA 47, 139; LW 22, 420. See Friedrich, 'Das Hör-Reich und das Sehe-Reich', 451–2. For another relevant sermon see WA 49, 'Predigt am Gründonnerstag, 25 March 1540. Die Coenae Domini', 72–8.

[48] See, for example, Thomas Lentes, 'Auf der Suche nach dem Ort des Gedächtnisses. Thesen zur Umwertung der symbolischen Formen in Abendmahlslehre, Bildtheorie und Bildandacht des 14. bis 16. Jahrhunderts', in Klaus Krüger and Alessandro Nova (eds), *Imagination und Wirklichkeit. Zum Verhältnis von mentalen und realen Bildern in der Kunst der frühen Neuzeit* (Mainz, 2000), 21–46. Gabriele Wimböck, ' "Durch die Augen in das Gemüt kommen": Sehen und Glauben—Grenzen und Reservate', in Wimböck et al. (eds), *Evidentia*, 427–52, here 427.

[49] WA 51, 'Predigt, in Merseburg gehalten', 11–22, here 11. See Koerner, *The Reformation of the Image*, 41–2.

this sermon as evidence of a piety that was fundamentally opposed to the visual, or that embraced hearing without qualification.[50] Luther spoke in this sermon of two kingdoms, 'the kingdom of Christ and the worldly kingdom', both of which are present on earth, but each of which is ruled in a different way. Christ rules 'spiritually and in a heavenly way, so that although one does not see his kingdom as one sees the worldly kingdom, one hears it nonetheless'. Secular government, by contrast, rested not on hearing alone, but on works and compulsion. Secular rulers must protect the pious, uphold law, maintain peace, and punish the godless and evil-doers: for this, hearing was not sufficient.[51] The temporal kingdom—the kingdom that could be grasped with all the senses—played an important role in disseminating belief and piety. Here, as elsewhere, Luther therefore accepted, as Markus Friedrich argues, 'the immediate fact of visual sensation as part of the work that must be done to create religious conviction'.[52]

PROCLAIMING THE GOSPEL

The role that images played in this spreading of evangelical religious conviction was explored by Bob Scribner in relation to Lutheran propaganda. Scribner showed the ways in which elements of late-medieval popular and religious culture were transformed 'on the propagandists' terms': familiar images and symbols were used to ridicule the Reformation's opponents and to present Luther himself as a teacher and prophet.[53] Humour, especially scatological humour, was used extensively: images of peasants farting at the pope and devils shitting monks inevitably linger in the minds of readers of Scribner's book. The woodcut became a means of mass communication, and was, as Scribner put it, 'like homemade gin . . . cheap, crude and effective'. Images also, however, helped to 'establish the Reformation in more positive terms, as a movement with a distinct theological viewpoint and definite religious characteristics of its own'.[54] Lucas Cranach's Law and Gospel, an iconography formulated in France during the early 1520s but disseminated through the Wittenberg artist's paintings and woodcuts, was the most famous visualization of the basic tenets of the evangelical faith. It became a staple of sixteenth-century Lutheran visual culture, adorning books, altarpieces, epitaphs, and items of household furnishing.[55]

In addition to this propaganda, however, the Wittenberg Reformation also produced, from its very beginning, illustrated Bibles, catechisms, and devotional

[50] Friedrich, 'Das Hör-Reich und das Sehe-Reich', 461.

[51] WA 51, esp. 11–14.

[52] Friedrich, 'Das Hör-Reich und das Sehe-Reich', 462–3.

[53] R. W. Scribner, 'Popular Piety and Modes of Visual Perception in Late-Medieval and Reformation Germany', *Journal of Religious History*, 15 (4) (1989), 448–69; Scribner, *For the Sake of Simple Folk*.

[54] Ibid., 5, 190.

[55] Heimo Reinitzer, *Gesetz und Evangelium: über ein reformatorisches Bildthema, seine Tradition, Funktion und Wirkungsgeschichte*, 2 vols. (Hamburg, 2006). On the Law and Gospel iconography see also Joseph Koerner, *The Moment of Self-Portraiture*, chapter 16; Martin Schwarz, *Martin Luther: Lehrer der christlichen Religion* (Tübingen, 2015), 187–95.

texts. It was the Bible that 'powered the very project of Reformation': the cry 'Scripture alone' underpinned every evangelical campaign, from Luther's moderate Wittenberg movement to the violent radicalism of Münzter and beyond; the authority of scripture, made available in accurate vernacular translation, was the cornerstone of every Protestant creed.[56] For Lutherans, this vernacular translation was, of course, the reformer's own, and a history of Lutheran confessional culture cannot be written without reference to Luther's Bible. It shaped early modern Lutheran theology and ecclesiology, but also became, during the late eighteenth and nineteenth centuries, a key part of the cultural patrimony of German Protestants. It was celebrated by Goethe and Herder as the birthplace of the German language, and also continued to fulfil an important role in domestic devotion, as Thomas Mann attests in his semi-autobiographical novel *Buddenbrooks*.[57] Mann describes the 'old Wittenberg Bible' which was, according to Consul Buddenbrook's grandfather, 'to descend to his eldest son, and thence from first-born to first-born in each generation'. This Bible, 'with the funny big letters', was a focal point for domestic religious ritual: the Frau Consul read from it at Christmas time before the servants and the poor, and at other times for the edification of the family. From the time of Luther to the time of Thomas Mann, it was part of the 'godly patrician house', part of the world whose demise *Buddenbrooks* chronicles.[58]

The story of Luther's Bible translations and their various editions has been told many times: it began with the September New Testament, prepared hurriedly before the reformer's return from the Wartburg in 1522 and published by Lucas Cranach and Christian Döring. This was followed by the revised December New Testament, another bestseller, and by editions of individual parts of the Old Testament: the Pentateuch (1523) and the books of history and poetry (1524). The translation of the Old Testament was a hard task, and alongside Luther's teaching commitments took twelve years to complete, even with the help of his Wittenberg colleagues: in 1532, a German edition of all of the Prophets appeared from Hans Lufft's print shop, followed in 1534 by the Apocrypha.[59] From the beginning Bible publishing was big business, and Wittenberg printers were in competition with those in other towns. The first complete German Bibles were produced in 1529

[56] Jonathan Sheehan, *The Enlightenment Bible: Translation, Scholarship, Culture* (Princeton, 2005), here 1.

[57] Ibid., 225. Luther's impact on the development of the German language is still debated, but there can be no doubt that, as Michael Beyer recently put it, 'im kulturellen Gedächtnis der Deutschen ist Luther als "Bibelübersetzer" fest verankert.' Michael Beyer, 'Übersetzer', in Volker Leppin and Gury Schneider-Ludorff (eds), *Das Luther-Lexikon* (Regensburg, 2014), 709–11, here 709. On the domestic use of Luther Bibles see Heimo Reinitzer, 'Leserspuren in Bibeln', *Wolfenbütteler Beiträge: aus den Schätzen der Herzog August Bibliothek* 13 (2005), 149–52, here 167–9. See also Etienne François, 'Das religiöse Buch als Nothelfer, Familienreliquie und Identitätssymbol im protestantischen Deutschland der Frühneuzeit (17.–19. Jahrhunderts)', in Ursula Brunold-Bigler and Hermann Bausinger (eds), *Hören Sagen Lesen Lernen. Bausteine zu einer Geschichte der kommunikativen Kultur* (Bern, 1995) 219–30.

[58] Thomas Mann, *Buddenbrooks*, tr. H. T. Lowe-Porter, (London, 1924), 63, 102–3, 276, 608–9, 318–19, 737.

[59] For a useful overview see Heimo Reinitzer, *Biblia deutsch: Luthers Bibelübersetzung und ihre Tradition*, exh. cat. (Wolfenbüttel and Hamburg, 1983), esp. 114–16. Hans Volz, *Martin Luthers deutsche Bibel* (Hamburg, 1978).

and 1530, substituting translations by other reformers for the parts that Luther and his team of theologians had not yet finished.[60] Finally, in 1534, the first full Bible using only Luther's translations was printed by Hans Lufft. More editions followed over the next decade, as Luther added revisions and his printers experimented with different formats. It was the 1545 Wittenberg Bible that finally achieved canonical status, since its text was (and is) regarded as the last fully authorized by Luther himself.[61]

Heimo Reinitzer estimates that between the publication of the September New Testament of 1522 and the reformer's death in 1546, 430 whole and part editions of the Luther Bible were printed in Wittenberg and elsewhere. By the mid-sixteenth century, he suggests that there were about half a million Luther Bibles in circulation, written in both High and Low German.[62] Sanctified by its wide dissemination and by long usage, Luther's translation became a 'Kleinod', a treasure, as the Wittenberg theology faculty put it in their introduction to a 1670 edition.[63] Johann Gottfried Zeidler, poet laureate from 1678, referred to it in the preface to his 1701 *Bilder-Bibel* as 'our Lutheran Vulgate'.[64] It was, as the Altdorf theology faculty wrote in 1702, a 'great and almost incomparable treasure of the church'. 'What a great blessing it is', the Altdorf theologians continued, 'for a house to have a well-thumbed, well-read, and properly used…German Bible'.[65] Luther's Bible was, as this comment suggests, not only the core of the religious life of the church but also the heart of domestic devotion, at least for the fortunate 'God-loving housefather' and his family who could afford to purchase such a precious item.[66]

In encomia to the Luther Bible, whether penned by early modern theologians or by modern authors, it is always the text that is praised. And yet many editions of Luther's Bible were illustrated, from the September and December New Testaments, with their famous woodcuts by Lucas Cranach the Elder, to the beautiful engraved

[60] Ph. Schmidt, *Die Illustration der Lutherbibel, 1522–1700. Ein Stück abendländische Kultur- und Kirchengeschichte* (Basel, 1962), 163.
[61] Stefan Michel, 'Bibel', in Leppin and Schneider-Ludorff (eds), *Das Luther-Lexikon*, 108–12, here 110–11.
[62] Reinitzer, *Biblia deutsch*, 116–27, based on WA DB 2, 201–727.
[63] *Biblia, das ist/die gantze Heilige Schrifft Alten und Neuen Testaments/Deutsch/D. Martin Luthers/ Sampt D. Hütteri Summarien/der Biblischen Bücher und Capitel richtiget Eintheilung…*(Wittenberg: Balth. Christ. Wust, 1670), Vorrede.
[64] *Johann Gottfried Zeidlers Neu=ausgefertigte Bilder=Bibel/darinnen Die denckwürdigsten Historien Heiliger Schrifft in vielen anmuthigen und künstlichen Biblischen Figuren vorgestellet…*(Magdeburg: Johann Daniel Müller, 1701), Vorrede. On Zeidler see John Flood, *Poets Laureate in the Holy Roman Empire. A Bio-bibliographical Handbook*, Volume 4: *S–Z* (Berlin and New York, 2006), 2288–93. Also Johann Heinrich Zedler, *Grosses vollständiges Universallexikon alle Wissenschaften und Künste*, 64 vols. (Leipzig, 1731–54), vol. LXI, 672–8. For a full discussion of Zeidler's two illustrated bibles (1691 and 1701), see Bridget Heal, 'Reformationsbilder in der Kunst der Aufklärung' in Wolf-Friedrich Schäufele and Christoph Strohm (eds), *Das Bild der Reformation in der Aufklärung* (Gütersloh, forthcoming).
[65] *Biblia, Das ist: Die gantze Heilige Schrifft/Alten und Neuen Testaments/Durch Herrn D. Martin Luthern verteutschet…auch mit 250. Schönen Kuper=Figuren eines berühmten Künstlers in Augspurg geziert…*(Nuremberg: Johann Leonhard Buggel, Moritz Hagen, 1702), Vorrede.
[66] For examples of 'fleißig durchblätterte' Lutheran Bibles, see Reinitzer, 'Leserspuren'. For an example of a Bible that was used as a family chronicle see Thomas Schauerte, 'Die Luther-Bibel des Hans Ulrich Krafft', *Wolfenbütteler Beiträge* 13, (2005), 256–307.

illustrations in Matthaeus Merian's 1630 Bible, and beyond. Lutherans were not, of course, the first to illustrate Scripture, any more than they were the first to translate it. Medieval picture Bibles, the *bible moralisée* and *biblia pauperum*, had placed images from the Old and New Testaments alongside brief texts, and full illustrated Bibles also existed. Both the Low German Bibles printed in Cologne in 1478–9 by Heinrich Quentel and the High German Bible printed by Anton Koberger in Nuremberg in 1483 used, for example, the same rich selection of woodcut images.[67] But the emphasis that the evangelical movement placed on providing access to Scripture, and the proliferation of the translations and formats in which it was now available, meant that, during the sixteenth century, Bible illustration reached the hands of the laity as never before. The layperson's encounter with the Word of God was, in many cases, mediated by images. Chapter 4 will consider lay responses to these biblical images, but evidence for this comes from a much later period. For the illustrated Bibles produced during Luther's lifetime we have only the woodcuts themselves and the reformer's reflections on them: it is from these that we must assess images' importance in constructing a Lutheran religious understanding and confessional identity.

Luther's 1522 September and December New Testaments each contained a cycle of twenty-one woodcuts by Lucas Cranach the Elder. These woodcuts illustrated only one book: the Apocalypse. This was the New Testament book that was, according to Luther, of least value. Luther's Bible prefaces do not talk explicitly about images, but his introduction to the Apocalypse suggests that he permitted it to be illustrated, probably at Melanchthon's behest, because it was highly visual and because it was difficult to interpret.[68] Revelation was, he wrote, neither apostolic nor prophetic. The apostles did not deal in visions:

> For it befits the apostolic office to speak clearly of Christ and his deeds, without images and visions. Moreover, there is no prophet in the Old Testament, to say nothing of the New, who deals so exclusively with visions and images.[69]

Cranach's illustrations have been thoroughly studied, and here we need only make a few brief observations about their significance for the broader history of Lutheran Bible illustration.

The woodcuts were, in many cases, simplified versions of the seminal images contained in Albrecht Dürer's 1498 series, with expansions and deviations intended to bring them more closely in line with the biblical text. Scriptural accuracy was, in theory, a requirement of Lutheran art, yet even here, in the Wittenberg of Cranach, Luther, and Melachthon, it was not fully achieved. For dramatic effect, for legibility, and above all to bring out the text's significance, Cranach introduced changes. Most notably, he gave the images a polemical, anti-Catholic flavour: in the September New Testament, which followed hard on the heels of his

---

[67] Reinitzer, *Biblia deutsch,* 69–71; Schmidt, *Die Illustration,* 66 ff. Walter Eichenberger and Henning Wendland, *Deutsche Bibeln vor Luther: die Buchkunst der achtzehn deutschen Bibeln zwischen 1466 und 1522,* 2nd ed. (Hamburg, 1977), especially 65–86, 91–6.

[68] Peter Martin, *Martin Luther und die Bilder zur Apokalypse* (Hamburg, 1983), 112–14.

[69] WA, DB 7, 'Vorrhede auf die offfinbarung Sanct Johannis', 404; LW 35, 398–411.

very successful *Passional Christi und Antichristi*, the whore of Babylon wore a papal tiara, for example.[70] The text may not, in itself, have been especially valuable in Luther's eyes, but its images, like its preface, could function as exegesis, directing the reader towards its proper interpretation. Although the anti-papal elements were toned down in the woodcuts for the December New Testament, Luther emphasized the significance of Revelation for the history of the present-day church increasingly strongly during the 1520s and in the preface to his 1530 edition.[71]

In 1523 and 1524, parts one, two, and three of the Old Testament followed. For the original Wittenberg printing, Luther himself specified a number of places where images should be inserted.[72] He had perhaps learned something from his experiences in 1519, when his sermon on the Eucharist appeared illustrated with two woodcuts of monstrances, one supposedly bearing a Hussite goose. On this occasion the reformer excused himself by saying that he really did not have the time to check 'what the printer takes as an image, as letters, inks or paper'.[73] Whether prompted by this incident, or by the radical challenges of 1521–2, Luther paid at least some attention to the illustration of the Bibles printed in Wittenberg, as we know from an account given in 1563 by Christoph Walther, formerly the corrector in Hans Lufft's print shop:

> The venerable Herr Doctor Martin Luther indicated in part himself how the figures in the Wittenberg Bible should be cut or painted, and recommended that one should cut and paint very simply the content of the text. He did not want them to be besmirched with superfluous and useless things that did not help the text.[74]

Walther's comment was, in part at least, a rhetorical device. The printing of German Bibles was a lucrative business, and Walther wanted to be seen as the true heir to the Luther–Lufft enterprise. He therefore launched an attack on the Solis-Feyerabend printing house in Frankfurt am Main, saying that these printers had made the figures in their Bibles 'very small and almost unrecognisable' and had surrounded them with 'foolishness, play things and works of the devil'.[75] Yet, Luther's engagement with the illustration of Bibles produced in Wittenberg is documented elsewhere too.

The images for the 1523–4 parts of the Old Testament were designed in Cranach's workshop, and were, like the Apocalypse illustrations from 1522, in many cases full-page and dramatic. The treatment of Noah's Ark, for example,

[70] On the *Passional Christi und Antichristi* see Scribner, *For the Sake of Simple Folk*, 149 ff.
[71] Volz, *Martin Luthers deutsche Bibel*, 154; Jörg Armbruster, *Luthers Bibelvorreden. Studien zu ihrer Theologie* (Stuttgart, 2005), esp. 257–69.
[72] WA, DB 2, 217–18; further illustrated editions 1523/4, WA, DB 2, 220–1, 261–2. Schmidt, *Die Illustration*, 137 ff.
[73] WA 6, 81–2. See Veronika Thum, *Die Zehn Gebote für die ungelehrten Leut'. Der Dekalog in der Graphik des späten Mittelalters und der frühen Neuzeit* (Munich and Berlin, 2006), 108.
[74] Walther, Christoph, *Bericht von vnterschied der biblien vnd anderer des Ehrnwirdigen vnd seligen Herrn Doct. Martini Lutheri Bücher/so zu Wittemberg vnd an andern enden gedruckt werden/dem Christlichen leser zu nutz. Durch Christoffel Walther/des Herrn Hans Luffts Corrector* (Wittenberg, 1563), B ii v. On the importance of Luther's close engagement with Wittenberg book production see Andrew Pettegree, *Brand Luther: 1517, Printing, and the Making of the Reformation* (New York, 2015).
[75] Ibid. See Reinitzer, *Biblia deustch*, cat. nos. 145 and 146.

unlike earlier German Bible illustrations, shows death and destruction: streams of rain and drowning animals and birds.[76] It was the illustrations for the story of Samson (Judges 13–16) that apparently interested Luther most: in the hand-written copy of his translation he here added marginal notes specifying what should be depicted.[77] Other woodcuts showed the sacred archaeology of the Old Testament, in particular the Tabernacle. Such images were not new, but these versions were very true to the text, and were reproduced in Lutheran Bibles into the seventeenth century. The third part of the Old Testament contained only two illustrations: a title page and a woodcut of Job.

It lies beyond the scope of this study to investigate in detail why Luther and his collaborators and successors chose to illustrate particular biblical scenes: tradition certainly played a role, as did the desire to visualize particularly dramatic events in biblical history, from Noah's Ark and Isaac's Sacrifice to the story of Samson and Delilah.[78] More complex theological and pastoral messages certainly stood behind some choices: Job, for example, was an important figure for Luther because of his suffering and his experience of the *Deus Absconditus*. Job could, Luther stated, be understood by those who 'experience and feel what it is to suffer the wrath and judgement of God, and to have His grace hidden from view'.[79] The title page to *Das Dritte teyl des allten Testaments* (*The Third Part of the Old Testament*) provides another example of careful theological communication. Above are kings and prophets from the Old Testament, two of whom, David and Moses, point to the scene beneath, which shows Christ about to be nailed to the cross (Fig. 1.1). Here, as with Cranach's Apocalypse cycle, images do not just illustrate, they interpret: they draw the eye, and therefore the mind and the heart, to the significance of a particular text. In this case, the title page shows the Old Testament's unity with the New, and its Christocentric significance: for Luther, the events of Christ's life were already present (not just foreshadowed) in Old Testament history.[80]

Already by 1525, therefore, images were part of the project to proclaim the Gospel, and to bring Scripture to the common man. In *Wider die himmlischen Propheten*, Luther reflected:

> I have myself seen and heard the iconoclasts read out of my German Bible. I know that they have read out of it, as one can easily determine from the words they use. Now there are a great many pictures in those books, both of God, the angels, men and animals, especially in the Revelation of John and in Moses and Joshua.

If the radicals read from his illustrated Bibles, he continued, then they should 'permit us to do what they themselves do, for we would paint such images on the walls for the sake of remembrance and better understanding'.[81] In 1534, Hans Lufft

[76] Carl Christensen, 'The Reformation of Bible Illustration: Genesis Woodcuts in Wittenberg, 1523–1534', *Archiv für Reformationsgeschichte* 90 (1990), 103–29, here 105.
[77] Schmidt, *Die Illustration,* 137–9.
[78] See Christenson, 'The Reformation of Bible Illustration'.   [79] LW 35, 252.
[80] Heinrich Bornkamm, *Luther und das Alte Testament* (Tübingen, 1948); on the significance of the Old Testament for Luther see also Schwarz, *Martin Luther*, 45–62.
[81] WA 18, 82–3; LW 40, 99.

Fig. 1.1. Lucas Cranach the Elder, title page from *Das dritte teyl des allten Testaments* (Wittenberg: Cranach und Döring, 1524).

issued the first complete Bible in Luther's High German translation. It contained
a cycle of 117 new images, produced in the Cranach workshop by an artist who
signed himself as 'Master MS'.[82] This cycle achieved 'virtually canonical status in
Wittenberg': it was reused in almost all of the complete High German Bibles
published there up to 1546.[83] The woodcuts deserve our attention partly because
of their seminal status, and partly because they provide the most wonderful
example of Lutheran visual exegesis, demonstrating the sophistication with which
images could be used in Luther's *milieu* during the early decades of the Reformation.

Even though Luther was not intrinsically opposed to depicting scenes from
Christ's life, as his 1529 prayer book showed, his New Testament remained sparsely
illustrated: it contained images of the evangelists at the start of each Gospel, of the
apostles (most notably Paul) at the start of the Letters, and a new cycle of Apocalypse
illustrations. The Old Testament was much more richly illustrated. The Genesis
cycle, for example, omits various traditional themes for doctrinal reasons or
because, as with some of the more entertaining Joseph stories, they add little to
theological understandings of Scripture. It introduces, however, some new elements: the rainbow in the story of Noah as a visible sign of God's covenant with
man; and the rarely illustrated story of Jacob and the Rods, that according to
Luther's gloss showed that through the Gospel souls are led away from legalists and
hypocrites and become 'coloured, speckled, and spotted—that is, adorned with
divers gifts of the Spirit'.[84] Like Cranach's 1522 Apocalypse illustrations, the 1534
images are not always entirely true to the text. Luther looked, as he translated, for
language that allowed him to speak 'as one speaks in the marketplace', and in his
prefaces, glosses, and marginalia he 'visualized . . . sacred Scripture, by speaking to
the present and making it relevant'.[85] The 1534 images were part of this process of
making the Bible more immediate. They are characterized above all by their narrative density and by their tendency to represent biblical stories in detailed (and
delightful) early modern settings.

Legibility, as Christoph Walther pointed out in 1563, and drama are key to the
images. Delilah's defeat of Samson (Judges 16: 16–19), for example, takes place in
a sixteenth-century living room, with a paper bearing the date 1532 and signature
MS on its wall. Delilah sits on the table cradling Samson's head in her lap and cuts
his hair, though the text records that she called for a helper to shave him, while
armed Philistines wait around the corner to capture him. The *Prophetenbilder*, in
particular the illustrations to the Twelve Minor Prophets, are particularly rich, and
show perhaps better than any others how images might work, as Luther had put it
in 1525, 'for remembrance and better understanding'. Each depicts a preaching
prophet and, where it can be visualized, the core of his prophecy in the background.[86] At the start of the Book of Hosea, for example, the prophet, dressed in
sixteenth-century costume, preaches to a group of listeners against the backdrop of

---

[82] WA, DB 2, 545–53.   [83] Christensen, 'The Reformation of Bible Illustration', 105.
[84] Ibid., 114.   [85] Reinitzer, *Biblia deutsch*, 112.
[86] On the Minor Prophets see Gerhard Krause, *Studien zu Luthers Auslegung der Kleinen Propheten*
(Tübingen, 1962).

a very German landscape (Plate 2). Behind, we see Christ's Crucifixion and resurrection: the image tells the reader, much more immediately than any para-text could do, that this book is about Christ. Luther's marginal glosses confirm this: Hosea, one emphasizes, 'foretells…of Christ and the Gospel'.[87]

For Luther, the Old Testament's Christocentric prophecies were key, but so too were its stories, its accounts of God's preservation of Israel against powerful enemies. These provided both warning and comfort to the Bible's sixteenth-century readers.[88] The illustration from the Book of Nahum, which tells of the destruction of Nineveh and God's righteous justice, shows the prophet, simply dressed, preaching in the harbour of a German town to a group of merchants while cargo is unloaded from a nearby ship by crane (Plate 3). This image, like many of the others, transports biblical history into the world of the viewer. The 'woe of the murderous city, which is full of lies and robbery' (Nahum 3:1) serves as a warning to the Bible's readers, inhabitants of prosperous mercantile communities just like the one depicted here. The woodcut that illustrates Revelation 20, Gog and Magog's Attack on the Beloved City, provides another dramatic example. In 1522, this scene had been omitted, but now it was visualized as the Turkish siege of Vienna of 1529: some copies include the inscription 'Wien', in case the turbans, caftans and Stefansdom were not indicative enough.[89] One final example draws together a number of these themes. In the woodcut of St Luke that adorns the start of his Gospel, the evangelist is seated in a sixteenth-century study, and gazes towards a crucifix outside his window. The theological significance is clear: it is Luke who provides the fullest account of Christ's death on the cross. Luke's ox, the attribute given to him in accordance with Ezekiel's vision, is present, but so, more surprisingly, is his artist's easel and palette. Here, in keeping with tradition and perhaps out of respect for his status as the patron saint of painters, Master MS moves well beyond the boundaries of scriptural accuracy.

The woodcuts in the 1534 complete Bible provide the gold standard by which Lutheran Bible illustration was, and still is, measured. They are more visually engaging than any other cycle, and also more carefully crafted in order to bring out the significance of the texts they illustrate. It is not surprising, therefore, that they dominated Wittenberg Bible production during Luther's lifetime and continued to be reproduced either as a group or individually long after his death. Yet, it would be a mistake to take them as representative. In their quest to make Bibles visually appealing and marketable, publishers drew on a very wide variety of woodcuts, both re-using old designs and commissioning new. In Basel, Thomas Wolff printed in 1523 a copy of Luther's September New Testament in octavo format, illustrated with woodcuts based on Cranach's but designed by Hans Holbein the Younger.[90] Holbein also designed the woodcuts for the translations of the first three parts of the Old Testament, also in octavo format, that Wolff printed in 1524. In Augsburg

[87] On this edition see WA, DB 2, 545–53.

[88] Krause, *Studien*, 121; Bornkamm, *Luther und das Alte Testament*.

[89] Schmidt, *Die Illustration*, 192.

[90] Schmidt, *Die Illustration*, 122 ff. These woodcuts reappeared in many later editions, including the Froschauer Bibles of 1531 and 1545.

in 1523, Silvan Othmar published the *Neue testament deutsch*, with illustrations to Revelation designed by Hans Burgkmair the Elder. In 1534, in Frankfurt am Main, Christian Egenolph's publishing house produced a *Lutherbibel*, with small-scale illustrations by Hans Sebald Beham.[91]

Even after the seminal 1534 Wittenberg complete Bible, diversity continued: in 1540 Hans Lufft, Luther's favoured Bible publisher, produced an edition with illustrations by Georg Lemberger. It seems that Luther rejected these: the editions that he oversaw in 1541 and 1545 returned to Master MS's 1534 woodcuts. But Lemberger's illustrations, which constituted a much fuller cycle, were reproduced again during the 1550s and 1560s.[92] Such examples could be multiplied: although the 1534 woodcuts were certainly highly valued in Luther's Wittenberg they, unlike Luther's text, never became canonical elsewhere. We will see in Chapter 4 how much variety there was by the 1560s, the age of artists such as Virgil Solis, Jost Amman, and Tobias Stimmer. After Luther's death publishers continued to adapt and to update. During the 1550s, Lufft used the Lemberger illustrations, alongside others by Hans Brosamer. Brosamer's illustration for Hosea remains true to the spirit of the 1534 cycle in that it depicts on the left the prophet preaching and the resurrected Christ. Now, however, two-thirds of the scene is given over to a depiction of the prophet's warning against the evil living of the children of Israel: before a trellis entwined with vines, the king, high priest, and others eat, drink, and lust after women.[93]

The Bible may have 'powered the very project of Reformation', and was certainly, by the mid-sixteenth century, widely available to lay Lutherans. But it remained expensive, and despite its increasingly rich para-textual material and guiding illustrations it was still not an easy book to use. Hartmann Beier, preacher and pastor in Frankfurt, reflected in the preface to his illustrated 1555 *Historien Bibel* that he had gathered together the stories of the Old Testament and put them 'in a proper order' so that they could be grasped more easily. His work had been undertaken for the benefit of 'those who do not wish to buy the whole Bible', and for 'those who have the whole Bible, which is not convenient to carry' but want to read its stories on their travels.[94] Beier's passing comment draws our attention to the fact that the full vernacular Bible, for all its theological and cultural significance, was not the way that most laymen and women experienced Scripture. If we wish to assess images' importance in this process, we need to look therefore not only at Bibles but also at the texts that would have been more easily available to them, above all at Luther's *Small Catechism*, which for 300 years was reprinted more than any other Lutheran catechism and which set the tone for a tradition of illustrated Lutheran school books that lasted into the nineteenth century.[95]

[91] Ibid., 158–61, 128–33, 175–8.   [92] Ibid., 217 ff.
[93] Schmidt, *Die Illustration*, 225.
[94] *Historien Bibel. Das ist/Alle vornemste Historien aller bücher des Alten Testaments/auß dem Text der Bibel gezogen …* (Frankfurt: Chr. Egen, 1555), Vorrede.
[95] Stefan Ehrenpreis, 'Teaching Religion in Early Modern Europe: Catechisms, Emblems and Local Traditions', in Heinz Schilling and István György Tóth (eds), *Cultural Exchange in Early Modern Europe*, vol. 1, *Religion and Cultural Exchange in Europe, 1400–1700* (Cambridge, 2006), 256–73,

In 1529, the year in which the expanded and illustrated edition of Luther's prayer book appeared, two other key volumes were also printed in Wittenberg in octavo format: a new hymnal, and the *Small Catechism*. As Christopher Boyd Brown has pointed out, all three were intended to bridge the gap between the public worship and teaching of the church and the private devotional life of the household, and all three reflected 'an enduring Lutheran commitment to the use of the arts in the proclamation of the gospel'.[96] Of the three the catechism was, for Luther, undoubtedly the most important: it was 'the layman's Bible, which contains the whole contents of Christian teaching, which every Christian needs to know for salvation'.[97] In response to 'the lamentable, miserable need' that he encountered during the visitations carried out in Electoral Saxony and in Meissen in 1528–9, Luther produced two catechisms in 1529: one short, in dialogue form; one longer (the *German Catechism*) giving more expansive explanations intended for pastors and preachers.[98] The common man knew nothing, Luther complained, of Christian teaching, and many pastors were not fit to remedy this lack. So here, in readily accessible question-and-answer form, Luther presented the Ten Commandments, the Creed, the Our Father, and explanations of baptism and the Eucharist, alongside prayers for domestic devotion.

Printed catechisms became, over the course of the sixteenth century, the key tools of Lutheran religious instruction in churches and schools, and also in the home where, as the preface the *German Catechism* stated, 'every housefather must ask and hear his children and servants at least once a week'.[99] Luther's catechisms were not the only ones available: Johannes Brenz's, first published in 1527, remained popular, and after the mid-sixteenth century, new editions, both Lutheran and Reformed, proliferated as confessional boundaries hardened and both ecclesiastical and secular authorities sought to impose particular doctrinal views and devotional practices.[100] The Catholic response was spearheaded by Peter Canisius's Latin catechisms, available in various vernacular editions.[101] Scholarly research has focused on the theological content of the evangelical catechisms, with some consideration of their production and use in particular regional contexts and of their significance for the history of Protestant pedagogy. But like the editions of

here 258; Ringshausen, *Von der Buchillustration zum Unterrichtsmedium*, 36. See also Lee Palmer Wandel, *Reading Catechisms, Teaching Religion* (Leiden, 2016), especially 296–325.

[96] Christopher Boyd Brown, 'Devotional Life in Hymns, Liturgy, Music, and Prayer', in Kolb (ed.), *Lutheran Ecclesiastical Culture*, 205–58, here 205–6.

[97] WA, TR 5, 581, no. 6288.

[98] Gerhard Bode, 'Instruction of the Christian Faith by Lutherans after Luther', in Kolb (ed.), *Lutheran Ecclesiastical Culture*, 159–204, here 164. WA 30/I, 123 ff.

[99] WA 30/1, 129.

[100] Ehrenpreis, 'Teaching Religion', 259–60; Bode, 'Instruction', 162. See also Ferdinand Cohrs, *Vierhundert Jahre Luthers Kleiner Katechismus. Kurze Geschichte seiner Entstehung und seines Gebrauchs* (Langensalza, 1929); Johann Michael Reu, *Quellen zur Geschichte des kirchlichen Unterrichts in der evangelischen Kirche Deutschlands zwischen 1530 und 1600* (Gütersloh, 1904–35). Reu's survey of catechisms suggests that in every decade between 1550 and 1600 thirty or forty new editions were published.

[101] Ehrenpreis, 'Teaching Religion', 262; Ringshausen, *Von der Buchillustration zum Unterrichtsmedium*, 40 ff.

Luther's vernacular Bible, versions of his catechism were frequently illustrated. In 1529, both the *German* and *Small Catechism* used a cycle of woodcuts based on a series produced by Lucas Cranach the Elder for a single-sheet explanation of the Ten Commandments and Our Father written by Philip Melanchthon and probably printed in 1527 for distribution during visitations. During Luther's and Melanchthon's lifetimes most of the catechisms printed in Wittenberg took these Cranach illustrations as their prototype.[102]

In Melanchthon's early catechetical works, image and text were closely integrated: the single-sheet catechism showed above each image the relevant plea or commandment, with an explanation beneath that made sense of the scene depicted.[103] The first plea of the Our Father, for example, 'your name is holy', was illustrated by a preacher and his congregation, with a crucifix between them, with the explanation: 'Your name is rightly known, through right teaching and faith, and thereby honoured and praised' (Fig. 1.2).[104] The Ten Commandments were illustrated with a cycle of Old Testament scenes. The significance of some is clear: the Dance around the Golden Calf, for example, as a warning against worshipping other gods. Others were more obscure, and when Melanchthon reused these images in 1528 and 1529 he added further explanations. The ninth commandment, 'You should not covet your neighbour's house', was illustrated, for example, with the story of Jacob and the Rods, a rare iconography that was chosen here as a warning against miserliness.[105]

In 1529, however, when Cranach's images were adapted for use in Luther's catechisms, the carefully formulated relationship between image and text was compromised. Here, in Luther's octavo book, the illustrations are full-page: in visual terms, image and text are given equal weight. But Luther's texts, unlike Melanchthon's, give no guidance as to the meaning of the accompanying images. Each opening in the Decalogue, for example, simply shows on one page a woodcut and on the other the Commandment and accompanying question and answer: 'What is that? Answer...'. Early editions did not even include the biblical citation that would have helped the reader to make sense of the passage being illustrated. Moreover the prefaces to Luther's *Small* and *German Catechism*, unlike that to his prayer book, give no justifications for including images, suggesting that they were perhaps inserted at the publisher's (Rhau's) behest.[106] Luther trusted, it seems, Melanchthon's choice of scenes, and presumably hoped that the preacher or housefather would be able to build the necessary intellectual bridge between the image and its accompanying text.

It is surely here, in Luther's *Small Catechism*, if anywhere, that we should find images being used 'for the sake of simple folk'? Even if children and the poor did not regularly hold these books in their hands, they would have been familiar

---

[102] Thum, *Die Zehn Gebote*, 37, 80, 127. Ernst Grüneisen, 'Grundlegendes für die Bilder in Luthers Katechismen', *Luther=Jahrbuch* 20 (1938), 1–44.

[103] Ringshausen, *Von der Buchillustration zum Unterrichtsmedium*, 37.

[104] Grüneisen, 'Grundlegendes', 12. See also Koerner, *The Reformation of the Image*, 252 ff.

[105] Thum, *Die Zehn Gebote*, 83; Grüneisen, 'Grundlegendes', 36. This scene was also depicted in the 1534 Wittenberg complete Bible.

[106] Ringshausen, *Von der Buchillustration zum Unterrichtsmedium*, 37–8.

**Das iſt/ Dein name werde recht erkand/ durch rechte
lere vnd glauben/vnd dadurch gelobet vnd gepreiſet.**

Fig. 1.2. Lucas Cranach the Elder, woodcut illustration for 'Your Name is Holy', second page in the series 'The Lord's Prayer', 1527.

Credit: © Kupferstich-Kabinett, Staatliche Kunstsammlungen Dresden, Inv. Nr. A 1905-372. Photo: Herbert Boswank.

objects, used in catechism instruction in churches, schools, and homes. The Saxon visitation articles for 1533 already specified that Luther's catechisms must be in every parish, and a visitation ordinance for Brandenburg stated that housefathers and housemothers should 'diligently make their children and servants attend church, and also memorize the main articles of the Christian faith, as they are succinctly contained in Luther's catechism'.[107] Yet, the 'children and servants' would not have understood many of their images, because once removed from Melanchthon's explanations their interpretation depended on an extensive knowledge of the Bible. Jacob with his rods and sheep, for example, can have done little to enrich most catechumens' understanding of the ninth commandment, against covetousness. The careful linking of text and image, and the refined visual exegesis that we encountered in at least some Lutheran Bibles is lacking here, yet the woodcuts are still lively and engaging, depicting in many cases Luther's world with contemporary costumes and German landscapes. They explain, in part, the *Small Catechism*'s success: as one recent study has argued, the text became a type of chapbook because it was illustrated with full-page woodcuts.[108]

Gradually, once the practice of catechism illustration was established, Lutheran authors, illustrators, and printers worked to develop its pedagogical potential. And while the cycle of images designed by Melanchthon remained seminal, there was variation.[109] In an edition of the *German Catechism*, for example, printed in Nuremberg in 1531, the Second Commandment ('You shall not take the name of your God in vain') is illustrated with a woodcut showing two men in sixteenth-century costume throwing dice before a crucifix, their right hands held out in gestures of swearing or cursing. Behind a merchant and a man with dogs make similar gestures. In the background is the scene that traditionally illustrated this commandment: the stoning of the blasphemer. Lines connect the swearing mouths and gesturing hands to Christ's wounds and to the admonitory figure of God the Father above: a visualization of the sixteenth-century practice of swearing by the wounds or by the name of God, and a reminder that Christ was crucified for our sins.[110] A modified version of this image was used to illustrate a Nuremberg edition of the *Enchiridion (Small Catechism)*, published in 1547. There the publisher added a decorative border and, more importantly, a biblical citation to locate the image: 'This figure is described in the Third Book of Moses, Leviticus chapter 24.'[111]

The custom of adding biblical citations to the woodcut images gradually became more widespread: in Leipzig in 1544–5, for example, Valentin Bapst printed an edition of the *Small Catechism* that followed Melanchthon's canonical selection of scenes, but enclosed them in decorative borders and added scriptural references (Fig. 1.3).[112] Such brief scriptural references had become standard by the later

[107] Cohrs, *Vierhundert Jahre*, 27.   [108] Thum, *Die Zehn Gebote*, 37.
[109] Ibid., 112–13.
[110] Thum, *Die Zehn Gebote*, 108–9. Gerd Schwerhoff, *Zungen wie Schwerter: Blasphemie in alteuropäischen Gesellschaften 1200–1650* (Konstanz, 2005).
[111] *Enchiridion. Der kleyn Catechismus für die gemeyne Pfarrherren vnnd Predigern. Auffs new zugericht. Marti. Luther* (Nuremberg: Christoff Gutknecht, 1547), reprint Nuremberg, 1980.
[112] Thum, *Die Zehn Gebote*, 114–15. Luther himself praised the beauty of Bapst's hymn book: WA 35, 477, preface to 1545 edition.

Fig. 1.3. Illustration from Martin Luther, *Enchiridion Der kleine Catechismus: Für die gemeine Pfarherr und Prediger* (Leipzig: Bapst, 1544).

sixteenth century, and some authors added other interpretative apparatus. An edition of the *Enchiridion* written by Petrus Victorius, pastor in Kyritz in Brandenburg, and printed in Leipzig in 1591 provides a good example.[113] It has attracted interest in the context of studies of Lutheran pedagogy because it combines the lessons of the catechism with testimony from the Bible, drawing on the tradition of biblical *Sprüchbücher* (collections of sayings taken from Scripture).[114] This book was intended for children who recited the catechism in church in front of the congregation, and in it images are thoroughly integrated into the process of learning and understanding. Beneath or alongside each woodcut not only the relevant biblical citation but also a summary of the biblical passage is given. The images, based in most cases on the visual canon established by Melanchthon and Cranach, guided Victorius's choice of biblical sayings. For the catechumens taught from Victorius's book, the experience of learning to be Lutheran was profoundly shaped by images as well as by words.

CONCLUSION

Luther's teachings set the scene for a rich tradition of Protestant visual piety: the association that he made between iconoclasm and radicalism encouraged moderation with regard to the visual heritage of the late-medieval church; his emphasis on Christian freedom resurfaced again during the second half of the sixteenth century in disputes with iconoclastic Calvinists; his belief in the efficacy of the preached Word was used to justify the preservation of pre-Reformation images; and his willingness to use images for instruction and commemoration inspired numerous illustrated Bibles and catechisms. Moreover, against the traditional notion of the Reformation's 'Entsinnlichung' and 'Entemotionalisierung' of Christianity—the loss of the sensual and emotional elements of late-medieval piety—we should place Luther's clear conviction that faith is felt and not learned. For him images—both physical and mental—helped the Christian to understand Scripture and experience faith, aiding in the process by which God's Word was impressed upon human hearts.

The illustrated Bibles and catechisms produced in Wittenberg during the reformer's lifetime provide physical testimony to images' importance, as well as setting the scene for the development of a rich tradition of illustrated Lutheran devotional works. The visual clarity and theological depth of the biblical images produced in the Wittenberg of Luther, Melanchthon, and Cranach was unique. While the illustrations to many religious texts did little more than decorate, making books visually appealing to potential buyers, these images aspired to do

---

[113] *Enchiridion. Der Kleine Catechismus des Hocherleuchten vnd Geistreichen Mannes D. Martini Lutheri…Fein richtig vnd ördentlich zusammen gezogen/vnd mit den allerschönsten/herrlichten vnd besten Sprüchen der heiligen Göttlichen Schrifft also gezieret/geschmücket vnd erwiesen…Durch Petrum Victorium Pfarrern zu Kyritz* (Leipzig: Michael Lantsenberger, 1591). See Reu, *Quellen*, II, XCVI.
[114] Christine Reents and Christoph Melchior, *Die Geschichte der Kinder- und Schulbibel. Evangelisch—katholisch—jüdisch* (Göttingen, 2011), 73.

much more: they guided the interpretation of particular parts of Scripture and helped to fix its meaning in frail human understanding. Of course Protestant piety was oriented strongly towards the Word, and of course books constituted a key part of Protestant religious identity. Yet, how many of us, when we pick up a book, turn first of all to its illustrations? As Grimmelshausen's account of Simplicissimus's encounter with an illustrated Bible suggests, images, even if they are few and far between, capture the reader's attention and draw him or her into a story in a much more immediate way than marginalia and textual glosses. The fact that Simplicissimus radically misinterpreted what he saw seems, however, to substantiate the arguments of the iconoclasts: without the hermit's guidance, he would certainly, as Karlstadt had feared, have learned nothing of salvation from that image. It was in the conjunction of seeing images, hearing the preached Word and reading texts that Lutheran confessional consciousness and religious identity was formed.

PART I

THE CONFESSIONAL IMAGE

2

Between Catholic Idolatry and Calvinist Iconoclasm

Images and Confessional Identity in the Sixteenth Century

Throughout the sixteenth century, the Wittenberg reformers trod a delicate line between Catholic idolatry on the one hand and radical iconoclasm on the other. Luther himself denied that he was a 'protector of images', and condemned idolatrous image worship. Yet, he also reacted strongly against Karlstadt's legalism and inflammatory preaching. Images were a matter of Christian freedom: they could be kept or they could be removed, provided that this was done without 'fanaticism' and violent destruction. As some of the Empire's princes and magistrates began to implement the Reformation within their territories during the 1520s and 1530s, images played an important part in defining religious allegiance. All evangelicals agreed on the need to eliminate idolatry. But the edicts, church ordinances, and instructions for visitations, through which theological theory was translated into devotional reality, adopted a variety of stances on images. In territories that were orientated towards Wittenberg, these normative documents were either silent on images—implicitly permitting their preservation—or attempted to draw a distinction between those that were idolatrous and those that were not.[1] In Electoral Saxony, for example, after the initial Wittenberg church ordinance of 1522, explicit prescriptive statements on images were rare. Brandenburg's highly conservative 1540 church ordinance, which prescribed the retention of vestments, church services conducted largely in Latin, and numerous feast-days, was also, not surprisingly, silent on images.[2]

Johannes Bugenhagen's 1529 church ordinance for Hamburg shows how idolatrous images might be defined within this Wittenberg circle, and also indicates images' importance for confessional demarcation. Bugenhagen lamented 'that we have in our churches many false images and many useless wooden statues'. The ordinance spoke of the removal of 'the images near and before which particular worship and idolatry and special honour with candles and lights have been practiced',

---

[1] Volker Leppin, 'Kirchenausstattungen in territorialen Kirchenordnungen bis 1548', in Sabine Arend and Gerald Dörner (eds), *Ordnungen für die Kirche—Wirkungen auf die Welt. Evangelische Kirchenordnungen des 16. Jahrhunderts* (Tübingen, 2015), 137–55.

[2] Leppin, 'Kirchenausstattungen', 154–5.

but also emphasized that 'we may not be iconoclasts'.[3] Elsewhere reformers advocated a more thorough cleansing of church space. In Hesse, for example, the Homberg Synod that met in 1526 at the behest of Landgrave Philipp made no concessions with regard to images: all should be removed, whatever their devotional status and subject matter. Although Luther objected to the conclusions reached by this synod, Philipp again decreed the removal of images in 1527. Here, as elsewhere, the impact of such normative prescriptions is hard to assess: many images seem to have survived, for in 1605 Landgrave Moritz found it necessary to undertake a thorough stripping of the territory's churches as part of his Calvinist-inspired Reformation.[4] In Württemberg, a 1536 ducal decree distinguished, as the Wittenberg reformers had done, between 'the images that are prayed to' and inoffensive ('unärgerliche') images, which could remain. Ultimately, however, Duke Ulrich decided in favour of the removal of all images, aligning the territory's churches not with those of distant Wittenberg but rather with those of the important Imperial and Free Cities nearby.[5]

Of course, decrees and ordinances provide access only to prescription and not to practice. The first section of this chapter will therefore investigate, briefly, the appearance of Lutheran churches in the mid-sixteenth century. The picture that emerges is incoherent in the extreme: the preservation of pre-Reformation images and furnishings in some cases; the rapid or more gradual cleansing of church space in others; and the occasional commissioning of new altars, pulpits, and fonts. This picture varied not just from territory to territory but also from church to church: once the intense debates of the 1520s had died down, local communities were often left to make their own decisions with regard to the images in their churches. The fact that local context was so crucial in determining images' fate complicates any sense that there was a coherent 'Lutheran' position on images, while the fact that Lutheran congregations frequently worshipped surrounded by late-medieval paintings and statues undermines any notion of a 'Lutheran' aesthetic. By the mid-sixteenth century, Lutheranism had certainly found no satisfactory solution to the image question.[6] The question may have lost some of its urgency when the iconoclasm of the 1520s came to an end, but it re-emerged with a vengeance against the backdrop of the confessional conflicts of the second half of the sixteenth century.

The mid-sixteenth century was a time of crisis for the Lutheran church. In the aftermath of his 1547 victory over the Schmalkaldic League, Charles V attempted to impose a provisional religious settlement, the Interim of Augsburg, throughout the Empire. As a result, Lutheranism entered an era of profound division and

---

[3] Sehling EKO 5, 513. See Bridget Heal, 'Kirchenordnungen und das Weiterbestehen religiöser Kunstwerke in lutherischen Kirchen, in Arend and Dörner (eds), *Ordnungen für die Kirche*, 157–74.

[4] Leppin, 'Kirchenausstattungen', 145–6.

[5] Ibid., 150–4; Gudrun Litz, *Die reformatorische Bilderfrage in den schwäbischen Reichsstädten* (Tübingen, 2006), 41–56. For a full exploration of the image question in Württemberg see Róisín Watson, 'Lutheran Piety and Visual Culture in the Duchy of Württemberg, 1534–*c*.1700' (unpublished PhD, University of St Andrews, 2015).

[6] Günther Wartenberg, 'Bilder in den Kirchen der Wittenberger Reformation', in Johann Michael Fritz (ed.), *Die bewahrende Kraft des Luthertums. Mittelalterliche Kunstwerke in evangelischen Kirchen* (Regensburg, 1997), 19–33, esp. 22.

discord. Although the Reformation's political gains could not, Charles discovered, be reversed, Luther's death in 1546 had deprived the church of its key source of authority. Under pressure from the Interim, Luther's heirs contested his legacy in key theological matters such as the role of adiaphora, the relationship between faith and works, the significance of the law in Christian life, human free will, and original sin. In addition, Andreas Osiander sparked a debate over justification; and, echoing earlier antagonism between Luther and Zwingli, disputes continued over the Lord's Supper and Christology.[7] Now, in this 'culture of conflict', the image question divided Lutheran from Lutheran as well as Lutheran from Catholic and Reformed. In Ernestine Saxony, for example, the heartland of Gnesio-Lutheranism, reformers campaigned against the images and altarpieces that had been allowed to survive the Reformation. The 1577 Formula of Concord, to which both Ernestine and Albertine Saxony subscribed, resolved many of the theological disputes within the Lutheran church. But by this time Germany's Lutherans were fighting a two-front war against a resurgent Catholic church on the one hand and a 'Second', Calvinist Reformation on the other. Images, which from the start had played a role in strategies of both alignment and demarcation, gained even more importance as Lutherans sought to define and defend their confessional identity.[8]

LUTHERAN CHURCHES IN THE MID-SIXTEENTH CENTURY

What, then, did the Empire's Lutheran churches look like at the time of the Luther's death in 1546? Reformers had sought to remove images that were the focus of pilgrimage, and had often, like Bugenhagen in his Hamburg church ordinance, campaigned against those that depicted non-scriptural subjects, stories that were, as a Franconian church ordinance of 1543 put it, 'unclear and full of lies'.[9] In reality, even the key objective of eliminating idolatrous practices proved hard to realize: visitation records indicate that in the countryside pilgrimage to cult images and the giving of votive offerings often continued for several decades after the Reformation, and sometimes even lasted until well into the seventeenth century. In the city churches where Lutheran pastors preached on a regular basis and where educated magistrates worshipped, images that had attracted idolatrous devotion were generally removed.[10] But even here, theory and practice did not necessarily coincide. The 'preserving power' of Lutheranism has been well documented: in

---

[7] Irene Dingel, 'Ablehnung und Aneignung. Die Bewertung der Autorität Martin Luthers in den Auseinandersetzungen um die Konkordienformel', *Zeitschrift für Kirchengeschichte*, 105 (1994), 35–57; Irene Dingel, 'The Culture of Conflict and the Controversies Leading to the Formula of Concord (1548–1580)', in Kolb (ed.), *Lutheran Ecclesiastical Culture*, 15–64. Robert Kolb, *Luther's Heirs Define His Legacy: Studies on Lutheran Confessionalization* (Aldershot, 1996); Luise Schorn-Schütte, *Das Interim 1548/50. Herrschaftskrise und Glaubenskonflikt* (Heidelberg, 2005).

[8] Leppin, 'Kirchenausstattungen'; Heal, 'Kirchenordnungen', 170–1.

[9] Sehling EKO 11, 630 (Schweinfurt).

[10] See, for example, Bridget Heal, *The Cult of the Virgin Mary in Early Modern Germany: Protestant and Catholic Piety, 1500–1648* (Cambridge, 2007), 110–14 on Nuremberg.

every Lutheran part of the Empire, from Württemberg in the south to the Hanseatic cities of Lübeck and Stralsund in the north and from Frankfurt am Main in the west to Upper Lusatia in the east, pre-Reformation images survived, many of them depicting non-scriptural subjects.[11] Their fate was, it seems, shaped as much by concern about order, by respect for private property, and by the power of communal memory as by the normative prescriptions of the reformers.

The extent of this preservation of course varied from place to place. Nuremberg's churches, for example, provide an astonishingly rich snapshot of late-medieval devotional life. Their furnishings were spared not only the predations of the iconoclasts but also the emendations of the baroque: in Nuremberg side altars, sacrament houses and saints' shrines provided (and continue to provide) the visual backdrop for evangelical worship.[12] In Berlin, even more pre-Reformation church furnishings survived Joachim II's 1539 Reformation, though many were dispersed or destroyed during the late-sixteenth and early-seventeenth centuries as Brandenburg's electors moved towards Calvinism. Joachim II had filled his newly built collegiate church (often referred to as Berlin's Cathedral) with valuable images, relics, textiles, and liturgical vessels. Its most famous furnishings were its winged altarpieces depicting scenes from the Passion and figures of saints produced by Lucas Cranach the Elder and his workshop in 1537–8 after the model of Albrecht of Brandenburg's commission for the Halle collegiate church.[13] The splendid visual environment of Berlin's Cathedral outlasted the introduction of evangelical services and the institutionalization of Brandenburg's Lutheran church. The Cranach panels remained intact and *in situ* until 1615, and visitors' accounts and inventories testify to the survival of many splendid treasures and vestments. In 1561, the papal nuncio Giovanni Francesco Commendone reported that Joachim II had showed him a chapel containing many silver statues of saints (some of which were still placed on the high altar at Christmas), as well as silver and gold crosses, chalices, candelabras, and monstrances. He also mentioned velvet vestments with images embroidered with gold and pearls.[14]

Nuremberg and Berlin provide two of the most extreme examples of Lutheranism's 'preserving power', but the phenomenon was widespread: in Saxony, at least

---

[11] Fritz, *Die bewahrende Kraft*; Caroline Walker Bynum, 'Are Things "Indifferent"? How Objects Change Our Understanding of Religious History', *German History* 34 (1) (2016), 88–112. The same was true beyond the Empire's borders—see, for example, Martin Jürgensen Wangsgaard, *Ritual and Art across the Danish Reformation: Changing Interiors of Village Churches, 1450–1600* (Turnhout, 2013).

[12] Heal, *The Cult of the Virgin Mary*, 64–115.

[13] Nikolaus Müller, *Der Dom zu Berlin* (Berlin, 1906), esp. 48–66; Agnieszka Gąsior, 'Der Reliquienschatz eines protestantischen Landesherren. Joachim II. von Brandenburg und Hedwig von Polen in Berlin', in Evelin Wetter (ed.), *Formierung des konfessionellen Raumes in Ostmitteleuropa* (Stuttgart, 2008), 237–50. Inventories from 1536, 1537, 1538, 1557, 1599 survive in GStPK, I. HA Rep. 2 Berliner Dom, Nr. 1: Etliche alte Dokumente des Domstifts, 1469–1609. On the Cranach altarpieces see Andreas Tacke, *Der katholische Cranach: zu zwei Grossaufträgen von Lucas Cranach d. Ä., Simon Franck und der Cranach-Werkstatt (1520–40)* (Mainz, 1992); Stiftung Preußische Schlösser und Gärten Berlin-Brandenburg, *Cranach und die Kunst der Renaissance unter den Hohenzollern. Kirche, Hof und Stadtkultur,* exh. cat. (Berlin, 2009), 213–21.

[14] Tacke, *Der katholische Cranach*, 208–9, 219.

230 altarpieces and 1000 individual carved figures and painted panels survive.[15] Nowhere, it seems, have so many medieval altar retables been preserved as in Lutheran churches.[16] Throughout this book, we will encounter examples of pre-Reformation images that were carefully conserved by Lutheran congregations, even though their subject matter was, to evangelical eyes, 'unclear and full of lies'. Yet, we need to qualify this picture of Lutheran preservation. There was very little Lutheran iconoclasm, but there was plenty of orderly removal and a good deal of long-term neglect. It is very difficult to reconstruct the pre- and post-Reformation furnishings of Lutheran churches. Even in Wittenberg's town church, the 'mother church of Protestantism', it is remarkably hard to be sure what was removed and when. On 24 January 1524, the town council decreed the removal of all images and retention of only three of the original nineteen altars.[17] Yet, on 13 February, the Elector ordered that surviving images should remain in the church, and it was not until 1536 and 1543 that all side altars were destroyed. Treasures and liturgical vessels were sold off gradually, and even in 1560 two images remained to be disposed of. By 1548, when Lucas Cranach's altarpiece was installed, the church was probably largely empty apart from a fifteenth-century font and some epitaphs.[18]

Elsewhere in the territory ruled over by the Ernestine electors until 1547 images' fate also hung by a thread. In Zwickau, for example, after an outbreak of iconoclasm in 1522, there was little popular destruction. An account of the history of St Katharine's Church given in the 1633 *Descriptio Urbis Cyneæ* suggests that there the transformation of church space was a gradual process, lasting more than two decades from the 1524 destruction of the altar at which early-morning Mass was read to the 1548 removal of the sacrament house.[19] In Zwickau, there were some spectacular survivals: the altar depicting Christ Washing the Disciples' Feet from the Cranach workshop, for example, which was moved in 1530 from the Marienkirche to the Franciscan cloister then in 1534 to St Katharine's; the elaborate carved Holy Sepulchre in the Marienkirche that had been used during the Easter liturgy; a carved *Vesperbild* (Mary with the body of Christ on her lap) that had been much venerated prior to the Reformation, and a life-sized crucifix in the same church.[20] But the numerous side altars in the Marienkirche were removed, along with most of its silver and gold treasures and precious textiles, and many of its images were hidden away. By the mid-seventeenth century the Holy Sepulchre and *Vesperbild*

[15] Ingo Sandner, *Spätgotische Tafelmalerei in Sachsen* (Dresden, 1993), 32–4. Sandner's study did not encompass the whole of Ernestine and Albertine Saxony, but focused on the areas of greatest artistic significance.

[16] Fritz, *Die bewahrende Kraft*, 17.   [17] Leppin, 'Kirchenausstattungen', 140–1.

[18] Insa Christiane Hennen, 'Die Wittenberger Stadtkirche: bauliche Situation und Wandel der Ausstattung', in Jan Harasimowicz and Bettina Seyderhelm (eds), *Cranachs Kirche: Begleitbuch zur Landesausstellung Sachsen-Anhalt Cranach der Jüngere 2015* (Markkleeberg, 2015), 21–6, esp. 23.

[19] *Descriptio Urbis Cyneæ. Das ist Warhafftige vnd Eigendliche Beschreibung/der vhralten Stadt Zwickau…Von Laurentio Wilhelmo Obern Cantori alhier* (Zwickau: Melchior Göpner, 1633), 220, 237. On Zwickau's medieval churches see Julia Sobotta, *Die Kirche der verhinderten Reichsstadt. Eine Untersuchung zur Geschichte der Kirchen in Zwickau im Mittelalter* (PhD, University of Leipzig, 2009).

[20] Otto Langer, 'Über drei Kunstwerke der Marienkirche zu Zwickau: den Altar, die Beweinung Christi und das heilige Grab', *Mitteilungen des Altertumsvereins für Zwickau und Umgegend*, 12 (1919), 75–101.

were in the sacristy, and other images languished in a room above the north porch that was known as the 'Götzenkammer' (idol chamber).[21] The church's most splendid pre-Reformation image, Michael Wolgemut's 1479 altarpiece, survived *in situ* but attracted considerable criticism, as we shall see (Plate 4). Here there were also some new commissions: epitaphs, a font, and a pulpit. The pulpit was donated in 1536, and used, according to later sources, the foundation stone from the recently destroyed Marian chapel in Zwickau's Töpfergasse at its base.[22]

In Albertine Saxony, the picture was equally complex. In Leipzig, the territory's commercial capital, side altars were removed from the Thomaskirche and Nikolaikirche, the city's two main parish churches, in 1540. Only one of the Thomaskirche's pre-Reformation altarpieces is known to have survived.[23] In the Nikolaikirche, the high altar's pre-Reformation winged retable remained in place until it was removed to make space for a new, evangelical altarpiece in the first decade of the seventeenth century. This church acquired various new furnishings including a font and, in the 1560s, four large Netherlandish tapestries and four large panels with Bible quotations that hung on the walls of the choir.[24] At the other extreme, the large-scale pre-Reformation furnishings of the parish church dedicated to St Anne in the mining town of Annaberg in the Erzgebirge survived into the seventeenth century largely undisturbed. These included six magnificent altarpieces. It is perhaps not surprising that Annaberg's town church, which had recently formed the focus of extensive investment by both the local community and its territorial overlord Duke Georg, was left more-or-less untouched by the Reformation.[25]

The situation was more varied in nearby Freiberg, a residential town for the Albertine Wettins and the administrative centre of the region's mining industry. Freiberg's Cathedral, from 1541 the burial place of the Albertine dukes and electors,

[21] On the pre-Reformation side altars see Langer, 'Über drei Kunstwerke', 79. For general discussions of the history of the church and its furnishings see 'Die Hauptkirche zu St. Marien in Zwickau', *Neue Sächsiche Kirchengalerie*, 1902, col. 71–106; Richard Steche, *Beschreibende Darstellung der älteren Bau- und Kunstdenkmäler des Königreichs Sachsen*, vol. 12 (Dresden, 1889), 80–124. On the *Vesperbild* see especially Langer, 'Über der Kunstwerke', 85–93. A rich collection of seventeenth-century inventories from the Marienkirche and the town's other churches survives: StadtAZw, III z 4 K Nr. 109, Kirchliche Inventarien 1675–1761. On the 'Götzenkammer' see also Joseph Koerner, 'The Icon as Iconoclash', in Bruno Latour and Peter Weibel (eds), *Iconoclash: Beyond the Image Wars in Science, Religion, and Art* (Karlsruhe and Cambridge, MA, 2002), 164–213, esp. 164–5.
[22] *Beschreibende Darstellung*, 111. M. T. W. Hildebrand, *Historische Nachrichten über die Kirchen der Stadt Zwickau* (Zwickau, 1819), 35.
[23] Cornelius Gurlitt (ed.), *Beschreibende Darstellung der älteren Bau- und Kunstdenkmäler des Königreichs Sachsen*, vol. 17, *Stadt Leipzig (I. Theil)* (Dresden, 1895), 52; Georg Dehio, *Handbuch der Deutschen Kunstdenkmäler. Sachsen II, Regierungsbezirke Leipzig und Chemnitz*, ed. Barbara Bechter et al. (Munich, 1998), 805–6, on the carved depiction of the Lamentation from *c.*1490/95 that was donated to the *Stadtkirche* of St John in Plauen near Zwickau in the 1720s.
[24] Frank Schmidt, 'Die Innenausstattung der Nikolaikirche im Wandel der Jahrhundert', in Armin Kohle (ed.), *St. Nikolai zu Leipzig. 850 Jahre Kirche in der Stadt* (Petersberg, 2015), 222–34, esp. 226–30. I am grateful to Professor Kohle for bringing this recent study to my attention.
[25] Bernd Moeller, 'Annaberg als Stadt der Reformation', in Harald Marx and Cecilie Holberg (eds), *Glaube und Macht: Sachsen in Europa der Reformationszeit. Aufsätze* (Dresden, 2004), 103–11. Georg Arnold, *Chronicon Annæbergense continuatum… biss uffs 1658. Jahr nach Christi Geburth* (reprint Stuttgart, 1812), 32–8.

Fig. 2.1. Hans Witten, Tulip Pulpit, *c.*1508–10 and Hans Fritzsche, Miner's Pulpit, 1638, Freiberg (Saxony), Cathedral.

Credit: © Bildarchiv Foto Marburg, Aufnahme-Nr.: B 4.965/1. Photo: Harald Busch.

lost its side altars. But its tulip-shaped pulpit survived (Fig. 2.1). It was a master-piece of late-gothic sculpture, created by Hans Witten in *c.*1508–10 and adorned with figures of four church fathers. What such portraits meant to a Lutheran audience we can only guess: Freiberg's chronicler Andreas Möller, writing in 1653, clearly had no idea of their significance, and identified them as Pope Sixtus IV, a cardinal and two bishops. In the same church, Möller records that statues of the apostles and saints also survived, and were 'beautiful and almost entirely covered with gold'. Yet, the other 'images and idols, which previously stood beside the Mass altars' were by Möller's time 'set aside in a special vault next to the large spiral staircase'.[26]

---

[26] On the Wettin burial chapel see in particular Monika Meine-Schawe, *Die Grablege der Wettiner im Dom zu Freiberg. Die Umgestaltung des Domchores durch Giovanni Maria Nosseni 1585–94* (Göttingen, 1989). Andreas Möller, *Theatrum Freibergense Chronicum. Beschreibung der alten löblichen BergHauptStadt Freyberg in Meissen...* (Freiberg: Georg Beuther, 1653), 58.

In each case, local context was key. Despite the attempts of some church ordinances and visitations to create a uniform environment of worship, decisions regarding altars, altarpieces, and other items of furnishing were generally made on an ad hoc basis by town councils, in response to the initiatives of individual pastors or parishioners. As a Franconian church ordinance of 1543 noted, 'there are some who break the images and throw them out of the churches. On the other hand, there are others who allow the images to remain. In this, one should diligently pay attention to the time, to people and to other circumstances'.[27] Perhaps the hardest aspect of all to document is the simple neglect of pre-Reformation images. Michael Wolgemut's Marian altar and Hans Witten's tulip-shaped pulpit were objects of local pride, valued by at least some Lutherans for their historical significance and beauty. Lesser images were not so carefully preserved. From the small town of Scheibenberg in the Erzgebirge, where he served as pastor from 1638 to 1688, the chronicler Christian Lehmann wrote of his experiences touring the region's churches:

> I found idolatrous images that had been used under the godless papacy for superstitious pilgrimages and self-chosen divine offices with the Gradual. Thereafter many of the images had been removed and placed in the corners or hidden in the sacristies.[28]

To a local schoolmaster who wrote to him asking what should be done with such images, Lehmann complained: 'It is annoying that some of the saints' images that were present in the old church are thrown back and forth beneath the old vault and are mutilated by some evil knaves'. They should, he argued, either be renovated 'and put up in the church in one place, or otherwise put away in an uncontested location'.[29] Though we can only occasionally glimpse what entered them and when, Freiberg's 'special vault', Zwickau's 'idol chamber', and the sacristy in Annaberg where, by the mid-seventeenth century, images and relics of saints had been hidden away, all testify to Lutherans' ambivalent attitude towards the material remnants of the pre-Reformation past.

AFTER THE INTERIM: CRISIS AND CONFLICT WITHIN LUTHERANISM

During the second half of the sixteenth century, the pre-Reformation images that many local Lutheran congregations had permitted to survive were given new significance by events occurring at the level of the Empire. On 25 April 1547 Charles V, his brother Ferdinand and Duke Moritz of Saxony defeated the Ernestine Elector Johann Friedrich of Saxony and the forces of the Schmalkaldic League at the Battle of Mühlberg. Johann Friedrich and Philip of Hesse, champions of the Protestant cause since the League's foundation in 1532, were captured

---

[27] Sehling EKO 11, 629.
[28] Quoted in Stephan Schmidt-Brücken and Karsten Richter, *Der Erzgebirgschronist Christian Lehmann: Leben und Werk* (Marienberg, 2011), 177. The Gradual is part of the Catholic Mass.
[29] Ibid., 172.

and imprisoned, and Johann Friedrich was forced to cede his electoral title and lands to his cousin, Moritz. At the 'armoured' Diet that met in Augsburg in 1547–8, Charles proclaimed a provisional religious settlement, the Interim, which was intended to last until the general council of the church, then underway at Trent, made final decisions concerning the religious schism. The Interim made minimal concession to Protestants on a married priesthood and communion in both kinds, but otherwise decreed a return to the doctrine and devotional life of the old church. It placed special emphasis on ceremony, 'without which religion cannot be properly fostered', re-imposing a full cycle of feast-days. And it affirmed the value of the images and other church furnishings that accompanied this ceremony, while attempting, as Trent did fifteen years later, to reform their use:

> The altars, priests' vestments, liturgical vessels of the churches, flags, and also crosses, candles, images and paintings should be kept in the churches, but they are only reminders and no divine honour is directed towards them. And no superstitious flocking to images and to paintings of the saints is to take place.[30]

Although some of the Empire's princes, notably Joachim II of Brandenburg and Friedrich II of the Palatinate, supported the Interim, there was plenty of political and popular resistance.[31] Many evangelical clergy from southern Germany chose exile over implementation, and the city of Magdeburg became a centre of literary opposition, thanks to the group of theologians assembled around Nikolaus von Amsdorf and Matthias Flacius Illyricus.[32] In Electoral Saxony, Moritz sought to negotiate a middle way between imperial pressure and the resistance of his Territorial Estates. In December 1548, an alternative to the Interim was presented to the Saxon Diet in Leipzig, a compromise based on the work of Philip Melanchthon and others, which proposed concessions to the Catholic party regarding traditional ceremonies and images in order to preserve the key teachings of the Lutheran Reformation. The so-called 'Leipzig Interim', which was published first of all by its opponent Flacius and then in abbreviated official form in 1549, avoided as far as possible controversial topics such as the ecclesiastical hierarchy. It relied on the concept of adiaphora, non-binding neutral practices, in order to facilitate compromise with the Catholic church, allowing amongst other things the preservation or reintroduction of vestments and images.[33]

The defeat of the Schmalkaldic League had created a crisis, a situation of widespread threat and persecution more acute than any that German Lutheranism had experienced before. While Melanchthon and the Wittenberg theologians saw compromise as the only possibility for preserving evangelical congregations, Flacius

[30] Joachim Mehlhausen (ed.), *Das Augsburger Interim von 1548. Nach den Reichstagsakten deutsch und lateinisch* (Neukirchen-Vluyn, 1970), 102 (22, 'Vom opffer der Meß'), 136 (26, 'Von den ceremonien und gebrauch der sacramenten').

[31] Schorn-Schütte, *Das Interim*; on Brandenburg see Bodo Nischan, *Prince, People, and Confession. The Second Reformation in Brandenburg* (Philadelphia, 1994), 25 ff.

[32] Thomas Kaufmann, *Das Ende der Reformation: Magdeburgs 'Herrgotts Kanzelei' (1548–51/2)* (Tübingen, 2003).

[33] Carl Gottlieb Bretschenider (ed.), *Corpus Reformatorum*, vol. 7 (Halle an der Saale, 1840), 258–64; 426–8.

and the Gnesio-Lutherans accused them of abandoning Luther's teachings. Amongst the theological controversies that arose in the wake of the Augsburg Interim, one, the adiaphora dispute, had particular significance for ecclesiastical images. The question of what was necessary for and what might be detrimental to faith, justification, and salvation had preoccupied the medieval church, and had resurfaced, as we have seen, during the early decades of the Reformation, when Luther had argued that in destroying images Karlstadt, just like the papists, had destroyed Christian freedom.[34] In the crisis situation of 1548, Melanchthon justified his concessions to the realities of imperial politics by distinguishing between matters of external order, such as the festal calendar and church furnishings, which could be determined by the state, and matters of evangelical teaching, which could not. For Flacius, on the other hand, the Interim and Leipzig response had created a situation in which the church needed to adopt a clear stance: 'In the case where confession of the faith is necessary there are no adiaphora'.[35] The Gnesio-Lutherans feared that Melanchthon's compromises would confuse the common people, obscuring the central evangelical principle of justification by faith alone. Adiaphora, they maintained, prevented a true public confession of faith once they were prescribed by the state.

Against this backdrop, the image question regained its urgency. In some evangelical territories, for example, Brandenburg, the Interim's injunction to retain 'altars...images and paintings' was easily observed, for very few had been removed in the first place; in others, for example Württemberg, various attempts were made to restore or replace images that had been neglected or destroyed.[36] Elsewhere, however, the removal of pre-Reformation images and altarpieces that had, up to that point, survived intact and *in situ* signalled opposition to the Interim. Reformers justified their removal on two grounds: an ongoing concern about idolatry; and a desire to be true to Luther's legacy by enabling pastors to celebrate communion facing towards the congregation. Luther had stated in his 1526 *German Mass* that 'in the true Mass amongst real Christians...the priest should always face the people, as Christ doubtlessly did in the Last Supper'.[37] Where retables remained, this was, of course, impossible. The removal of altarpieces, the repositioning of altars, and the suppression of all remaining 'unchristian ceremonies and idolatry' became, as we shall see in the case of Ernestine Saxony, a way of signalling opposition to the 'Adiaphoristen', to those who were prepared to make dangerous concessions to the Catholic church.[38]

---

[34] Dingel, 'The culture of conflict', 34 ff.; Joachim Mehlhausen, 'Der Streit um die Adiaphora', in ibid., *Vestigia Verbi: Aufsätze zur Geschichte der evangelischen Theologie* (Tübingen, 1998), 64–92. On the conflict in the Wettin terriotries see in particular E. Koch, 'Der Ausbruch des adiaphoristischen Streits und seine Folgewirkung', in Irene Dingel and Günther Wartenberg (eds), *Politik und Bekenntnis. Die Reaktion auf das Interim von 1548* (Leipzig, 2007), 179–90. See also Reimund Sdzuj, *Adiaphorie und Kunst: Studien zur Genealogie ästhetischen Denkens* (Tübingen, 2005), 111, 117.
[35] Dingel, 'The culture of conflict', 37.   [36] Watson, 'Lutheran Piety', 49–53.
[37] WA 19, 80; LW 53, 69.   [38] Heal, 'Kirchenordnungen', 168–9.

ERNESTINE SAXONY: WEIMAR AND BEYOND

When Duke Johann Friedrich I ('the Magnanimous'), who had been celebrated as champion of the true faith since his capture at Mühlberg, died in 1554 his three sons continued his political and religious policies. The eldest, Johann Friedrich II, was determined to regain his father's lost electoral title. His military support for the revolt led by the Imperial Knight Wilhelm von Grumbach ended in defeat in 1567, and he spent the remainder of his life (to 1595) as an imperial prisoner. Under both Johann Friedrich II and his successor, his brother Johann Wilhelm I, the religious life of Ernestine Saxony was shaped by the dukes' determination to draw boundaries between themselves and their Albertine cousin and neighbour, the Saxon Elector August I. While August styled himself as the protector of Melanchthon and his successors in Wittenberg, the Ernestine dukes promoted the Gnesio-Lutheran cause and resisted the Interim.[39] In 1557, Flacius was called to Johann Friedrich II's university in Jena, where he remained until 1561. He was dismissed in 1561, accused of having attempted to circumscribe the duke's authority as head of the territorial church. But those who supported Flacius's cause returned to favour in 1567 under Johann Wilhelm, and remained until 1573 when August I took over as regent at the duke's death and steered the territory firmly away from Gnesio-Lutheranism.[40]

The most famous visual expression of Ernestine religious identity is the Weimar Altarpiece, possibly planned before the death of Lucas Cranach the Elder in 1553 but completed by his son and workshop in 1555 (Fig. 2.2). Installed behind the high altar of Weimar's main church, St Peter and Paul, it served as a memorial to Duke Johann Friedrich I who is depicted with his wife, Sibylle of Cleves, on its left wing. It was commissioned—according to its Latin inscription—by the duke's three sons to commemorate the loyal faith of their parents; the sons appear on the altarpiece's right wing.[41] The central panel shows an allegory of salvation: from the side wound of the crucified Christ redeeming blood falls onto a full-length depiction of Cranach the Elder, who is flanked by John the Baptist and Luther.[42] To the left of the crucifix the resurrected Christ tramples death and devil, and behind is a version of the Law and Gospel iconography. In this image, the rulers of Ernestine Saxony lay claim to the Wittenberg legacy, depicting not only Luther himself but also his friend and ally, Cranach the Elder, who had followed the defeated Johann Friedrich I into exile after 1547. In 1572, the church also acquired an extraordinary triple portrait of Luther, attributed to the Weimar artist Veit Thim and his workshop. Here Luther is portrayed as a monk, as a pastor, and as Junker Jörg, with texts below giving the key dates and events of his life. As Joseph Koerner has pointed

---

[39] Dingel, 'The culture of conflict', 25 ff.

[40] Rudolf Herrmann, *Thüringische Kirchengeschichte,* vol. 2 (Weimar, 1947; reprint Waltrop, 2000), esp. 150–72.

[41] Ingrid Schulze, *Lucas Cranach d. J. und die protestantische Bildkunst in Sachsen und Thüringen: Frömmigkeit, Theologie, Fürstenreform* (Bucha nr. Jena, 2004), 106.

[42] See Heike Schlie, 'Blut und Farbe. Sakramentale Dimensionen der frühneuzeitlichen Bild- und Kunsttheorie', in Stefanie Ertz, Heike Schlie, and Daniel Weidner (eds), *Sakramentale Repräsentation. Substanz, Zeichen und Präsenz in der Frühen Neuzeit* (Munich, 2012), 51–80.

Fig. 2.2. Lucas Cranach the Younger, Weimar Altarpiece, 1555.
Credit: © Evangelisch-Lutherische Kirchengemeinde Weimar.

out, this triptych blurs the lines between 'exemplification and hagiography'.[43] Like the Cranach altarpiece, it provides eloquent testimony to the desire of Ernestine Saxony's evangelicals to be seen as Luther's true heirs.

---

[43] Koerner, *The Reformation of the Image*, 389.

If we look beyond these famous images we can see, however, that elsewhere in Ernestine Saxony images' role in Lutheran worship was contested during this period.[44] Flacius and his supporters wanted to cleanse the territory's churches of all remnants of the papist past, but Lutheran congregations—especially their more prosperous members—were reluctant to comply. Jena's main church, St Michael, provides one example. In 1558, Flacius, Jena's deacon Balthasar Winter, and a professor of law Basilius Monner wrote to the duke to try to dissuade him from returning an altarpiece—a 'papist panel', as the letter described it—to the church. Flacius, Winter, and Monner trod a typically Lutheran line between idolatry and iconoclasm, distancing themselves not only from 'papists' but also from 'icono-clasts', who reject all images including crucifixes. They opposed the Jena altarpiece for a variety of reasons: it was 'papist, mangled, broken, deformed and offensive', and the Christ Child had been taken from it, which they considered to be a bad omen; the retable had been removed recently at the behest of the court preacher Johann Stoltz, and to restore it would suggest division amongst the territory's theologians and cause confusion; and above all the duke must be true to Luther's memory, and ensure that 'the abandoned papist ceremonies and adiaphora' were not reintroduced. The danger of idolatry was still, for the authors of this letter, very real: restoring the altarpiece would, they argued, 'give simple Christians or secret papists, or at least their descendants…occasion and reason to pray with abominable sin to Joseph and Mary, who are carved and gilded on this panel'. They had witnessed, they said, only four years previously, 'that on a feast-day at meal time, women here knelt before the high altar and prayed to the saints'. And they feared that such people (the association between women and superstition was a common one) still had 'the old abomination of the papacy' hidden secretly in their hearts.[45]

Such concerns found expression in visitation articles too: images received an unusual amount of attention in the visitations conducted in the Ernestine lands during the mid-sixteenth century.[46] The instructions for the 1554–5 general vis-itation, drawn up by Johann Stoltz, stated that 'the pastors should not tolerate any papist or idolatrous images and paintings in their churches'. Instructions for individual towns sometimes specified that it was images that did not accord with biblical stories that were to be removed; and those for Coburg, Eisfeld, and Gotha also prescribed that altars should be arranged so that 'the ministers may perform all

---

[44] These controversies are described in Ernst Koch, 'Die Beseitigung der "abgöttischen Bilder" und ihre Folgen im ernestinischen Thüringen', in Hans-Jörg Nieden and Marcel Nieden (eds), *Praxis Pietatis: Beiträge zu Theologie und Frömmigkeit in der Frühen Neuzeit: Wolfgang Sommer zum 60. Geburtstag* (Stuttgart, 1999), 225–41.

[45] Thür HStA Weimar, Abteilung A, Ernestinisches Gesamtarchiv (hereafter EGA), Religionswesen, Registrande N. Nr. 183.

[46] On these visitations see Arno Heerdegen, 'Geschichte der allgemeinen Kirchen Visitation in den ernestinischen Landen im Jahre 1554/55, nach Akten des Sachsen-Ernestinischen Gesamt-Archivs in Weimar', *Zeitschrift des Vereins für Thüringische Geschichte und Altertumskunde* N. F. 6. Supplementheft (Jena, 1914); Rudolf Herrmann, 'Die Generalvisitationen in den Ernestinischen Landen zur Zeit der Lehrstreitigkeiten des 16. Jahrhunderts (1554/55, 1562, 1569/70, 1573)', *Zeitschrift des Vereins für Thüringische Geschichte und Altertumskunde*, N. F. 22 (1915), 75–156.

their services facing towards the people'.[47] Some pastors and congregations complied, but many did not. In 1559, Balthasar Winter, by that point superintendent in Jena, complained to the duke that in churches outside Jena the changes with regard to altars had not been implemented. If these changes were not made, the 'Adiaphoristen' would, he feared, return to papist ceremonies, to a form of celebrating communion that 'is like an ostentatious Mass rather than the original last supper of Christ'.[48] In 1560, Johann Friedrich ordered another visitation. In a provision that captures beautifully the shift that theologians wished to achieve from a visual to a verbal form of piety, the 1560 visitation stated that churches were to sell superfluous furnishings, images, and other objects, 'in favour of the acquisition of German Bibles, the *Hauspostille* and the volumes of the Jena edition of Luther's works that have appeared already'.[49]

This visitation, and subsequent local visitations, produced a series of responses from secular officials that document the survival of images and, in some cases, hint at their significance for Lutheran congregations. In Körner, for example, a community with two churches that lay within the *Amt* (administrative district) of Volkenroda, the parish church of St Wigbert still contained plenty of pre-Reformation images and artefacts. According to the list submitted to the duke by Volkenroda's tax collector in 1560, these included altar cloths, vestments, dresses for an image of the Christ Child, two monstrances, and liturgical vessels, amongst which were a container for holy water, a censer for incense, and a chalice for taking communion to the sick. The list contrasted 'papist books'—chiefly missals—with 'good books', including the German Bible and Luther's *German Catechism*. Amongst the church's surviving images were two altarpieces with 'papist images', a hanging candelabra made of stags' antlers with a statue of the Virgin Mary in it, and a Lenten cloth painted with scenes of the Passion.[50]

It is difficult to reconstruct what such images meant for their viewers a generation after the Reformation. Not surprisingly, traditional forms of piety persisted. There is no mention in these records of pilgrimage, but in Wickerstedt the congregation apparently used an old statue of St Boniface in their annual kermis celebrations.[51] In general, however, it is the reluctance of landowners—the *Adel* and *Junker*—to comply with the visitors' instructions that emerges most clearly from the records. In 1560, Bartholomäus Rosinus, superintendent of Weimar, ordered a special visitation for the area that lay within his jurisdiction. Alongside the usual complaints about ignorant and lazy pastors, Rosinus documented local nobles' determination to defend the traditional appearance of their churches: 'In many places, especially where they have been given by nobles, the altars have not yet been changed, or arranged like our Weimar altar in our parish church'. Some, he said, justified their resistance on the grounds that 'the altar in Your Grace's castle chapel has not yet been changed'. Even the duke, it seems, liked his altar the way it had always been.

[47] Koch, 'Die Beseitigung', 227–9; Sehling EKO 1, 545, 562, 569.
[48] Thür HStA Weimar, EGA, Reg. Jl 432.   [49] Koch, 'Die Beseitigung', 233.
[50] Thür HStA Weimar, EGA, Reg. Ji, Nr. 2770, fol. 2r–3v.
[51] Thür HStA Weimar, EGA, Reg. Ll 667; Koch, 'Die Beseitigung', 234.

Rosinus also complained that elsewhere the *Junker* 'hang up trophies of war, brought by themselves or their parents and ancestors from war or captured in battle, in the choir above the altar as a spectacle, or have other odd images painted in the churches'.[52] The role that images played in dynastic commemoration will be explored in Chapter 6, but here already it is clear that the desire for representation and commemoration shaped Lutheran visual culture. In Cralwitz, it was the local innkeeper who protected both the altar and an image of St George in the community's filial church.[53]

Throughout, Rosinus and his fellow reformers were concerned to eliminate all images and ceremonies that were unnecessary and that 'reek of the papacy and *Adiaphoristen*'. Even in 1570, however, it was still necessary for the authors of Weimar's new church ordinance to prescribe the removal of 'idolatrous altars and images'.[54] Ernestine Saxony's Flacian interlude came to an end with Duke Johann Wilhelm's death in 1573 and the beginning of Elector August's regency. The interlude had a lasting impact on the territory's churches: in many, old altarpieces, statues, and paintings were either removed entirely or banished to side aisles and galleries. Yet, it did not, in the long run, determine the nature of Lutheran visual culture. In Jena's main church, where Flacius and his supporters had campaigned against the reinstallation of a gothic altarpiece in 1558, August's reign brought a change in attitude. In 1573, the new rector and professors at the university wrote to August, stating that the church's altar had been removed by 'tumultuous people' and that both Johann Friedrich II and Johann Wilhelm I had intended to replace it. Without it, the church was 'disfigured', and attracted negative comments from outsiders. They asked the Elector to step in, and to provide the funds that had been promised but never delivered, for the church urgently needed a panel on its altar.[55] In a church now oriented towards Albertine Saxony and Wittenberg, an altarpiece was a requirement.

ALBERTINE SAXONY: THE EXAMPLE OF ZWICKAU

In Zwickau, which lay within the territories that were transferred from the Ernestine to the Albertine Wettins at the 1547 Capitulation of Wittenberg, there had been some popular iconoclasm during the early years of the Reformation.[56] Thereafter, side altars and some images were, as we have seen, removed, but there were plenty of survivals and also some new commissions. The disputes that arose during the 1560s concerning the altarpiece that adorned the high altar of the

---

[52] Thür HStA Weimar, EGA, Reg. Ll 841, fol. 3r–3v. I am very grateful to Frau Dagmar Blaha for bringing these sources to my attention. On the Weimar castle chapel see Niels Fleck, *Fürstliche Repräsentation im Sakralraum. Die Schlosskirchen der thüringisch-ernestinischen Residenzen im 17. und beginnenden 18. Jahrhundert* (Munich, 2015), 25–7, though Fleck's claim that the positioning of the altarpiece was changed here first of all is disproved by the records of the 1560 visitation.
[53] Thür HStA Weimar, EGA, Reg. Ll 841, fol. 43r.
[54] Sehling EKO 1, 689.   [55] Thür HSta Weimar, EGA, Reg. Ji, Nr. 2864.
[56] Susan Karant-Nunn, *Zwickau in Transition, 1500–47: The Reformation as an Agent of Change* (Columbus, 1987).

Marienkirche, which are documented in unusual detail in the minutes and correspondence of the town council, demonstrate the ongoing incoherence of the Lutheran
position. These disputes allow a rare glimpse into lay Lutherans' attitudes towards
pre-Reformation images, and indicate the extent to which the fate of such works
could be determined by forces beyond the control of pastors and theologians.

The altarpiece, shown in Plate 4, had been commissioned from Michael Wolgemut
in Nuremberg by the prominent Zwickau citizen Martin Römer, acting on behalf of
the Marienkirche's congregation, who provided the 1400 *Gulden* required to finance
it.[57] It had been installed in 1479. It shows in its carved inner shrine the Virgin and
Child, standing on a sickle moon and surrounded by rays of sun. Mary is crowned
and adored by angels and flanked by eight female saints. In the predella are carved
figures of Christ and the apostles, and on the altar's four painted moveable wings
are scenes from Christ's Nativity and Passion. The whole altarpiece was originally
crowned by a *Gesprenge*, a decorative wooden pinnacle.

In 1554, Master Johann Petrejus was called from Ehrensfriedersdorf near
Annaberg to become pastor and superintendent in Zwickau.[58] He was a difficult
man. Already by 1563, when the disputes over the Wolgemut altar broke out,
Petrejus had been in conflict with the council several times over what he regarded
as their unwarranted interventions in church affairs. These conflicts continued
until Petrejus's departure for Mühlhausen in 1570: the altar disputes of the 1560s
played out against a backdrop of hostile exchanges concerning issues such as
church accounts, the activities of local preachers, the organization of the local
library, appointments to ecclesiastical positions, and Petrejus's own privileges and
status. In 1563, the council decided that the Marienkirche needed restoring. In
particular, the choir area in which the Wolgemut altar stood was urgently in need
of work because its vaulting had developed cracks. The altar itself was dismantled,
and Wolgemut's retable was moved to the nave. Petrejus took this opportunity to
start a campaign against it, and approached the council who agreed on 23 August
1564 that the 'old altar with the idols' should not be put back once the choir's restoration was completed. The mayor, Dr Funck, suggested instead that the council
could order a replacement, an alabaster altar from Antorff like the one in the new
church in Marienberg.[59]

Here, in the opening salvoes, the main themes of a debate that continued, on
and off, for the next five years can already be identified. Petrejus believed that
the altar's images were idolatrous not because they were worshipped—there is no
hint anywhere in the records that the altar was the focus of inappropriate prayer
or pilgrimage—but because they depicted non-scriptural subjects. The council
were inclined to agree with him, but maintained that the choir area needed an

---

[57] Sobotta, *Die Kirche der verhinderten Reichsstadt*, 252 ff. See also Landesamt für Denkmalpflege
Sachsen (ed.), *Der Zwickauer Wolgemut-Altar: Beiträge zu Geschichte, Ikonographie, Autorschaft und
Restaurierung* (Görlitz and Zittau, 2008).

[58] For an overview of these events see Otto Langer, 'Der Kampf des Pfarrers Joh. Petrejus gegen
den Wohlgemutschen Altar in der Marienkirche', *Mitteilungen des Altertumsvereins für Zwickau und
Umgebung*, 11 (1914), 31–49.

[59] Ibid., 33–4.

altarpiece: if the Wolgemut altar was removed, it must be replaced. Both pastor and magistrates therefore attempted to identify and (above all) finance a suitable replacement. At this point the council suggested an alabaster altar that was more up-to-date in its appearance; later Petrejus proposed commissioning the Cranach workshop and provided plans for a winged retable based in part on the example in the Wittenberg parish church.[60] In 1564, however, the council reached no decision, and as the choir restoration was completed, Petrejus repeated his request. This time he argued that if the Wolgemut altar were to be put back, it would give the impression to outsiders and to Zwickau's opponents, the papists, 'that we wanted to willingly follow the papacy again and honour the saints and trust in them'.[61] In the discussions surrounding the Wolgemut altar, there is no explicit mention of the post-Interim adiaphora dispute, but here, as elsewhere, Petrejus showed an awareness of images' significance as confessional markers.

The council members agreed, once again, that the old panel was incompatible with their religion, but decided that because they did not at that time have enough money to replace it, it would be best to put back the old altar 'and let it stand for a while longer'. They stated that in order to make use of it, the gold should be scraped from its *Gesprenge*. If this process proved successful, it could be repeated on the altar itself.[62] Such comments warn us against assuming that the survival of images such as the Wolgemut altar was determined by the aesthetic sensibilities of sixteenth-century Lutherans: for the council it was, it seems, at this point more an inconvenience than an artwork. The Marienkirche's congregation felt differently however. The altar was reinstalled but with its wings closed and without its worm-eaten original *Gesprenge*. With resentment growing, and with Petrejus causing more trouble with regard to appointments and financial accounts, the council turned in July 1568 to Dr Paul Eber, Melanchthon's successor in Wittenberg, for advice. Eber responded that because the altar had not been deemed offensive by previous pastors, and because other similar examples existed elsewhere, it should be allowed to remain. Petrejus conceded, at this point, that the altar could be opened again, 'but with his knowledge and not at all frequently'.[63]

On 6 January 1569, the feast of Epiphany, Petrejus preached a sermon in which he made public his true feelings regarding the altar. We learn of its content from the council's records. Petrejus emphasized that he was not opposed to images *per se*. He was aware that just as retaining images could indicate loyalty to Catholicism, so removing them could suggest more radical affiliations. With regard to the Wolgemut altar, Petrejus now distinguished between its innermost opening, which contained 'idols', and its outer openings, which had 'fine, godly paintings, i.e. the histories of our Lord Christ'. He proposed, therefore, either replacing the whole altarpiece or 'taking the idols out and having beautiful panels painted in their

[60] StadtAZw, A * A III 3, Nr. 12 'Bedencken, was für Gemeld an die Newe tafel des altars zu malen'.
[61] Langer, 'Der Kampf', 35.
[62] StadtAZw, III x 68, Ratsprotokolle 1554 bis 1560, fol. 213r.
[63] StadtAZw, III x 69a, Ratsprotokolle (Konzept), 1567–70, fol. 420r–420v (1568), fol. 38r (1570).

place'.[64] In response, the council turned to the citizenry, asking the congregation and its representatives, the guilds' *Viermeister*, if the altar should remain. The council suggested that it could, 'because one is taught by God's word that one does not need to be troubled by such images, and [because] this altar was set up with these images in honour of the church that is named after Our Lady'. The *Viermeister* responded with the request that 'we ask you to leave the altar and to adorn it with a *Gesprenge*'. And then, because Petrejus apparently now refused to let the altar be opened on feast days, Georg Tröger appeared before the council with the wish that 'the altar be opened on the most important feasts for the adornment of the church and in honour of our dear ancestors'.[65]

On one side of this lengthy debate stood Petrejus, concerned to demonstrate his and his church's true Lutheran credentials; on the other stood his congregation, committed to the continued display and liturgical use—opening and closing—of the splendid altarpiece that had, for nearly a century, adorned their church. The town council, perhaps not surprisingly given its ongoing conflicts with Petrejus, decided in favour of the congregation: on 6 August 1569, they determined that 'because it [the altar] is not offensive to anyone, it will remain as it is and be adorned with a *Gesprenge*'.[66] The design of the new *Gesprenge* caused further conflict: on 13 August, the council decided that it must be made smaller and more transparent. Petrejus remained unconvinced: he complained to the council that for the cost of the new *Gesprenge* one could almost commission a new panel by Lucas Cranach. When the council refused to give way, Petrejus appealed to Dresden, bringing to the Elector's attention not only this case but also several other conflicts with the council. When the Elector called both parties to Dresden, Zwickau's council responded with a full account of events. They gave a detailed description of the altar, emphasizing that it had never before been disputed or labelled as idolatrous, and that Luther himself, who knew the Zwickau church and its ceremonies well, had never objected to it. The altar had, they stated, cost 1400 *Gulden*, and they did not wish to remove or damage it. There were many other similar altars to be found elsewhere in the Elector's territory, and it posed no danger to true faith: 'Both we and our congregation are taught so much through God's grace that this altar and similar images do not hinder us at all from knowing how to praise God'. Elector August I decided in their favour, and the altar's new *Gesprenge* was completed.[67]

The five-year dispute over Michael Wolgemut's Zwickau altar provides a wonderful insight into the complexities of Lutheran attitudes towards images. Of course, Lutheran theology provided the precondition for its survival: its central, carved images of saints may, as both Petrejus and the council acknowledged, have been idols, but the preaching of God's Word would, the council argued, render them harmless. Luther's own teaching and authority remained key, as the council's letter

[64] StadtAZw, III x 69, Ratsprotokolle von 1566/67 bis 1568/69, fol. 241r–241v.
[65] Langer, 'Der Kampf', 37–8; StadtAZw, III x 69a, Ratsprotokolle (Konzept), 1567–70, 233v.
[66] StadtAZw, III x 69a, Ratsprotokolle (Konzept), 1567–70, fol. 258r.
[67] Langer, 'Der Kampf', 44–6.

to the Saxon court shows. The altar's survival was by no means, however, a fore-gone conclusion. Ultimately, its fate was determined as much by the congregation's feeling that it should be kept 'for the adornment of the church and in honour of our dear ancestors' as by Lutheran theological moderation. This desire for adorn-ment and commemoration will be explored more fully in Chapter 6, but here we should note in particular the congregation's desire to have the *Gesprenge* replaced, and the council's determination to make the whole *ensemble* visually appealing. The council minutes for 9 September 1570 note, for example, their decision to restore the altarpiece itself, 'so that the colours answer [those of] the upper *Gespreng*'.[68]

The restored altar remained as the focal point of the church's interior. The 1633 *Descriptio Urbis Cyneæ* described it *in situ*, and suggests that at that time the open-ing and closing for which the congregation had campaigned still continued. The chronicle's author referred to the altar's 'innermost part that is opened only on feast days', and said, as the congregation had effectively done in 1569, that the inner opening, with its nine carved images of female saints, was 'the most beautiful'.[69] By the mid-seventeenth century, Zwickau's citizens had donated a variety of images and objects that complemented this exquisite altar, and provided a rich visual environment for the Lutheran liturgy. The pulpit and font acquired additional adornment. There were some spectacular epitaphs, including one painted by the Cranach workshop for Mayor Johann Unruh (d. 1556) showing Christ amongst the Children.[70] In the seventeenth century, there were other major donations, in particular the richly carved council pew (1617) and the burial chapel, tomb, and epitaph of Carl von Bose, colonel in the Saxony army, Zwickau's *Amtshauptmann* (district administrator), and one of Saxony's richest noblemen.[71] Church inven-tories also testify to the existence of many smaller images and artefacts: crucifixes, richly decorated vestments, altar cloths, candlesticks, and liturgical vessels, many given during the seventeenth century by both male and female members of the congregation. In particular, the inventories record two carved *Bornkinnel*, figures of the Christ Child, one of which stood on the altar, and an image of the Resurrected Christ.[72]

The lengthy dispute over the Wolgemut altar demonstrates the extent to which in Zwickau in the 1560s, as in Wittenberg in the 1520s and in Weimar in the 1550s, behaviour towards images could serve as an indication of religious allegiance. Although the post-Interim conflicts over adiaphora and other matters are not explicitly invoked in the Zwickau records, this backdrop of crisis and conflict explains Petrejus's 1564 concern that reinstalling the altar would suggest to outsiders that the congregation wished to return to the papal fold.[73] Petrejus's criticisms

[68] Langer, 'Der Kampf', 48.   [69] *Descriptio Urbis Cyneæ*, 71.
[70] Gurlitt (ed.), *Beschreibende Darstellung*, vol. 17, *Stadt Leipzig (I. Theil)*, 111, 114–15.
[71] On Carl von Bose see Bridget Heal, '"Zum Andenken und zur Ehre Gottes": Kunst und Frömmigkeit im frühneuzeitlichen Luthertum', *Archiv für Reformationsgeschichte*, 104 (2013), 185–210, here 203. Also Bruno Sobotka and Jürgen Strauss, *Burgen Schlösser Gutshäuser in Sachsen-Anhalt* (Stuttgart, 1994), 107–8.
[72] StadtAZw, III z 4 K Nr. 109, Kirchliche Inventarien 1675–1761.
[73] StadtAZw, A * A III, Nr. 12.

reflected common Lutheran themes: the Weimar reformers had, just like him, expressed fear of idolatry and a desire to tolerate only biblical images. In Ernestine Saxony, however, at least some of this anti-image polemic was explicitly directed against 'Adiaphoristen'. Petrejus, by contrast, despite being a thorn in the side of the Zwickau council and causing trouble in both Wittenberg and Dresden, ultimately took care to align himself with Albertine religious politics. In 1570, he was called to Mühlhausen, but before his departure he wrote a brief treatise, published in Wittenberg in 1571, warning against turning towards the 'unremitting cries of the Flacians'. In this attack on the Gnesio-Lutherans, Petrejus looked back with nostalgia to Luther's lifetime: 'The land was cleansed of the great idolatry of the pope. God's Word was still new, and the people held it dear'. Since then, he lamented, much conflict had arisen. The Interim was viewed by many people as an expression of the Emperor's determination to bring the church back to Rome and to unite it in one faith. It had provoked debates between princes and their theologians and preachers over what concessions could be made with regard to instruction and ceremony without damaging godly truth, and these debates had resulted in 'much misunderstanding and mistrust, not only amongst the common people, but also amongst some teachers'. The restoration of some traditional ceremonies suggested to them that there was an intention to restore the papacy, whereas in fact it was merely an act of obedience to the Emperor.[74]

CONFESSIONAL DELINEATION AND THE RISE OF CALVINISM

While Albertine and Ernestine post-Interim politics provided the immediate context for the mid-sixteenth-century conflicts over church furnishings in Weimar and Zwickau, renewed Lutheran interest in the image question must also be set against the broader backdrop of the revival of Catholicism and the rise of Calvinism within the Empire.[75] The Interim failed in its attempt to re-impose Catholic doctrine and devotion throughout the Empire, but during the second half of the sixteenth century Lutherans witnessed the conclusion of the Council of Trent (1563) and the acceleration of a Catholic counter-offensive in parts of Germany and in the Habsburgs's own hereditary lands. In Central Europe, Catholic revival brought with it not only the persecution of Protestants but also the development of popular Catholic consciousness. Confraternal life, pilgrimages, the cult of saints, Eucharistic piety, and processions flourished, and images played an important part in all of these devotional practices. In such circumstances, it is scarcely surprising that Germany's Lutherans showed an ongoing concern to distinguish their image use

[74] Johannes Petrejus, *Warnung und Vermanung: Das man an das Vnauffhörliche Schreien der Flacianer...sich nicht keren...* (Wittenberg, 1571), Vorrede, A iiiir, Cr, D iiiv.
[75] For an overview of the theological conflicts over images during this period see Irene Dingel, '"Daß wir Gott in keiner Weise verbilden". Die Bilderfrage zwischen Calvinismus und Luthertum', in Andreas Wagner, Volker Hörner, and Günter Geisthardt (eds), *Gott im Wort—Gott im Bild: Bilderlosigkeit als Bedingung des Monotheismus?* (Neukirchen-Vluyn, 2005), 97–111.

from that of the Catholics: Petrejus was certainly not alone in his concern that the retention of old images made Lutherans look 'papist', even amongst those who professed allegiance to the Albertine Elector and to Wittenberg.

On 3 December 1563, at its 25th session, the Council of Trent promulgated resolutions that reaffirmed the value of the veneration of saints and relics and the honouring of sacred images.[76] At the level of theological debate, Martin Chemnitz's four-volume *Examen Concilii Tridentini* (1565–73) was Lutheranism's most important response to Trent's codification of Catholic belief and practice. Chemnitz's discussion of images, and its significance for later commentators such as Johann Arndt and Simon Gedicke, have been explored in detail by Thomas Kaufmann, and need only brief discussion here.[77] Most of Chemnitz's polemic was directed against the papists, who in their Tridentine decree 'make a necessity of having and retaining images in the churches, as though they were an important part of religion, piety, and divine worship'. Chemnitz provided a detailed history of the cult of images, from its origins amongst the heathen, whose divine worship at shrines was very similar to that 'now seen at the statues in the churches of the papalists', through the disputes of the Byzantine period and Middle Ages.[78] Of course Scripture always provided his key point of reference: the Decalogue

> forbids every kind of worship of religious objects by means of two words: 'You shall not adore or worship them'. The first of these signifies bowing down, all outward gestures and rites of worship; the second embraces the inner affections and devotions of worship.

And Chemnitz always emphasized the primacy of the Word. In his discussion of Gregory the Great, he wrote that 'whatever may be said about teaching and communicating through pictures, in no way is a picture to be compared with the Word of God (written, preached, read, heard, and meditated upon), least of all preferred to it'.[79]

Chemnitz's defence of images is lukewarm at best. There is little here that can be read as a positive theology of images, and he is concerned above all to show 'the fundamental independence of the Christian religion from images'.[80] But Chemnitz's text did, through its engagement with the iconoclastic as well as the Tridentine position, provide a 'reasoned manual' for Lutherans who championed images in theological controversies with Reformed Protestants during the later sixteenth and seventeenth centuries.[81] Chemnitz, like Luther, condemns those who argue that no images can be tolerated, and 'therefore lay on consciences the necessity that images per se are neither to be made, nor possessed, nor tolerated, and place an important part of piety in demolishing images'. Images were adiaphora, and those that depicted 'true and useful histories' could, as Luther had argued, be kept 'for

[76] Christian Hecht, *Katholische Bildertheologie im Zeitalter von Gegenreformation und Barock: Studien zu Traktaten von Johannes Molanus, Gabriele Paleotti und anderen Autoren* (Berlin, 1997).

[77] Kaufmann, *Konfession und Kultur*, 167–73.

[78] Martin Chemnitz, *Examination of the Council of Trent Part IV*, tr. Fred Kramer (St Louis, 1986), 55, 64.

[79] Ibid., 75, 103.   [80] Kaufmann, *Konfession und Kultur*, 168.   [81] Ibid., 164–5.

the sake of beautification, remembrance, or history'. Chemnitz drew, throughout his discussion, on historical instances of the proper use of images, citing, for example, the 794 Synod of Frankfurt, which steered a middle course between condemnation and worship.[82] He sought to justify the Lutheran position on images against the backdrop of church history, and to show that the Lutheran position was the only one that was biblically legitimate and historically proven.[83] The condemnation of iconoclasm in Chemnitz's *Examen Concilii Tridentini* proved timely: with its discussion of adiaphora and of the historical use of images, the work became the most important handbook for Lutheran theologians confronted, during the later decades of the sixteenth century, by the rise of Calvinism.[84]

Images were a matter of Christian freedom, but the Eucharistic disputes of the second half of the sixteenth century added another layer to their confessional significance. These disputes were not, of course, new. In his impassioned responses to the 'Sacramentarians'—above all Karlstadt and Zwingli—Luther had always defended Christ's true, physical presence. It is an article of our faith, 'clearly and powerfully attested to in Scripture', that 'Christ's body and blood are at the same time in heaven and in the Supper', he wrote in 1527.[85] Because of the words of institution, 'This is my body, which was given for you', Christ was present in the Eucharistic elements. The exact nature of this presence was not, for Luther, something that humans should speculate upon: 'let us not dabble in too much philosophy'. Christ 'desired to keep us in a simple faith, sufficient to believe that his blood was in the cup', he wrote in *The Babylonian Captivity of the Church*.[86] God's omnipotence made it possible for the bread and wine to convey his body and blood if he so wished. The soteriological importance that Luther accorded to the 'graspable and perceptible' ritual of the Eucharist, and the belief, expressed succinctly in his *Small Catechism*, that at that ritual the Christian consumed Christ both spiritually and physically, had important implications for ecclesiastical visual culture. For Lutherans the ritual of communion was crucial, and the adornment of the altar at which it was performed became, as we will see, a marker of true faith.

Understandings of the Eucharist of course divided Lutheran from Reformed, but even within Wittenberg, Luther's views were not universally accepted. Melanchthon developed a more spiritualized understanding of communion, and the *Augustana Variata* (the Varied Augsburg Confession) that he drew up in 1540 contained a Eucharistic formula to which Calvin, with his denial of Christ's physical presence, was able to subscribe. This *Variata* came to play an important part in imperial politics, allowing, for a time at least, Calvinist princes to claim protection under the terms of the Peace of Augsburg. The Eucharistic and Christological disputes continued into the post-Interim period. While the Gnesio-Lutherans continued to argue that Christ's words of institution could be trusted in their literal form, and

[82] Chemnitz, *Examination*, 55–6; 127–8.
[83] Kaufmann, *Konfession und Kultur*, esp. 173.   [84] Ibid., 164.
[85] WA 23, 'Daß diese Wort Christi "Das ist mein Leib" noch fest stehen wider die Schwärmgeister', 38–320, here 137; LW 37, 59.
[86] WA 6, 511; LW 36, 34.

that we must put our trust in God's reliability and omnipresence, some of Melanchthon's heirs promoted a more spiritualizing view of Christ's presence in the Lord's Supper which led to them being accused of crypto-Calvinism. The 'Wittenberg Catechism' that they produced in 1571 was thought to endanger the status of Electoral Saxony under the terms of the Peace of Augsburg. The controversy came to a head with the publication of an anonymous tract on the Lord's Supper by Ernst Vögelin's print house in Leipzig in 1573. Elector August, convinced that his theologians were conspiring to change the teaching of the land, reacted harshly with sentences of imprisonment and exile and called Jakob Andreae from Tübingen, who began in Wittenberg his efforts to produce the Formula of Concord.[87]

A polemical image, produced in Saxony in the wake of this 'crypto-Calvinist' episode, gives visual expression to a number of these theological debates and indicates some of the ways in which they shaped Lutheran culture (Fig. 2.3).[88] Following the binary format and rich use of textual inscriptions beloved of Lutheran propagandists since the early decades of the Reformation, the painting opposes Calvinists on the left with Lutherans on the right. Behind the Calvinists stands the devil, with two of his victims, one in a cage and one captured in a net, prostrate on the floor. The image is divided by a heavenly ladder, at the top of which a Calvinist plunders a chest. Zwingli has also started to climb this ladder, but it collapses beneath him. The Reformed are opposed by Luther, brandishing a sword representing God's word, and his supporters. One key message here concerns the role of faith: the Calvinists' chief error is to place too much emphasis on human reason. One takes an apple from the serpent entwining the Tree of Knowledge; another searches in the chest containing the secrets of God at the top of the ladder.[89] With its representation of Christ chained to God's throne, the image also ridicules the Reformed view that Christ's human nature had ascended to sit at God's right hand, and could not therefore be present in the Eucharist. In the middle ground are two depictions of communion: the Calvinists meet secretly in a tent, with the devil as a guest; the Lutherans celebrate before a magnificent

---

[87] See Irene Dingel (ed.), *Die Debatte um die Wittenberger Abendmahlslehre und Christologie (1570–1574)* (Göttingen, 2008); Johannes Hund, *Das Wort ward Fleisch: eine systematisch-theologische Untersuchung zur Debatte um die Wittenberger Christologie und Abendmahlslehre in den Jahren 1567 bis 1574* (Göttingen, 2006), 206 ff. I am grateful to Dr. Henning Jürgens for these references. Ernst Koch 'Ausbau, Gefährdung und Festigung der lutherischen Landeskirche von 1553 bis 1601', in Helmar Junghans (ed.), *Das Jahrhundert der Reformation in Sachsen*, 2nd ed. (Leipzig, 2005), 191–218, here 203.

[88] For the most recent discussions of this image see Ansgar Reißand and Sabine Witt (eds), *Calvinismus. Die Reformierten in Deutschland und Europa,* exh. cat. (Berlin, 2009), 336–7 and Stiftung Preußische Schlösser und Gärten Berlin-Brandenburg, *Cranach und die Kunst der Renaissance*, 311. See also J. Bulisch and F. C. Ilgner, 'Der Tanzende Zwingli. Zwei lutherische Spottbilder auf das Abendmahl der Reformierten', *Das Münster: Zeitschrift für christliche Kunst und Kunstwissenschaft*, 1 (1999), 66–74, which dates the image to 1577–80; G. Wustmann, 'Geschichte der Heimlichen Calvinisten (Kryptocalvinisten) in Leipzig. 1574 bis 1593', *Neujahrsblätter der Bibliothek und des Archivs der Stadt Leipzig* 1 (1905), 1–94.

[89] The inscriptions in the cartouches at the bottom drive home this message. Volker Rodekamp (ed.), *Leipzig Original: Stadtgeschichte vom Mittelalter zur Völkerschlacht* (Altenburg, 2006), 129–31, gives a full transcription of the inscriptions.

Fig. 2.3. Anon., polemical, anti-Calvinist image (*Spottbild*), *c.*1574.

Credit: © Stadtgeschichtliches Museum Leipzig. Photo: Christoph Sandig.

Renaissance altar.[90] The Lutherans' two-tier altar shows Christ's ascension, with a crucifix above. Here communion is administered in both kinds by pastors wearing

---

[90] The Calvinists' devilish communion has inscriptions that emphasize its status as a commemorative sign, while its Lutheran equivalent has the words of institution from Matthew 26:26–7.

vestments to kneeling men while women look on. Lutherans' distinctive visual and ceremonial life was developed, this image suggests, not only in response to the teachings of Luther and his heirs but also through the process of confessional conflict.

The Leipzig polemical image captures a moment at which divisions within Lutheranism had already been overshadowed by the rise of Calvinism. Significantly, Melanchthon's distinctively gaunt figure is missing from the Lutheran crowd. We cannot date the image precisely, but it is possible that the two figures standing behind Luther and holding books represent Nikolaus Selnecker and Jakob Andreae, fathers of the Formula of Concord. The image may, therefore, be intended to instantiate a moment at which a degree of unity had been achieved within the Lutheran Church after decades of division and discord. After a series of failed efforts to achieve consensus during the 1550s and 1560s, a settlement was finally agreed in 1577. The Formula of Concord (1577) and the *Book of Concord* (1580) represented the culmination of years of tireless ecclesiastical diplomacy on the part of Andreae and others: approximately two-thirds of Germany's evangelical churches declared their support.[91] With regard to adiaphora, the Formula endorsed the Gnesio-Lutheran position: adiaphora were truly harmless only if they were truly free, for 'in a time of persecution, when an unequivocal confession of the faith is demanded of us, we dare not yield to the opponents in such indifferent matters'. In such a situation, adiaphora are no longer indifferent, for then 'the truth of the gospel and Christian freedom are at stake. The confirmation of open idolatry, as well as the protection of the weak in faith from offense, is at stake'. And with regard to the Eucharist, the Formula confirmed that at communion the Christian—even the impious Christian—encountered and consumed orally, not just spiritually, Christ, true God and true man, 'in one person, undivided and inseparable'.[92]

With the Formula and *Book of Concord*, Lutheranism achieved if not complete theological unity then at least a broad degree of consensus. But now, more than ever, Lutherans found themselves with their backs against the wall, threatened on one side by Catholics and on the other by Calvinists. The spread of Germany's 'Second Reformation' gave new significance to debates over images and ritual. Its proponents were determined to complete what they saw as Luther's half-finished Reformation by purging religious life of the remnants of papal superstition, thereby fortifying German Protestantism against the assaults of the resurgent Catholic church.[93] Reformed principalities only ever occupied a relatively small proportion of the Empire's territory, and Germany's Lutherans, unlike its Calvinists, continued to enjoy relative security under the terms of the Religious Peace of Augsburg (1555). Yet, the advance of Calvinism, with its 'Sacramentarian' attacks on traditional liturgy and images, was perceived as an immediate threat to the Lutheran faith.

---

[91] Dingel, 'The Culture of Conflict', 61–4.

[92] Robert Kolb and Timothy Wengert (eds), *The Book of Concord. The Confessions of the Evangelical Lutheran Church* (Minneapolis, 2000), 516, 505–6.

[93] Thomas A. Brady Jr., *German Histories in the Age of Reformations, 1400–1650* (Cambridge, 2009), 271. Heinz Schilling, *Religion, Political Culture and the Emergence of Early Modern Society* (Leiden, 1992), 265.

The Rhineland Palatinate, which had adopted the Augsburg Confession in 1556 under Elector Ottheinrich, was the first German territory to experience a Calvinist 'cleansing'. Ottheinrich's successor, Friedrich III 'the Pious' (r. 1559–76), brought Calvinism to Heidelberg.[94] In 1565, Friedrich issued an injunction against images, altars and other forms of church decoration. The Elector had a deep hatred of Catholic Eucharistic teaching, and did all he could to purify his churches of incitements to idolatry, participating himself in a number of iconoclastic incidents.[95] Other princes followed suit: in Anhalt, for example, Johann Georg ordered in November 1596 that churches should be cleansed of the 'remaining papist leaven' through the abolition of altar lights and vestments, the removal of altar panels and carved crucifixes, and the introduction of the *fractio panis* (the breaking of bread at communion).[96] And Landgrave Moritz of Hesse-Kassel introduced in 1605 a series of measures—the 'Verbesserungspunkte'—that included the reform of liturgy and removal of images. In 1613, another Imperial Elector, Johann Sigismund of Brandenburg, converted to Calvinism, and a number of other dukes, imperial counts and cities also introduced Calvinist reforms.[97] Even Electoral Saxony seemed in danger in 1586–91: there Christian I's attempts to introduce a Calvinist Reformation were brought to a halt by his untimely death.

As contemporaries noted, Calvinism and iconoclasm inevitably went hand-in-hand. German Lutherans had already watched what Jakob Andreae described in 1586 as the 'wild destruction of churches' in France and the Netherlands.[98] While the iconoclasm of Germany's Second Reformation was orderly by comparison—conducted not by rowdy mobs but by princes and magistrates—theologians and pastors feared its alienating effects. It would, Simon Gedicke argued in 1597, 'annoy the simple folk without reason'.[99] Lutheran responses to Calvinist iconoclasm have been explored at the level of theological polemic by Thomas Kaufmann. The 1586 Colloquy of Montbéliard, at which Jakob Andreae and Theodore Beza, Calvin's successor in Geneva, debated at the behest of the Lutheran Duke Ludwig III of Württemberg, achieved paradigmatic status, its formulations on images frequently cited in later works.[100] The events in Anhalt in 1596 produced polemical works by

---

[94] The 1556 church ordinance was Lutheran, but with strong Swiss influences. On Ottheinrich's initial actions against images see Hans Rott, 'Kirchen- und Bildersturm bei der Einführung der Reformation in der Pfalz', *Neues Archiv für die Geschichte der Stadt Heidelberg und der rheinischen Pfalz*, 6 (1905), 229–54, here 231–41.

[95] Heal, 'Kirchenordnungen', 169–70; Joh. B. Götz, *Die erste Einführung des Kalvinismus in der Oberpfalz 1559–76* (Münster, 1933), 21.

[96] Quoted in Kaufmann, *Konfession und Kultur*, 179–80. See also Nadine Jaser, '*Fugite idola!* Reformierte Bildentfernungen in Anhalt', in Norbert Michels (ed.), *Cranach in Anhalt: Vom alten zum neuen Glauben* (Petersberg, 2015), 77–84.

[97] For a list see J. F. Gerhard Goeters, 'Genesis, Formen und Hauptthemen des reformierten Bekenntnisses in Deutschland', in Schilling (ed.), *Die reformierte Konfessionalisierung*, 44–59, here 46.

[98] Jacob Andreae, *Colloquium Mompelgartense … Auß dem Latein Verdeutscht* (Tübingen: Georg Gruppenbach, 1587), 711.

[99] Simon Gedicke, *Von Bildern vnd Altarn/In den Euangelischen Kirchen Augspurgischer Confession* (Magdeburg: Johann Francke, 1597), Tii; see also Abraham Taurer, *Hochnothwendigster Bericht/Wider den newen Bildstürmerischen Carlstadtischen Geist in Fürstenthumb Anhald* (Eisleben, 1597), Kiii; Andreae, *Colloquium Mompelgartense*, 721.

[100] Kaufmann, *Konfession und Kultur*, 174, n. 55.

Johann Olearius, Abraham Lange, Simon Gedicke, Johann Arndt, and Abraham Taurer, while in Brandenburg in 1615 and 1616 Peter Conovius, Lutheran superintendent, wrote in defence of images.[101]

Many of the arguments made in defence of images during the era of the Second Reformation were familiar. Images were adiaphora, 'evidence of Christian freedom', as Abraham Lange, court preacher in Altenburg, wrote in his 1597 *Christlicher/ lutherischer Gegenbericht* (*Christian, Lutheran Riposte*).[102] They could be used to teach, and for Gedicke they constituted an inevitable part of religious devotion: 'for in people's soul there is an image, when the heart thinks something and envisages it, so a form and pattern imprints in it'.[103] Other arguments were new, or were at least developed well beyond Luther's original formulations. The polemic was strong. During the Anhalt controversy, Lutheran commentators compared the Calvinist innovators to the Turks who, during the capture of Constantinople in 1453, had mocked and destroyed images of Christ (a comparison given extra weight by the renewal of the Imperial/Ottoman Wars in 1593).[104] They defended images' value for adornment: Abraham Taurer, pastor in the village of Schwertzau in the diocese of Magdeburg, complained, for example, that the Calvinists' churches 'resembled a public beer hall rather than a temple of the Lord'.[105] And they argued that images, like music, could move the heart, a recognition of their affective power that will be explored in detail in Chapter 4. Yet, all Lutheran commentators remained conscious of the dangers inherent in such arguments: authorities must always, Andreae emphasized, take action against images that were the focus of idolatrous veneration, and must 'forbid the common rabble this wilfulness, that they follow their thirst for images'.[106]

The Calvinist-Lutheran debate over images was not confined to the level of the theological elite. In the Upper Palatinate, Danzig, Anhalt, Hesse, Lippe, and Brandenburg, Calvinist attempts to cleanse Lutheran churches of remnants of the 'papist' past met with fierce opposition.[107] We know that Calvinist attempts to reform traditional Lutheran liturgies were deeply unpopular. The abolition of the elevation of the consecrated host and the introduction of the breaking of bread or *fractio panis* at communion—both external signs of Calvinist rejection of the doctrine of Christ's real presence in the sacrament—caused particular resentment amongst Lutheran congregations. The deletion of the exorcism rite from baptism

---

[101] On Conovius and his interlocutor, who published as Georg Gottfried, see Stiftung Preußische Schlösser und Gärten Berlin-Brandenburg, *Cranach und die Kunst der Renaissance*, 306–7.

[102] Kaufmann, *Konfession und Kultur*, 187. See also Simon Gedicke, *Calviniana oder Calvinisterey/ So fälschlich die Reformirte Religion genennet wird...* (Leipzig: Abraham Lamberg, 1615), 507; Andreae, *Colloquium Mompelgartense*, 695.

[103] Kaufmann, *Konfession und Kultur*, 196.   [104] Ibid., 183–6.

[105] Taurer, *Hochnothwendigster Bericht*, AIII, E.

[106] Andreae, *Colloquium Mompelgartense*, 757.

[107] See, for example, Jan Harasimowicz, *Kunst als Glaubensbekenntnis: Beiträge zur Kunst- und Kulturgeschichte der Reformationszeit* (Baden-Baden, 1996), 33; Sergiusz Michalski, 'Die lutherisch-katholisch-reformierte Rivalität im Bereich der Bildenden Kunst im Gebiet von Danzig um 1600', in J. Bahlcke and A. Stromeyer (eds), *Konfessionalisierung in Ostmitteleuropa* (Stuttgart, 1999), 267–87.

was also highly controversial.[108] Attacks on images aroused similar sentiments. In cases of conflict between Lutheran subjects and Calvinist princes it was, of course, not just liturgy and images that were at stake. Resistance to religious reforms often provided a focal point for protest against an increase in princely or central state authority. Yet, the fact that this resistance coalesced around the attempted reform of liturgy and iconoclasm demonstrates the importance of images and ritual to Lutheran congregations.

In Hesse-Kassel, for example, when Landgrave Moritz introduced his Calvinist reforms in 1605–8, he encountered opposition from Lutheran Upper Hesse in particular. On 6 August 1605 resistance in Marburg reached a high point when rumours circulated that the Marienkirche, the town's main parish church, was about to be stripped of images. Lutheran citizens boycotted the Calvinist service, and attacked the preacher who had preached on the problem of the Eucharist. They then took the keys of the church and locked it. Moritz threatened to use military force against them if necessary, and preached in the church himself. After this display of princely authority, a group of artisans were commissioned to destroy the contested images.[109] In Schmalkalden, a Hessian exclave in Thuringia, there were revolts in 1608 triggered by the prospect of the introduction of the *fractio panis* and the removal of images.[110] Elsewhere, resistance was less dramatic: in Dillich, a small community between Marburg and Kassel, the *Kirchenbuch* (church register) for 1606 reports that

> In this year no children were confirmed because they did not want to accept the *Verbesserungspunkte*, and especially the other commandment added in, De non colen-dis imaginibus et fractionem panis [against worshipping images and on the breaking of the bread].[111]

When Marburg and Upper Hesse fell to the Lutheran Landgrave Ludwig V of Hesse-Darmstadt in 1624, altars and altarpieces were replaced.[112] In Marburg's parish church, the site of the 1605 disturbances, a new high altar and retable was

---

[108] Bodo Nischan, *Lutherans and Calvinists in the Age of Confessionalism* (Aldershot, 1999), esp. 1–27 on the elevation.

[109] Bettina Wischhöfer, 'Kirche als Ort von Disziplinierung und Verweigerung. Die Einführung der "Zweiten Reformation" in Hessen-Kassel 1605', in Andrea Bendlage, Andreas Priever, and Peter Schuster (eds), *Recht und verhalten in vormodernen Gesellschaften. Festschrift für Neithard Bulst* (Bielefeld, 2008), 223–31, here 226. Gerhard Menk, 'Landgraf Moritz und die Rolle Marburgs bei der Einführung der "Verbesserungspunkte"', in Hans-Joachim Kunst and Eckart Glockzin (eds), *Kirche Zwischen Schloß und Markt. Die Lutherische Pfarrkirche St. Marien zu Marburg* (Marburg, 1997), 48–57, esp. 52. A Calvinist account of events is given in Gregor Schönfeld, *Historischer Bericht der Newlichen Monats Augusti zugetragenen Marpurgischen Kirchen Händel* (Marburg, 1605), esp. 20–6. See also B. Kümmel, *Der Ikonoklast als Kunstliebhaber: Studien zu Landgraf Moritz von Hessen-Kassel (1592–1627)* (Marburg, 1996), 20–68.

[110] D. Mayes, *Communal Christianity: The Life and Loss of a Peasant Vision in Early Modern Germany* (Boston and Leiden, 2004), 97–8. Mayes highlights the differences between urban and rural Upper Hesse, arguing that because of their 'aconfessional' attitudes rural communities were much less likely to manifest a strong attachment to Lutheran images and rituals in the face of Calvinist threat. For a fuller discussion of the events in Schmalkalden see W. Troßbach, 'Volkskultur und Gewissensnot. Zum Bilderstreit in der "zweiten Reformation"', *Zeitschrift für Historische Forschung*, 23 (1988), 473–500.

[111] Wischhöfer, 'Kirche als Ort', 230.   [112] Ibid., 231.

Fig. 2.4. Adam and Philipp Franck, altarpiece from the parish church of St Marien, Marburg, 1626.

Credit: © Bildarchiv Foto Marburg, Aufnahme-Nr.: 810.278. Photo: Ludwig Bickell.

installed (Fig. 2.4). It was created by Adam and Philipp Franck, and shows in its centre sculptured figures of Christ on the cross between Mary and John. An angel collecting Christ's blood in a chalice to makes clear the scene's Eucharistic significance, and in the predella is the Last Supper.[113]

---

[113] Theodor Mahlmann, 'Stein gewordene Christologie. Balthasar Mentzer und der Altar der Lutherischen Pfarrkirche St. Marien', in Kunst and Glockzin (eds), *Kirche zwischen Schloß und Markt*, 70–104.

Marburg's parish church provides a suitable end-point for this chapter's discussion of Lutheran visual culture between idolatry and iconoclasm. Here the only item that we might read as evidence of Lutheranism's preserving power is a fourteenth-century sacrament house, which survived the both the Lutheran Reformation of 1527 and the Calvinist unrest of 1605. Until 1605, however, the choir area was dominated by a 'golden panel' (altarpiece) and a triumphal cross, both of which escaped Philipp of Hesse's initial attempt to abolish idolatrous images. Today the church contains two spectacular dynastic memorials and the Franck altarpiece. The burial chapel of Landgrave Ludwig IV of Hesse-Marburg (d. 1604) and his wife, Hedwig of Württemberg (d. 1590) was installed in 1590–2, and, like most noble dynastic memorials, survived the era of Calvinist cleansing.[114] The memorial to Ludwig V of Hesse-Darmstadt (d. 1626) and his wife Magdalena of Brandenburg (d. 1616) was commissioned in 1627 by Ludwig's successor, Georg II, as part of his quest to legitimate his dynastic claim to the territory. The altar, commissioned by Ludwig V and installed in 1626, was a clear statement of Lutheran belief and a symbol of the rejection of the Reformed church politics of his predecessor.[115] Here images' significance in the struggle against Calvinism is revealed in microcosm, from the Lutheran congregation's attempted defence of images in 1605 to the post-iconoclastic installation of an altar that celebrated Lutheran Eucharistic teaching in 1626.

CONCLUSION

By the time of Luther's death in 1546 the first steps had been taken along the path by which images became an important part of Lutheran confessional culture. Events of the later sixteenth and seventeenth centuries accelerated progress along that path. Lutherans had, during the first decades of the Reformation, found theological justifications for images, defended them as signs of religious moderation and used them in pastoral care and instruction, in the crucial work of disseminating the Gospel. There was no clear consensus on the question of images, however, either at the level of theological discourse or at the level of lived piety. The normative prescriptions contained in church ordinances and mandates varied greatly: some condemned all non-scriptural images; others gave at least tacit permission for their preservation. At the level of devotional practice, decisions about images were often made locally, by congregations and their pastors and town magistrates. Some kept almost all pre-Reformation images, as in Annaberg; others gradually removed them and replaced them with new, evangelical images, as in Wittenberg. In the

---

[114] Nadine Lehmann, 'Reformierte Bildersturm und Herrschaftsrepräsentation: Der Umgang mit fürstlichen Grabmälern während der obrigkeitlichen Bildentfernung im Zuge der Zweiten Reformation', in Anna-Maria Blank, Vera Isaiasz, and Nadine Lehmann (eds), *Bild—Macht—UnOrdnung. Visuelle Repräsentationen zwischen Stabilität und Konflikt* (Frankfurt am Main, 2011), 165–93.

[115] Oliver Meys, *Memoria und Bekenntnis: die Grabdenkmäler evangelischer Landesherren im Heiligen Römischen Reich Deutscher Nation im Zeitalter der Konfessionalisierung* (Regensburg, 2009), 566–7.

aftermath of the 1548 Interim, this incoherence became problematic. As Luther's heirs contested his legacy, the treatment of images served as a way of signalling allegiance to either Wittenberg or the Gnesio-Lutheran cause. This was most obvious in Saxony, divided now between the Albertine Elector who tended—as in case of Zwickau's Wolgemut altar (Plate 4)—towards the preservation of old images, and the Ernestine dukes, who were pushed by their Flacian advisors to cleanse their territory's churches of papist images and rearrange their altars, often against the wishes of local congregations.

The 1550s and 1560s were a period of uncertainly with regard to images and rituals. Thereafter, however, disputes over adiaphora within Lutheranism were overshadowed by the threat of Calvinist iconoclasm. Lutheran theologians never stopped worrying about the dangers of idolatry. In 1597, for example, the Wittenberg theology faculty advised that even though Lutherans, fortified by God's Word, could enter image-filled Catholic churches without endangering their souls, such visits were not to be recommended for the 'weak'.[116] But conflict between Lutheran and Calvinist, which was most acute between the 1560s and the 1630s, constituted a turning point for Lutheran visual culture. The series of princely conversions within the Empire, with their attendant iconoclasms, reaffirmed the Lutheran conviction that images were necessary signs of religious moderation. They, like particular liturgical rituals, became litmus tests of confessional allegiance in the struggle against Calvinist reform. Images might have been indifferent in salvific terms, but they were nonetheless, as the Marburg example suggests, an important part of what it meant to be Lutheran. In Electoral Saxony and Brandenburg, which we will now examine in greater detail, moments of confessional conflict not only revealed the strength of Lutheran attachment to images, but also left a lasting legacy, embedding images more firmly than ever in Lutheran confessional consciousness.

---

[116] Kaufmann, *Konfession und Kultur*, 195, n. 34.

3

The Desire for Images
Lutheran Identity in Electoral Saxony and Brandenburg

At the 1586 Colloquy of Montbéliard, the Württemberg theologian Jakob Andreae defended Lutherans' use of paintings and sculptures against his Reformed opponent, Theodore Beza, but also warned of a 'thirst for images' that was to be found amongst the 'common people'.[1] Andreae was afraid that images might continue to form the focus of idolatrous worship, a fear that sixteenth-century visitation records suggest was justified, at least in rural areas. But while the persistence of superstitious practices preoccupied reformers and has attracted considerable attention from Reformation historians, the Lutheran 'thirst for images' was not just the result of evangelical failure to eradicate traditional beliefs and practices. To state, as Calvinists did, that Lutherans were 'half-papists' and 'idolaters' is to misrepresent the nature of their attachment to images. The Lutheran Reformation, in whatever local context we encounter it, was an incoherent process: the breaks that it engendered with Catholic tradition were often gradual or incomplete. But Lutheran defences of images and liturgy should not be read simply as evidence of a 'failed' Reformation. Rather, they testify to the extent to which images had become a part of Lutheran confessional culture by the late sixteenth century. The main phase of Lutheran/Reformed conflict within the Empire lasted for only one long generation: rapprochement began in the 1630s, thanks to irenicism and the political pressures of the Thirty Years' War. But as this chapter will show, in Saxony and Brandenburg this period conflict left a lasting legacy: a determination on the part of the territories' Lutheran inhabitants to defend images and to use them to express their loyalty to the Unaltered Augsburg Confession.

Electoral Saxony never experienced a fully fledged Second Reformation, but it was by no means immune to the confessional currents of the time. Elector August I (r. 1553–86) had consolidated Saxony's territorial church, protecting Luther's heritage as he understood it during a time of crisis and conflict. After the Philippist or cryto-Calvinist episode of 1571–4 August watched carefully for any signs of the renewal of such tendencies. He called Jakob Andreae to Saxony and financed the production of the *Book of Concord* in 1580. In the same year, he issued a new church ordinance to enforce orthodoxy and uniformity throughout his territory. August's successor, Christian I (r. 1586–91), inclined, however, towards Calvinism. Encouraged by his chancellor, Dr Nikolaus Krell, he abandoned the mandatory

---

[1] Andreae, *Colloquium Mompelgartense*, 757.

swearing of allegiance of pastors and professors to the Formula of Concord. He purged the court clergy and removed key opponents in the universities. Christian I and Krell dissolved the consistories, issued a new prayer book, catechism, and hymnal, and secretly ordered a new Bible translation. Christian I died in 1591; Krell, who had aroused the fury of the nobility through his authoritarian reforms of the territory's political as well as its religious life, was imprisoned and finally executed in 1601. Under the regency of Duke Friedrich Wilhelm I of Sachsen-Weimar-Altenburg, Electoral Saxony returned to the Lutheran fold, with a territory-wide visitation in 1592. From this time on all pastors and secular officials had to subscribe not only to the *Book of Concord* but also to Andreae's 1586 'Four Articles' on the Eucharist, Christology, baptism, and predestination, formulated at Montbéliard.[2] Thereafter, Electoral Saxony remained a bastion of Lutheran Orthodoxy until the conversion of Elector Friedrich August I to Catholicsm in 1697.

Lutherans in the Mark Brandenburg operated in a very different confessional environment to their Saxon co-religionists. Here the Second Reformation brought about a lasting confessional division within the territory. Joachim II's moderate Reformation had permitted the preservation of numerous traditional images and rituals, and this visual and ceremonial traditionalism persisted under his successor, Johann Georg (r. 1571–98). At the end of the sixteenth century, Joachim Friedrich (r. 1598–1608) undertook a modest reform of the church, eliminating some of its most anomalous forms of visual piety. Under Johann Sigismund, his son, the break with tradition was much more dramatic. Johann Sigismund's conversion to Calvinism was made public with a Reformed Christmas communion in Berlin's so-called Cathedral in 1613. Abraham Scultetus, Germany's leading Reformed theologian, came to Berlin in 1614, and pushed for a full cleansing of Brandenburg's religious life, focusing on Eucharistic teaching, on liturgical ritual, and on images. Johann Sigismund was reluctant to comply. In 1615, however, his brother, an ardent Calvinist, ordered the stripping of the Cathedral. The riot that followed exposed popular Lutheran attachment to images and marked a turning point in Brandenburg's confessional history. Johann Sigismund's hope that his Lutheran subjects would follow his example and convert proved ill-founded: Calvinism remained confined to the ruling elite of the court.[3] In the long run, the religious history of Hohenzollern Brandenburg-Prussia was characterized by toleration, by the integration of religious refugees from France and the Netherlands and by the flourishing of Pietism. During the first decades of the seventeenth century, however, Brandenburg's story was one of confessional delineation. Here, 'Lutherans and Reformed clashed head to head as in no other major Protestant territory'.[4] Brandenburg's history therefore illustrates, perhaps better than that of any other

---

[2] For overviews see Koch, 'Ausbau, Gefährdung und Festigung'; Smolinsky, 'Albertinisches Sachsen'.

[3] Nischan, *Prince, People, and Confession*; Brady, *German Histories*, 271 ff.; Rudersdorf and Schindling, 'Kurbrandenburg'; Thomas Klein, *Der Kampf um die zweite Reformation in Kursachsen, 1586–1591* (Cologne and Graz, 1962).

[4] Brady, *German Histories*, 274.

part of the Empire, the role that Calvinism played in the creation of Lutheran confessional consciousness.

SAXONY

Electoral Saxony's Calvinist episode was short-lived, but it nonetheless had a lasting impact on the territory's religious culture. At the level of the nobility, the reforms of theology and piety planned and partially executed under Christian I 'acted like a trauma'.[5] Conscious of their Reformation heritage and sensitized by the crypto-Calvinism of 1571–4, the Saxon nobility became, after the caesura of Christian I's reign, determined supporters of Lutheran Orthodoxy.[6] Both textual and visual sources from the milieu of the lesser nobility testify to the extent to which their religious identity was defined in opposition to Calvinism, with its attacks on liturgy and images. Hildebrand von Einsiedel (1528–98), a member of one of the territory's leading Lutheran dynasties, advisor to the Elector, senior tax collector, and head of the consistory in Leipzig, wrote an account of the state of Saxony following Christian I's death, in which he lamented the 'turmoil' of the territory's churches and schools. He and his fellow nobles' ancestors had, he stated, presented the Augsburg Confession to Emperor Charles V in 1530, 'not without great effort and danger'. Since then, however, a few 'tumultuous people' had tried to introduce Calvinism into the territory in a concealed manner.[7] At this difficult moment, Hildebrand presented himself and his fellow nobles as the guardians of right belief. They had resolved to promote and protect the *Book of Concord,* and to forbid the introduction of

> any foreign religion, rejected according to the guidance of God's word…through which churches and schools are brought into disorder, the common man offended and a dangerous lack of concern created, from which nothing will result other than contempt for God and his Word and the confusion and burdening of poor simple consciences.

Reiterating his loyalty to the 'Unaltered Augsburg Confession' and the Formula of Concord, Hildebrand ended with a plea that justice and peace should prevail.[8]

Such protestations should not, of course, always be taken at face value. There were political as well as religious reasons for supporting orthodox Lutheranism in Christian II's Saxony. As Johann Zörler, pastor in Finsterwalde, remarked in his funeral sermon for Otto II von Dieskau (d. 1597), 'it is now unfortunately common

---

[5] Koch, 'Ausbau, Gefährdung und Festigung', 221. On the conservative religous attitude of the nobility see Johannes Herrmann, 'Beobachtungen zur Kontinuität von Frömmigkeit. Leipziger Land vor und nach der Reformation', in Gerhard Graf (ed.), *Vestigia Pietatis. Studien zur Geschichte der Frömmigkeit in Thüringen und Sachsen* (Leipzig, 2000), 61–76.

[6] Martina Schattkowsky, *Zwischen Rittergut, Residenz und Reich: die Lebenswelt des kursächsischen Landadligen Christoph von Loß auf Schleinitz (1574–1620)* (Leipzig, 2007), 57, 143–4.

[7] SStAL, Rittergut Gnandstein 20392, Nr. 814, here fol. 25v–26r. On the von Einsiedel family see Chapter 6.

[8] SStAL, Rittergut Gnandstein 20392, Nr. 814, fol. 26r–27r.

that when one wants to suppress someone, one says he is a Calvinist'.[9] The 1599 will of Carl Freiherr von Friesen auf Rötha, gives a good insight into the mixture of motives that might shape nobles' statements of confessional loyalty.[10] Carl was the first of the von Friesen family to occupy a senior position at the electoral court, serving as kitchen master to Christian I from 1588. After Christian's death and the dissolution of his court, Carl became advisor to Duke Johann of Sachsen-Altenburg.[11] In his will, he prayed that God should stand by his Lutheran churches, protecting them from all 'dangers of the devil, in particular…Calvinism'. In a passage that highlights the significance of Eucharistic piety for Lutheran confessional identity, Carl wrote of the need to trust God's word rather than in human reason. He pledged to believe simply in God's promises regarding communion

> without any of the interpretation of human reason of damned Calvinism…to remain constantly loyal to this and to end my life blessedly with it, and not to concern myself and pursue reason with regard to how it is that God the Almighty is simultaneously in heaven and in his Holy Supper, and is received at communion substantially and truly in and with the bread and wine according to Christ's institution.[12]

His instructions concerning his own burial show the extent to which political loyalty and religious piety might merge. Carl asked to be buried in the church over which he exercised patronal rights in Rötha in front of the altar, with a small chain bearing images of Christian II and Duke Friedrich Wilhelm but otherwise with 'no jewellery at all nor my sword, but my prayer book'.[13] He also, like a number of other nobles of the period, tried to ensure that his heirs would uphold his confessional stance. His sons should, he wrote, 'let themselves be bound in all seriousness to God's Word as the greatest treasure, and protect themselves from Calvinist rubbish and other sects'.[14] Carl's son Heinrich the Elder (1578–1659), who was, according to the will, to be provided with a teacher who was an adherent of the pure evangelical religion and no Calvinist, wrote, in around 1600, a lengthy *Gutachten zum Calvinismus* (*Opinion Concerning Calvinism*).[15]

The loyalty of members of the Saxon nobility to orthodox Lutheranism and their professed abhorrence of Calvinism explains, in part at least, their patronage of church art. Altars and other church furnishings became visual confessions of

[9] Johann Zörler, *Zwo Leichpredigten Uber den vnuerhofften Tödlichen…abgang der beyden Christlichen…Eheleut, des…Otto von Diskaw…und auch der…Ursulae* (Eisleben, 1599), Dr.

[10] SStAL, Sonstige Herrschaften, 20532 Rittergut Rötha mit Trachenau, Nr. 2251.

[11] Jens Kunze, 'Friesen, Carl von (zu Kauern, später zu Rötha)', Institut für Sächsische Geschichte und Volkskunde e.V. (ed.), *Sächsische Biografie*, online-edition: *http://www.isgv.de/saebi/* (18.10.2013).

[12] SStAL, Sonstige Herrschaften, 20532 Rittergut Rötha mit Trachenau, Nr. 2251, fol. 2v–3v.

[13] SStAL, Sonstige Herrschaften, 20532 Rittergut Rötha mit Trachenau, Nr. 2251, fol. 3v–4v. On his church see Dehio, *Sachsen II*, 856.

[14] SStAL, Sonstige Herrschaften, 20532 Rittergut Rötha mit Trachenau, Nr. 2251, fol. 14v–15r.

[15] SStAL, Sonstige Herrschaften, 20532 Rittergut Rötha mit Trachenau, Nr. 2251, fol. 16v–17r. Trained in law, Heinrich became in 1629 Präsident des Appellationsgerichts, rose eventually to the position of chancellor (1640) and played a key role in persuading Elector Johann Georg I to take up the leadership of the *Corpus Evangelicorum* at the Diet of Regensburg in 1653. Jens Kunze, 'Friesen, Heinrich d.Ä. Freiherr von (zu Rötha)', *Sächsische Biografie*, online edition: *http://www.isgv.de/saebi/* (18.10.2013). For the 'Gutachten' see SStAL, Sonstige Herrschaften, 20532 Rittergut Rötha mit Trachenau, Nr. 5462.

faith.[16] Where both textual and visual sources relating to a particular patron survive, we can examine in detail this relationship between images and confessional identity. The castle church in Planitz near Zwickau, for example, contains a number of explicit visual reminders of the loyalty of its patronal family to Luther's Reformation. The lordship of Planitz was acquired by Joachim von Beust in 1579, and the church was renovated between 1585 and 1588 by Joachim and his son Heinrich.[17] Joachim had studied law in Leipzig and in Bologna, taught and for a time served as rector in Wittenberg, acted as advisor to the electors of Saxony and the prince of Anhalt, was a member of the upper consistory in Dresden and played an important role in the 1592 general visitation. In his professional life, Joachim was therefore closely involved in upholding Lutheran teaching, participating in, for example, the Colloquy of Quedlinburg in 1583, which produced an apology for the *Book of Concord*. He was also a very pious man himself, author of the *Enchiridion de arte bene beateque moriendi*, published first in Leipzig in 1593.[18] The furnishings of the Planitz church testify to the deep attachment that Joachim and his son felt for Luther's Reformation.

In 1588, Joachim gave full-figure and life-sized portraits of Luther and Melanchthon to his newly restored church. These unusual images, originating in the Cranach workshop, are composed of woodcuts, partially coloured and assembled in wooden frames. In bringing reformer portraits into his church, Joachim was following a well-established tradition.[19] The portraits indicate, however, not only Joachim's Wittenberg affiliation but also his deep personal admiration for Luther, whom he had first encountered in 1539 during his studies in Leipzig. Joachim had stated, according to Pastor Peter Willich, who preached his funeral sermon, that 'he could not look at Doctor Luther, the holy man of God, enough, for a truly lion-like courage and heroic heart shone from his eyes, words and gestures'.[20] The Bible that Joachim donated to the church, a richly illustrated folio edition of Luther's translation printed by Zacharias Lehmann in Wittenberg in 1594, also attests to his Lutheran piety. On its front pages the church's patron wrote in his own hand an address to the clergy who used it:

> Our Saviour Jesus Christ … recommended searching in Scripture, which gives evidence of him. Therefore I, who already have one foot in the grave, admonish you, the

[16] Jan Harasimowicz, *Kunst als Glaubensbekenntnis: Beiträge zur Kunst- und Kulturgeschichte der Reformationszeit* (Baden-Baden, 1996).

[17] Günter Zorn, *Die Schlosskirche zu Zwickau—Planitz. Der kleine sakrale Kunstführer 5* (Altenburg, 2003).

[18] On Joachim see Inga Brinkmann, *Grabdenkmäler, Grablegen und Begräbniswesen des lutherischen Adels: adelige Funeralrepräsentation im Spannungsfeld von Kontinuität und Wandel im 16. und beginnenden 17. Jahrhundert* (Berlin, 2010), 89–95. Peter Willich, *Leichbegängnis vnd Ehren=predigt/bey der Begrebnis des weyland Edlen/Gestrengen/Ehrnvehsten vnd Hochgelahrten Herrn IOACHIMI von Beust/ Auff Planitz …* (Leipzig, 1597) gives an account of his life and his funeral.

[19] Zorn, *Die Schlosskirche*, 19–20. See also Ruth Slenczka, 'Cranach der Jüngere im Dienst der Reformation', in Roland Enke, Katja Schneider, and Jutta Strehle (eds), *Cranach der Jüngere. Entdeckung eines Meisters* (Munich, 2015), 125–37, esp. 126; Kaufmann, *Konfession und Kultur*, 199–200, n. 160.

[20] Willich, *Leichbegängnis vnd Ehren=predigt*, Jr.

servants of the divine word in this church, to persist with reading and exhortation, as the teacher of the heathen urged   (1 Timothy 4:13).[21]

Most interesting, however, is the church's carved sandstone altar, erected in 1592 in the immediate aftermath of Christian I's death and attributed to the Freiberg sculptor Samuel Lorentz (Fig. 3.1). The patrons were Joachim's son, Heinrich von Beust and his wife Barbara, and the immediate occasion for their donation was, according to an inscription on the reverse of the altar, the birth of their son: 'for the little son Heinrich Friedrich, given by God, they fulfil their vow in honour of the Holy Trinity and the saving testament of Jesus Christ the Redeemer, and have therefore had this altar built out of thankfulness'.[22] The fact that Lutheran patrons could give an altar in fulfilment of a vow reveals the deeply personal circumstances that might motivate individual commissions, circumstances that can only very rarely be reconstructed from surviving documents. The front of the altar, by contrast, is a very public statement of Lutheran confessional identity. It shows in its central shrine, as Luther would have wished, the Last Supper. Beneath is an inscription, unusually not taken from the Bible and perhaps composed by Joachim, that invokes a specifically Lutheran understanding of the Eucharist, stating that Christ gives his body through the bread and his blood through the wine, and that the viewer must believe the Word of God.[23] Heinrich and his wife kneel on either side of the inscription, and above them are reliefs showing baptism and confession. Beneath is the Birth of Christ and above his Resurrection, flanked by Moses and John the Baptist representing the Law and Gospel.

The Last Supper—the scriptural record of the institution of communion—was, of course, one possible iconography for presenting a visual confession of Lutheranism. In his 1530 commentary on Psalm 111, Luther himself had recommended the Last Supper as the most appropriate image to adorn an altar, and in Saxony the iconography had a distinguished pedigree, going back to the 1547 Cranach altarpiece in Wittenberg's parish church.[24] During the era of the Second Reformation it was, however, the crucifix rather than the Last Supper that became the most powerful symbol of Lutheran confessional identity. Even during the early decades of the Reformation Lutherans had routinely adorned their altars with small, sculpted crucifixes (*Altarkreuze*). The Wittenberg altarpiece bears a painted version, a visual representation of Luther's Hidden God.[25] But as Calvinist criticism of idolatry mounted, and debates over the nature of Christ's presence at communion intensified, Lutherans reaffirmed their commitment to visual representations of the crucified Christ.

Crucifixes were objects of particular hatred for Reformed Protestants. At Montbéliard Beza, for example, argued that amongst all the images that profaned

---

[21] 'Die Parochie Planitz', *Neue Sächsische Kirchengalerie: Die Ephorie Zwickau* (Leipzig, 1902), cols 162–200, here col. 167. The Bible is preserved today in the *Pfarramt*.
[22] For a full discussion see Heal, ' "Zum Andencken und zur Ehre Gottes" ', 203–4.
[23] CHRISTVS DAT CORPVS CVM PANE MEROQVE CRVOREM CREDE DEI VERBO, COETERA MONSTRA FUGE.
[24] WA 31/1, 415.   [25] Koerner, *The Reformation of the Image*, chapter 13.

Fig. 3.1. Samuel Lorentz, altarpiece from the castle church in Zwickau-Planitz, 1592.

Credit: Photo: author's own, with permission from the Pfarramt Planitz-Rottmannsdorf.

churches, crosses and crucifixes were especially dangerous: 'I believe that an image will not soon be found that the papists have misused more than the crucifix'.[26] Crucifixes were often, as we shall see in Berlin in 1615, the first images to fall victim to Calvinist iconoclasm, and were keenly defended by Lutherans. A pastor from Anhalt, for example, who was prepared to accept the breaking of bread as an adiaphoron, took the removal of his crucifix to be an intolerable offense.[27] Abraham Taurer, responding to the Anhalt iconoclasm, also identified the crucifix as a particular point of conflict: the Anhalt Calvinists—the new 'Karlstadtians', as he described them—had polluted God's sacred temple by throwing from it the crucifix and 'all other Christian images'.[28] Were the Anhalt reformers really Calvinists, Tauerer asked? Were they as bad as those in the Palatinate? Yes, for they could not tolerate images of the crucified Christ, and this showed that they had 'Calvinist blasphemy' in their hearts.[29]

Rejected by Calvinists, the crucifix became a Lutheran confessional image. The town church in Finsterwalde, a small town near Electoral Saxony's border with Lower Lusatia, provides a particularly good example of its confessional use. The Finsterwalde castle was in the hands of the von Dieskau family from 1533 to 1625, and at the behest of Otto II (d. 1597) a new church, St Trinitatis, was built between 1584 and 1593 to replace the pre-Reformation church of Sankt Marien that had grown too small for its congregation. St Trinitatis is a fascinating church, rich not only in images but also in inscriptions that direct the educated viewer towards their proper Lutheran use. On the exterior, for example, was an image of the Trinity with the instruction: 'It is God that the image depicts, but we do not pray to it. Look at it, and worship in spirit what you regard in the image'. The church's altar was given in 1594 by Otto II's sons, according to an inscription on a panel in the choir area, 'guided by pious feeling towards their forefathers' (Fig. 3.2). The donors addressed the altar's viewers explicitly:

> You, traveller, do not strive too busily for empty pomp, but think rather that all worldly goods are dreams, shadows and smoke, and prepare yourself thus through this example and true trust in God, so that you, freed from the bonds of the mortal body, enjoy immortality and eternal happiness with the angels.[30]

The altarpiece shows a life-sized sculpted crucifix (now with a new townscape behind), accompanied by the biblical words of institution beside and beneath it. Above is a text from Psalm 111: 'He has given a remembrance of his wonders, the gracious and merciful Lord'.[31]

Finsterwalde's biblical inscriptions do not provide as immediate a link to the Lutheran–Calvinist conflict as those on the von Beust altar in Planitz. But the 1597 funeral sermon for Otto II von Dieskau, preached by Pastor Johann Zörler, provides

---

[26] Andreae, *Colloquium Mompelgartense*, 742.   [27] Kaufmann, *Konfession und Kultur*, 181.
[28] Taurer, *Hochnothwendigster Bericht*, Vorrede, ii r–v.   [29] Ibid., X iv v.
[30] On the Finsterwalde church see Angela Beeskow, *St. Trinitatis in Finsterwalde, Grosse Baudenkmäler 485* (Munich and Berlin, 1993). The various inscriptions are given in Theodor Goecke (ed.), *Die Kunstdenkmäler der Provinz Brandenburg*, vol. 5/1 (Berlin, 1917), 151–65.
[31] Ps 111:4.

Fig. 3.2. M. Brauer and S. Herber, altarpiece from the parish church of St Trinitatis, Finsterwalde, 1594.

Credit: Photo: author's own, with permission from the Ev. Kirchengemeinde Finsterwalde.

the necessary context for their interpretation. Otto II had been educated in theology and law in Wittenberg, and served as a councillor to Elector August, rising to become a member of the privy council under Christian I. After remarking that an accusation of Calvinism was a good way to ruin a reputation, Zörler stated:

> I can say in truth of our dear lord and Christian *Junker*, and give witness before God and this congregation, that he was not a follower of this error. For whenever he made his confession before me, his unworthy pastor, he always distinguished and set apart his belief in the article of the Eucharist from the errors of the Calvinists.[32]

Zörler took care to emphasize that Otto II had bought the Formula of Concord for his library. In his account of Otto II's death, Zörler describes his last communion and his desperate desire to die as a true Christian, crying out 'Herr Pastor, not in a Calvinist manner, not in a Calvinist manner, but as Jesus Christ instituted it, I too wish to receive it as a true Christian'.[33] It is not clear whether we should interpret the Finsterwalde altar as a genuine sign of Otto II's commitment, after a successful career made serving a Calvinist prince, to a Lutheran understanding of communion. It could equally well be read as an attempt on the part of his sons to clear his, and his family's, reputation and to bind the von Dieskau family firmly to Christian II's new political order. Either way, however, the role that images, especially altar-pieces and crucifixes, played in expressing Lutheran identity is beyond doubt.

It is unusual to be able to reconstruct the context of a particular commission in such rich detail. But examples of church furnishings that deliberately demonstrated their patrons' loyalty to Lutheranism could certainly be multiplied. The church in Seifersdorf near Dresden contains an altar that incorporates, as its central image, an epitaph for Dietrich von Grünrod who died in 1603 (Fig. 3.3). Dietrich kneels, clad in armour, before a crucifix made of wood and alabaster. Beneath is a relief of the Last Supper, with inscriptions that emphasize a Lutheran understanding of communion, based on Luke 18:27 ('what is impossible with men, is possible with God'), Isaiah 45:9 ('woe to him, who quarrels with his creator'), and Psalm 33:4 ('the word of the Lord is truthful'). After Dietrich's death his epitaph was incorporated into an altarpiece bearing paintings of his descendants and another inscription:

> The honourable Joachim Heinrich and Wolf Dietrich, the von Grünrod brothers, built this altar for the Christian commemoration of their pious father, as a testimony to their Christian faith in remembrance of their mortality and steadfast confession, until their blessed end, of the Unaltered Augsburg Confession. 1604.[34]

Dietrich had spent his career in the service Emperor Charles V and of the electoral houses of Saxony and Brandenburg. His funeral sermon, preached by Seifersdorf's pastor Johannes Lindener, emphasized his service to August I of Saxony and Johann Georg of Brandenburg, and passed over in silence the years of Christian I's

---

[32] Zörler, *Zwo Leichpredigten*, Dv.   [33] Ibid., D 3v.
[34] Cornelius Gurlitt (ed.), *Beschreibende Darstellung der älteren Bau- und Kunstdenkmäler des Königreichs Sachsen*, vol. 26, *Amtshauptmannschaft Dresden-Neustadt* (Dresden, 1904), 230 ff.

Fig. 3.3. Anon., altarpiece and epitaph for Dietrich von Grünrod from the parish church of Seifersdorf near Radeberg, 1604.

Credit: © SLUB/Deutsche Fotothek.

reign.[35] In Seifersdorf, as in Finsterwalde, the heirs of a member of the nobility whose political career had spanned Saxony's Calvinist interlude used images to demonstrate their dynasty's loyalty to orthodox Lutheranism.

BRANDENBURG

Brandenburg's sixteenth-century Lutherans worshipped in a remarkably traditional visual environment. Although Brandenburg sided with the Gnesio-Lutheran cause after 1548, Joachim II was harsh in his condemnation of iconoclasm and defended the doctrine of the real presence against the 'Sacramentarian' threat. His church placed great emphasis on seeing. In 1562, the Elector replaced the simple elevation, approved by Luther and in use in a number of territories, with the *ostensio*, a rite

---

[35] Johannes Lindener, *Christliche Leichpredigt von dem letzten Wort... Bey Leichbestattung des Dietrich von Grünraden auff Seyffersdorf u. Widerode* (Dresden: Stöckel, 1603).

derived from the liturgy of the Greek Orthodox Church. After reciting the words of institution, the officiating minister not only held the consecrated elements aloft but also turned to the congregation and addressed them with the following words: 'See, dear Christians, this is the true body of Christ given for us, and this is the true blood of Christ shed for us'.[36] The Elector did this, according to his public confession of faith made in Berlin's Cathedral on 19 April 1563, to counter 'enthusiasts and profaners of the Sacrament'. In the same confession of faith, he defended the continued use of the crucifix:

> All my life during papist times I was never taught that I should pray to that wood, rather that it was a reminder, as Augustine said: 'not this, but the heart of Christ through this', so every Christian should have a crucifix before him every day, to remind himself of the martyrdom of the Son of God.[37]

Joachim II's son, Johann Georg (r. 1571–98), moved the church more firmly towards Gnesio-Lutheranism, appointing Andreas Musculus as superintendent-general and participating actively in the drafting and dissemination of the Formula of Concord. In his view, however, doctrinal orthodoxy still had to be reinforced by ceremonial and visual traditionalism in order to keep Calvinism at bay. In 1572, he produced a revised version of the 1540 church ordinance, which reformed some of the most controversial elements of Joachim's ceremonial but left the majority of the ritual and visual life of the church untouched.[38] The Eucharist continued to be celebrated as it had been under Joachim II, and processions and para-liturgical dramas such as those performed at the Holy Sepulchre in Berlin's Cathedral on Good Friday and Easter Saturday persisted.[39] In 1593, the Elector compelled his heirs to sign a pledge that committed them 'to abide faithfully by the Formula of Concord ... and to allow no changes in our schools and churches that would violate this confession'. And Johann Georg's 1596 testament specified that 'church vestments, ornaments, silverware, treasures, vessels, paintings, and other church decorations' should remain in the Cathedral after his death, and that his successors should 'maintain and preserve the current liturgy and ceremonies' there also.[40]

As in Electoral Saxony, images were used by the nobility to express loyalty to orthodox Lutheranism during this period. Lampert Distelmeyer (d. 1588), who had served during his career as court councillor (*Hofrat*) and chancellor to Joachim II and Johann Georg, gave a painted epitaph for Berlin's Nikolaikirche that shows the crucified Christ before the city of Jerusalem, flanked by two angels, one collecting blood in a chalice. The epitaph indicates a pronounced Eucharistic piety: it expresses visually the belief that Christ's body and blood were truly present in the

---

[36] Nischan, *Lutherans and Calvinists*, 15. See also Müller, *Der Dom*, 391–3.
[37] Paul Steinmüller, 'Das Bekenntnis Joachims II', *Forschungen zur Brandenburgischen und Preußischen Geschichte*, 17 (1) (1904), 237–46, here 241–2; GStAPK I. HA Rep. 2 Berliner Dom, 77–102, fol. 89r, 87r.
[38] Nischan, *Prince, People, and Confession*, 46–7.   [39] Müller, *Der Dom*, 445 ff.
[40] Quoted in Nischan, *Prince, People, and Confession*, 54.

bread and wine.[41] Lampert's 1587 will, in which he left 300 *Thaler* for his 'grave stone and handsome epitaph', professes his loyalty

> to the true Christian religion, as it is written and gathered together in the three chief confessions, the Apostolic, Nicene and Athanasian, the Augsburg Confession and Luther's catechism, in simple understanding of the same, without all the dangerous disputations and quarrels that have been stirred up during our times.[42]

Lampert Distelmeyer's son, Christian, who served as chancellor after his father's death until 1598, also gave a painted epitaph to the Nikolaikirche. It was commissioned shortly before Johann Sigismund's 1613 public conversion to Calvinism, and shows the crucified Christ with angels carrying the *Arma Christi*.[43] Christian's image, like his will which speaks merely of his 'Christian and blessed departure', is less explicitly confessional than that of his father.[44] Yet, even without an explicit linking of blood and communion, its monumental depiction of Christ's body serves, like the crucifix on the Finsterwalde altar (Fig. 3.2), to visualize Christ's real presence.

Brandenburg's conservative liturgical and visual environment provided the backdrop for the territory's particularly dramatic encounter with Calvinism. Johann Georg's successor, Joachim Friedrich (r. 1598–1608), had served as administrator of the Archbishopric of Magdeburg for thirty-two years. He was more afraid of Catholic renewal and of its international supporters, the Guise and Habsburgs, than of Calvinism, and favoured, therefore, a pan-Protestant confessional stance.[45] In his own territory, he stated in 1598, he did not wish for any changes in religious matters, but rather to preserve the example of his grandfather and father and to uphold the pure Augsburg Confession and Formula of Concord. Above all, however, he was determined 'not to allow any Papist, Calvinist or other errors to be introduced into churches and schools', and in order to achieve this he was minded to undertake a modest reform of the church.[46]

An 'Opinion' (*Gutachten*) written by Christoph Pelargus, Simon Gedicke, and others in March 1598, listed the measures that the Elector's theologians considered necessary to achieve this. They emphasized the need for uniformity in teaching, in ceremonial, and in matters of indifference to salvation. They recommended the abolition of some ceremonies, including the *ostensio*, which was the cause of particular superstition: 'As soon as those lacking in understanding, especially among the women, hearken [to it] they beat their breasts or raise their hands up or make another sign, which is sufficient to show [their] superstition'.[47]

---

[41] Maria Deiters, 'Individuum—Gemeinde—Raum. Zur nachreformatorischen Ausstattungen von St. Marien und St. Nikolai in Berlin', in Evelin Wetter (ed.), *Formierung des konfessionellen Raumes in Ostmitteleuropa* (Stuttgart, 2008), 41–56.
[42] BLHA, Rep. 37 Lübbenau, Familienarchiv der Grafen zu Lynar auf Lübbenau, Nr. 1605, fol. 1v.
[43] Deiters, 'Individuum'; see also Stiftung Preußische Schlösser und Gärten Berlin-Brandenburg, *Cranach und die Kunst der Renaissance,* 38.
[44] BLHA, Rep. 37 Lübbenau, Familienarchiv der Grafen zu Lynar auf Lübbenau, Nr. 1605, fol. 24 ff.
[45] Nischan, *Prince, People, and Confession*, 62.
[46] GStAK PK I. HA Rep. 2 Berliner Dom, 110–52, No. 70: 'Reformation des Dombstieffs czue Collen an der Sprew Anno 1598', (27 February).
[47] Ibid., 30 March.

The theologians had nothing specific to say on images, but their comments on the spectacle of Brandenburg's church services indicate a growing suspicion of visual piety. The para-liturgical rituals on Palm Sunday should be abolished, they wrote, because 'no creature in heaven or on earth' can depict the sufferings of Christ without hindering their spiritual contemplation and turning them into a 'comedy play'. The use of the Holy Sepulchre on Good Friday should also be abandoned, 'because this happened once and is to be believed, and appropriated for our consolation and not depicted with external gestures'. The rituals of Ascension Day, when a figure of Christ was pulled up into the roof of the Cathedral, allowed their opponents to label them as 'servants of idols', and as for Pentecost: 'That is almost like puppetry, raising and lowering the Holy Ghost as a wooden figure, which can create no devotion at all amongst believers and for the simple folk is much more harmful than pious'.

Even while they approved the continued use of vestments, the theologians emphasized that pastors should remember that they were a matter of Christian freedom and 'look more to the inner adornment of the heart'. Pelargus, a disciple of Melanchthon who by 1613 had moved towards a Calvinist understanding of the Lord's Supper, wrote a separate letter explaining his objections to the *ostensio*, emphasizing 'that it makes visible what we cannot see with our bodily eyes, but rather must believe with certainty, as the ancient little verse says: that what you do not perceive, what you do not see, bold faith affirms'. The rite was, he believed, of no use against Calvinism for 'all errors and perversities must be put down again through the Word of God alone'. Moreover, seeing did nothing to generate piety, which must 'come from Christ, his Word and the diligent contemplation of the same, rather than [from] the bodily seeing of the bread', and which will 'not be improved by such seeing'.[48]

Joachim Friedrich proceeded with caution, implementing only some of his theologians' recommendations. The *ostensio* was abolished in Berlin in 1598 and elsewhere in the Mark by the early seventeenth century, though even in 1633 Frankfurt an der Oder's theological faculty found it necessary to advise that 'the elevation and *ostensio*, where they are found, must without doubt be forbidden, for they point souls towards the earthly elements'.[49] There was a territory-wide visitation in 1600 that 'suggested a subtle yet important shift in the Mark's confessional orientation'.[50] It sought to enforce the Formula of Concord, but paid particular attention to popular piety and ceremony, condemning not only the *ostensio* but also processions in its attempt to distinguish the territory's church clearly from its papist predecessor. The Elector re-dedicated Berlin's Cathedral in 1598, which had, 'during the papacy', been consecrated in honour of Saints Erasmus and Mary Magdalene. Now 'such an idolatrous name should be removed entirely', and

---

[48] GStAK PK I. HA Rep. 2 Berliner Dom, 110–52, No. 70: 'Reformation des Dombstieffs czue Collen an der Sprew Anno 1598', (21 May).

[49] *Fortgesetzte Sammlung von Alten und Neuen Theologischen Sachen, Büchern, Uhrkunden, Controversien, Veränderungen, Anmerckungen, Vorschlägen, u. d. g. zur geheiligten Ubung in beliebigem Beytrag ertheilet von Einigen Dienern des Göttlichen Wortes* (Leipzig, 1728), 29.

[50] Nischan, *Prince, People, and Confession*, 70.

henceforth the church should 'have and keep the name of the Holy Trinity'.[51] There was, as yet, no sustained campaign against images. An inventory of the Cathedral from 1599 lists numerous elaborate liturgical vessels, monstrances, para-liturgical props such as a rainbow and a wooden dove for Ascension and Pentecost, a 'gilded wooden crucifix, used when oaths are made', another wooden crucifix with 'bloody drops of sweat', and a rich collection of vestments and textiles.[52] But during the final years of his reign Joachim Friedrich did take steps to renovate the Cathedral. The preface to his successor's confession of faith, drafted by Reformed theologians, praised Joachim Friedrich not only for his liturgical reforms but also for removing idols and monstrances from Berlin's main church.[53]

If the confessional shift that occurred under Joachim Friedrich was subtle, the transformation that his son Johann Sigismund (r. 1608–19) brought about was anything but. Johann Sigismund's religious education had been entrusted to Simon Gedicke, but this fanatically anti-Calvinist preacher failed, ultimately, to instil in his charge a sense of loyalty to the Lutheran church. The future Elector converted secretly to Calvinism, probably during a visit to the Palatinate in 1606, and made a public declaration of his Reformed faith through his Christmas communion in Berlin's Cathedral in 1613.[54] In preparation for this public declaration of faith, the Elector promised that he would leave his subjects' freedom of conscience untouched, and that his Lutheran subjects could retain 'their ceremonies, with altars, lights, images, vestments and all else'.[55] They would, he hoped, follow his example and convert of their own volition. Yet, from the perspective of his Reformed advisors, such an accommodating approach was not acceptable. Clearer confessional lines needed to be drawn, for 'when papists come here and see the ceremonies, they will think nothing other than that it is still papist here'.[56]

In 1614, the Elector called Abraham Scultetus to Berlin, and the pressure for a full purging of papist remnants increased.[57] Not surprisingly, images were one of Scultetus's main targets. In his response to a list of issues sent to him for consideration by the council, Scultetus recommended a colloquium with the Lutherans at which seven points should be discussed. The first was communion, the second exorcism at baptism, and the third 'the keeping of the pope's idols in evangelical churches'. Scultetus went on to urge the Elector to make the Cathedral into an exemplary church 'that is cleansed of all idols'. There could be, he wrote, no proper

---

[51] GStAPK, I. HA Rep. 2 Berliner Dom, 106r–106v.

[52] GStAPK, I. HA Rep. 2 Berliner Dom, 153–64. For a discussion of another crucifix used in a Lutheran context for oath swearing see Bridget Heal, 'Seeing Christ: Visual Piety in Saxony's Erzgebirge', in Jeffrey Chipps Smith (ed.), *Visual Acuity and the Arts of Communication in Early Modern Germany* (Farnham, 2014).

[53] Nischan, *Prince, People, and Confession*, 72; GStAPK, I HA Rep. 47, Tit. 16 Reformierte Religion 1613–1749, 137–9.

[54] Nischan, *Prince, People, and Confession*, 92 ff.

[55] GStAPK, I HA Rep. 47, Tit. 16 Reformierte Religion 1613–1749, fol. 8r.

[56] GStAPK, I HA Rep. 47, Tit. 16 Reformierte Religion 1613–1749, 137–9.

[57] Karl Pahncke 'Abraham Scultetus in Berlin', *Forschungen zur Brandenburgischen und Preußischen Geschichte*, 23 (1910), 35–53.

start to the Reformation while there was no single place that had been entirely purged of the papacy and its relics.[58] During Scultetus's six-month stay in Berlin, key parts of the work of reformation were undertaken.[59] But the Elector did not move against images. On 27 June 1614, he wrote to his brother 'that we are not disinclined to remove the idols and images from our Cathedral Church, but that we have not yet had time for this, and would prefer to be present in person at the removal'.[60]

BERLIN 1615

Johann Sigismund was right to be cautious. In March 1615, nearly a year after the Elector had given the Cathedral over to Reformed worship and while he was away on a hunting trip, his regent, his ardently Calvinist brother Margrave Johann Georg of Brandenburg, ordered that all images and liturgical paraphernalia were to be removed from the church.[61] A report dated 13 April 1615, probably written by Johann Sigismund's Calvinist advisor Abraham von Dohna, records that about five weeks previously the Margrave had 'had the large wooden crucifix, which was attached to the iron railing in front of the choir in the Cathedral, broken, smashed and thrown in pieces into the [River] Spree'. The remainder of the Cathedral was stripped on 30 March. On Palm Sunday, 2 April, the Elector's court preacher, Martin Füssel, delivered a sermon that sought to justify the Berlin iconoclasm. Images were, he complained, not lay Bibles; that idea was not to be found anywhere in sacred Scripture, but rather 'came from the devil'. Füssel criticized in particular a stone image on a pillar 'here in Cölln in St Peter's church', depicting two people committing adultery.[62]

The Lutheran preacher Peter Stuler responded immediately, preaching later that morning in St Peter's against Füssel, saying, according to Dohna, that 'the Calvinists vilify our churches as a brothel, wherein all sorts of ignominy and vice are committed, they destroy the images from the churches, [and] they also wish to tear the Lord Christ from our hearts'.[63] Stuler also, according to various accounts, criticized the Elector's actions, saying: 'if you want to reform, go to Jülich: there you have reforming to do'. With the Treaty of Xanten of 12 November 1614, Johann Sigismund had surrendered his claims to the Catholic provinces of Jülich and Berg to Wolfgang Wilhelm of Neuburg, receiving in return the predominantly Protestant regions of Cleves, Mark, and Ravensberg. Stuler was suggesting, therefore, that the

---

[58] GStAPK, I HA Rep. 2 Berliner Dom, Nr. 37: 'Acta betreffend den Hofprediger Scultetus, 1614–1617', fol. 10r–10v. See Pahncke, 'Abraham Scultetus', 44–5 on context.

[59] Ibid., 51–2.   [60] GStAPK, I HA Rep. 47, Tit. 16 Reformierte Religion 1613–1749, 149.

[61] Nischan, *Prince, People, and Confession*, 185 ff.

[62] Printed in 'Extract schreibens sub dato Cöln an der Sprew den 13. aprilis a. 1615', *Forschungen zur Brandenburgischen und Preußischen Geschichte*, 9 (1) (1896), 18–21, here 19; see Harasimowicz, *Kunst als Galubensbekenntnis*, 33–4.

[63] 'Extract schreibens', 19.

Elector should focus his reforming efforts on real Catholics rather than on his Lutheran subjects in Berlin.[64]

On the following Monday, 3 April, in response to rumours that the Lutheran Stuler was about to be arrested, 'a common cry went out amongst the people'. That evening there was a riot: the Lutherans assembled before Stuler's door, where they were served beer by his wife, and then started to attack the houses of prominent Calvinists, Dr Saffius and Salomon Finck. In response, Johann Georg, who had apparently spent the evening reading Scultetus's Passion sermons, rode with his companions to meet the crowd.[65] 'Citizens and ragamuffins' confronted the margrave, crying 'you black Calvinist ... you destroyed our images and our crucifix; we want to attack you and your Calvinist priests'. After further threats, Johann Georg and his companions fired warning shots. The rabble rang the storm bells, and more rebels arrived; the crowd eventually, according to Dohna, numbered 600 or 700 in total. Johann Georg was forced to retreat, and the crowd went on to plunder the houses of the Calvinist preachers Füssel and Carl Sachse. Füssel lost everything, to the extent that he had to preach on the following Friday 'in underwear and a green vest', to which he added a borrowed coat.[66]

The situation remained critical on Tuesday, but Johann Sigismund's swift return, his issuing of arrest warrants and his raising of a 300-man militia successfully restored the peace.[67] Thereafter, the Elector proceeded with caution against the Lutheran rioters. He compelled the city's magistrates and burghers to sign an oath pledging that they had not been involved, and ordered an investigation which interrogated 150 witnesses about the events of 3 April.[68] The investigators focused on a number of ring leaders and on the actions of the Lutheran Electress Anna of Prussia, whom they suspected of inciting or encouraging the riot.[69] In the end, they concluded that Stuler, who had already fled the territory, was largely responsible. It was he who had, in the words of a later commentator, 'poured oil onto the fire'.[70]

In an already tense confessional situation, the removal of images from the Cathedral provided the spark that ignited the tinderbox of Lutheran fear. Contemporary commentators differed in how much weight they assigned to that one issue. The Calvinist Dohna mocked the popular Lutheran response to the iconoclasm, saying that when the crucifix was removed 'the common folk lamented much that Our Lord God was treated so badly'. When the remainder

[64] Nischan, *Prince, People, and Confession*, 206. Beckmann's (1641–1717) *Kirchengeschichte* gives a full account of events: GStAPK, VI. HA (Familienarchive und Nachlässe), NI Johann Christopher Beckmann, J. Ch. Nr. 20.
[65] Daniel Heinrich Hering, *Historische Nachricht von dem ersten Anfang der Evangelisch-Reformirten Kirche in Brandenburg und Preußen* (Halle: Johann Jacob Curt, 1778), 293.
[66] Ibid., 290.   [67] Nischan, *Prince, People, and Confession*, 190.
[68] GStAPK, I. HA GR, Rep. 49 Fiscalia M, 13–17 (Aufruhr, Tumult), M 16. I am very grateful to Nadine Jaser for bringing this collection to my attention.
[69] On Anna of Prussia see recently: Christian Wieland, 'Spielräume und Grenzen religiöser Selbstbestimmung der Fürstin im konfessionellen Zeitalter: Renée de France und Anna von Preußen', in Irene Dingel and Ute Lotz-Heumann (eds), *Entfaltung und zeitgenössische Wirkung der Reformation im europäischen Kontext* (Gütersloh, 2015), 233–48.
[70] Hering, *Historische Nachricht*, 291.

of the Cathedral was stripped many of those who saw the paintings, images, and altars being destroyed 'shed tears, especially however the women, because the image of Our God (as they call it) was so mercilessly treated'. They also called on God to punish the iconoclasts.[71] Dohna's account, which implies that in their ignorance and superstition the Lutheran population conflated images with their prototypes and expected divine punishment for those who attacked them, finds no corroboration in other sources. But Berlin's Lutherans were deeply attached to their images, and Johann Georg's iconoclasm was certainly a major cause of the unrest.

A number of accounts agree that 'iconoclast' was one of the insults hurled at Johann Georg. And when the 150 witnesses were asked, amongst other things, what caused the riot, many pointed to the image question. Most blamed 'sharp' preaching by Füssel and Stuler, compounded by Lutheran fear that Stuler was about to be arrested.[72] The minority who admitted to any detailed knowledge of the events reported that Füssel had preached against images, and that Stuler had responded with an explanation of the controversial image in St Peter's (a depiction of adultery), stated that images should be left in peace and argued that if reform was required then it was in Jülich rather than here in Berlin.[73] One, a servant Michell Schmidt, aged 19, stated that he had been told by his tailor that the attack on Füssel's house pleased him, for 'they had taken the crucifixes from the churches and smashed them apart', and therefore the same must be done to the crosses (i.e. the bars) in their windows.[74]

The threat of further iconoclasm was also important. Friederich Buchfelder, aged 55, scribe to Abraham von Dohna, gave a long account of Johann Georg's confrontation with the crowd, in which he reported that 'one amongst the mob [subsequently identified as the tailor Ernst Löeckel], who had a halberd in his hands, began and said, why should we be peaceful, the Cathedral is destroyed, soon they will come and destroy our churches too'. Catharina Schulzen, wife of Salomon Finck, reported that Michell Aschenbrenner had warned her three days before the riot that 'they will take the images out of the churches, at which the people will be angry; they will wish to do it in the other churches, at this the common servants will awake, beat the drum, and break the Calvinists' necks'.[75] Some reports exaggerated the extent of the iconoclasm. In his account of the events, the Lutheran mayor stated that epitaphs, as well as crucifixes, altars, and other images, had been removed from the Cathedral, which, as Peter Conovius and other commentators

---

[71] *Extract*, 18.
[72] GStAPK, I. HA Geheimer Rat, Rep. 49 Fiscalia M, Nr. 16. See, for example, witnesses 15 and 22.
[73] e.g. ibid., witness 37: Walpurg Schmiels, aged 40, widow of the *Bürgermeister*; witness 47, Michell Poenes, aged 33, 'Marck vnd Wagemeister' for Cölln's council; also 45; 53; 54. See also set 2: no. 2, no. 5. Also set 32: no. 18, no. 36. On the Petrikirche image see Beckmann's *Kirchengeschichte*, GStAPK, VI. HA (Familienarchive und Nachlässe), NI Johann Christopher Beckmann, J. Ch. Nr. 20, fol. 165; Hering, *Historische Nachricht*, 284.
[74] GStAPK, I. HA Geheimer Rat, Rep. 49 Fiscalia M Nr. 16, set 2, witness no. 12.
[75] Ibid., set 2, witness no. 6.

noted, was not true: many epitaphs remained in place until 1717, when they were removed to create space for more pews.[76]

LEGACIES OF CONFLICT

The April 1615 'great unrest', as documents placed in the capsule at the top of the Nikolaikirche's tower described it, marked, for both Lutherans and Calvinists, a turning point in the history of the Brandenburg's churches.[77] Johann Christoph Beckmann (1641–1717), Reformed theologian at the university in Frankfurt an der Oder, devoted twenty-five pages of his church history to a full description of the events.[78] 'There has been no greater and more dangerous rebellion and tumult than that on the 3rd April 1615', he concluded.[79] Beckman emphasized, not surprisingly, the guilt of the Lutheran preacher Stuler: 'It was not the business with the images that caused the tumult, but Stuler's thoughtless speech: if you want to reform go to Jülich, there you have enough to reform', combined with the rumour that he was about to be arrested.[80] Beckmann argued that it was misguided to blame Reformed iconoclasm, because 'it never happened, and perhaps was never thought about; the images in St Peter's, St Mary's and St Nicholas' are still standing, as they stood then'.[81]

Although Beckmann's suggestion that the Reformed never intended to remove the images from Berlin's parish churches is an oversimplification, his account does provide a necessary corrective to some of the most impassioned Lutheran rhetoric. In 1615, the majority of the images that were removed from Berlin's Cathedral were not destroyed; this was no discriminate act of violent iconoclasm. Some, notably the Cranach altarpieces, were transferred to the castle chapel, which served the Lutheran Electress Anna and her daughters, or to other Lutheran churches.[82] Treasures were removed to the electoral residence in Cölln or dispatched to Custrin then melted down; some eventually became part of the Electors' art collection, some were dispersed, for example, a gilded silver pax from which the cross and relics had been removed, given to the Archduke of Florence in or before 1624.[83] Without doubt, however, the stripping of the Cathedral represented a triumph for

---

[76] Peter Conovius, *Bescheidentliche Abfertigunge eines Tractetleins Georgii Gottfrieden Berlinensis, Theologiae Studiosi. Die Ausmusterung der Bilder/So wol Die Abschaffung des Exorcismi Betreffence…* (Wittenberg: Georg Kelner, 1615), A iii v.

[77] Johann Christoph Müller and Georg Gottfried Küster, *Altes und Neues Berlin. Das ist: vollständige Nachricht von der Stadt Berlin, derselben Erbauen, Lage, Kirchen…Erster Theil* (Berlin: Johann Peter Schmid, 1737), 274.

[78] On Beckmann see H. U. Delius, 'Johann Christoph Beckmann's handschriftliche "Brandenburgische Kirchengeschichte"', *Jahrbuch für Berlin-Brandenburgische Kirchengeschichte*, 47 (1972), 71–91. It was never published but was used extensively by later commentators.

[79] GStAPK, VI. HA (Familienarchive und Nachlässe), NI Johann Christopher Beckmann, J. Ch. Nr. 20, fol. 165v.

[80] Ibid., fol. 178v.   [81] Ibid., fol. 178r. See also Hering, *Historische Nachricht*, 96, 279, 281.

[82] Tacke, *Der katholische Cranach*, 221–5.

[83] GStAPK, I. HA, Rep. 2 Berliner Dom, 90 ff. See also Hering, *Historische Nachricht*, 281–2.

the Reformed party. Shortly afterwards, the Augsburg art agent Philip Hainhofer reported on its appearance: 'It is a beautiful, huge bright church, from which all altars, panels, pictures, and crucifixes have been removed. Except for the green railings and carpets, it is now completely white inside'.[84]

The contrast between the appearance of the Cathedral and that of Berlin's two medieval parish churches, which remained in Lutheran hands, was enormous. In 1613, both parish churches had been renovated at the behest of the city council: in St Marien the font had been moved, pews built in the middle of the church and 'the papist altars torn out of it'.[85] But some pre-Reformation furnishings remained intact and *in situ*, and these were augmented by the post-Reformation donations of prosperous Lutheran parishioners. In St Marien, for example, the medieval high altar showing the Virgin and Child, described in Johann Christoph Müller and Georg Gottfried Küster's 1752 *Fortgesetztes Altes und Neues Berlin* as 'a work built in Roman-Catholic times', survived until 1762 when it was replaced by a new altar adorned with paintings by Bernhard Rode.[86] The Marienkirche's gothic high altar was perhaps still used for communion on feast days, and the church also had a second altar: it had been given in 1587 by the electoral secretary Joachim Steinbrecher, and was situated underneath the medieval triumphal cross at the crossing between the nave and the choir.[87]

The Nikolaikirche was also, as we saw with the Distelmeyer epitaphs, used as a site for representation by Berlin's Lutheran elite. Another epitaph, possibly commissioned by Christian Distelmeyer in 1612 alongside his own, shows Johann von Kötteritz (d. 1609), an electoral advisor, and his wife, Caritas Distelmeyer (d. 1615), Christian's sister (Plate 5).[88] They kneel between Moses and John the Baptist, allegorical personifications of the Law and Gospel. In the background, there is a minutely detailed depiction of the interior of the Nikolaikirche, richly adorned with images providing a suitable setting for the key rites of the Lutheran liturgy. A baptism enclosure with its font, dating from 1563, occupies the centre of the church; to the left is a confessional or a private pew. Communion is being celebrated at the medieval high altar in the choir. A triumphal cross rises above the rood screen, and the von Kötteritz family chapel, in which the epitaph originally hung, can be seen on the right.[89] While the interior that is represented here is, of course, an imagined ideal rather than a straightforward depiction of reality, inventories confirm that in the Nikolaikirche the liturgy of the Lutheran church was carried out with proper visual solemnity. In addition to its large-scale images and

---

[84] Quoted in Nischan, *Prince, People, and Confession*, 186.

[85] Müller and Küster, *Fortgesetzes Altes und Neues Berlin* (Berlin, 1752), 463.

[86] See Chapter 7.   [87] Deiters, 'Individuum', 44.

[88] J. Becken, 'Die Epitaphien Distelmeyer-Kötteritzsch in der Nikolaikirche Berlin-Mitte', *Jahrbuch Stiftung Stadtmuseum Berlin*, 10 (2004/5), 73–95. BLHA, Rep. 37 Lübbenau, Familienarchiv der Grafen zu Lynar auf Lübbenau, Nr. 6114/1. For a recent discussion of this image see Maria Deiters, 'Hof- und Stadtgesellschaft im Kirchenraum. Gedächtnismale residenzstädtischer Eliten in der Berliner Nikolaikirche', in Stiftung Preußische Schlösser und Gärten Berlin-Brandenburg, *Cranach und die Kunst der Renaissance*, 39.

[89] On the chapel see EKLAB, Repositur I, 1423–1945, Nikolaikirche, Nr. 603, 'Legat des Kurfürstlichen Brandenburger Rats Johann von Kötteritz, 1612–1845'.

furnishings, the church had a rich collection of vestments and other textiles, some of which were probably pre-Reformation survivals and some of which had been given by members of its Lutheran congregation. It also had a silver crucifix—especially provocative to a Calvinist audience—that was listed in inventories from both 1614 and 1631.[90]

The von Kötteritz epitaph was, according to its inscription, completed in 1616, that is, after the Berlin tumult. It provides a wonderful glimpse of the role images and liturgy played in defining and expressing elite Lutheran identity in Berlin. Lutherans in the Mark's smaller cities were equally resistant to Calvinism. There anti-Calvinist protest might be sparked by a number of different things: the manner in which communion was celebrated; a threat, or perceived threat to a Lutheran preacher or the attempt to install a preacher suspected of Calvinism; the deletion of the exorcism rite from baptism; the introduction of a new prayer formula.[91] But as in the residential city, Lutheran identity tended to coalesce around liturgy and images. Parish churches in Brandenburg an der Havel and Frankfurt an der Oder remained richly furnished, partly with surviving medieval images and partly with Lutheran altars, pulpits, and epitaphs. In Brandenburg an der Havel, for example, pre-Reformation altarpieces survived in the Cathedral, alongside a sacrament house and triumphal cross, a spectacular collection of vestments, and a Lenten cloth.[92] The parish church of St Gotthardt had a remarkably rich collection of Lutheran epitaphs, most dating from the late sixteenth and early seventeenth centuries.[93] The Mark's Lutheran village churches were also, if they had sufficiently wealthy and dedicated patrons, well furnished. Inventories made during visitations carried out in the late sixteenth and early seventeenth centuries record that many had not only the liturgical vessels that were essential to the administration of Lutheran communion—chalices and patens—but also crucifixes and vestments. In some cases, medieval monstrances survived.[94] Not surprisingly, Lutheran images and ceremonies remained a thorn in the side of Brandenburg's Reformed theologians. In a visitation carried out in 1633, Frankfurt an der Oder's theology faculty complained, for example, about 'offensive idols', and in 1639 they produced a *Gutachten* prohibiting images of the Trinity and Mary and banning (once again) exorcism in baptism and the elevation of the consecrated host.[95]

[90] EKLAB, Repositur I, 1423–1945, Nikolaikirche, Nr. 122, 'Inventarium der Nikolaikirche I, 1575–1812'.
[91] Hering, *Historische Nachricht*, 275, 320 ff., 301 ff., 313 ff. Nischan, *Lutherans and Calvinists*.
[92] Marcus Cante (ed.), *Denkmaltopographie Bundesrepublik Deutschland. Denkmale in Brandenburg. Band 1.1. Stadt Brandenburg an der Havel. Teil 1* (Worms am Rhein, 1994), 61–77.
[93] For an overview see Renate Johne, *Reformatorisches Gedankengut in der St. Gotthardtkirche zu Brandenburg an der Havel: Die Epitaphien* (Berlin, 2008). See also Gerlinde Strohmaier-Wiederanders, '"Vera Euangely doctrina" im Bild: Evangelische Bildprogramme auf Altar und Grabbildern in St. Gotthard, Brandenburg', in Katharina Gaede (ed.), *Spuren in der Vergangenheit—Begegnungen in der Gegenwart. Glauben, Lehren und Leben in orthodoxen, altorientalischen und evangelischen Kirchen* (Berlin, 1999), 147–53.
[94] GStAPK, I HA, Rep. 47, Tit. 15, Kirchenvisitationen 1540–1602.
[95] *Fortgesetzte Sammlung*, 28. On the 1639 Gutachten see Gerlinde Strohmaier-Wiederanders, 'Beobachtungen zur protestantischen Ikonographie an Altar- und Kanzelgestaltungen in Kirchen der

CONCLUSION

For Lutheran theologians confronted by Calvinism, religious images—especially altarpieces and crucifixes—served as confessional markers. The iconoclasts of the later sixteenth and seventeeth centuries were equated in Lutheran polemic with the radicals of the 1520s, with Karlstadt and his supporters. Now, even more than during the early decades of the Reformation, images were part of Lutheran confessional identity, and those who attacked them were labelled as dangerous radicals. In 1616, Simon Gedicke preached a sermon in the Cathedral at Meißen in Electoral Saxony on the occasion of its restoration, in which he recounted the traumas that the church and its furnishings had endured, including the Peasants' War and the Schmalkaldic War. In particular, Gedicke referred to its survival during the 'Calvinist poison' of 1590–1, when proponents of the Reformed faith had wished to attack the altar, organ, images, and especially the crucifix. 'God protect us', he pleaded, 'from their zeal and venom'.[96] Members of the political elite in both Electoral Saxony and Brandenburg shared, this chapter has shown, theologians' sense of what it meant to be Lutheran, even if they did not engage in subtle doctrinal disputation. In their wills, they professed their loyalty to the Unaltered Augsburg Confession and to a specifically Lutheran understanding of the Eucharist, and through their commissioning of epitaphs and altarpieces they gave visual expression to their beliefs, placing images of the Last Supper and the crucified Christ before their subjects' eyes. Further down the social scale images were, the Berlin riot of 1615 suggests, equally integral to Lutheran identity.

An altarpiece commissioned by Hans Friedrich von Stutterheim (d. 1616) for the village church in Drahnsdorf near Luckau in Lower Lusatia brings together many of the themes of the last two chapters (Fig. 3.4). At the centre of this altarpiece, enclosed within a richly decorated architectural frame in late-Renaissance style, is a fifteenth-century statue of Mary as the Queen of Heaven, holding the Christ Child and a sceptre.[97] This is an image that would have been described by the Flacian reformers in Ernestine Saxony or by Johann Petrejus, zealous pastor in Zwickau, as an idol. Yet, in the Drahnsdorf retable, it is flanked by two clear statements of Lutheran confessional identity, one in Latin and one in the vernacular. They ask God to protect the church and its altar from all dangers and to drive from it 'the Romanists, the Jesuits and Calvinists'. By 1619, when this altarpiece was installed, the Thirty Years' War had begun. The altarpiece's plea that God should protect the church and its altar from Catholics and Calvinists was the product of a

---

Mark Brandenburg vom 16. bis zum 18. Jahrhundert', in Tatjana Bartsch and Jörg Meiner (eds), *Kunst: Kontext: Geschichte. Festgabe für Hubert Faensen zum 75. Geburtstag* (Berlin, 2003), 156–77, here 161.

[96] Simon Gedicke, *Encaenia Sacra, oder christliche Predigt bey Renovatio oder Ernewerung der großen herrlichen Dom Kirche zu Meissen* (Freiberg: Melchior Hoffmann, 1616), 30–7.

[97] Theodor Goecke, *Die Kunstdenkmäler der Provinz Brandenburg*, vol. 5/1, *Luckau* (Berlin, 1917), 97–8; Strohmaier-Wiederanders, 'Beobachtungen', 170–1.

Fig. 3.4. B. Böttger, altarpiece from the village church in Drahnsdorf near Luckau, *c.*1440 (Virgin and Child) and 1619.

Credit: © SLUB/Deutsche Fotothek.

particular historical moment, a moment at which the Word and sacrament, central pillars of the Lutheran faith, seemed in jeopardy. Yet, as a Lutheran patron, von Stutterheim chose to demonstrate his loyalty to the church not by commissioning a portrait of Luther or an image of the Last Supper but rather by a confident reuse of a pre-Reformation image, by re-setting a statue that in other circumstances would surely have fallen victim to the purifying zeal of the reformers.

PART II

THE DEVOTIONAL IMAGE

4

Image, Instruction, and Emotion
Visual Piety during the Seventeenth Century

At the height of Lutheran–Calvinist conflict within the Holy Roman Empire, Johann Arndt, pastor in Quedlinburg, published a brief tract, the *Ikonographia* (Halberstadt, 1597).[1] Unlike Arndt's other works, this tract was not especially widely disseminated: it was never reprinted during his lifetime. But it nonetheless marked an important turning point on the path that led from Luther to Dresden's Frauenkirche. The Lutheran baroque, with both its splendour and its pathos, would have been unthinkable without the changes in piety that occurred during the late sixteenth and seventeenth centuries, and Arndt was their greatest exponent. Arndt was a controversial figure: proper evangelical teaching on justification seemed, to some, to have disappeared beneath his extensive discussions of spiritual renewal.[2] Yet, he was also, without doubt, one of the most important influences on post-Reformation Protestantism, central to the new piety—the *Frömmigkeitsbewegung*— that fed, during the later seventeenth century, into Pietism. *Ikonographia* was Arndt's response to the confessional conflicts examined in Chapters 2 and 3, but his most influential writings, *Vier Bücher vom Wahren Christentum* (*True Christianity*, 1605–10) and *Paradiesgärtlein voller christlicher Tugenden* (*Little Garden of Paradise full of Christian Virtues*, 1612), presented not confessional polemic but rather prescriptions, based in part on the writings of late-medieval mystics, for true piety, for the internalization of Christian teaching and the transformation of Christian life.[3]

The significance of this *Frömmigkeitsbewegung* for Lutheran visual culture is explored here through writings on images and through illustrated texts, and in Chapter 5 through a consideration of transformations in both verbal and visual Passion piety. In its quest to understand images' role in seventeenth-century Lutheran

---

[1] Johann Arndt, *Ikonographia (1597). Kritisch herausgegeben, kommentiert und mit einem Nachwort versehen von Johann Anselm Steiger* (Hildesheim etc., 2014).

[2] On Arndt's relationship to the orthodox Lutheran tradition see Eric Lund, '*modus docendi mysticus*. The Interpretation of the Bible in Johann Arndt's Postilla', in Torbjörn Johansson, Robert Kolb, and Johann Anselm Steiger (eds), *Hermeneutica Sacra. Studien zur Auslegung der heiligen Schrift im 16. und 17. Jahrhundert/Studies of the Interpretation of Scripture in the Sixteenth and Seventeenth Centuries* (Berlin, 2010), 223–45.

[3] On Arndt see Johannes Wallmann, 'Johann Arndt und die protestantische Frömmigkeit. Zur Rezeption der mittelalterliche Mystic im Luthertum', in Dieter Bauer (ed.), *Frömmigkeit in der frühen Neuzeit. Studien zur religiösen Literatur des 17. Jahrhunderts in Deutschland (Chloe. Beihefte zum Daphnis. Band 2)* (Amsterdam, 1984), 50–74.

piety, this chapter draws on a variety of sources: on polemical works such as Arndt's *Ikonographia*, on illustrated Bibles and catechisms, and on prayer books and other texts intended for individual contemplation. Encouraged by interest in the history of emotions, recent literature has dispelled the myth of Protestantism as a religion of the head and not the heart, of understanding rather than feeling. For Luther the two were inseparable, as we saw in Chapter 1. The heart was, for him, the seat of the soul and the mind, of emotion and will, and it was there that the Word of God must operate. The distinction that historians and art historians have tended to draw between didactic and devotional texts and images is one that early modern commentators would not have recognized, for to them memory and understanding as well as spiritual affections and desires resided in the heart.

In the writings of Arndt and his followers, the heart featured especially prominently. It represented for Arndt 'all the powers of the soul: understanding, will, affections, and desires', and it was central to his programme of spiritual renewal.[4] *True Christianity* aimed to show 'how true repentance must proceed from the innermost source of the heart; how the heart, mind, and affections must be changed, so that we might be conformed to Christ and his holy Gospel'.[5] Against this backdrop, the language used to justify religious images took on new inflections. Lutheran images had aimed, from the start, to stimulate memory by imprinting their messages on their viewers' hearts and souls. But Arndt and his contemporaries endowed them with a new spiritual significance. Images now played a more important part in *Einbildung* or *Verinnerlichung*, in the process by which the intellectual—knowledge of God—became the affective—his presence in the soul. Lutheran defences of images became more like Lutheran defences of music, which had always been ascribed a strong affective role and praised for its ability to penetrate Christians' thoughts and emotions. Lutheran religious texts of the seventeenth century presented their readers with a great variety of images, from detailed narrative woodcuts and engravings such as those found in Matthaeus Merian's famous 1630 Bible to emblems, symbolic images combined with brief texts that invited prolonged contemplation. Images had long been integral to Lutheran confessional identity; during the seventeenth century, the era of the devotional image, they became increasingly important to Lutheran piety.

THE DEVOTIONAL CONTEXT

The late sixteenth and seventeenth centuries witnessed a great increase in the production of devotional writings aimed primarily at the laity, from prayer books and hymn collections to novels and dramas. Of course lay devotional literature was not, in itself, a novelty, as Luther's prayer book, his *Small Catechism*, and his hymnal demonstrate. These texts had always enjoyed an 'amphibious existence' between church and home, and they provided the foundation for a Lutheran tradition of

---

[4] Johann Arndt, *True Christianity*, tr. Peter Erb (London, 1979), 186.   [5] Ibid., 21.

song and prayer that encompassed the domestic as well as the public sphere.[6] During the later sixteenth century, there was, however, not only a quantitative increase in the amount of lay devotional literature produced but also a qualitative change in its content. Private prayer was distinguished increasingly strongly from public: the new devotional literature placed greater emphasis on individual experience, on internal piety and on themes such as sin and repentance, communion, love of God (*unio mystica*), eschatology, and the rejection of the world. There was a 'renaissance of mysticism', a renewed and widespread interest amongst Lutherans in the writings of medieval authors such as Bernard of Clairvaux, Johannes Tauler, and Thomas à Kempis, and in the experiential knowledge of God that they described.[7] And this recourse to pre-Reformation mysticism was reinforced, in at least some cases, by borrowings from contemporary Catholic (above all Jesuit) sources.[8] This mystical turn in Reformation piety was initiated by Andreas Musculus (d. 1581), Philip Nicolai (1556–1608), Philipp Kegel (d. after 1611), and Martin Moller (1547–1606), and reached its culmination in the works of Arndt (1555–1621). The texts on which these authors drew were not, of course, new discoveries—Luther himself had edited the anonymous *Theologia Deutsch* in 1516—but they were now used to encourage individual spiritual development. Their renaissance was accompanied by a new emphasis on individual meditation, an emphasis that was also to be found in Catholic and Reformed spirituality of the period.[9]

Church historians and theologians have explained the origins and dissemination of this new piety in a number of ways. Winfried Zeller, looking primarily at the internal development of Lutheranism, spoke of a *Frömmigkeitskrise* (crisis of piety) amongst the third generation of Lutheran pastors and theologians, a crisis that reflected, he suggested, the separation of theology and lived piety during the 'age of Orthodoxy'.[10] This separation has, however, been overstated: the picture of a monolithic Lutheran Orthodoxy, focused on doctrine rather than devotion, on the university rather than the parish, was a distortion, a caricature produced by its Pietist and Enlightenment critics. In fact, this was an age of pluralization within Lutheran confessional culture, of numerous and varied calls for renewal and reform from inside as well as outside the bounds of Lutheran Orthodoxy.[11] Elke Axmacher attributes the new piety not to a third-generation crisis, but rather to a long-term pastoral problem that had confronted the early reformers as well: the gap between the promised (imputed) and actual existence of the Christian. She highlights the early

---

[6] Boyd Brown, 'Devotional Life', 205–6.

[7] Winfried Zeller, 'Protestantische Frömmigkeit im 17. Jahrhundert', in ibid., *Theologie und Frömmigkeit. Gesammelte Aufsätze*, vol. 1, ed. Bernd Jaspert (Marburg, 1971), 85–116, here 92. See also Elke Axmacher, *Praxis Evangeliorum. Theologie und Frömmigkeit bei Martin Moller (1547–1606)* (Göttingen, 1989), esp. 314.

[8] Udo Sträter, *Meditation und Kirchenreform in der lutherischen Kirche des 17. Jahrhunderts* (Tübingen, 1995), here esp. 2.

[9] Sträter, *Meditation*; ibid., '"Wie bringen wir den Kopff in das Hertz?" Meditation in der Lutherischen Kirche des 17. Jahhunderts', in Gerhard Kurz (ed.), *Meditation und Erinnerung in der Frühen Neuzeit* (Göttingen, 2000), 11–35.

[10] Zeller, 'Protestantische Frömmigkeit'.

[11] Thomas Kaufmann, *Dreißigjähriger Krieg und Westfälischer Friede: kirchengeschichtliche Studien zur lutherischen Konfessionskultur* (Tübingen, 1998), 78 ff.

history of the reception of mysticism within Lutheranism and argues that eschato-logical thinking—eternal life and its contemplation as consolation—resurfaced as pastors recognized the 'religious and moral failure of preaching on justification'.[12] Udo Sträter refers to a perceived deficit of *Kirchlichkeit* (churchliness) amongst seventeenth-century Lutherans, suggesting that the literature of devotion and meditation was primarily an attempt to supply this deficit.[13]

Any attempt to move beyond an inner history of Lutheran theology and piety and to link spiritual changes to concrete historical events is inevitably fraught with difficulty. Like Zeller, Hartmut Lehmann sees the flourishing of devotional litera-ture as a response to crisis, but crisis of a much broader nature. This was a period during which a little ice age caused poor harvests and famine, and during which economic and social dislocation was compounded by the effects of war. Theology and devotional practice responded, Lehmann suggests, to these seventeenth-century crises by offering consolation.[14] The impact of the Thirty Years' War is, however, probably best understood in narrower terms: seventeenth-century sources are full of references to punishment and of calls to repentance; and there were plenty of attempts to appease God through services with special pleas and prayers (*Bittgottesdiensten*), through processions, and through alms-giving.[15]

It is very difficult to determine whether the experiences of war—the loss and suffering that it engendered in many parts of the Empire—shaped Lutheran piety in more lasting and fundamental ways. In order to understand images' new devotional role during the seventeenth century, we must recognize that the striv-ings for a renewal of piety began well before the traumas of the seventeenth century: Arndt himself wrote during a time of relative peace and prosperity, and made very little reference to external hardship or anxiety. Lutheran authors clearly inclined towards mysticism, and from the time of Martin Moller onwards we can speak of a Lutheran 'theology and spirituality of desire'.[16] This was expressed, as we will see in Chapter 5, in Passion piety; here broad devotional patterns were sometimes given local inflections by experiences of individual and communal suffering.

Whatever its cause or causes, the new piety had, at its core, one key task: to bridge the gap between between 'intellect and affect, between understanding and volition, between teaching and living'. The quest to bridge this gap 'runs through the writings of Lutheran theologians of the seventeenth century'.[17]

---

[12] Axmacher, *Praxis Evangeliorum*, 135, 307–16.   [13] Strater, *Meditation*, 31.

[14] Hartmut Lehmann, *Das Zeitalter des Absolutismus. Gottesgnadentum und Kriegsnot* (Stuttgart etc., 1980), esp. 105–22. For a recent discussion see Sträter, *Meditation*, 9–22.

[15] Kaufmann, *Dreißigjähriger Krieg*; Matthias Asche and Anton Schindling (eds), *Strafgericht Gottes: Kriegserfahrungen und Religion im Heiligen Römischen Reich Deutscher Nation im Zeitalter des Dreißigjährigen Krieges* (Münster, 2001); for a detailed case study see Bernd Roeck, *Eine Stadt in Krieg und Frieden: Studien zur Geschichte der Reichsstadt Augsburg zwischen Kalenderstreit und Parität* (Göttingen, 1989).

[16] Ronald Rittgers, 'Mystical Union and Spiritual Desire in Late Reformation Devotion: The Case of Martin Moller's *The Great Mystery* (1595)', *Reformation & Renaissance Review*, 17 (3) (2015), 214–29.

[17] Sträter, *Meditation,* 1.

Arndt, for example, lamented in the preface to the third book of his *True Christianity* that:

> Many believe that it is enough and more than enough if they grasp Christ with their understanding by reading and disputing. This is now the general study of theology, and it consists in mere theory and knowledge. They do not think that the other chief power of the soul, namely the will, and deep love belong to faith.[18]

This desire on the part of Lutheran pastors to bring, as the early Pietist Philip Spener later put it, 'the head into the heart' was hardly new.[19] Protestantism had certainly never been austere and rationalist, a religion of the head and not the heart, the intellect and not the emotions. Luther himself used mystical language, emphasized the senses and emotions, and referred frequently to the heart.[20] As he observed in his 1528 *Winterpostille*, cold faith in particular doctrines was not enough: one needed a 'living perfect trust in the heart…towards Christ'.[21] But how did this trust, this knowledge and understanding of God, reach the heart and soul? For Luther, the work was done by the Word. The visual could play a part in disseminating the Gospel, in 'the work of religious persuasion', but faith came not from seeing or from understanding but from the Word.[22] As he stated in his 1528 sermon for Palm Sunday, the Christian must 'hang onto the simple words, close the eyes, blindfold reason, and reach out only our ears and grasp onto the Word and write it in our hearts'.[23]

Of course the primacy accorded to the Word never diminished. Arndt stated in *True Christianity* that 'the new birth in a spiritual manner…occurs through the Word of God…This Word awakens faith and faith clings to this Word and grasps in the Word Jesus Christ together with the Holy Spirit. Through the Holy Spirit's power and activity, man is new-born'.[24] But for Arndt and his contemporaries Lutheran preaching of the Word had not achieved enough. 'Where', Arndt asked, 'are the fruits of righteousness? Where is the demonstration of living active faith, which alone makes a true Christian?'[25] Theology must be no 'mere science, or rhetoric' but rather 'a living experience and practice'. *Verinnerlichung* emerged as a key

---

[18] Arndt, *True Christianity*, 221.

[19] Sträter, '"Wie bringen wir den Kopff in das Hertz?"'; see also Catherine Newmark, *Passion—Affekt—Gefühl. Philosophische Theorien der Emotionen zwischen Aristoteles und Kant* (Hamburg, 2008), 67. On *Einbildung*—mediation between the intellectual and affective faculties of soul—see Günter Butzer, 'Rhetorik der Meditation. Martin Mollers "Soliloqvia de Passione Iesu Christi" und die Tradition der *eloquentia sacra*', in Kurz (ed.), *Meditation*, 57–78, here 66 ff.

[20] See Kaufmann, 'Die Sinn- und Leiblichkeit'; Stolt, *Martin Luthers Rhetorik des Herzens*; Karl-Heinz zur Mühlen, 'Die Affektenlehre im Spätmittelalter und in der Reformationszeit', *Archiv für Begriffsgeschichte*, 35 (1992), 93–114.

[21] Renate Dürr, 'Laienprophetien. Zur Emotionalisierung politischer Phantasien im 17. Jahrhundert', in Claudia Jarzebowski and Anne Kwaschik (eds), *Performing Emotions. Interdisziplinäre Perspektiven auf das Verhältnis von Politik und Emotion in der Frühen Neuzeit und in der Moderne* (Göttingen, 2013), 17–41, here 19–24.

[22] Friedrich, 'Das Hör-Reich und das Sehe-Reich', 462–3.

[23] WA 21, 147–55, here 149.   [24] Arndt, *True Christianity*, 37.

[25] Quoted in Johannes Wallmann, 'Johann Arndt (1555–1621)', in Carter Lindberg (ed.), *The Pietist Theologians* (Malden, MA, 2004), 27.

theme: true repentance and spiritual renewal must, Arndt argued, proceed from 'the innermost source of the heart'.[26]

In his quest to achieve this, Arndt made extensive use of earlier mystical writings, especially those of Johannes Tauler and Thomas à Kempis. His account of union with God was presented in a way that eliminated any suggestion of human synergism, of co-operation in the process of salvation. It took justifying faith as its precondition: 'Faith is a deep assent and unhesitating trust in God's grace promised in Christ and in the forgiveness of sins and eternal life. It is ignited by the Word of God and the Holy Spirit'.[27] But it then described a path to closer union with God and to true *pietas* via daily repentance, self-denial (the rejection of the flesh and of temporal goods), and individual meditation and prayer.[28] 'No one', he wrote in book one of *True Christianity*, 'is more certain or more at rest than when he is at home and when he keeps his thoughts, words, and meditation in the house of his heart'.[29] Book five describes in some detail the experience of mystical union, of God 'dwelling and indwelling' in man, and draws on the nuptial imagery of the Song of Songs so beloved of medieval mystics. When Christ approaches, wrote Arndt: 'The soul melts for love, the spirit rejoices, the affections and the desires become fervid, love is ignited, the mind rejoices, the mouth gives praise and honour, man takes vows, and all the powers of the soul rejoice in and because of the bridegroom'.[30]

Although *True Christianity* did not explicitly dwell on the role of either music or images in devotional practice, other texts certainly acknowledged their potential to move the heart. Music's pedigree was, of course, impeccable. Luther, himself an accomplished musician, had recognized its affective power, famously describing it, in the preface to Georg Rhau's *Symphoniae iucundae* (1538), as 'the mistress and governess of human emotions'. He praised its ability to make the sad joyful and the joyful sad, and to strengthen the hearts of those who despaired.[31] Music was, for Luther, a creation and a gift of God, and it served its highest purpose when it was used to proclaim the Gospel, to convey God's Word.[32] Philipp Melanchthon reflected on the value of verse and music together, which, he argued 'impress themselves on the mind and move the heart more strongly than words without music'.[33] Such defences echoed throughout the sixteenth century and beyond: Johann Mathesius wrote in 1562 that while scriptural texts are in themselves beautiful

---

[26] Arndt, *True Christianity*, 21.   [27] Ibid., 45.

[28] Wallmann, 'Johann Arndt und die protestantische Frömmigkeit', 72; see also Christian Braw, *Bücher im Staube. Die Theologie Johann Arndts in ihrem Verhältnis zur Mystic* (Leiden, 1986), 220.

[29] Arndt, *True Christianity*, 121.   [30] Ibid., 255 ff.

[31] Jochen Arnold, '"…eine Regiererin des menschlichen Herzen"—ein Versuch zu Martin Luthers Theologie der Musik', in Jochen M. Arnold, Konrad Küster, and Hans Otte (eds), *Singen, Beten, Musizieren. Theologische Grundlagen der Kirchenmusik in Nord- und Mitteldeutschland zwischen Reformation und Pietismus (1530–1750)* (Göttingen, 2014), 13–34. See also Joyce Irwin, *Neither Voice nor Heart Alone. German Lutheran Theology of Music in the Age of the Baroque* (New York, 1993).

[32] Boyd Brown, 'Devotional Life', 208–19.

[33] Quoted in Elke Axmacher, *Johann Arndt und Paul Gerhardt. Studien zur Theologie, Frömmigkeit und geistlichen Dichtung des 17. Jahrhunderts* (Tübingen and Basel, 2001), 80.

music 'when a sweet and heartfelt tune is added…then the song acquires a new force and enters more deeply into the heart'.[34]

During the seventeenth century, Lutheran commentators continued to argue that music helped in the process of *Einbildung*, impressing God's word upon its hearers' hearts.[35] The Ulm superintendent Conrad Dieterich stated, for example, in a sermon preached sometime before 1629, that the average person is moved by figural music, even without understanding it.[36] And Johann Olearius, court preacher to Duke August of Sachsen-Weißenfels, aimed in his *Geistliche Singe-Kunst*, one of the most important hymn collections of its time, to 'move the heart…through the ears'.[37] The music of the period *c.*1635–80 not only developed new styles but also drew on a new range of texts: prayers in the form of personal supplications that expressed the individual Christian's fervent love for Christ.[38] The parallels between the musical and visual culture of the period are, as we shall see in Chapter 5, fascinating: both aimed to create a more immediate, more mystical form of piety, focused on Christ's Passion.

IMAGE AND AFFECT: THEORY

What, then, of images? Their power to move the heart and soul had, like that of music, been recognized since Antiquity. It underpinned the critiques of the sixteenth-century iconoclasts: at the 1586 Colloquy of Montbeliard the Genevan theologian Theodore Beza argued, for example, that images had the power to 'seduce' the hearts of mortals 'through stimulation and quick moving of the soul'.[39] But for Lutheran commentators of the late sixteenth and seventeenth centuries this power could be put to positive use. Arndt's *Ikonographia*, which addressed a number of Beza's criticisms directly, was without doubt the most interesting defence of images generated by the confessional controversies of the period.[40] *Ikonographia* was Arndt's first publication and his only contribution to confessional polemics. He wrote the tract in Quedlinburg, having been dismissed from his post as pastor in Baderborn in Anhalt in 1590 because of his resistance to Duke Johann Georg's (r. 1586–1618) Calvinist liturgical reforms. Six years later, when Johann Georg moved to complete Anhalt's Second Reformation by stripping altars, crucifixes, and images from churches and introducing further

---

[34] Boyd Brown, 'Devotional Life', 219; see also Sven Rune Havsteen, 'Das "Music-Büchlein" (1631) von Christopher Frick' in Arnold et al. (eds), *Singen, Beten, Musizieren*, 53–74, here 71.

[35] Ibid., 66.

[36] Joseph Herl, *Worship Wars in Early Lutheranism: Choir, Congregation, and Three Centuries of Conflict* (Oxford, 2004), 117.

[37] Johannes Olearius, *Geistliche Singe-Kunst, und ordentlich verfassetes vollständiges Gesang-Buch* (Leipzig: Caspar Lunitius, 1671), Ciii recto ('Erinnerung an den Christlichen Leser').

[38] Mary Frandsen, 'Music and Lutheran Devotion in the Schütz Era', unpublished paper.

[39] Kaufmann, *Konfession und Kultur*, 176.

[40] Arndt, *Ikonographia (1597)*, esp. 54 ff., 60–1, 187–8.

reforms of ritual life, Arndt watched from exile.[41] *Ikonographia* was his response to the unfolding of events in his native land. In it, he defends not only images but also altars, the making of the sign of the cross, genuflection, and the Lutheran numbering of the Ten Commandments, all of which had been abolished in Anhalt. With regard to images, Arndt sought a 'proper middle way' between compulsion and honour, preached by the papists, and destruction, practised by the Calvinists.[42] Here, at least, Arndt showed himself to be an orthodox Lutheran: images were for him, as for many others with direct experience of Reformed Protestantism, an expression of confessional identity. But Arndt's discussion of images went well beyond that of previous Lutheran commentators.

Ikonographia combined traditional Lutheran defences of images, most of them based on Martin Chemnitz's *Examen Concilii Tridentini*, with arguments derived from very different sources, above all the writings of Paracelsus, Agrippa von Nettesheim, and the alchemist and hermetic philosopher Heinrich Khunrath.[43] On the basis of this rich mixture of sources Arndt discussed different types of images: *Imagines mysticae*, which were both visual and verbal and were used by God in the Old and New Testaments; *Imagines Historicae* from the time of the early church; and 'images that have their source in nature'. In his discussion of the last type, images in nature, he was especially dependent on Paracelsus and Khunrath, and argued that creation could be deciphered and could offer wisdom to those who could read its writing. From his discussion of the spiritual use of images, one theme emerged particularly strongly: the need for external (physical) and internal (spiritual) images to be in harmony.[44] In chapter 5, Arndt argued that God had revealed the Holy Ghost in the form of a dove and his Son in the form of a lamb. He had also taught both the apostles and the prophets through images. He continued:

> Christ left images in our hearts of his suffering and death, which the Holy Spirit renews and clarifies daily, 2 Corinthians 3. It follows, therefore, that no Christian heart, in which the Holy Spirit depicts Christ's Passion internally, can feel disgust, revulsion and horror at external images of Christ's Passion for this reason: the Holy Spirit forms in your heart that which you see externally.

The conviction that only an enemy of Christ's Passion—here he named Beza—could object to images of the Crucifixion was reinforced by the teachings of nature, for 'no man can be hostile to the image of that which he loves in his heart'.[45]

---

[41] On the text's immediate context see Arndt, *Ikonographia (1597)*, 181–5. See also Hans Schneider, *Der fremde Arndt. Studien zu Leben, Werk und Wirkung Johann Arndts (1555–1621)* (Göttingen, 2006), esp. 58–9.

[42] Arndt, *Ikonographia (1597)*, 79.

[43] Inge Mager, 'Johann Arndts Bildfrömmigkeit' in Udo Sträter (ed.), *Pietas in der lutherischen Orthodoxie* (Wittenberg, 1998), 41–60. See also Arndt, *Ikonographia (1597)*, 192–201; Kaufmann, *Konfession und Kultur*, 197–8.

[44] Arndt, *Ikonographia (1597)*, 195. See also Mager, 'Johann Arndts Bildfrömmigkeit', 53.

[45] Arndt, *Ikonographia (1597)*, 60, 64.

Arndt did not, ultimately, seek to re-evaluate the relative importance of hearing and seeing in the process of *Einbildung*. In his summing-up at the end of *Ikonographia,* he emphasized that:

> I know very well that true worship may happen without images. I also teach daily that true faith must be awakened by God's Word and that the Holy Spirit is also given and goes into the heart through the Word, and not through images.[46]

But the emphasis that he placed on the relationship between external and internal images, and on images' ability to move the heart, did constitute a turning point in Lutheran theology of images. Luther's rather cautious endorsement of images' ability to stimulate memory and devotion was given new vitality, for, as Arndt argued, what one sees 'truly goes to the heart'.[47] In his discussion of the many verbal images used in the Bible, Arndt argued that:

> Just as a figurative speech…paints an image in the heart through hearing, and forms it so that it remains in the mind, so looking at a beautiful image and painting forms in a person's heart in a spiritual manner that which it signifies.[48]

God's Word kindled faith, but the work of the artist could complement that of the preacher.

Unlike Luther's seminal writings on images, *Ikonographia* was not regularly cited by later iconophiles, and unlike *True Christianity* and the *Paradiesgärtelin* it did not enjoy broad popular appeal.[49] But in his interest in outer and inner images and in images' ability to move the heart, Arndt was certainly not alone. In 1597, Simon Gedicke (1551–1631) published in Magdeburg his *Von Bildern vnd Altarn/In den Euangelischen Kirchen Augspurgischer Confession* (*On Images and Altars in the Evangelical Churches of the Augsburg Confession*). This tract was, like *Ikonographia,* prompted by events in Anhalt, which Gedicke observed from his post as senior court preacher to Elector Johann Georg of Brandenburg.[50] Gedicke's tracts were much more overtly polemical than Arndt's: they were written to show that adherents of the Augsburg Confession were not, as the Reformed suggested, 'half papist' and still mired in Catholic idolatry.[51] They mobilized defences of images that were, by now, traditional in Lutheran theology, but they also, like other writings of the time, invoked images' affective power.

For Gedicke, art was, as music had been for Luther, a divine gift. Echoing Exodus 31:5 (in which God calls Bezaleel and Oholiab to decorate the Tabernacle), Gedicke wrote that 'sculpture, painting, casting, cutting and setting stone artfully are special gifts from God'.[52] These gifts could be put to good use, in the service of true piety:

> And just as it is a special art in all paintings, if one expresses emotions and thereby moves the beholder's or viewer's heart and soul somewhat…So God is especially to be thanked for the fine paintings of biblical stories, above all of the bitter suffering and

---

[46] Ibid., 121.   [47] Ibid., 63.   [48] Ibid., 78.   [49] Ibid., 190–1.
[50] With the conversion of Elector Johann Sigismund, Gedicke experienced Calvinism at first hand: in 1614 he fled to Saxony, and from there he continued to agitate against the Reformed. Nischan, *Prince, People, and Confession,* 114–15.
[51] Gedicke, *Von Bildern und Altarn,* Biiv.   [52] Ibid., Giiiiv.

death and joyful resurrection of our dear Lord…so whenever pious Christians see
them, they feel as a result of them good thoughts and movement of the heart.[53]

A Christian should contemplate the life and death of Christ daily; this 'meditation
and taking to heart' would then bring about the 'impressing (*Einbildung*) of the
histories and stories'. Echoing Luther, Gedicke argued that: 'Whenever a Christian
thinks of the cross of Christ, he produces in his heart just through his thoughts the
shape of the cross, and also the form of the eternal Son of God our redeemer and
saviour, as he hung there naked and bare on the cross'. And if internal images were
an inevitable part of devotion, then external images were not only permitted but
also, in Gedicke's view, necessary, for one who has never seen Christ's cross cannot
'express [it] with his heart and thoughts' as well as one who 'sees it so finely made
through the carver's or painter's art and diligence'.[54] Images were not, Gedicke
stressed, the Bibles of the laity. But they were of particular use to the 'simple folk',
for 'what often comes before one's eyes holds fast and remains in the soul'.[55] When
Christ is depicted before our eyes, we are awakened to greater piety, 'for it is said:
Obiecta mouent sensus. What someone sees before his eyes goes into his heart and
moves him'.[56]

   In the same year (1597), Abraham Taurer, pastor in the village of Schwertzau
in the diocese of Magdeburg, published his *Hochnothwendigster Bericht/Wider
den newen Bildstürmerischen Carlstadtischen Geist im Fürstenthumb Anhald* (*Most
Necessary Exposition, against the new iconoclastic, Karlstadt-like spirit in the Principality
of Anhalt*). Taurer, like Gedicke, believed that images could move the heart, and he
also, like Arndt, emphasized the role of the Holy Spirit in this process of *Einbildung*.
Every Christian must confess, he wrote, that when they see a crucifix or another
image of Christ or biblical story, their 'heart is stirred through the movement of
the Holy Spirit'. Taurer also followed Arndt in asserting that images were of value
not only 'for the sake of simple folk' but also for educated Christians:

> images have this salutary benefit not only amongst the young and old, for they are
> the Bibles of the common folk, but the learned too will be stimulated to remember
> Christ's deeds through looking at images, for it is said: *Obiecta movent sensus*, one is
> moved by what one sees constantly before one's eyes.[57]

The formulation used by both Gedicke and Taurer, 'Obiecta movent sensus',
derived ultimately, as Gabriele Wimböck has suggested, from Aristotelian cogni-
tive theory, mediated via medieval interpreters, most notably Thomas Aquinas.
According to this theory, objects and images acted on passive recipients via the
eyes, leaving impressions in their viewers' senses and intellects just as solid objects
left impressions in wax.[58] Sixteenth-century Lutheran pastors rarely engaged with
the theoretical discussions of vision found in the works of Roger Bacon, William

---

[53] Ibid., H v.   [54] Ibid., J iii r–v.   [55] Ibid., J iv v.
[56] Ibid., K r. Gedicke repeated this phrase in his 1615 *Calviniana oder Calvinisterey*, 500.
[57] Taurer, *Hochnothwendigster Bericht*, Mii.
[58] Wimböck, '"Durch die Augen"', 440. See Stuart Clark, *Vanities of the Eye: Vision in Early Modern
European Culture* (Oxford, 2007), 15–16; David Lindberg, *Theories of Vision from Al-Kindi to Kepler*
(Chicago, 1976), especially 139–46.

of Ockham, and other medieval commentators. But the phrase 'Obiecta mouent sensus' had by now become, as the preacher Peter Streuber put it in a 1593 consecration sermon, a 'Sprichwort', a common justification for the use of religious images amongst Lutheran as well as Catholic authors.[59]

Taurer went on to identify images that were particularly effective in moving their viewers' hearts: 'What Christian will not reflect a little, when he sees painted in front of his eyes how Christ the Lord sweated bloody sweat because of our sins...It would be an *adamantinum cor*, a stone heart, that did not consider: Ah, Christ suffered that for our sins'. Taurer also mentioned images of the Last Judgement that would help with the internalization of Christian piety: 'who amongst true Christians would not examine themselves concerning this, and therefore be moved to piety?' He also praised images of the Baptism, Resurrection, and Ascension of Christ, which would 'stimulate a Christian heart to all piety and honour'.[60]

For all Lutheran commentators images of the Passion remained most important, as we shall see in Chapter 5. In 1619, for example, the Württemberg reformer Johann Valentin Andreae published *Christianopolis*, a Utopian description of an imaginary ideal community that was dedicated to, amongst others, Johann Arndt. Andreae's account of the city was by no means free from confessional polemic. As a visitor he could not, he wrote, admire the art and beauty sufficiently, 'especially because I remembered those who, under the pretext of religion, plunder the churches and then, when the desolation of the sacred places is complete, do not forget the luxury of their homes'.[61] But in his account of images' role in religious devotion, Andreae echoes Arndt and his contemporaries. *Christianopolis*'s temple was, he wrote, 'a royally magnificent building' the walls of which were 'bright and elegant with beautiful paintings of religious subjects or scenes from stories in the Bible'. 'I did not see any statues', he added, 'except for the crucified Christ, so skilfully made as to move even the hardest of hearts'.[62]

The changing relationship between image and affect is difficult to delineate. We should not conclude, because of the prevalence of polemical and allegorical images during the early decades of the Reformation or because of the simple style of the Cranach school, that Lutheran art was intended to deflect emotional responses. Luther, as we have seen, acknowledged images' ability to move their viewers, and wrote at least a little of their relationship to the heart. It is clear, however, that images' affective power, their ability to incite devotion in the heart, was articulated with new vigour by Lutheran authors during the late sixteenth and early seventeenth centuries. Indeed, some even endorsed tears as an external expression of this affective response. By the seventeenth century, there was a 'conspicuous culture

---

[59] Peter Streuber, *Einweyhung der New erbawten Schloßkirchen zu Sora* (Sora, 1593), B vi v. On the Ulm superintendent Conrad Dieterich and his discussion of sensory perception see Philip Hahn, 'Sensing Sacred Space: Ulm Minster, the Reformation, and Parishioners' Sensory Perception, *c*.1470 to 1640', *Archiv für Reformationsgeschichte* 105 (2014), 55–91, esp. 82.

[60] Taurer, *Hochnothwendigster Bericht*, M ii v.

[61] Quoted in Kaufmann, *Konfession und Kultur*, 164.

[62] Translation from J. V. Andreae, *Christianopolis*, ed. Edward H. Thompson (Dordrecht, 1999), 257–8.

of crying' within Protestantism. A number of Lutheran pastors and theologians, including Arndt, Heinrich Müller (1631–1675), and Christian Scriver (1629–1693), wrote about tears in their devotional works.[63] Tears were, as Arndt argued, an external expression of internal contrition, and a means of achieving spiritual renewal and union with God.[64] They could also, on occasion, be provoked by images. Drawing on a story recounted by Chemnitz, both Arndt in his *Ikonographia* and Gedicke in his *Von Bildern und Altaren* described Gregory of Nyssa's encounter with an image of the Sacrifice of Isaac: 'As Gregory of Nyssa saw the holy Abraham's likeness, and remembered thereby his wondrous story, he began to cry'.[65] As we shall see in Chapter 5, it was above all images of Christ's Passion that provoked similar responses in seventeenth-century Lutherans, causing them to weep for their sins, the sins that had caused Christ's suffering.

IMAGE AND AFFECT: PRACTICE

Chapter 4 has focused up to this point on writings *about* images, on works by pastors and theologians published for polemical purposes, to defend Lutheran image use in the face of Calvinist threat. What of the prints, paintings, and statues themselves? Did the changing religious environment of the late sixteenth and seventeenth centuries create new types of image or new types of visual piety?[66] This question can be addressed in part through an examination of illustrated texts: the devotional literature, illustrated Bibles, and books of biblical instruction that continued the traditions begun in Wittenberg during Luther's lifetime. In their prefaces, such texts often reflected on images' role in religious devotion. Their defences of sacred images were not, of course, as detailed or as sophisticated as those of the great Catholic apologists of the time, men such as Johannes Molanus and Gabriele Paleotti. But they did nonetheless help to construct and to disseminate a specifically Lutheran theology of images. And the images that Lutheran authors chose to accompany these devotional texts testify to the breadth and diversity of Lutheran visual piety, and to the extent to which these images were much more than mere pedagogical aids for 'simple folk'.

Bilderbibeln—copiously illustrated collections of biblical stories or sayings—were often described, in their prefaces, as 'lay Bibles'.[67] They were always intended at

---

[63] Claudia Ulbrich, 'Tränenspektakel. Die Lebensgeschichte der Luise Charlotte von Schwerin (1731) zwischen Frömmigkeitspraxis und Selbstinszenierung', in Mineke Bosch, Hanna Hacker and Ulrike Krampl (eds), *Spektakel (L'Homme. Europäische Zeitschrift für Feministische Geschichtswissenschaft)*, 23 (1) (2012), 27–42, here 31. See also Christian Soboth, 'Tränen des Auges, Tränen des Herzens. Anatomien des Weinens in Pietismus, Aufklärung und Empfindsamkeit', in Jürgen Helm and Karin Stukenbrock (eds), *Anatomie. Sektionen einer medizinischen Wissenschaft im 18. Jahrhundert* (Stuttgart, 2003), 293–315, esp. 296–7.

[64] Arndt, *True Christianity*, 118, 188.   [65] Gedicke, *Von Bildern und Altaren*, H v.

[66] For a useful discussion of single-leaf prints see Eva-Maria Bangerter-Schmid, *Erbauliche illustrierte Flugblätter aus den Jahren 1570–1670* (Frankfurt am Main, 1986).

[67] See Richard Gassen, 'Die Leien Bibel des Straßburger Druckers Wendelin Rihel. Kunst, Religion, Pädagogik und Buchdruck in der Reformation', *Memminger Geschichtsblätter* (1983/84), 5–271, esp. 20 ff.

least in part, as Virgil Solis's 1560 *Biblische Figuren* put it, 'for the sake of simple Christians who cannot read Scripture'.[68] Both Gregory the Great's defence of images as Bibles of the illiterate and Luther's 1529 prayer book, the first Lutheran 'lay Bible', provided points of reference until well into the seventeenth century. Some prefaces also reflected in greater detail on the ways in which images functioned to capture their viewers' attention, imprinting sacred stories on human hearts and souls. Words such as *reitzen* (stimulate) and *erwecken* (awaken) appear with increasing frequency from the 1560s onwards. Johann Bocksberger's and Jost Amman's biblical prints, first published in 1564, were, for example, to 'delight' viewers' eyes, and 'to stimulate their hearts'.[69] In the preface to Tobias Stimmer's *Neue Künstliche Figuren*, printed in Basel in 1576 and again in Straßburg in 1590, Johann Fischart emphasized images' moral significance: 'painting tells the soul how to avoid fault and choose good'. Fischart referred to the classical equation of art with poetry. In his preface, the ancient valorization of sight as the most important of the senses was given, as it had been during the Middle Ages, a Christian gloss. The Ancients knew, Fischart wrote, 'that painting moves the soul and inclines [it] towards that which it depicts and shows: so the biblical figures will certainly awaken holy thoughts'.[70]

Matthäus Merian's 1625–27 *Icones biblicae* deserves particular mention here (Fig. 4.1). The engraver is famed today above all for his topographical works, which looked back to the prosperity and glory of the Holy Roman Empire before the destruction of the Thirty Years' War. Merian was born in Basel, studied in Paris and elsewhere, and spent most of his career in Frankfurt, where in 1623 he took over the de Bry publishing house.[71] The *Icones biblicae* was an album of scriptural images, each of which was accompanied by short verses in Latin, German, and French. Its engravings were subsequently incorporated into the famous Merian Bible of 1630. In his preface, Merian, like Solis and others before him, praised images' aesthetic and pedagogical value. Merian, who was himself eventually accused of associating with Spiritualist followers of Valentin Weigel, also, however,

---

[68] *Biblische Figuren des Alten und Newen Testaments/gantz künstlich gerissen. Durch den weitberümpten Vergilium Solis zu Nürnberg* (Frankfurt am Main: David Zöpfel, Johann Rasch, Sigmund Feyerabend, 1560), A ii v.

[69] See Reinitzer, *Biblia deutsch*, 244–6.

[70] *Neue Künstliche Figuren Biblischer Historien/grüntlich von Tobia Stimmer gerissen: Vnd zu Gotsförchtiger ergetzung andächtiger hertzen/mit artigen Reimen begriffen*…(Basel, Thomas Guarin, 1576), Vorrede. On the classical prioritization of sight see, for example, Frances Yates, *The Art of Memory* (Chicago, 1966); Clark, *Vanities of the Eye*. On Johann Fischart, who converted from Lutheranism to Calvinism during the first half of the 1570s, see Ulrich Schöntube, 'Transkonfessionalität und Konfessionskonformität am Beispiel literarischer Quellen von Emporenbilderzyklen der Region des Kurfürstentums Brandenburg', in Thomas Kaufmann, Anselm Schubert, and Kaspar von Greyerz (eds), *Frühneuzeitliche Konfessionskulturen* (Gütersloh, 2008), 347–74, especially 351–4. Schöntube argues that Fischart's comments in the preface reflect Calvin's teachings, in particular his prohibition on images in churches. The poems that accompany the images are, however, 'confessionally unspecific' and the text as a whole is suited to a 'transconfessional reading'.

[71] On the *Topographia Germaniae* see Ulrike Valerie Fuss, *Matthaeus Merian der Ältere. Von der lieblichen Landschaft zum Kriegsschauplatz—Landschaft als Kulisse des 30 jährigen Krieges* (Frankfurt am Main, 2000), here 133. On Merian, who is discussed more fully in Chapter 7, see Lucas Heinrich Wüthrich, *Matthaeus Merian d. Ä. Eine Biographie* (Hamburg, 2007).

Fig. 4.1. Matthäus Merian, title page from the *Icones Biblicae Præcipuas Sacræ Scripturæ Historias eleganter & graphice repræsentantes...* (Strassburg: Lazari Zetzners sel. Erben, [1625]–1630).

Credit: © Zentralbibliothek Zürich, shelfmark Rv 76.

drew on the ideas of the *Frömmigkeitsbewegung*: 'without a doubt', he wrote, 'obiecta moueant sensus'. Religious images were important, for through 'straightforward contemplation of these figures the soul will find itself very differently engaged than in consideration of frivolous paintings of Venus, the shameful obscenities of Pietro Aretino and similar scandalous inventions'.[72]

The engravings themselves, which were frequently reproduced not only in other biblical works but also in painted form on church furnishings, are exquisite. They are set apart from what had gone before above all by their detailed depiction of nature; in this regard they constitute a visual precursor to the physico-theology of the Enlightenment era.[73] Here in 1625–27, however, Merian was perhaps drawing on the ideas of the *Frömmigkeitsbewegung* and of Arndt in particular, who had written in his *Ikonographia* of images in nature that were 'God's letters, through

---

[72] *Icones Biblicæ Præcipuas Sacræ Scripturæ Historias eleganter & graphice repræsentantes...* (Frankfurt am Main: De Bry, 1625), A iii r.

[73] On physico-theology see Jonathan Sheehan, *The Enlightenment Bible: Translation, Scholarship, Culture* (Princeton, 2005), 124; Irmgard Müsch, *Geheiligte Naturwissenschaft. Die Kupfer-Bibel des Johann Jakob Scheuchzer* (Göttingen, 2000), especially 107–14 on Scheuchzer's illustrations.

which he sets forth nature...to all those who understand it, and are able to read this wondrous writing'.[74]

A few years later, in 1629, a Nuremberg preacher, Johannes Saubert, published his *Icones Precantium*, a series of images of Christian figures to be contemplated during prayer hours, 'in which the examples of the honest supplicants and penitent hearts from sacred Scripture are depicted and put before the eyes to awaken greater devotion'.[75] Like Merian's *Icones biblicae*, Saubert's work appeared during the traumas of the Thirty Years' War. In his preface, Saubert writes of the 'troubled times (when nothing is more necessary than prayer)', and states that to meet this need he has portrayed praying figures from Scripture 'so that Christian eyes take delight, are refreshed, and may be helpful to the heart for greater devotion in prayer'. The book contains a series of images of Old Testament figures such as Jacob, Moses, Samson, and Samuel at prayer, with relevant biblical texts and explanations taken from 'distinguished evangelical teachers', from Luther to Arndt. A pastor wished, according to Saubert, to ensure that all the senses of his hearers were filled with the godly Word, especially, however, hearing and seeing, 'because it is certain that sacred Scripture cannot reach human hearts other than through diligent ears during preaching or through alert eyes'. The eyes and ears are, he added, the main gates to the heart.[76]

Preaching and reading were to occupy the senses of hearing and sight. But Saubert then turned to images: 'Alongside Scripture, beautiful scriptural figures or images can awaken the eyes of godly people, and, with God's help, make them long for piety'. He, like Johann Fischart, drew on Classical Antiquity, citing the 'heathen' Horace, and also Clement of Alexandria in support of images' ability to move the heart, arguing that 'what comes through the ears often does not touch the heart as much as when an image presents itself to the face'. Images and examples are necessary to proper teaching, because they 'penetrate strongly through the eyes to the heart'.[77]

Most of Saubert's illustrations were straightforward depictions of Old Testament figures in prayer before narrative backdrops. The *Icones Precantium* opens, however, with a symbolic image accompanied, in the tradition of the religious emblem, by two texts. The image shows a lighted candle held by two joined hands, surrounded by winds trying to extinguish it. Above is a biblical passage, Proverbs 13:9, and below an explanation: the light of faith remains strong against the storms on all sides, because we 'remain strong with sighing and prayers, and beseech God for his grace early and late'. Interest in emblems dated back to the Renaissance, and during the seventeenth century they enjoyed great popularity throughout Europe. Much has been written about their significance, and here we need only observe the

---

[74] Arndt, *Ikongraphia (1597)*, 81–2.
[75] Johannes Saubert, *Icones precantium: das ist: Christliche Figuren, zur Gebetstund angesehen* (Nuremberg: Endter, 1629), title page.
[76] Johannes Saubert, *Icones precantium: das ist: Christliche Figuren, zur Gebetstund angesehen*, (Nuremberg: Endter, 1637), Vorrede.
[77] Ibid.

vogue for emblems in religious instruction characteristic of the period.[78] Nuremberg was at the forefront of this development: there Saubert's successor, Johann Michael Dilherr (1604–69), published devotional works illustrated with emblems and Georg Philipp Harsdörffer's published in 1641 his *Frauenzimmer Gesprächspiele* (*Women's Conversation Games*), which dealt in two of its eight volumes with 'Geistliche Gemählde' (spiritual pictures) and 'Andachts-Gemählde' (devotional pictures).[79] Harsdörffer's text describes women conversing with men on religion and the arts and sciences, serving as active interlocutors in discussions of the fashionable topics of the day. Emblems enjoyed widespread appeal amongst the educated elite, but women—especially Lutheran noble-women—did, as we shall see in Chapter 5, make particularly extensive use of them in their devotional practices.

The image, authors such as Dilherr believed, worked more quickly and more immediately than the word, but must be given its meaning by an accompanying text. As Harsdörffer expressed it, the image was the unintelligible, opaque body; the text its necessary soul.[80] The widespread spiritual use of emblems was, in part at least, a natural culmination of the image theology developed by Johann Arndt and his contemporaries. And indeed in 1679 an edition of Arndt's *True Christianity* richly illustrated with emblems was published in Riga. The edition's preface and the explanations of its emblems were provided by Johann Fischer, superintendent in Livland.[81] Fischer had contact with Harsdörffer and Dilherr, as well as with the fathers of the Pietist movement, Philipp Jakob Spener and August Hermann Francke, whom we will encounter in the final chapters of this book.[82] The preface explained that illustrations had been added so that the lover of *True Christianity* would discover 'how he can at any time awaken his soul to devotion through contemplation of the things existing in nature or art, and can withdraw it from the earth and raise it to God'.[83] For more than 200 years thereafter, new editions of the illustrated *True Christianity* were printed. Its images, the contemplation of which raised the soul to God, helped determine its popular appeal.

Alongside the production of such illustrated devotional works, sophisticated experiments in visual pedagogy began during the seventeenth century. These merged the traditions of illustrated Bibles and catechisms that went back to Luther's Wittenberg with contemporary interest in allegories and emblems. Texts such as Sigismund Evenius's *Christliche Gottselige Bilder Schule* (Jena, 1636), Johannes Buno's *Bilder-Bibel* (Hamburg, 1680), and Melchior Mattsperger's *Geistliche*

---

[78] See, for example, Dietmar Peil, *Zur »angewandten Emblematik« in protestantischen Erbauungsbüchern. Dilherr—Arndt—Francisci—Scriver* (Heidelberg, 1978); Bettina Bannasch, 'Von der »Tunckelheit« der Bilder. Das Emblem als Gegenstand der Meditation bei Harsdörffer', in Kurz (ed.), *Meditation*, 307–25, esp. 312–13. Gerhard Strasser and Mara Wade (eds), *Die Domänen des Emblems: Außerliterarische Anwendungen der Emblematik* (Wiesbaden, 2004).

[79] Georg Philipp Harsdörffer, *Frauenzimmer Gesprechspiele*, IV and VI (Nuremberg: Endter, 1643, 1646).

[80] Bannasch, 'Von der »Tunckelheit« der Bilder', 312–13.

[81] Peil, *Zur »angewandten Emblematik«*, 46 ff.

[82] Axmacher, *Johann Arndt und Paul Gerhardt*, 31–5.

[83] Quotes in Winfried Zeller, 'Protestantische Frömmigkeit im 17. Jahrhundert', in ibid., *Theologie und Frömmigkeit*, 166.

Herzens-Einbildungen (Augsburg, 1685) suggest that while the seventeenth century may have been an age of stagnation in terms of biblical scholarship, it was an age that witnessed some creative innovation with regard to biblical instruction and images' use therein. In general, these texts were intended, like Luther's prayer book, for domestic use.[84] But some, such as Evenius's, bridged the gap between home and school.

Evenius had studied in Wittenberg and had served as rector of the Latin schools in Halle (1613–22) and Magdeburg (1622–31). In 1634, Duke Ernst the Pious called him to Weimar to serve as his advisor, a position that he held until his death in 1639.[85] He was a theologian and pastor, but above all a pedagogue and reformer who wrote extensively about the need for general Christian instruction as well as the organization of Lutheran schools. The *Christliche Gottselige Bilder Schule* (*Christian, Pious Picture School*) was intended for teaching children as young as three, four, and five at school and in the home, children whose understanding was 'still very tender and weak' and who were likely to be led astray by the bad examples set by their parents, siblings, and friends.

Three full-page emblematic 'general images' introduce the main body of the work, which consists of 54 so-called 'special images' presented in groups of six (Fig. 4.2). The introductory images visualize theological concepts in allegorical form, and represent fear of God, prayer, and the catechism, while the 'special images' and their accompanying texts describe the story of man's salvation, from pre-lapsarian innocence via the Fall to the Resurrection and Last Judgement. As Fig. 4.2 shows, each image is interpreted in minute detail, with biblical citations, a recapitulation of its story, a description of its relationship to the catechism, and an assessment of its 'Gebrauch' or application. This process of interpretation is facilitated by the introduction of numbers, a practice also used in illustrations for scientific and medical works.[86] Evenius proposed that the work should be used in five successive stages. During the first the children should be shown only the images, and their numbers and explanations should be read out by the teacher. The second should focus on the stories, which should be recounted slowly and explained where necessary. The third focused on the biblical citations that should be related back to the images and stories studied previously. The fourth course progressed to the passages from the catechism that accompanied each image, while the fifth required children to learn and understand the work's application for religious *praxis*.[87] By the end, children should be able to recapitulate each stage without recourse to either image or text.

---

[84] Gerhard F. Strasser, *Emblematik und Mnemonik der Frühen Neuzeit im Zusammenspiel: Johannes Buno und Johann Justus Winckelmann* (Wiesbaden, 2000), esp. 86–7.

[85] For a discussion of his life and works see Ludolf Bremer, *Sigismund Evenius (1585/89–1639). Ein Pädagoge des 17. Jahrhunderts* (Cologne and Vienna, 2001). For a general discussion of the *Christliche Gottselige Bilder Schule* see Ingrid Hruby, '1636. Sigismund Evenius: Christliche / Gottselige Bilder Schule' in Theodor Brüggemann (ed.), *Handbuch zur Kinder- und Jugendliteratur. Von 1570 bis 1750* (Stuttgart, 1991), cols 145–156.

[86] For a full discussion see Ringshausen, *Von der Buchillustration,* 58–70.

[87] Hruby, '1636. Sigismund Evenius', 151–2.

Fig. 4.2. Sigismund Evenius, *Christliche/Gottselige BilderSchule/Das ist/Anführung der Ersten Jugend zur Gottseligkeit in und durch Biblische Bilder…* (Jena: Reiffenberger, 1636), p. 84.
Credit: © Klassik Stiftung Weimar, Herzogin Anna Amalia Bibliothek, shelfmark Cat XVI: 173 [a].

In his preface, Evenius situated his work within a tradition of Christian image use that had started with St Paul preaching so vividly that it seemed as if his hearers, the Galatians, had stood beneath Christ's cross and seen it for themselves (Galatians 3:1). Echoing Luther, Evenius argued that 'the natural understanding of man cannot grasp or understand such stories' other than through an internal image in the soul. He went on to write of the use of physical images from the time of the apostles to Luther and beyond. Biblical images were, he wrote, published during Luther's life time 'and thereafter from year to year increased and improved'. The Lutheran tradition of image use reached its high point, he believed, with emblems accompanied by clear explanations and indications of their use, such as those given in his first three 'Generalbilder'.[88] Although Evenius clearly did not think that images alone could teach—each of his has an over-abundance of interpretative texts—his work pushed visual pedagogy in new

---

[88] Evenius, *Christliche Gottselige Bilder Schule*, A 3 v.

directions, making physical images the very centre-pieces of memorizing and understanding. His experiment enjoyed some success: new editions of the *Bilder Schule* were printed in Nuremberg in 1637 and in 1670, and French and Italian translations appeared in 1662 and 1671.[89] Moerover, Evenius's method—his use of numbered images and texts—helped inspire one of the most important illustrated educational texts of the early modern period, Johann Amos Comenius's 1658 *Orbis Sensualium Pictus*.[90]

Johannes Buno's *Bilder-Bibel* (*Picture Bible*) was a much more complex work—so complex, in fact, that contemporaries already wrote scathingly of its limited pedagogical potential.[91] Buno had studied in Marburg and Helmstedt and spent most of his career teaching. From positions in Königsberg and Danzig he published pedagogical works on grammar, history, and law. In 1674, Buno started to apply his methods to sacred history, producing first of all a New Testament and then in 1680 a full *Bilder-Bibel*. This *Bilder-Bibel* is an extraordinary work. Buno stated that it could be used as a guide to the full Bible that every 'God-loving housefather' had already in his home, but at over 1,000 sides of octavo text, with a separate volume of 70 images, it was also a very substantial work in its own right. Buno sought to do very much more than merely illustrate the Bible. He sought to put before his readers' eyes things that were 'difficult to grasp . . . and escape the memory again quickly, such as numbers, strange and unknown names and words, and the like'. Whereas previous Bible illustrations had shown particular histories and stories, in Buno's book 'all chapters of the whole Bible . . . are presented in pictures and images, so that the reader can bring and keep in his memory the contents and summaries of the chapters', as well as their numbering and the order in which they occur.[92]

Fig. 4.3 shows an example, the Book of Genesis. Each biblical book was visualized against the backdrop of a particular image to make it more memorable, here a round globe because Genesis 1 describes the creation of the world. Buno used a system of 'counting words', which he explained in his preface, to remind his readers of chapter numbers and to summarize their content. Genesis, for example, has the *Zahlwort* 'KInder Jacob', because KI, according to Buno's scheme, denotes '50', the number of chapters in the book, and the last of these fifty chapters tells the story of Jacob's children. Buno's *Bilder- Bibel* took the Lutheran art of visual mnemonics to a new level, but beneath its innovations the work's fundamental principle remained that articulated by many earlier commentators: what is read in Scripture should 'be depicted in images and pictures before the eyes, and looked at with desire' so that it can be understood better and more firmly held in the mind. Images were, for Buno as for earlier iconophiles, necessary aids to fallible human memory.

---

[89] Bremer, *Sigismund Evenius*, 155.

[90] Hruby, '1636. Sigismund Evenius', 155–6; Bremer, *Sigismund Evenius*, 163–8.

[91] Strasser, *Emblematik und Mnemonik*, 67. On Buno see also Marion Keuchen, *Bild-Konzeptionen in Bilder- und Kinderbibeln: die historische Anfänge und ihre Wiederentdeckung in der Gegenwart* (Göttingen, 2016), 143–58.

[92] Buno, *Bilder-Bibel*, Vorrede.

Fig. 4.3. Johannes Buno, *Bilder-Bibel: darinn die Bücher Altes und Neuen Testaments durch Alle Capitel in annemliche Bilder kürtzlich gebracht/und also fürgestellet sind…* (Hamburg: Lichtenstein, 1680), Genesis.

Credit: © Herzog August Bibliothek Wolfenbüttel, shelfmark A 178.2° Helmst.

Melchior Mattsperger's *Geistliche Herzens-Einbildungen* (*Spiritual Figures for the Heart*), first printed in Augsburg in 1685, also used symbolic images to shore up memory of sacred Scripture. Mattsperger, merchant and later councillor and mayor in Augsburg, had, according to his preface, from his youth onwards collected 'Sprüche', scriptural passages relating to particular points of faith, which had become so familiar to him that it was as if they were 'painted in the heart and in the mind'.[93] His *Geistliche Herzens-Einbildungen* represented an attempt to convey

---

[93] Mattsperger, *Die Geistliche Herzens=Einbildung*, Vorbericht. See Ulrich Kreidt, '1684/92. Melchior Mattsperger: Geistliche Herzens = Einbildungen', in Brüggemann (ed.), *Handbuch*, cols 171–90.

Fig. 4.4. Melchior Mattsperger, *Geistliche Herzens-Einbildungen Inn Zweihundert und Fünfzig Biblischen Figur-Sprüchen angedeutet…*(Augsburg: Bodenehr, 1688).

Credit: © Herzog August Bibliothek Wolfenbüttel, shelfmark Xb 7191 (1).

these *Sprüche* to others, in particular to young and simple folk, through 250 emblems. The heart is central to both its visual and verbal discourses. On its elaborate title page are no fewer than 12 hearts bearing emblems, those on the left representing the five senses. The main body of Mattsperger's work uses *Figursprüche*: each page shows three emblems, with individual words replaced by small images that function as hieroglyphs (Fig. 4.4). As the preface remarked, 'when this or that word is expressed through a figure, it will lie and imprint itself even more within the heart'.[94] When the reader lingered on the images and took pleasure in them the biblical messages would be properly assimilated. As Mattsperger's brother commented in a dedicatory poem, the objects were depicted 'so that you [the reader] spend time, and thus playfully—as through a permitted joke—the noble Bible plants itself in the heart'.[95]

The heart was also a key theme in Johann Ludwig Prasch's *Emblematischer Catechismus* (*Emblematic Catechism*), printed in Nuremberg in 1683. Here Luther's catechism was illustrated with 27 emblems and explanations. The book's title page is illustrated with a burning heart, intended, according to Prasch's explanation, to show that 'the heart must go to school and be improved'. The fire that 'enlightens and sets aflame' it is the Holy Spirit, 'or divine grace, love and devotion'. Fig. 4.5 shows the third of the Ten Commandments, 'Remember the Sabbath, and keep it holy'. On an altar with a retable depicting the Crucifixion rests an open book with a heart on top of it. 'Where better can our heart rest than in the church, in God's word and in communion, signified by the open book and altar?', asks its accompanying commentary. Prasch stated that his work was intended for 'high and low,

[94] Quoted in ibid., col. 176.
[95] Mattsperger, *Die Geistliche Herzens=Einbildung*, 'Ehren-Gedicht' by Marx Mattsperger.

Fig. 4.5. Johann Ludwig Prasch, *Emblematischer Catechismus/Oder Geist und Sinnreiche Gedancken…*(Nuremberg: Endter, 1683), p. 33.

learned and unlearned, old and young'. The catechism was, he lamented, despised as 'a children's book, learned by heart', but should be studied every day. The emblematic mode of teaching would help, the author reflected, for it 'tempts and pleasures both the eyes and the soul, strengthens and enflames the spirit, explains and makes accessible the things [that it depicts], and impresses them better in the heart and in the memory, just like everything that is seen with the eyes'.[96]

Where did such celebrations of visual piety lead? By the end of the seventeenth century, Lutheran authors were operating within a new devotional and pedagogical environment thanks to the emergence of Pietism and the early stirrings of Enlightenment thought, neither of which encouraged the use of religious images.[97] Lutherans continued, however, to use images in their attempts to reform and re-invigorate religious instruction. In his *Bilder-Büchlein* (Magdeburg 1691, revised edition 1701) the theologian, pastor and poet laureate Johann Gottfried Zeidler recommended the traditional use of the catechism, but simultaneously, like many of his contemporaries, lamented the state of Lutheran domestic instruction, which was conducted by lazy and ill-educated parents.[98] Biblical images provided, for him, a solution to this problem: 'When the child who looks at the image wants to know everything, the tongues of the negligent and ineloquent parents will be loosed for they will have to answer'. When they do this, they themselves will become well-versed in the Bible.[99] In 1691, Zeidler spoke of children's love of images. In 1701, he went further, recommending that anyone who had enough time and aptitude should illuminate the images with 'lively colours' in order to make them more appealing to children. He himself had, he added, experienced this with his own children, 'with great profit'.[100] Zeidler's comment provides a lovely glimpse into the realities of domestic religious instruction: between 1691 and 1701 he had clearly had direct personal experience of entertaining young children with images. Zeidler's book, written by a pastor and a father, testifies to the creative ways in which images might be used in Lutheran religious instruction.

CONCLUSION

The seventeenth century was the era of the devotional image. Images had, since the time of Luther's illustrated Bibles and catechisms, formed part of Lutheran piety. But their affective power, their ability to move the heart and soul, was articulated with new vigour during the seventeenth century. Johann Arndt was a key figure

---

[96] *Emblematischer Catechismus/Oder Geist= und Sinnreiche Gedancken. Uber die Hauptstücke Christlicher Lehrer…*(Nuremberg: Johann Andreæ Endters Söhne, 1683), Zuschrifft and 33–6.

[97] Reents and Melchior, *Die Geschichte der Kinder- und Schulbibel*, 158, 202, 205.

[98] On Zeidler see Flood, *Poets Laureate*, vol. 4: S-Z, 2288–93. Elmar Lechner, *Pädagogik und Kulturkritik in der deutschen Frühaufklärung: Johann Gottfried Zeidler (1655–1711). Zehn Thesen und Edition einiger seiner autobiographischen, pädagogischen und historischen sowie aphoristischen Schriften* (Frankfurt am Main, 2008), esp. 53–77. Also Zedler, *Grosses vollständiges Universallexikon*, LXI, 672–8. For a full discussion of Zeidler's two illustrated Bibles (1691 and 1701), see Heal, 'Reformationsbilder in der Kunst der Aufklärung'.

[99] *Johann Gottfried Zeidlers Neu=ausgefertigte Bilder=Bibel*, Vorrede.   [100] Ibid.

here. His 1597 *Ikonographia* was shaped by his desire to defend images from Calvinist iconoclasm but drew on an eclectic mixture of sources to provide an account of images' spiritual significance that was without precedent in Lutheran thought. Arndt always emphasized the primary importance of the Word. But he also described the connection between external (physical) and internal (spiritual) images in new ways. The two were inextricably linked, for 'the Holy Spirit forms in your heart that which you see externally'. Arndt's belief that the contemplation of art and of nature could help raise the soul to God encouraged the use of religious emblems. His desire for spiritual renewal, his determination to close the gap between the teaching of Christianity and its realization in the life of the Christian, led him to encourage the renewal of mysticism, albeit in attenuated Lutheran form. This had important implications for Passion piety, as we shall see in the next chapter.

Yet, we should not think in terms of a straightforward transition from a didactic image during the early decades of the Reformation to a devotional image during the seventeenth century. Religious images were always both: even Cranach's Law and Gospel iconography, the ultimate aid to Lutheran teaching, invited the (literate) viewer to read and look, to use image and text together as part of religious devotion. Seventeenth-century Lutherans produced some remarkable works of visual pedagogy. Evenius's *Bilder Schule* and Buno's *Bilder-Bibel*—two of the most spectacular—cited traditional Lutheran defences of images, but also went well beyond these. They prescribed complex mnemonic practices that made images into the focal points of religious learning and pious practice. Mattsperger's *Geistliche Herzens-Einbildungen* was the precursor to a whole genre of illustrated collections of biblical texts that remained popular in Europe and North America for more than 200 years. This work celebrated, both verbally and visually, images' ability to penetrate the heart. Several of these authors also acknowledged the pleasure that images afforded: Johann Gottfried Zeidler, for example, whose children loved their father's hand-coloured woodcuts of biblical scenes. Others recognized the importance of artistry, such as Johann Valentin Andreae, who wrote that the crucifix in Christianopolis' temple was 'so skilfully made as to move even the hardest of hearts'. Lutheran artists no longer needed, it seems, to employ 'insulating strategies' to protect their images from idolatrous worship.[101] To make sense of Andreae's celebration of skilful fabrication, of the creation of a life-like crucifix that provoked compassion in its viewer, we need to turn now to Passion piety, to an examination of the ways in which it was transformed by the new piety of the later sixteenth and seventeenth centuries.

---

[101] Christopher Wood, 'Iconoclasm and Iconophobia' in Michael Kelly ed., *Encyclopedia of Aesthetics*, (Oxford, 2014).

5

Lutherans and the Suffering of Christ

Fig. 5.1 shows a life-sized (250 × 156 cm) painting of Christ on the Cross, produced in the Wittenberg workshop of Lucas Cranach the Younger. It is inscribed with the date 1571, and was probably painted for Luther's house, which had been sold in 1564 by the reformer's heirs to Wittenberg University. Given the painting's dimensions, it was most likely intended for a large room, perhaps for the recently renovated *Lutherhörsaal* (lecture room).[1] This is the archetypal Lutheran Crucifixion: not only was it was produced by the Cranach workshop for the building that became the focal point of Luther's cult; it also depicts the crucified Christ in a characteristically 'Lutheran' way. The 1571 Crucifixion can be read as representative of the broad shifts in Passion piety and in visual culture brought about by the Reformation. Its inscription, attributed to the Wittenberg professor of poetry Johannes Maior, emphasizes mankind's sin and responsibility for Christ's suffering. It addresses the viewer directly: 'O man, you who look at me: look at yourself and your own guilt, for I would not have to die were you not death worthy'; 'do not avert your eyes, because I am hanging on the cross for you'.[2] The text then offers a detailed description of the events of the Passion, starting with Christ's face that was spat upon and beaten. There is no lack of emotion in this verbal account. Yet, the visual representation of the crucified Christ is remarkably whole. There is little evidence of physical suffering: there is no side wound; blood trickles only gently from the wounds in Christ's hands and feet and from his crown of thorns; his expression is distant and contemplative.

The image invites comparison with Matthias Grünewald's famously gruesome Isenheim Altarpiece, or with Cranach the Elder's early Crucifixion scenes, which depict suffering in much more graphic terms and use the emotional reactions of the surrounding figures to awaken compassion in the viewer. Joseph Koerner has insisted that inscriptions are the 'aesthetic bane of Lutheran art': they deaden the image, collapse pictorial space and, in the case of the 1571 Crucifixion, turn 'the canvas into a page, and the picture into text or hieroglyph'.[3] They constitute one of the 'insulating strategies' that artists working for Lutheran patrons used in order

---

[1] Enke et al. (eds), *Lucas Cranach der Jüngere*, cat. No. 3/43; Stefan Laube, *Das Lutherhaus Wittenberg. Eine Museumsgeschichte* (Leipzig, 2003), 149 ff.

[2] Koerner, *The Reformation of the Image*, 222; Gabriele Wimböck, 'Wort für Wort, Punkt für Punkt. Darstellung der Kreuzigung im 16. Jahrhundert in Deutschland', in Johann Anselm Steiger and Ulrich Heinen (eds), *Golgatha in den Konfession und Medien der Frühen Neuzeit* (Berlin and New York, 2010), 161–85, here 171–8.

[3] Koerner, *The Reformation of the Image*, 226, 221–3.

Fig. 5.1. Lucas Cranach the Younger, Christ on the Cross, 1571.
Credit: © Stiftung Luthergedenkstätten in Sachsen-Anhalt.

to reduce verisimilitude and deflect idolatrous worship.[4] In this image, concludes one recent commentator, Christ's presence can no longer be affectively experienced.[5] Koerner writes in similar mode of other Cranach Crucifixions. Cranach the Younger's 1584 altarpiece, for example, which shows a multi-figure Crucifixion within a heart, is, he suggests, a paradox: 'Despite its format, Cranach's panel is an emotional blank, a litany of passion motifs to be learned by heart'. 'Where is the feeling in Cranach's heart altarpiece?', he asks. The figures are not portrayed in a manner that invites the viewer to experience emotion in his or her heart.[6]

The implied distinction between the head and the heart, between intellect and emotion, that underpins many discussions of Lutheran images is, as we have seen, problematic. Yet, there can be no doubt that the serene Christ of Cranach's 1571 Crucifixion represents a significant departure from the tortured figures depicted in many pre-Reformation images. Figs. 5.2 and 5.3 show, for example, two sculptures of Christ created around 1500. In the first, a 116 cm high limewood sculpture, Christ is depicted resting on the way to Golgotha. He is seated on a rock, alone and sorrowful. He wears the crown of thorns, and his body is covered in scourge marks. His right hand supports his head, with its expression of mournful contemplation; his left reaches for support from the ground beneath him. The second is a life-sized image of the crucified Christ, again carved from limewood. Blood runs down his arms and flows from the wound in his side. His parted lips, downcast eyes, and pallid face express his physical suffering. The verisimilitude of the image is heightened by Christ's woven crown of thorns and by his wig, fashioned (as often with such images) from real human hair. Both images display a preoccupation with Christ's suffering that was entirely characteristic of the late Middle Ages; both are *Andachtsbilder*, devotional images that sought, through their subject matter and through their modes of representation, to encourage contemplative immersion in their content.[7] Their artists generated compassion in the viewer through isolating one key moment—Christ seated in contemplation; Christ alone on the cross—from the narrative of the Passion, and through using all available means to highlight physical suffering.

Fig. 5.2 is attributed to the Zwickau artist Peter Breuer (*c.*1472–1541), and was probably made for the Nikolaikirche in Freiberg (Erzgebirge). This iconography, known as *Christus in der Rast*, was particularly favoured in the Freiberg region, but similar images could also be found throughout Saxony and beyond.[8] The carved crucifix (Fig. 5.3) comes from the Laurentiuskirche in Pegau just south of Leipzig. Such life-sized crucifixes were standard elements of the furnishing of Gothic churches, and were often displayed either above the choir screen or in the choir area. As carriers of feeling, as incitements to compassion expressed through tears,

---

[4] Wood, 'Iconoclasm and Iconophobia'.
[5] Norbert Michels, 'Einführung', in ibid. (ed.), *Cranach in Anhalt*, 13–16, here 14.
[6] Koerner, *The Reformation of the Image*, 218–19.
[7] For a useful discussion of this term see Karl Schade, *Andachtsbild. Die Geschichte eines kunsthistorischen Begriffs* (Weimar, 1996). See also Bernhard Decker, *Das Ende des mittelalterlichen Kultbildes und die Plastik Hans Leinbergers* (Bamberg, 1985), esp. 92–8.
[8] Ulrich Thiel, *Stadt- und Bergbaumuseum Freiberg* (Chemnitz, 2005), 100–2.

Fig. 5.2. Peter Breuer, Christ Resting on the Way to Golgotha, *c.*1500.
Credit: © Stadt- und Bergbaumuseum Freiberg.

such late-medieval Passion images surely had little part to play in a post-Reformation visual culture that sought to avoid the dangers of idolatry by rejecting seductive realism? Yet, both of these images, and many more like them, survived the
transition to Lutheranism intact and *in situ*.

Luther himself valued depictions of the Crucifixion as memorials and as reminders,
but was horrified by images such as the Pegau one. He wrote of the crucifix in
the Erfurt cloister where he was a novice: 'When I saw his picture or image, as
He hung on the cross, I was frightened by it and lowered my eyes and would rather
have seen the devil'.[9] His Passion preaching focused not on the type of compassion
for the suffering Christ that the Freiberg and Pegau images were intended to generate, but on internal sorrow and remorse for mankind's sins. By the mid-seventeenth
century, however, such images, and the affective responses they created, had been
thoroughly integrated into Lutheran culture. Changes in Lutheran piety played
an important part in this process. Authors such as Martin Moller, Johann Arndt,

---

[9] WA 37, 310. Koerner, *The Reformation of the Image*, 178–9; Dieter Koepplin, 'Kommet her zu
mir alle. Das tröstliche Bild des Gekreuzigten nach dem Verständnis Luthers', in Kurt Löscher (ed.),
*Martin Luther und die Reformation in Deutschland. Vorträge zur Ausstellung im Germanischen
Nationalmusuem Nürnberg 1983* (Schweinfurt, 1983), 153–99, esp. 154.

Fig. 5.3. Anon., crucifix from the parish church of St Laurentius, Pegau, early sixteenth century.

Credit: Photo: author's own, with permission from the Ev.-Luth. Kirchspiel Pegau.

Johann Gerhard, Paul Gerhardt, and Christian Scriver sought, through their devotional writings, to create an immediate encounter between the Christian and the crucified Christ, hoping thereby to reform Christian life. Some were, as we have seen, prepared to use images to achieve this: Johann Valentin Andreae, for example, who wrote of the crucifix in *Christianopolis* that was 'so skilfully made as to move even the hardest of hearts'.

This desire for spiritual renewal was intensified by the unfolding of historical events during the seventeenth century, in particular by the catastrophe of the Thirty Years' War. The practical implications of this catastrophe were clear: in affected areas both religious and secular authorities were confronted by the need to rebuild or restore churches and schools and re-cultivate proper religious customs. The psychological trauma, and its impact on inner spiritual life, is much harder to pin down. Thomas Kaufmann points to an increased 'pluralisation' of devotional types within Lutheran confessional culture, to the simultaneous reception during the 1630s, for example, of English religious literature, of Arndt's works and of Valentin Weigel's spiritualism. In the hymns and poetry of the period, particular themes emerge more strongly: war as punishment for sin, the need for penance,

apocalypticism, and 'a honed, individualized sense of self on the part of the sinner'.[10]
The war also, it seems, encouraged the type of intense Passion piety promoted by
the *Frömmigkeitsbewegung*. It provided the backdrop for the writings of several of the
pastors examined here and for the visual and verbal Passion piety of lay Lutherans
such as the Austrian noblewoman Catharina Regina von Greiffenberg and Georg
Planck, chancellor of Lower Lusatia. As a result of the *Frömmigkeitsbewegung*, with
its emphasis on inner renewal, and of the widespread suffering of the Thirty Years'
War, the crucifix became much more than just a confessional marker: it became
a Lutheran *Andachtsbild*.

PASSION PIETY

Martin Luther's *Eyn Sermon von der Betrachtung des heyligen Leidens Christi* (*A Sermon
on the Contemplation of the Passion of Christ*) published in 1519 and reprinted more
than 20 times up to 1524, became the classic text for Lutheran Passion preaching.[11]
In this brief sermon, Luther criticized the Passion piety of the late Middle Ages,
which aimed, above all, to awaken in man a deep sense of compassion with Christ
and with the Virgin Mary. Passion piety should, he believed, be directed not towards
achieving compassion with the suffering Christ, but rather towards experiencing
sorrow over one's own sins.[12] The Christian must recognize that 'it is you who
has martyred Christ, because your sins are certainly responsible'. 'When you see
Christ's nails piercing his hands, be sure that they are your works; when you see His
crown of thorns, believe it is your evil thoughts'.[13] This sense of the Passion as a
mirror—of God's wrath and of our own sinfulness—and the sense of *pro me* or *pro
nobis*, the thoughts of the believer's own guilt and of his or her responsibility for

---

[10] Kaufmann, *Dreißigjähriger Krieg*, esp. 34–6, 76. See also Asche and Schindling (eds), *Das
Strafgericht Gottes*; Hartmut Lehmann, 'Europäisches Christentum im Zeichen der Krise' in Hartmut
Lehmann and Anne-Charlott Trepp (eds), *Im Zeichen der Krise. Religiosität im Europa des 17.
Jahrhunderts* (Göttingen, 1999), 9–15; Bernd Roeck, 'Der Dreißigjährige Krieg und die Menschen im
Reich. Überlegungen zu den Formen psychischer Krisenbewältigung in der ersten Hälfte des 17.
Jahrhunderts', in Bernhard R. Kroener and Ralf Pröve (eds), *Krieg und Frieden. Militär und Gesellschaft
in der Frühen Neuzeit* (Paderborn etc., 1996), 265–79.

[11] WA 2, 136–42. I. Mager, 'Weshalb hat Martin Luther kein Passionslied geschrieben?', in Johann
Anselm Steiger (ed.), *Passion, Affekt und Leidenschaft in der frühen Neuzeit,* vol. 1 (Wiesbaden, 2005),
405–22, esp. 412; Johann Anselm Steiger, 'Zorn Gottes, Leiden Christi und die Affekte der
Passionsbetrachtung bei Luther und im Luthertum des 17. Jahrhunderts', in ibid. (ed.), *Passion, Affekt
und Leidenschaft*, 179–202, esp. 184. See also Birgit Ulrike Münch, *Geteiltes Leid: Die Passion Christi
in Bildern und Texten der Konfessionalisierung* (Regensburg, 2009).

[12] For discussions of Luther's Passion piety see, for example, Martin Elze, 'Das Verständnis der
Passion Jesu im ausgehenden Mittelalter und bei Luther', in Heinz Liebing and Klaus Scholder (eds),
Geist und Geschichte der Reformation. Festgabe Hanns Rückert zum 65. Geburtstag (Berlin, 1966), 127–51,
esp. 138–45; Robert Kolb, 'Passionsmeditation. Luthers und Melanchthons Schüler predigen und
beten die Passion', in Michael Beyer and Günther Wartenberg (eds), *Humanismus und Wittenberger
Reformation: Festgabe anläßlich des 500. Geburtstages des Praeceptor Germaniae Philipp Melanchthon am 16.
Februar 1997* (Leipzig, 1996), 267–93; Axmacher, *Johann Arndt und Paul Gerhardt,* 186 ff; Mager,
'Weshalb', 412; Susan Karant-Nunn, *The Reformation of Feeling: Shaping the Religious Emotions in
Early Modern Germany* (Oxford, 2010), 78–83.

[13] WA 2, 137.

Christ's suffering, remained a constant of Lutheran Passion piety. It was reflected, for example, in the text inscribed on Cranach's 1571 Crucifixion (Fig. 5.1). Christ's cross was ultimately, however, a consoling and strengthening image for Luther. In his *Sermon von der bereytung zum sterben* (*Sermon on Preparing to Die*), also published in 1519, he referred to it as a 'gnaden bild', an image of grace: it contained within it all that Christ had done and would do for him.[14] In the Cranach image, the figure of Christ, with its open eyes and almost bloodless body, is not disturbing: it seems to echo Luther's conviction that the cross should comfort, not repel. This is an image to teach remorse for our own sin and to commemorate Christ's atoning sacrifice.

Pain and tears were undoubtedly less central to Lutheran Passion preaching than to Catholic. This should not lead us to conclude, however, that Lutheran Passion piety was less affective than its Catholic counterpart. The emotions were essential for Luther: fear was a necessary precondition for recognizing man's sinfulness, sorrow was an inevitable response to that recognition and certainty of the grace of God ultimately brought joy.[15] Even within early Lutheranism, Christ's Passion and man's own passions were closely linked. Yet, there was, without doubt, a shift in the nature and tone of Lutheran Passion piety during the late sixteenth and seventeenth centuries. Sermons, devotional literature, prayers, poetry, music, and images of the period manifested a clear tendency towards a more immediate Passion piety, a Passion piety that sought to install its hearers in the scene at Golgotha.[16] There was a new, or better said, renewed willingness to use vivid, mystical, or even erotic language (often inspired by the Song of Songs) to describe the individual encounter with Christ.[17] This intense Passion piety accorded spiritual and moral benefits to the contemplation of Christ's cross, and reflected, as Ron Rittgers has suggested, a new 'theology and spirituality of desire'.[18] This shift could be illustrated through an examination of the works of many different authors—the Lutheran reception of mystical texts, for example, went back as far as Andreas Musculus (1514–81), writing in the mid-sixteenth century.[19] Here, however, I have chosen to focus on authors whose writings were not only influential in devotional terms but also related in direct ways to visual manifestations of Passion piety.

One key figure was Martin Moller (1547–1600), a theologian and pastor who spent much of his life in Görlitz at the eastern edge of Upper Lusatia. Moller's writings were shaped by the spiritual environment in the remote part of the Empire in which he worked, with its inclinations towards Philippism and irenicism and its

[14] WA 2, 685–97, especially 689.
[15] See Dürr, 'Laienprophetien', 19–24; Kaufmann, 'Die Sinn- und Leiblichkeit', esp. 24–30.
[16] Johann Anselm Steiger, 'Christus Pictor. Der Gekreuzigte auf Golgatha als Bilder schaffendes Bild. Zur Entzifferung der Kreuzigungserzählung bei Luther und im barocken Luthertum sowie deren medientheoretischen Implikationen', in Johann Anselm Steiger and Ulrich Heinen (eds), *Golgatha in den Konfessionen und Medien der Frühen Neuzeit* (Berlin and New York, 2010), 93–127, esp. 106.
[17] For a useful discussion of the stylistic differences between the Passion accounts of, for example, Johann Gerhard and Martin Moller see Elke Axmacher, *'Aus Liebe will mein Heyland sterben'. Untersuchungen zum Wandel des Passionsverständnisses im frühen 18. Jahrhundert*, 2nd ed., (Stuttgart, 2001), 74–84.
[18] Rittgers, 'Mystical Union'. [19] Axmacher, *Praxis Evangeliorum*, 307 ff.

support for mystical movements, from the Schwenckfelders to the followers of Valentin Weigel and Jakob Böhme.[20] Moller's works, which eschewed doctrinal conflict and focused instead on inner piety, were received and praised by a wide spectrum of theologians, not only fellow Lutherans (including Arndt and Paul Gerhardt) but also Catholics and Calvinists. Like Arndt's writings, Moller's key texts were widely reproduced: the *Soliloquia de passion Jesu Christi* (1590), the *Manuale de praeperatione ad mortem* (1593), and the *Praxis Evangeliorum* (1601) each went through around 42 editions. They seem, judging by references in funeral sermons and elsewhere, to have been used in domestic contexts, and their content was taken up in devotional literature, in spiritual poetry and in music.[21] Moller's first work, the *Meditationes sanctorum partum*, was a prayer book compiled from writings of the church fathers. Here Moller used the language of medieval mysticism, drawing on authors such as Bernhard of Clairvaux and Johannes Tauler to describe a burning love of Jesus.[22] The *Soliloquia*, which is of most relevance to us here, draws on the earlier *Meditationes* both in its content and in its style.[23]

In the *Soliloquia*, Moller strove to put the image of Christ crucified as forcefully as possible before his readers' eyes. This text was not intended, he emphasized in his preface, as an interpretation of the Passion, but as 'an introduction, [to how] a simple Christian should themselves contemplate daily and use fruitfully the history of the Passion of Jesus Christ with pious prayers and comforting sighs'. It is an instruction in how the Passion, read in books and heard in sermons, should be used by Christians 'in their temptations [*Anfechtungen*], in prayers, in suffering [*Creutze vnd Hertzenleyd*], in life and in death'.[24] Despite Moller's emphasis on reading and hearing, the text opens with an image, an *Ecce Homo*, in fact not, as the title suggests, an illustration of Christ as he appeared before Pilate but of the ultimate *Andachtsbild*: the Man of Sorrows or *Imago Pietatis*. In this image, Christ is entirely removed from the narrative context of the Passion. He is not the *Ecce Homo*, because he already has the wounds of the Crucifixion; he is not the resurrected Christ because he wears the crown of thorns.[25] Moller remarked that such images were, in former times 'found in almost all churches'. He then directed his readers to their proper evangelical use: 'When you, Christian person, look at this image or another painted crucifix, you must not allow your thoughts to remain stuck to it, but move yourself to the writings of the sacred prophets and apostles, which represent for you the true, living ECCE HOMO'.[26]

---

[20] Axmacher, *Praxis Evangeliorum*, 68–70. See also Paul Althaus, *Forschungen zu evangelischen Gebetsliteratur* (Hildesheim, 1966), 134–5.

[21] Axmacher, *Praxis Evangeliorum*, esp. 15–7.   [22] Ibid., 103–31.

[23] Ibid., 92. 168 ff. Günter Butzer, 'Rhetorik der Meditation. Martin Mollers »Soliloqvia de Passione Iesu Christi« und die Tradition der *eloquentia sacra*', in Kurz (ed.), *Meditation*, 57–78.

[24] Martin Moller, *Soliloquia de passion Iesu Christi* (Görlitz: Fritsch, 1590), D vi r-v. See Axmacher, *Praxis Evangeliorum*, 171.

[25] For other examples see Dieter Koepplin, 'Lutherische Glaubensbilder' in Gerhard Bott (ed), *Martin Luther und die Reformation in Deutschland. Vorträge zur Ausstellung im Germanischen Nationalmusuem Nürnberg 1983* (Schweinfurt, 1983), 352–63. Koepplin gives the example of a 1521 edition of Luther's *Eyn sermon von der betrachtung des heyligen leydens christi* published in Nuremberg and illustrated on its title page with an *Ecce Homo* and the instruments of the Passion.

[26] Moller, *Soliloquia*, Vorrede.

Moller proceeded to examine the story of the Passion in twenty-one chapters, using a few narrative woodcuts as illustration. In particular, he included a sudden concentration of images during the account of Christ's Judgement before Pilate, heightening the dramatic intensity of the narrative.[27] Even where there are no images, Moller's use of medieval mystical texts leads to an increase in affective engagement with the Passion.[28] In part of chapter 17, entitled 'How one should contemplate the Lord on his cross', Moller writes, for example, 'now lift up your eyes, dear soul, and see the Prince of Life hanging on the stem of the cross'. He goes on to evoke Christ's suffering in detail, and describes himself falling beneath the cross at Christ's feet and finding refuge in his wounds.[29] In such texts, there is no sense of distance, of observing the Crucifixion from afar. Rather, the hearer or reader approaches the cross, embraces it, and even enters into Christ's wounds.

With the *Frömmigkeitsbewegung*, this spirituality of desire and this interest in *unio mystica* flourished. Immersion in the inner (spiritual) image of the crucified Christ, in his wounds, his blood, and the instruments of his Passion, distinguished the Passion piety of this period from that of the early sixteenth century. Arndt dedicated a prayer in his 1612 *Paradiesgärtlein*, a key text in the development of private prayer collections, to the contemplation of Christ's wounds, asking his Saviour to 'show me Your hands and feet and Your side, because I wish to see in this comforting mirror the merciful, paternal heart of my dear Father in heaven'. In another prayer of thanks for Christ's suffering, he asked: 'nail me to Your cross with the nails of love, so that Your Crucifixion always hangs before my eyes and in my heart'.[30] The experience of Christ dwelling in the soul, the climax of mystical spirituality, was for Arndt a necessary part of the process of *Verinnerlichung* and a step on the path to ethical renewal.

The desire for an intensification and individualization of piety, coupled with a quest for a more effective morality, was not, however, confined to a small minority of 'Arndtian' reformers. It can be found in Johann Gerhard (1582–1637), perhaps the most learned and famous representative of Lutheran Orthodoxy, as well as in Arndt. Gerhard was a native of Quedlinburg, and was influenced at an early stage by Arndt. He studied in Wittenberg, Jena and Marburg, became in 1615 superintendent in Coburg then returned in 1616 to Jena. Gerhard is famed above all for his *Loci theologici* (1610–22), a thorough exposition of Lutheran dogmatic theology.[31] He was also, however, deeply concerned with pastoral care, and wrote a number of devotional texts that were widely disseminated. Like Moller and Arndt, Gerhard drew on the church's pre-Reformation mystical traditions, and he also cited contemporary

---

[27] Ibid., 169 ff.   [28] Axmacher, *Praxis Evangeliroum*, 175.
[29] Moller, *Soliloquia*, 193 ff. For a discussion of Moller's sources here see Axmacher, 'Aus Liebe', 81–3.
[30] Johann Arndt, *Paradies=Gärtlein, Voller Christlicher Tugenden, Wie solche, Zur Ubung des wahren Christethums, Durch Andächtige, lehrhaffte und trostreiche Gebete in die Seele zu pflantzen* (Leipzig: Johann Samuel Heins, 1753), 235, 245. For full analysis see Axmacher, *Johann Arndt und Paul Gerhardt*, 43–71.
[31] On Gerhard see Johann Anselm Steiger, *Johann Gerhard (1582–1637). Studien zu Theologie und Frömmigkeit des Kirchenvaters der lutherischen Orthodoxie* (Stuttgart, 1997).

Catholic sources.[32] He dwelt on Christ's blood and wounds giving, for example in his 1611 *Erklärung der Historien des Leidens vnnd Sterbens vnsers Herrn Christi Jesu*, graphic descriptions of his suffering. Like Arndt, Gerhard employed very visual language to impress this suffering on his readers' hearts. After Christ had been nailed to the cross and his side wounded with the spear:

> His whole body was naked and covered in weals, His bones were pitifully stretched out on the cross, so that all of them could be counted, His veins shed blood abundantly, all limbs were dried out like potsherds, His tongue cleaved to the roof of his mouth, His heart was like melted wax in his body, His eyes shed tears and darkened in death.[33]

Gerhard also invoked the power of the cross to reform morality: 'If the sorrowful image of the crucified Christ hovers before our hearts at all times, then all evil desires will be easily extinguished'.[34] And although he made no use of physical images, his pupil Johann Michael Dilherr translated his ideas into the realm of the visual through his use of emblems.

The culmination, in cultural terms, of this evocative Passion piety was undoubtedly the poetry of Paul Gerhardt (1607–76). Gerhardt studied in Wittenberg and from 1657 served as deacon at the Nikolaikirche in Berlin. A staunch defender of the Formula of Concord, Gerhardt was dismissed from his post in Berlin in 1666 for his resistance to Elector Friedrich Wilhelm's attempts to promote a union amongst his Reformed and Lutheran subjects. He was called in 1668 to Lübben in the Spreewald, where he spent the rest of his career.[35] Fig. 5.4 shows a portrait of him from around 1675, still located in his church in Lübben. In this portrait, he points to a small, silver crucifix. Beneath is a Latin epigram that tells the Christian viewer to sing Gerhardt's songs frequently, for through them God's spirit will penetrate the heart.

Gerhardt drew on Arndt, writing six songs based on prayers in the *Paradiesgärtlein*.[36] His desire to create an immediate encounter between the Christian and the crucified Christ is expressed most famously in his *Passions-Salve an die leidenden Glieder*, parts of which remain well-known today because of its later use in J. S. Bach's St Matthew Passion. Here Gerhardt reworked a medieval Latin hymn, attributed in his time to Bernard of Clairvaux, with greetings to Christ's feet, knees, hands, sides, breast, heart, and face. The experience of seeing Christ is key throughout. In verse three, for example, Gerhardt writes: 'Look here, here I stand a wretch, who has earned wrath: Give me, O my Merciful One, sight of Your grace'.[37] And in verse ten, when the poem has turned to contemplation of death, he adds: 'Appear

---

[32] Steiger, *Johann Gerhard*, esp. 28, 31, 54, 70.

[33] Johann Gerhard, *Erklärung der Historien des Leidens vnnd Sterbens vnsers Herrn Christi Jesu nach den vier Evangelisten…*(Jena: Tobias Steinmann, 1611), 7 ff.

[34] Ibid., 13.

[35] Johannes Ruschke, *Paul Gerhardt und der Berliner Kirchenstreit. Eine Untersuchung der konfessionellen Auseinandersetzung über die kurfürstliche verordnete 'mutua tolerantia'* (Tübingen, 2012), especially 436–43 on his dismissal, and 469–72 on Lübben.

[36] Axmacher, *Johann Arndt und Paul Gerhardt*, xi.

[37] 'Schau her, hie steh ich armer, / Der zorn verdienet hat: / Gib mir, o mein Erbarmer, / Den anblick deiner gnad'.

Fig. 5.4. Anon., portrait of Paul Gerhardt from the parish church of St Nikolai, Lübben, *c.*1676.

Credit: © SLUB/Deutsche Fotothek.

to me for protection, for comfort at my death, and let me see Your image, in Your sorrow on the cross. Then I will look to You, then full of faith I will press You to my heart. Whoever dies thus dies well'.[38]

Amongst the theologians and pastors who reflected in writing on the Passion during this period one more deserves mention: Christian Scriver (1629–93). Scriver was another representative of Lutheran Orthodoxy. His writings were much admired by Philipp Jakob Spener and he therefore provides a direct link to the pastoral

---

[38] 'Erscheine mir zum schilde, Zum trost in meinem tod / Unnd laß mich sehn dein bilde / In deiner creutzesnoth. / Da wil ich nach dir blicken, / Da wil ich glaubensvoll / Dich vest an mein hertz drücken / Wer so stirbt, der stirbt wol'. For a detailed analysis of this poem see Axmacher, *Johann Arndt und Paul Gerhardt*, 183–207, here 184.

concerns of the Pietists. Scriver, who had studied in Rostock, served from 1653 as archdeacon of St Jakob's Church in Stendal, a former Hanseatic city within Brandenburg's Altmark, before moving in 1667 to become pastor and eventually *Senior*, leader of the local pastorate, in Magdeburg.[39] As newly-appointed pastor in Stendal, Scriver preached, in 1653, three sermons for Lent subsequently published under the title *Das Blutrünstige Bild Jesu Christi des Gekreutzigten (The Wounded Image of Christ Crucified)*.[40] Scriver's description of Christ's suffering was graphic: 'The sacred head is lacerated by thorns, and so that they penetrate deeply enough, it is terribly beaten, so that without doubt blood flowed abundantly down over the lovely face'. He invoked the senses in his account, describing not only what Christ heard and saw but also what he felt and tasted, from the kiss of Judas on his mouth and the scourge on his body to the gall and vinegar on his tongue.[41] We know that Scriver stood, to preach these sermons, in the pulpit located on the north side of the nave in the St Jakobskirche. Above the choir screen was a monumental crucifix. As the preacher asked his congregation to 'stand quietly with me … and look with weeping eyes and lamenting heart at the person who is your Saviour' and to contemplate the details of Christ's suffering, including the blood running down his face surely some, at least, of his hearers raised their eyes to the monumental crucifix above the choir screen?[42]

Between 1675 and 1696 Scriver published a monumental sermon collection, the *Seelenschatz*. This collection of 74 sermons totalling around 3,000 pages, described, like John Bunyan's contemporary *Pilgrim's Progress* (1678), the soul's journey from suffering to the glory of eternal life.[43] Its focus throughout was on internal, individual piety, and it advocated daily self-examination. Like Arndt, Scriver made frequent reference to the heart, and invoked visual images: 'My heart is a panel, upon which and image of my crucified Saviour is delineated and drawn'.[44] For Scriver, such internal (spiritual) images were closely linked to their external (physical) counterparts. In a story that points to the loosening of confessional boundaries in the devotional literature of this period, Scriver tells of a priest in Rome who, when his body was opened up after his death, proved to have no heart. This priest had, Scriver reported, during his lifetime, directed his eyes and heart only towards the crucified Christ. His heart was, as a result, found by those present at the foot of a crucifix that he had used for his devotions. Scriver's own heart would, he added, be found in the wounds of Christ.[45] In another vignette,

---

[39] H. Müller, *Seelsorge und Tröstung. Christian Scriver (1629–1693)* (Waltrop, 2005).

[40] Müller, *Seelsorge*, 48. The introit for the third Sunday in Lent set the tone for these sermons: 'Occuli mei semper ad Dominum – meine Augen schauen stets auf den Herrn' (Psalm 25:15).

[41] Christian Scriver, *Das Blut=rünstige Bild Jesu Christi des Gecreutzigten…* (Magdeburg: Müller, 1728), 77.

[42] Scriver, *Das Blut=rünstige Bild*, 31. Georg Dehio, *Handbuch der Deutschen Kunstdenkmäler. Sachsen-Anhalt I, Regierungsbezirk Magdeburg* (Munich and Berlin, 2002), 881–8.

[43] Martin Brecht, 'Ein "Gastmahl" an Predigten. Christian Scrivers *Seelenschatz* (1675–1692)', *Pietismus und Neuzeit* 28 (2002), 72–117, here 78.

[44] Christian Scriver, *Seelen=Schatz…*, (Leipzig: Johann Melchior Süstermann and Christoph Seidel, 1698), 623.

[45] Ibid., 589.

Scriver told the story of a good Lutheran housefather who, on his deathbed, directed his impoverished wife and child to his hidden treasure. Expecting gold or jewels, his family was initially disappointed but ultimately strengthened and comforted by the contents of his hidden store: 'they found nothing in it', Scriver reported, 'but the Bible, a crucifix, and a piece of cloth that had been made quite yellow by many tears, in which was wrapped a prayer book'.[46] The proper implements of Lutheran devotion included, for Scriver, not only the Bible and a prayer book but also the crucifix. And the proper response to their use included tears.

This examination of Lutheran Passion piety has focused so far on theologians and pastors, the group rightly described by Thomas Kaufmann as the architects of confessional culture. Amongst the lay authors of devotional texts on Christ's Passion one was particularly important in the seventeenth century and is particularly well-known today: Catharina Regina von Greiffenberg (1633–94). Von Greiffenberg was a Lutheran noblewoman, born in Lower Austria during the era of militant Habsburg recatholicization. Eventually in 1678, as a widow, she fled to Nuremberg. Von Greiffenberg was both highly educated and extremely devout: her religious reading included the writings of medieval mystics as well as Luther's works and texts by Arndt, Harsdörffer and Dilherr. She published in 1662 a collection of spiritual sonnets, and then in 1672 *Des Allerheiligst- und Allerheilsamsten Leidens und Sterbens Jesu Christi, Zwölf andächtige Betrachtungen* (*Twelve Pious Meditations on the Supremely Holy and Supremely Salvific Suffering and Dying of Jesus Christ*), the first part of a series of meditations on the life and miracles of Christ. Von Greiffenberg's works were widely received during her lifetime, and she prided herself on the fact that they were read by Catholics as well as Protestants.[47]

Each of the *andächtige Betrachtungen* is introduced by an emblem, designed by von Greiffenberg's friend and mentor Sigmund von Birken: the work belongs, therefore, in the tradition of illustrated devotional works discussed in Chapter 4. Each emblem is followed by an explanation, a passage from Scripture and a lengthy commentary. Von Greiffenberg's commentaries place a distinctive emphasis on women's participation in biblical history and on spiritual equality: the Holy Spirit 'works, sings, plays, shouts for joy, and jubilates in their [women's] hearts as in men's'. In her discussion of Christ's Nativity and Passion, von Greiffenberg also places a very clear emphasis on somatic experience. She is, as Lynne Tatlock points out, 'at her most eloquent when she contemplates incarnation, pregnancy, and gestation; Jesus as fetus in the womb; the corporeal experience of pain and sorrow; martyrdom; and burial'.[48] She also enlists all parts of her own body in her devotional practice, for example, in her contemplation of Christ on the Mount of Olives.[49]

Such somatic engagement was, to an extent, characteristic of the period: male-authored Passion texts described, as we have seen, the devotee falling at Christ's

---

[46] Ibid., 236.
[47] Catharina Regina von Greiffenberg, *Meditations on the Incarnation, Passion, and Death of Jesus Christ*, ed. and tr. Lynne Tatlock (Chicago, 2009).
[48] Greiffenberg, *Meditations*, 'Volume Editor's Introduction', 29.
[49] Karant-Nunn, *The Reformation of Feeling*, 231.

feet and finding refuge in his wounds. Like all Lutheran commentators, von Greiffenberg also emphasized human sin and culpability and the comfort that could be derived from Christ's cross. But her account of the Passion is suffused to an unusual extent by reflections on physical suffering and on the importance of compassion:

> Now, dearest Lord Jesus, wilt Thou experience terrible agony, and I will agonize in my heart. Oh! It is a cross for me to bear to name Thy Crucifixion and agony for me to imagine it. How can my hands describe the pain of Thine without trembling and shaking with pain? How can I recall the stripping of Thee without dying of sheer horror?

She writes of Christ's nakedness, of his bloody wounds, and of the splintered cross to which he was nailed. She writes of his veins cracking, his sinews crunching, the marrow in his bones trembling, and his blood boiling and flowing to his heart, 'which trembles and hammers in pure pain as if it would burst into a thousand pieces'. The reader's compassion is increased by her account of the emotions of those present at the Crucifixion, in particular the Virgin Mary, Mary Cleophas, and Mary Magdalen, whose 'eyes and began to weep as much white blood as He could spill red blood'. These three women 'endlessly embraced the wooden cross spattered with His blood'.[50] Susan Karant-Nunn describes von Greiffenberg as exceptional, not only in her knowledge and eloquence but also in the nature of her piety. She had, Karant-Nunn suggests, absorbed the doctrinal core of Lutheranism, but the 'culture of that creed [had] not developed fully around her'.[51] Yet, as we have seen, the cross-confessional borrowing that underpinned von Greiffenberg's Passion piety was an established part of Lutheran culture by the seventeenth century.

A 'culture of devotion' focused on the Passion arose amongst seventeenth-century Lutheran noblewomen.[52] Von Greiffenberg was certainly its most famous representative, but other women also wrote and published on the Passion: Aemilia Juliana von Schwarzburg-Rudolstadt (1637–1706); Henrietta Katharina von Gersdorf (1648–1726); Magdalena Sibylla von Württemberg (1652–1712), to name but a few. Aemilia Juliana was a prolific author of music and poetry, and commissioned images that showed her and her family in scriptural scenes, including scenes from the Passion.[53] Henrietta Katharina, grandmother of Count Nikolaus Ludwig von Zinzendorf and an important influence on his childhood spirituality, published verses on the Passion.[54] Amongst Magdalena Sibylla's devotional writings was *Das mit Jesu gekreutzigte Hertz* (*The Heart Crucified with Jesus*), printed in 1689 and illustrated with a frontispiece that showed the author embracing the foot of Christ's cross.[55] By the early eighteenth century this composition, which emphasized the

---

[50] Greiffenberg, *Meditations*, 99.
[51] Karant-Nunn, *The Reformation of Feeling*, 234.   [52] Ibid., 235.
[53] Judith P. Aikin, *A Ruler's Consort in Early Modern Germany: Aemilia Juliana of Schwarzburg-Rudolstadt* (Farnham, 2014).
[54] Karant-Nunn, *The Reformation of Feeling*, 235 ff.; Erika Geiger, *Nikolaus Ludwig Graf von Zinzendorf*, 4th ed. (Holzgerlingen, 2009), 15 ff.
[55] Watson, 'Lutheran Piety', esp. 174–6.

depth and intimacy of the devotee's relationship with Christ, was not uncommon in Lutheran art. Although the most widely circulated Passion texts of the period were, of course, penned by men, the works of von Greiffenberg and her fellow noblewomen remind us that women were far from just passive recipients, a silent audience for the religious writings of churchmen and theologians. These women, thanks to their exceptional education and to the financial resources at their disposal, were able to play an active part in shaping Lutheran confessional culture.

SEEING CHRIST

Seventeenth-century Lutheran Passion piety was characterized by the use of highly emotional language and by emphasis on Christ's physical suffering. Emphasis on themes such as Christ's wounds, inspired by a renaissance of medieval mysticism, provided a way to engage Christians' hearts as well as their minds, to generate a deeper individual devotion and thereby a renewal of moral and ethical life. In their desire to intensify the encounter between the Christian and the crucified Christ, Lutheran authors sometimes, as with Moller's *Soliloquia*, made use of printed images. Yet, as we saw with Scriver's description of a house father praying with a Bible and a prayer book before a crucifix, or with the paintings commissioned by Aemilia Juliana von Schwarzburg-Rudolstadt, Lutheran Passion piety made use not only of woodcuts and engravings but also of paintings and sculptures. We need to consider not just verbal enjoinders to imagine oneself before the cross but also Lutheran experiences of physically standing or kneeling before the cross, before Arndt's 'externally-formed images and paintings'. We need to take seriously what Lutherans, again in Arndt's words, 'saw externally', because it was these physical images that, according to contemporary understandings, the Holy Spirit inscribed on their hearts.[56]

Lutherans saw Christ often: many saw him in their homes, most saw him in their local churches, and all saw him when they attended communion. The Erzegebirge, the prosperous mining region of Southern Saxony that had Freiberg as its administrative centre, provides an example. Recent work on the material culture and archaeology of the Reformation has shown that Lutheran homes were often adorned with biblical images.[57] Amongst these images, depictions of the Crucifixion were prominent. In Freiberg, for example, miners and smelters had themselves painted on the walls of their homes kneeling in prayer before Christ's cross. Fig. 5.5 shows one such painting from around 1570, located in a house that was owned by Paul Klotz, a financial supervisor for a smelting work; here a miner (left) and a smelter (right) flank a crucifix.[58] Crucifixion scenes could also be found on objects

---

[56] See Chapter 4.
[57] See, for example, Siegfried Müller, 'Repräsentationen des Luthertums – Disziplinierung und konfessionelle Kultur in Bildern', *Zeitschrift für historische Forschung*, 29 (2002), 215–55.
[58] On such images see Angelica Dülberg, 'Wand- und Deckenmalereien vom 15. bis zum ausgehenden 17. Jahrhundert in Freiberger Bürgerhäusern', in Yves Hoffmann and Uwe Richter (eds), *Denkmale in Sachsen. Stadt Freiberg. Beiträge Band III* (Freiberg, 2004), 828–68.

Fig. 5.5. Anon., Wall Painting, Pfarrgasse 20, Freiberg (Saxony), *c.*1570.
Credit: Photo: Antje Ciecior, Freiberg.

such as ceramic stoves.[59] Other domestic devotional images are harder to trace, but certainly existed: an inventory of the possessions of Valerius Segebald, a Freiberg goldsmith, drawn up in 1667 mentions, for example, in addition to his extensive collection of Lutheran books, and image of the Wise and Foolish Virgins and 'a wooden crucifix in the living room'.[60]

Evidence of the actual *use* of crucifixes in domestic devotion, rather than their mere presence on walls and furniture, is hard to come by. Did they, as the devotional writer Scriver suggested, form a focal point for prayer, or were they merely a norm for interior decoration? Here, in the absence of a comprehensive study of Lutheran domestic inventories, all we can draw on is anecdote. Wenzeslaus Bergmann, pastor of Gerlachsheim in Upper Lusatia, reported, for example, that his father, a Bohemian exile who died in 1648 in Breslau, had a crucifix painted on the wall opposite his bed during his last illness and had the hymn 'Herr Jesu Christ, mein Lebenslicht' ('Lord Jesus Christ, my life's light') sung 'so that he could derive

---

[59] H. Meller, *Fundsache Luther. Archäologen auf den Spuren des Reformators* (Stuttgart, 2009), 274–84. See also J. Hallenkamp-Lumpe, 'Das Bekenntnis am Kachelofen? Überlegungen zu den sogenannten "Reformationskacheln"' in Carola Jäggi and Jörn Staecker (eds), *Archäologie der Reformation. Studien zu den Auswirkungen des Konfessionswechsels auf die materielle Kultur* (Berlin, 2007), 323–43.

[60] StadtAFr, Aa Ib VII 67VI (Akten des Stadtrats zu Freiberg, Testaments- und Erbschaftssachen, 1656/72): 'ein holzern Crucifix in der Wohnstube'. On Segebald see K. Knebel, 'Die Freiberger Goldschmiedeinnung, ihre Mester und deren Werke', *Mitteilungen des Freiberger Altertumsvereins*, 31 (1894), 1–116, here 52.

Fig. 5.6. Georg Hoffman, *Ein Christliches vnd andechtiges Bergkgebet* (Freiberg, 1625).
Credit: © Germanisches Nationalmuseum Nürnberg, HB. 14161.

comfort and strength in his sufferings from the sufferings of Christ on the cross'.[61] The connection between Christ's cross and the death of the individual Christian was, not surprisingly, a strong one: not only was the use of a *Vorträgekreuz* (crucifix) in funeral processions fiercely defended as an essential component of an honourable burial, but the use of small crosses or crucifixes at the deathbed, recommended by Luther, also remained current, described by some theologians as an adiaphoron and recorded in visual depictions.[62]

Fine paintings and sculptures were, of course, relatively costly, but devotional woodcuts were easily available. Fig. 5.6 shows a woodcut produced by the Freiberg printer Georg Hoffman in 1625 entitled 'A Christian and pious mining prayer'. It is a wonderful expression of the Lutheran spirituality of the region's miners.[63] In the Erzgebirge, saints' protection had traditionally been invoked above all during the miners' dangerous journeys into and out of the pits. Christian Lehmann, who served as pastor in the village of Scheibenberg from 1638 to 1688, condemned, for example, the misuse of Marian images that had occurred before the Reformation. Miners had, he said, 'put her image in spooky shafts and in sinister routes, in the hope of being saved from the kobold of the mine, but in vain'.[64] Lutheran pastors encouraged their congregations to put their trust instead in Christ. In Joachimsthal, Johann Mathesius advocated the recitation of prayers, especially the Our Father, at the moment of entry into the mine and after the miner's safe

[61] E. E. Koch, *Geschichte des Kirchenlieds und Kirchengesangs mit besonderer Rücksicht auf Württemberg. Zweiter Teil. Die Lieder und Weisen* (Stuttgart, 1847), 457–8.

[62] WA 46, 664–5 (*Auslegung des ersten und zweiten Kapitels Johannis in Predigten 1537 und 1538*). See in particular H. Grün 'Die kirchliche Beerdigung im 16. Jahrhundert', *Theologische Studien und Kritiken*, 105 (2) (1933), 138–209, esp. 141. For a case of Lutheran-Calvinist conflict over the use of a *Vorträgekreuz* see Nischan, *Prince, People, and Confession*, 49–50.

[63] Dorothy Alexander and Walter L. Strauss, *The German Single-Leaf Woodcut, 1600–1700*, vol. 1 (New York, 1977), 261–2.

[64] Schmidt-Brücken and Richter, *Der Erzgebirgschronist*, 173.

return. He also reassured his congregation that miners were protected by God's angels at these crucial moments.[65] Hoffman's print instructs the pious miner on how to prepare his heart for his entry and work in the mine:

> He should have God before his eyes, and undertake everything in the fear and in the name of God, and should not forget his mine light, but think about his catechism, and from it learn to recognize a true highest creator, claim blessing and prosperity from him, and moreover work faithfully.

The text goes on to talk of God creating the mountains and valleys and letting silver fall from his hand into the mines, and prays: 'Protect me at my going in and coming out, through Your angels'. This piety is characteristically Christocentric and Protestant, but seeing is key: in the middle of Hoffman's print is Christ on the cross, with wheat and bones (a device used in emblem books) and 'spes altera vitae'. The broadsheet therefore allows the pious miner to have God literally 'before his eyes' as he starts his journey into the mine.

Having perhaps encountered Christ's image at home and during his working day, the Freiberg miner would also, of course, have 'God before his eyes' in church. The Cathedral provides the most spectacular example. In the choir area stands the tomb of Elector Moritz of Saxony, commissioned in 1555 by his brother and successor Elector August (Fig. 5.7). Moritz kneels with his electoral sword in perpetual prayer beneath a three-dimensional crucifix. The depiction of the crucified Christ was the central focus of the iconographical programme of innumerable Lutheran epitaphs, here and elsewhere.[66] From 1589 to 1594 the choir where Moritz's monument sits was converted into a splendid burial chapel for his Wettin descendants by Giovanni Maria Nosseni. Beyond Moritz's crucifix, on the ceiling of the choir, we see the Resurrected Christ surrounded by angels carrying the instruments of the Passion. On the altar stands a bronze crucifix, produced in 1590–93 by Carlo di Cesare.[67] Crucifixes also adorned the surviving medieval rood screen, the communion altar and the *Bergmannskanzel* (miner's pulpit) given in 1638 by the mayor Jonas Schönlebe (Fig. 2.1). Schönlebe had also paid for the restoration of Freiberg's *Ratskruzifix* (council crucifix), a late-gothic rock crystal cross kept in the room where the council met and possibly used for oath taking.[68]

Freiberg's Cathedral was exceptionally richly decorated, but local village churches also provided ample opportunity for seeing Christ. The church in Scheibenberg, for example, where the chronicler Christian Lehmann served as pastor, had a late-gothic altar cross, a life-sized crucifix from *c.*1522 that was renovated in 1670 at the expense of one Barbara Heinrich, and a processional cross from 1628 commissioned by the mining supervisor Christoph Dietrich. The processional cross had an

---

[65] Johann Mathesius, *Sarepta oder Bergpostill Sampt der Joachimßthalischen kurtzen Chronicken* (Nuremberg, 1564; reprint Prague, 1975), XXV v.

[66] Meys, *Memoria und Bekenntnis*, 255–60.

[67] Meine-Schawe, *Die Grablege*. There is a wonderful list of visitors to the chapel: StadtAFr, Abteilung II (Kirchensachen), Section I. FAV-HS Aa 131 'Verzeichniß des Tranck Geldes, so der Dom-Glöckner, wegen Eröffnung der Churfstl Begräbnuß Capelle, von Anno 1594 genoßen'.

[68] On Freiberg Catherdal see Heinrich Magirius, *Der Dom zu Frieberg* (Leipzig, 1986). On the *Ratskruzifix* see Heal, 'Seeing Christ'.

Fig. 5.7. Choir Area of the Cathedral, Freiberg (Saxony), with the monument for Elector Moritz of Saxony in the centre, 1563.
Credit: © Otto Schröder.

inscription that linked it to the miners' devotion: 'until death knocks for us [*auspochen* – the signal to leave the mine], grant Jesus that your light, like our cross, goes before, illuminates us, and does not go out'.[69] Lehmann's own epitaph, originally located in a niche in the wall of the graveyard and probably produced in 1689 by a Schneeberg artist, also shows Christ crucified between the bust-length portraits of the pastor and his wife Euphrosyna (né Kreusel).

These visual encounters with Christ were quotidian, constant elements of the lives of the Lutheran inhabitants of the Erzgebirge and of their co-religionists elsewhere in the Empire during the sixteenth and seventeenth centuries. What of the emergence of new types of image or image use that might have accompanied the changes in Passion piety taking place from the late sixteenth century onwards? Here we need to cast our net more widely, and draw on examples from elsewhere in Saxony and Brandenburg. We have already, with the Freiberg *Christus in der Rast* (Fig. 5.2) and the Pegau crucifix (Fig. 5.3), noted the survival of pre-Reformation images. We do not know the precise history of the Pegau image, but church accounts tell us that the crucifix in nearby Geithain was moved in 1597 from a 'freestanding' position, presumably in the nave, to the baptism chapel on the south side of the church.[70] Such images were not, then, accidental survivals, objects that were bundled away in the sacristy or 'idol chamber' in the early decades

---

[69] Schmidt-Brücken and Richter, *Der Erzgebirgschronist*, 247–52.
[70] Pfarrarchiv Geithain, Kirchenrechnungen, 1597.

of the Reformation and forgotten about. An example from Görlitz in Upper Lusatia, a territory sandwiched between Habsburg Bohemia and Electoral Saxony, shows the importance that Lutheran congregations might accord them. In 1559, a large wooden crucifix that had stood in a small chapel dedicated to St Anne was moved into the main church of St Peter and Paul and placed on the pillar beside the councillors' pew. There it attracted the attention of the city's Habsburg over-lords: at the wish of the Emperor's mother it had to be sent to Madrid as a gift. It was, however, replaced by another wooden crucifix—church accounts from 1572 record payments for its painting and gilding with gold leaf. This one fared no better: Adam von Dietrichstein, chief chamberlain at the imperial court, took a fancy to it, and asked that it be given to him for the new church he was building in Austria. Again it was replaced, this time with a clay version (1581).[71] Görlitz's Lutherans not only preserved but twice replaced their life-sized crucifix.

Pre-Reformation survivals did, on occasion, attract criticism. In the *Ikonographia*, Arndt complained that 'one often finds old images, so large, monstrous, [and] badly formed, that they are very offensive to look upon'. These old images should, he argued, be removed by the authorities.[72] Other pastors were willing, however, to incorporate them into the devotional life of the Lutheran church. Christian Lehmann provides a fascinating example. Between 1632 and 1647 the towns and villages in which Lehmann exercised his ministry were frequently plundered and burned, their populations decimated by plague. Lehmann was forced to flee into the mountains with his Scheibenberg congregation on several occasions in order to escape the predations of Swedish troops. Lehmann's copious writings testify to the difficulties he faced in trying to eradicate 'superstitious' beliefs and renew proper devotional practice in his remote and war-torn territory.[73] While Lehmann advocated the removal of 'idols', he also praised particular pre-Reformation images of Christ's Passion. Lehmann described a 'Jammerbild Jesu' (image of Christ's suffering) from 1536 that was life-sized with a crown of thorns. Christ's body was naked, covered in scourge marks, and his right hand showed the wound made by the nail. He held the whip and switch used at the Flagellation in his left arm, and wore a bloody loin cloth. This 'Jammerbild', a Man of Sorrows or *Imago Pietatis*, had, Lehmann said, 'such life-like colours, limbs, streams of blood etc. that you could not look at it for long without compassion and tears'.[74] Lehmann also commented on an *Ölberg*—a sculpture of Christ on the Mount of Olives—from Annaberg that was transferred to the nearby village of Geyer. This image, which would have played a role in the paraliturgical rituals of Holy Week before the Reformation, was according to Lehmann restored in 1657 'to preserve the contemplation of the sacred Passion and the old piety'.[75] Old images of Christ's

---

[71] RatsAG, Varia 98, 10a and lib. Miss. 1581=1586, fol. 46r–46v. See Alfred Zobel, 'Beiträge zur Geschichte der Peterskirche in Görlitz in den Jahren 1498–1624', *Neues Lausitzisches Magazin*, 108 (1932), 1–86, here 75.

[72] Arndt, *Ikonographia (1597)*, 66.

[73] Fritz Roth, *Christian Lehmanns Leben und Werke und seine Stellung zum Aberglauben* (Marburg, 1933).

[74] Schmidt-Brücken and Richter, *Der Erzgebirgschronist,* 176–7.   [75] Ibid., 178.

Passion were, Lehmann's comments suggest, reanimated in response to the changing devotional climate of the seventeenth century.

GÖRLITZ'S HOLY SEPULCHRE

The Holy Sepulchre in Görlitz (Upper Lusatia) is perhaps the most spectacular example of a pre-Reformation Passion monument that was incorporated, from the later sixteenth century onwards, into the devotional life of a Lutheran community.[76] The Holy Sepulchre had been built between 1481 and *c.*1520 just outside Görlitz's city walls. The ensemble of buildings consisted of a copy of Christ's grave, as recoded in the illustrations of contemporary pilgrimage books, a small *Salbungshaus* (anointing house) containing a sculpture of the *Pietà* and a two-story chapel dedicated to the Holy Cross. The grave and *Salbungshaus* had been given by the local patrician Georg Emmerich after a visit to the Holy Land. Until the Reformation the site formed the focus of Görlitz's annual Holy Week rituals. On Good Friday a wooden figure of Christ was taken down from the cross in the chapel and placed in the grave; on Easter Sunday it was resurrected, carried in procession through the town and returned to the chapel. In 1525, as the Reformation gained ground in Görlitz, the council stopped the procession and the wooden figure of Christ was destroyed by a lightning strike in 1537, according to the *Stadtschreiber* (town scribe) Johannes Haß. The ensemble of buildings survived under the protection of the donor family, but was not used.[77]

From the last third of the sixteenth century onwards, however, the Görlitz Holy Sepulchre 'cult' was reanimated. This was not a renewal of pre-Reformation Passion piety, but rather its reinterpretation in a Lutheran sense. In 1573, the pastor Sigismund Suevus published the *Gesitliche Wallfarth oder Pilgerschafft zum heiligen Grabe* (*Spiritual Journey or Pilgrimage to the Holy Sepulchre*), which described the Holy Sepulchre as a memorial (*Gedenckzeichen*), to be used properly by its visitors, 'so that they think comfortingly, as with a beautiful image, of the proper grave of Christ and its great fruit'.[78] The core of Suevus's text was an account of a spiritual pilgrimage to the Holy Sepulchre. For him, 'viewing the place where Christ lay' did not consist simply of external contemplation of a stone grave, but rather of internal contemplation of God's Word and faith. The pilgrim's mantel must be 'the

---

[76] In Frankfurt (Oder) a *Kruzifixhäuschen*, a small chapel with almost life-sized figures of Christ on the cross and the Virgin Mary and Mary Magdalen to either side, was maintained after the Reformation by donations from members of the congregation of St Georgen. In 1660 a local merchant even replaced the crucifix at his own cost after it had been stolen. Theodor Goecke, *Die Kunstdenkmäler der Provinz Brandenburg,* vol. 6/2, *Stadt Frankfurt a. O.* (Berlin, 1912), 38–9.

[77] For a detailed history of the site see Kai Wenzel, 'Die Bautzener Taucherkirche und das Görlitzer heilige Grab. Räumliche Reorganisationen zweier Orte spätmittelalterlicher Frömmigkeit im konfessionellen Zeitalter', in Wetter (ed.), *Formierung des konfessionellen Raumes,* 167–92, esp. 177–9. On Johannes Haß see Martin Christ, 'The Town Chronicle of Johannes Hass: History Writing and Divine Intervention in the Early Sixteenth Century', *German History* 35 (1) (2017), 1–20.

[78] Sigismund Suevus, *Geistliche Wallfarth oder Pilgerschafft zum heiligen Grabe* (1573), Vorrede. On this text see Kai, 'Die Bautzenner Taucherkirche', 182.

innocence and salvation of Christ our Saviour', his bag right belief, his hat hope, his staff God's Word and his boots preaching. This spiritual pilgrimage would lead the Christian to the 'beautiful pleasure garden beside Christ's grave', that is, to Holy Scripture, to the fountain of life and to the true church.[79]

In 1595, ownership of the grave was transferred to the city council, who pledged to maintain it as a 'public and sacred place' and put it under the administration of the parish church of St Peter and Paul. It was actively promoted as a place of pilgrimage, perhaps in part because of the emergence of a rival Holy Sepulchre site erected in nearby Catholic Sagan in 1598–1600.[80] Fig. 5.8, for example, shows a woodcut that was reproduced repeatedly during the seventeenth century, with the chapel, *Salbungshaus* (with figures kneeling in prayer before it) and grave.[81] Another woodcut from *c*.1600 offered a Lutheran interpretation of the *Salbunghaus* with its *Pietà*. Two men kneel in prayer before the chapel. The inscription beneath gives an appropriate prayer for the contemplation of Christ's anointing, and describes the process by which the contemplation of the image leads to a *Verinnerlichung*, an engagement of the heart:

> This good woman took You, Jesus, on her lap, and anointed You well! With this I will reflect: Your bitter death on the cross freed me from sin, and through this You give me salvation, grace and life. I can have no greater riches in this world. In thanks I will bury You in my heart.[82]

In 1625, a pillar bearing an image—probably of Christ Carrying the Cross—was built to provide a focus for a Way of the Cross that led from the town church to the Holy Sepulchre site. A written account of 1666 by the schoolmaster Gottfried Tschirche gave a precise prescription for the contemplation of particular scenes from the Passion as the pilgrim proceeded along this path.[83] By the late seventeenth century the site clearly had cross-confessional appeal. In 1688, the council agreed to accept gifts for its maintenance, even if they were from Catholics, and in 1690–91 a donor gave 300 *Gulden* out of special devotion to the site, which, he noted, was frequently 'held in honour even by the non-Catholics'.[84] In around 1700, a painted *Christus in der Rast* was put into the Kreuz-Kapelle, and sculpted figures of the three Maries and an angel were placed at the tomb to heighten its verisimilitude.[85]

By the early eighteenth century the site was famous, and once again played an important part in the town's Easter celebrations. The council ruled in 1705 that as in previous years the Holy Sepulchre should be open on Easter Sunday, 'so that the people can look at it', but cautioned that no food should be sold there.[86] This was a sacred site, a site for devotion not commerce. In 1723, the council granted

---

[79] Suevus, *Geistliche Wallfarth*, Section IX, A iii r ff., Q v r.

[80] Kai, 'Die Bautzenner Taucherkirche', 181.

[81] I. Anders, and M. Winzeler (eds), *Lausitzer Jerusalem. 500 Jahre Heiliges Grab zu Görlitz* (Görlitz and Zittau, 2005), 57–65.

[82] Ibid., 62.   [83] Kai, 'Die Bautzenner Taucherkirche', 184.

[84] RatsAG, Ratsprotokolle Varia 133, fol. 141r, Varia 135, fol. 2r–v and also recorded in a separate document: Akten Rep I Seite 250 Nr. 212.

[85] Anders and Winzeler, *Lausitzer Jerusalem*, 90–9; Kai, 'Die Bautzenner Taucherkirche', 190–1.

[86] RatsAG, Ratsprotokolle Varia 135, 18r.

Fig. 5.8. Anon., 'Eigendlicher Abris des heiligen Grabes zu Görlitz . . .', (Görlitz: Christoph Zippern, n.d.), between 1663 and 1677.

Credit: Görlitz, Kulturhistorisches Museum, Inv.-Nr. 40-10. © Görlitzer Sammlungen für Geschichte und Kultur, Verlag Gunter Oettel.

permission for a cantor to sing 'a couple of sacred songs' from the Holy Sepulchre on Good Friday. In 1752, however, they refused to approve the Passion devotion proposed for the site on Holy Saturday, in order to avoid 'criticisms and false inter-pretations'.[87] Images and texts recorded its appearance and offered instructions for its use. A richly illustrated pamphlet, *Eigentliche Bechreibung des Görlitzschen Heiligen Grabes (Proper Description of Görlitz's Holy Sepulchre)*, which was first pub-lished in 1718 and went through 17 editions during the eighteenth century, spoke of the close relationship between external and internal images:

> Christians should always have their Saviour's death and resurrection before their eyes and in their hearts…Although the eyes of faith of our soul, which is joined to our Saviour, must contribute most to this remembrance, so also our bodily eyes serve to make visible external things to remind us of the death and resurrection of Christ. They are like awakeners that stir up the eyes of the soul to contemplate their duty.[88]

An engraving of 1719 served in part as a pilgrimage memento, but also offered plenty for the 'bodily eyes' to make use of (Fig. 5.9). Entitled 'Image of Christ

Fig. 5.9. Anon., 'Abbildung der Ausführung Christi zu seinem schmertzl. Leyden…', 1719.

Credit: Görlitz, Kulturhistorisches Museum, Inv.-Nr. 6 -49 © Görlitzer Sammlungen für Geschichte und Kultur, Verlag Gunter Oettel.

---

[87] RatsAG, Ratsprotokolle Varia 135, 64r, 195v.
[88] Kai, 'Die Bautzenner Taucherkirche', 189.

being led to his painful Passion, with a representation of the so-called Holy Sepulchre and Holy Cross Church in Görlitz' it shows each of the individual scenes of Christ's journey to Calvary, from him being led away from Pilate, before the portal of Görlitz's town church, to him being carried to the Holy Sepulchre.[89] In Görlitz, in confessionally mixed Upper Lusatia, there were good commercial as well as good devotional reasons for granting the Holy Sepulchre a new lease of life.

ALTARPIECES

The re-articulation of pre-Reformation images and sacred sites was, in part at least, a response to the changing devotional climate of the later sixteenth and seventeenth centuries. These physical reminders of Christ's Passion, these 'externally formed images' (Arndt), provided another means, beyond devotional literature, music and preaching, of intensifying individual piety, of encouraging *Verinnnerlichung*. Newly created altarpieces also reflected this shift: they increasingly presented the Crucifixion in ways that were intended to generate compassion. Altars provided the backdrop for the physical encounter with Christ that occurred at communion, and were central to Lutheran piety. The Lutheran altar, though no longer filled with relics, was still consecrated and still sacred: Superintendent Helwig Garth wrote, for example, in his consecration sermon for an altar in Freiberg (Fig. 5.10), that any attack on the altar was an attack on the 'sacred and worthy Sacrament, for the administration of which it is primarily built'.[90] Most Lutheran altarpieces created between the mid-sixteenth and early-seventeenth centuries have, in accordance with Luther's own prescription, the Last Supper somewhere on them. Yet, the Crucifixion was a more popular choice of subject for the main panel.[91] Initially, these Crucifixions tended to be painted scenes, framed by complex explications of Lutheran theology, by cycles of narrative scenes and by texts. By the later sixteenth century, however, altars' iconographic programmes tended to be simpler, focusing on three key salvific events: the Last Supper in the predella, the Crucifixion in the central shrine and the Resurrection above.[92]

There was also a significant change in medium. During the early decades of the Reformation, Lutherans had routinely adorned their altars with small, three-dimensional crucifixes or *Altarkreuze*, but the first Lutheran altarpieces were painted,

[89] Anders and Winzeler, *Lausitzer Jerusalem,* 62–5. III.19.

[90] Helwig Garth, *Christliche/Evangelische Altar=Weyhe...* (Freiberg: Hoffman, 1611), E ii r-v. The church accounts from the Nikolaikirche in Geithain near Leipzig provide a wonderful glimpse of the significance that a Lutheran altar might have. In 1592 a carpenter was paid for making a small box that was then walled up in the altar. This box contained not, as its Catholic equivalent would have done, relics, but instead a copy of the Bible and of Veit Dietrich's *Summarien.*

[91] See, for example, H. C. von Haebler, *Das Bild in der evangelischen Kirche,* (Berlin, 1957), 33 for a survey of the subject matter of epitaph altars in eastern Germany between 1560 and 1660.

[92] See, for example, P. Packeiser, 'Umschlagende Fülle als Autorität des Einen: Abundanz, Inversion und Zentrierung in den Tafelaltären Heinrich Füllmaurers', in Frank Büttner and Gabriele Wimböck (eds), *Das Bild als Autorität. Die normierende Kraft des Bildes* (Münster, 2004), 401–45, esp. 402; Peter Poscharsky, 'Das lutherische Bildprogramm' in ibid., *Die Bilder in den lutherischen Kirchen. Ikonographische Studien* (Munich, 1998), 21–34, esp. 21.

Fig. 5.10. Bernhard Ditterich and Sebastian Grösgen, altarpiece from the parish church of St Jakobi, Freiberg (Saxony), 1610.
Credit: © SLUB/Deutsche Fotothek.

not sculpted.[93] During the later sixteenth and seventeenth centuries, sculpted Crucifixion scenes became more common. Some, as we have seen, expressed a specifically Lutheran sense of confessional identity in the face of Calvinist threat, emphasizing Christ's real presence at communion.[94] Others depicted narrative scenes: the 1609 altarpiece from the Nikolaikirche in Lübben (Lower Lusatia), where Paul Gerhardt served from 1669 until his death in 1676, or the carved altarpiece from Freiberg's Jakobikirche, produced in 1610 by Bernhard Ditterich and financed by Elector Christian (Fig. 5.10). In these images, a multi-figured, coloured Crucifixion relief is surrounded by smaller scenes: the Last Supper below and the Burial of Christ above. The Lübben image also shows the Annunciation, Christ's Birth and typological precedents for the Crucifixion.[95] Garth's consecration

---

[93] On *Altarkreuze* see P. Graff, *Geschichte der Auflösung der alten gottesdienstlichen Formen in der evangelischen Kirche Deutschlands bis zum Eintritt der Aufklärung und des Rationalismus* (Göttingen, 1921), 100.
[94] For example, Finsterwalde, Chapter 3.
[95] For another example see Wolfgang Gericke, Heinrich-Volker Schlieff and Winfried Wendland, *Brandenburgische Dorfkirchen* (Berlin, 1975), 89. The altar at Lauta-Dorf, commissioned 1654 by the

sermon for the Freiberg altar gives an insight into the purpose of its images. The 'panels of beautiful images and carvings, painted with several colours, gold and silver' were intended, Garth stated, to awaken 'in the hearts of the communicants, and of other pious Christians, good and useful thoughts of the Last Supper of Christ and his bitter Suffering and Death, Resurrection and Ascension'.[96]

From the early seventeenth century onwards, some Lutheran altars abandoned such narrative compositions, and focused instead on isolated images of the suffering or dying Christ.[97] Plate 6 shows a remarkable example from the village church in Kemmen (Lower Lusatia), produced in 1649–52 by the local sculptor Andreas Schulze. The form is so odd that it looks as though this altar has been put together from left-over bits and pieces, though in fact only the resurrected Christ is a later addition.[98] This altarpiece is immediately identifiable as a Lutheran work because of the prominence of the depiction of the Last Supper on the predella, but above we see a fully three-dimensional, life-sized image of Christ flanked by angels bearing the instruments of the Passion. There is no narrative or allegory here—none of the didacticism characteristic of early Reformation images—but only a series of objects intended for devout contemplation, to encourage thoughts of Christ's suffering and sacrifice, and therefore of God's mercy.

Kemmen's church had been destroyed during the Thirty Years' War, and was rebuilt and refurbished, as a written statement concealed in the hollow of the angel's column records, by Georg Plank, chancellor of Lower Lusatia and lord of the local manor. Here we can draw a concrete link between Passion piety and the suffering of war. Planck kept a diary, and we know that he was deeply affected by the war. In particular, in 1626, his three-year-old son died from smallpox when the family was forced to flee from the approaching Swedish army. Only those, Plank wrote, who had experienced and survived domestic affliction (*Hauskreuz*) like his could properly understand the fear of God, but also his goodness and the hope that he provides in time of sorrow.[99] Religion served in this text as a coping strategy, helping Planck come to terms with his loss. The image that he chose to adorn the altar of his rebuilt church served a similar purpose: in Kemmen the devout

village congregation, shows the Last Supper, Crucifixion and Last Judgement crowned by angels bearing the instruments of Christ's Passion.

[96] Garth, *Christliche/Evangelische Altar=Weyhe*, Dii.

[97] For a discussion of the formal development of Saxon altarpieces see Heinrich Magirius, 'Die Werke der Freiberger Bildhauerfamilie Ditterich und die lutherische Altarkunst in Obersachsen zwischen 1550 und 1650', in Hans-Herbert Möller (ed.), *Die Hauptkirche Beatae Mariae Virginis in Wolfenbüttel* (Hannover, 1987), 169–78; W. Törmer-Balogh, 'Zur Entwicklung des protestantischen Altars in Sachsen während des 16. und beginnenden 17. Jahrhunderts. Versuch einer Typologie der Aufbaukonzepte' in Landesamt für Denkmalpflege Sachsen (ed.), *Denkmalpflege in Sachsen 1894–1994. 2. Teil* (Halle an der Saale, 1998), 411–36.

[98] F. Böhnisch, *Andreas Schultze—ein Niederlausitzer Bildhauer des 17. Jahrhunderts* (Cottbus, 1984), esp. 14–21.

[99] Gustav Wustmann, 'Das Tagebuch einer Leipziger Bürgerfamilie aus dem 16. und 17. Jahrhundert', *Schriften des Vereins für die Geschichte Leipzigs*, 2 (1878), 62–81, esp. 71–3. See also Benigna von Krusenstjern, 'Seliges Sterben und böser Tod: Tod und Sterben in der Zeit des Dreißigjährigen Krieges', in Benigna von Krusenstjern and Hans Medick (eds), *Zwischen Alltag und Katastrophe. Der Dreißigjährige Krieg aus der Nähe* (Göttingen, 1999), 469–96, here 492. Thank you to Dr Nikolas Funke for guiding me to this material.

Lutheran was encouraged, through contemplating the image of the Crucifixion, to remember the spiritual significance of suffering and death.

Kemmen is exceptional; Schulze's altar for the village church in nearby Freienhufen is more typical, with a conventional structure and crucifix framed by the figures of Moses and John the Baptist (Fig. 5.11).[100] But both reflect a trend towards altarpieces that depicted the Crucifixion in a simpler and more immediate way, a trend that owed its origins to both long-term changes in Lutheran piety and the more immediate trauma of war. In 1649, the year in which the Kemmen altarpiece was commissioned, Joseph Furttenbach the Younger published a tract written by his father, the *KirchenGebäw*, intended as a guide for the reconstruction of the churches in Augsburg that had been destroyed during the war. Furttenbach was concerned above all with the quick and cheap provision of a physical space that was suitable and comfortable for worship. In addition to the essential elements—altar, pulpit, pews—he also, however, included in his plan a chapel with an altar on which stood a 'beautiful crucifix' in a frame covered with black velvet. Here those waiting to receive communion could sit 'in a still, secluded and pleasing place...to remember with heartfelt sighs the most sacred suffering and death of our Saviour Jesus Christ'.[101] Furttenbach's tract was dedicated to Johann Valentin Andreae, who in his 1619 *Christianopolis*, had written of a crucifix 'so skilfully made as to move even the hardest of hearts'. Here, in Furttenbach's prescription for an *Andachtsbild*, the new piety and the needs of post-war Lutheran congregations coalesced.

During the later sixteenth and seventeenth centuries, Lutherans' encounter with the suffering Christ was also intensified by the return of particular iconographies on and around altars, for example the *Arma Christi* or *Leidenswerkzeuge*, the tools with which Christ's suffering had been inflicted and his victory achieved. Luther himself had not encouraged the visual depiction of the *Leidenswerkzeuge*—'I and all Christians must have the signs imprinted on our flesh and blood, not painted on the wall', he preached in 1538—but they were, by the late sixteenth century, a popular Lutheran theme.[102] Fig. 5.12 shows a wonderful example from Zittau in Upper Lusatia. It is a *Fastentuch*, a cloth commissioned in 1573 to cover the altar of the Johanniskirche during Lent. Such cloths were common during the Middle Ages, though few survive. Possibly inspired by the survival of a splendid late-medieval cloth, Zittau's Lutherans commissioned their own example, at a time during which the solemn celebration of Passiontide was becoming a part of Lutheran liturgical life.[103] The Zittau Lenten cloth shows in its centre the Crucifixion with Mary Magdalene, the Virgin Mary and John, and its broad border is filled with the *Arma Christi*. By the seventeenth century the *Arma Christi*

[100] Böhnisch, *Andreas Schultze*, 29–37.

[101] Joseph Furttenbach, *KirchenGebäu: Der Erste Theil…* (Augsburg: Schultes, 1649), n. p. See also Joseph Furttenbach, *Lebenslauff 1652–1664,* ed. Kaspar von Greyerz, Kim Siebenhüner and Roberto Zaugg (Cologne etc., 2013).

[102] WA 41, 304, 'Ein Christlicher schoener trost jnn allerley leiden und trübsal', 1535.

[103] CWB Zittau, A240, *Geschichte der Kirche zu St. Johannes*, fol.38r and v. For a general discussion of Zittau's Lutheran Lenten cloth see *Zittauer Geschichtsblätter*, 38 (2009), especially 18–26. For a brief discussion of Saxon Passion piety see Koch, 'Ausbau, Gefährdung und Festigung', 217–18.

Fig. 5.11. Andreas Schulze, altarpiece from the Village Church in Freienhufen (Großräschen), 1656–57.

Credit: Photo: author's own, with permission from the Ev. Pfarramt Klettwitz.

Fig. 5.12. Lenten Cloth (the so-called 'Kleines Zittauer Fastentuch'), Zittau, 1573.

Credit: © Abegg-Stiftung, CH-3132 Riggisberg, 1996 (photo: Christoph von Viràg), reproduced with the permission of the Städtische Museen Zittau.

could also be seen on pulpits, painted on walls and carved on altarpieces as at Kemmen and Freienhufen.

Another theme that gained new currency during the seventeenth century was the *Ecce Homo*, showing Christ bound, scourged and crowned with thorns.[104]

---

[104] Lutheran patrons also commissioned cycles of paintings showing Christ's Passion for the galleries of their churches—some examples date from the sixteenth and early seventeenth centuries, but

Like the crucifix, the *Ecce Homo* was intended to arouse compassion and to awaken thoughts of the viewer's own responsibility for Christ's Passion. A 1611 engraving from Nuremberg shows, for example, the *Ecce Homo* with the title 'Mirror of the Sufferings of Christ'. The accompanying poem begins 'Look into yourself, my soul. Look at your saviour'.[105] A half-length painted *Ecce Homo* adorns the altarpiece installed in 1623 in Bad Freienwalde (Oder), while sculpted, full-length figures occupied the shrines of the altarpieces created by Valentin Otte during the 1650s and 1660s for the Saxon churches of St Afra in Meißen, of Mittweida and of Leisnig.[106] The Meißen Altarpiece (Plate 7) contains some characteristically Lutheran motifs: the Last Supper in its predella, and Moses and John the Baptist, representatives of the Law and Gospel, flanking its third tier. In its centre is a life-sized image of the *Ecce Homo*, framed by elaborate columns and scenes of the *Noli me Tangere* and the Incredulity of Thomas. Beneath is a painted panel showing Christ in the Garden of Gethsemane and above is a crucifix. In comparison with some medieval images of the *Ecce Homo*, Christ's suffering here is not extreme. But as the congregant approaches the altar to receive communion he or she experiences the presence of this life-sized figure, his foot stepping forward out of the altar, his hands bound and his body covered in blood.

Abraham Werdemann's 1653 consecration sermon refers to the Meißen altar as a peace altar after the traumas of the Thirty Years' War, during which soldiers had turned the choir into a pigsty, and praises its subject matter: 'For here we see nothing heathen, nothing idolatrous, nothing obscene…but images, which are the laity's Bible, taken from sacred, divine Scripture'. Werdemann's invocation of the images of the Passion story emphasizes once again the role of the visual in arousing emotion and devotion:

> See how fervently and piteously He prays in His bloody sweat of fear on the Mount of Olives to his Heavenly Father? Look at His wounds and nails, how freely He shed His blood for us on the altar of the cross?…Whoever sees it with the eyes of faith must weep for pain and joy: for pain, because he through his sins prepared such terrible suffering for the Eternal Son of God; with joy, because Christ was awakened again for our salvation. Through external ornament man is easily moved to internal adornment of the heart.[107]

Ten years later the pastor in Jessen near Wittenberg echoed Simon Gedicke and preached a similar message when he consecrated his church's new altar. It was, he stated, a particular art

---

this iconography became more common after the Thirty Years' War. See R. Lieske, *Protestantische Frömmigkeit im Spiegel der kirchlichen Kunst des Herzogtums Württemberg* (Munich, 1973), 195; C. Unger, *Barocke Emporenmalerei in Dorfkirchen des Herzogtums Sachsen-Gotha. Bedeutung, Entstehung und Gestaltung* (Weimar, 2006), 64 ff.

[105] Ernst Koch, 'Passion und Affekte in der lutherischen Erbauungsliteratur des 17. Jahrhunderts' in Steiger (ed.), *Passion*, 509–18, here 510.

[106] Ernst Badstübner, *Stadtkirchen der Mark Brandenburg* (Berlin, 1982), 74; Mario Titze, 'Der Altar von Valentin Otte und die Kanzel von Abraham Conrad Buchau in der Stadtkirche Unser Lieben Frauen in Mittweida', *Sächsische Heimatblätter: Zeitschrift für sächsische Geschichte, Denkmalpflege, Natur und Umwelt*, 55 (3) (2009), 222–36.

[107] Abraham Werdemann, *Altar Afranum, Oder Schrifftmessige Einweihungs-Predigt des Neuen Altars…* (Dresden: Bergen, 1653), C v and D iii v.

when one can express the emotions, and thereby move the viewer's heart and soul somewhat: So God is to be especially thanked that through sculpture and painting biblical histories, especially the bitter suffering and death [of Christ], can be so finely depicted that whenever pious Christians see them, they feel as a result of them good thoughts and movement of the heart.[108]

That such representations of the *Ecce Homo* and of other moments in Christ's Passion did, as these pastors hoped, provoke empathetic sorrow is suggested by a vignette from Grimmelhausen's *Simplicissiumus*. As pageboy to the Swedish commander in Hannau, Simplicissimus is shown around an art collection by a 'noble gentleman'. 'Among his paintings', the hero comments, 'there was none I liked better than an *Ecce Homo* because it was painted in such a way as to arouse the compassion of those who looked at it'.[109]

CONCLUSION

To characterize Lutheran art as an emotional blank and to refer to its remoteness, or to conceive of it as dry and intended only to teach the basic precepts of the faith is misguided. What was missing during the early decades of the Reformation was not an awareness of images' psychological power—Lutheran willingness to use visual propaganda demonstrates this beyond doubt—but rather a desire to harness that power fully in the service of true piety. With authors such as Johann Arndt this desire returned. Images could, Arndt and his contemporaries believed, move the heart to proper devotion. External images could create internal images and the presence of physical objects could awaken the senses, the gateways to the soul. Such convictions, which drew on age-old valorisations of the sense of sight, were articulated by Lutheran authors as they sought to defend religious images from Calvinist attack. They also, however, owed much to a new willingness on the part of Lutheran pastors and theologians to borrow both from medieval mystical and contemporary Catholic sources in their quests for spiritual and moral renewal. The new willingness to harness images' emotive power for devotional purposes found visual expression not only in book illustration and in the widespread use of emblems but also in the re-articulation of pre-Reformation Passion images such as Görlitz's Holy Sepulchre and in the production of new painted and sculpted images, for example on Crucifixion altarpieces. Sometimes, as at Kemmen (Plate 6), these broad devotional shifts were given very personal inflections by the trauma and suffering of the Thirty Years' War.

---

[108] Christianus Parneman, *Consecrationum Quaternio, Das ist/Vierfache Einweyhung...* (Wittenberg: Hartmann, 1663), F2r. For the Gedicke text on which this is based see above, 109–10.

[109] Grimmelshausen, *The Adventures of Simplicissimus*, 77. Much later, in 1719, Nikolaus Ludwig, Graf von Zinzendorf, had a similar response to an *Ecce Homo* by Domenico Felti in the picture gallery at the *Stadtschloß* in Düsseldorf. Zinzendorf, who was in Düsseldorf on a *Kavaliersreise* through Germany, the Netherlands and France, recorded in his diary that 'Unter vielen Hunderten der herrlichsten Porträts auf der Galerie...zog das einzige Ecce Homo [sein] Auge und Gemüt [an]'. Geiger, *Nikolaus Ludwig Graf von Zinzendorf*, 59.

By the seventeenth century Passion iconography was deeply embedded in Lutheran confessional culture. The crucifix continued to function as a confessional marker until at least the middle of the century. In 1642, for example, Superintendent Nicodemus Lappe consecrated a splendid Crucifixion altar in the Oberkirche in Arnstadt. After lamenting the destruction of the Thirty Years' War, Lappe described the altar as a rebuttal of Calvinist teachers, 'who tolerate in their churches no carved, painted or in other ways artistically-made histories and images'.[110] By this point, however, the crucifix was also a Lutheran *Andachtsbild*. Sermons, prayer collections, Passion treatises and hymns encouraged individual contemplation of Christ's Passion, inviting their readers and hearers to imagine themselves present at Golgotha, falling at Christ's feet, embracing his cross and entering into his wounds. The Passion piety of Catharina Regina von Greiffenberg, with its emphasis on bodily suffering and on compassion, provides a particularly spectacular example, but von Greiffenberg's writings reflected the devotional preoccupations of the period. Images—printed, painted, sculpted—gave visual expression to these shifts in Passion piety. Allegorical images did not disappear, neither did narrative Crucifixion scenes. Yet, significant changes occurred between the era of Lucas Cranach and that of Andreas Schulze and Valentin Otte: sculpture, despite all its idolatrous connotations, returned; there was a new focus on Christ's physical suffering; and Lutherans made new use of traditional iconographies, in particular the *Arma Christi* and the *Ecce Homo*. In devotional terms, it was a relatively short step from the works of Schulze and Otte to the 'lonely' crucifixes of the baroque, examined in the final chapters of this book, that borrowed from contemporary Catholic models and placed the encounter of the individual believer with the crucified Christ absolutely centre stage.[111]

---

[110] Nicodemus Lappe, *Inauguratio Renocati Altari Arnstadiensis...* (1642), C iiir.

[111] Peter Poscharsky, 'Ikonographische Beobachtungen an lutherischen Altarretabeln in Sachsen bis zum Ende des Barock', in Jens Bulisch (ed.), *Kirchliche Kunst in Sachsen: Festgabe für Hartmut Mai zum 65. Geburtstag* (Beucha, 2002), 111–28, here 124.

6

Visual Commemoration

The late sixteenth and early seventeenth centuries constituted a turning point in the history of Lutheran piety. As we saw in Chapter 5, a new 'spirituality of desire', a longing for immediacy and intimacy in the individual Christian's encounter with Christ, shaped both verbal and visual accounts of the Passion. The commemorative practice that lay at the very heart of the Christian tradition—reflection on Christ's redeeming sacrifice—was transformed as a result. This chapter turns from sacred memory to collective or social memory, exploring the ways in which Lutherans used images to shape understandings of their more recent past.[1] We know that Lutheran commemorative practices were not, as one might expect from a confession that privileged the Word so highly, dematerialized: they revolved around images and rituals as well as preaching and printed texts. History writing, from civic histories to martyrologies and the monumental work of the Magdeburg Centuriators, of course played an important role in legitimating the Lutheran church and in creating a sense of confessional belonging amongst its educated elite.[2] By the seventeenth century, however, such written histories constituted only one part of a rich commemorative culture. In 1617 and 1630, at a time of acute political crisis, Wittenberg's theologians and the Saxon Elector Johann Georg I instituted centennial celebrations of the Ninety-Five Theses and Augsburg Confession. Jubilees multiplied thereafter, from the annual observance of Reformation Day at the Dresden court to the numerous municipal and parochial celebrations organized by local Lutheran pastors. Throughout, images served to reinforce the construction of the historical past offered in printed texts and preached sermons: commemorative coins and medals were struck in 1617 and 1630; painted and printed images

---

[1] For a useful general overview of the huge literature on memory studies see Astrid Erll, *Memory in Culture*, tr. Sara Young (Basingstoke, 2011). Gadi Algazi, 'Forget Memory: Some Critical Remarks on Memory, Forgetting and History', in Sebastian Scholz, Gerald Schwedler and Kai-Michael Sprenger (eds), *Damnatio in Memoria: Deformation und Gegenkonstruktionen in der Geschichte* (Vienna, Cologne and Weimar, 2014), 25–34 and 'Forum: Memory before Modernity: Cultures and Practices in Early Modern Germany', *German History* 33 (1) (2015), 100–22.

[2] See, for example, Bruce Gordon (ed.), *Protestant History and Identity in Sixteenth-Century Europe* (Aldershot, 1998); Susanne Rau, *Geschichte und Konfession: städtische Geschichtsschreibung und Erinnerungskultur im Zeitalter von Reformation und Konfessionalisierung in Bremen, Breslau, Hamburg und Köln* (Hamburg, 2002); Thomas Fuchs, 'Reformation, Tradition und Geschichte. Erinnerungsstrategien der reformatorischen Bewegung', in Joachim Eibach and Marcus Sandl (eds), *Protestantische Identität und Erinnerung. Von der Reformation bis zur Bürgerrechtsbewegung in der DDR* (Göttingen, 2003), 71–89; Matthias Pohlig, *Zwischen Gelehrsamkeit und konfessioneller Identitätsstiftung: Lutherische Kirchen- und Universalgeschichtsschreibung 1546–1617* (Tübingen 2007); Kerstin Armborst-Weihs and Judith Becker (eds), *Toleranz und Identität: Geschichtsschreibung und Geschichtsbewusstsein zwischen religiösem Anspruch und historischer Erfahrung* (Göttingen, 2010).

depicted the handing-over of the Augsburg Confession; representations of Luther and Melanchthon multiplied; and parish churches acquired their own series of pastor portraits. Images, just like texts, could, it seems, be 'entrusted with the charge of collective memory'.[3]

With temporal distance from the Reformation, second- and third-generation Lutherans certainly developed a strong sense of history, and recognized its potential for reinforcing religious cohesion. History writing, Reformation jubilees, and the visual depiction of the church's key figures and events all served to create and to nurture a Lutheran identity, to build some kind of collective self-understanding, whether at the level of the local congregation, the town, the territory, or the supra-regional confession. Yet, we should not assume that this process, this verbal and visual construction of the past, resulted in a stable and homogenous sense of what it meant to be Lutheran. Normative invocations of Lutheranism's foundational history and defining doctrines and rituals in fact masked variations and instabilities in confessional culture.[4] The centennial celebrations of 1617, for example, papered over Electoral Saxony's ambivalent political situation: representing itself as the motherland of the Reformation, the territory had nonetheless refused to join the Protestant Union in 1608. Likewise invocations of the Augsburg Confession implied a theological unity within the Lutheran church that had never been fully achieved.[5] This chapter focuses most of its attention, therefore, *not* on iconic representations of the 'founding fathers' of the Reformation and the events of 1530, but rather on one very specific type of Lutheran memory work: the commemoration of the dead.

The commemoration of the dead was 'the most reflective and past-minded of activities'.[6] It was always a matter for both the individual and the community: here personal memories and experiences of loss were inevitably shaped by broader cultural expectations. The Reformation, as we know, transformed these cultural expectations, rewriting the rules that had underpinned late-medieval religious commemoration. Funerary images, rituals, and texts no longer served a salvific purpose; they no longer invited intercessory prayer or sought to speed the deceased's passage through purgatory. Commemoration of the dead continued within the evangelical confessions, and indeed flourished during the seventeenth century. But it was now 'directed entirely towards the world of the living', towards the bereaved

---

[3] Christopher Wood, *Forgery, Replica, Fiction: Temporalities of German Renaissance Art* (Chicago, 2008), 77. Susan Boettcher, 'Von der Trägheit der Memoria. Cranachs Lutheraltarbilder im Zusammenhang der evangelischen Luther-Memoria im späten 16. Jahrhundert' in Eibach and Sandl (eds), *Protestantische Identität*, 47–69; Wolfgang Flügel, *Konfession und Jubiläum: zur Institutionalisierung der lutherischen Gedenkkultur in Sachsen 1617–1830* (Leipzig, 2005); Stefan Dornheim, *Der Pfarrer als Arbeiter am Gedächtnis. Lutherische Erinnerungskultur in der Frühen Neuzeit zwischen Religion und sozialer Kohäsion* (Leipzig, 2013).

[4] See, for example, von Greyerz et al. (eds), *Interkonfessionalität*; Andreas Pietsch and Barbara Stollberg-Rilinger (eds), *Konfessionelle Ambiguität. Uneindeutigkeit und Verstellung als religiöse Praxis in der Frühen Neuzeit* (Gütersloh, 2013), especially Barbara Stollberg-Rilinger, 'Einleitung', 9–26.

[5] Dornheim, *Der Pfarrer als Arbeiter*, 41. On the persistence of theological plurality in the aftermath of the Formula of Concord see Irene Dingel, *Concordia controversa. Die öffentlichen Diskussionen um das lutherische Konkordienwerk am Ende des 16. Jahrhunderts* (Gütersloh, 1996).

[6] Bruce Gordon and Peter Marshall (eds), *The Place of the Dead in Late Medieval and Early Modern Europe* (Cambridge, 2000), 5–7.

and his or her community.[7] Scholarship tends to suggest that the Reformation
brought about a secularization or naturalization of commemoration; that when
Protestants remembered their dead they were concerned above all with reputation
and fame. Recent studies of the memorials constructed for Germany's Lutheran
nobles during the confessional age emphasize the theme of representation: the
instrumentalization of epitaphs for the display of social prestige and confessional
orthodoxy.[8] The importance of such representation is undeniable. But the case
studies presented here, which follow the commemorative patronage of two families
from Saxony's lesser nobility *across* the hiatus of the Reformation, suggest that
Lutheran memorials, like their medieval predecessors, not only fulfilled social roles
but also met individual needs. Lutheran commemorative culture provided, this
chapter will argue, a visual as well as a verbal language that allowed patrons not
only to express social and religious distinction but also to narrate grief and sometimes even to mitigate death's power to separate the living and the dead.

Studying the commemorative patronage of the nobility also provides a way of
addressing broader questions about Lutheran attitudes towards visual relics of the
pre-Reformation past. As we saw in Chapter 2, Lutheranism displayed a remarkable 'preserving power': hundreds of medieval altarpieces, statues, and paintings
remained intact and *in situ*, especially in the northern and eastern parts of the
Empire. This 'preserving power' can be rationalized in all kinds of ways: Lutherans
wanted to display religious moderation; images were matters of indifference to
salvation; some could be reinterpreted to fit with evangelical teaching. These pre-
Reformation images were also, however, bearers of collective memory. For the
nobility, dynastic memory was, of course, key. Lordship was justified through
historical continuity, and this continuity was demonstrated through the commissioning of family trees, series of ancestral portraits and written histories. Dynastic
memory cut across both the spiritual caesura of the Reformation and the social
and economic traumas of the Thirty Years' War. It dictated not only the survival
of particular religious monuments during the early decades of the Reformation
but also their long-term preservation. By the later sixteenth century, some nobles
were paying close attention to the religious art that they had inherited: in the
churches over which they exercised patronal rights they restored damaged images,
re-set them in new frames and even augmented them with collections of medieval
paintings and sculptures acquired from elsewhere. Through such anachronistic
refurbishments they honoured their families' cultural heritage. The visual evidence
presented in this chapter also suggests that although this interest in continuity,
this awareness of history, has traditionally been associated with the clergy and
nobility, it in fact extended further down the social scale, at least to the level of the
mercantile elite and guilds.

---

[7] Doreen Zerbe, 'Memorialkunst im Wandel. Die Ausbildung eines lutherischen Typus des Grab-
und Gedächtnismals im 16. Jahrhundert', in Jäggi and Staecker (eds), *Archäologie der Reformation*,
117–63, here 124. See also Koerner, *The Reformation of the Image*, 388.
[8] Inga Brinkmann, *Grabdenkmäler*, 11; Meys, *Memoria und Bekenntnis*, 86. Otto Gerhard Oexle,
'Memoria und Memorialbild', in Karl Schmid and Joachim Wollasch (eds), *Memoria. Der geschichtliche
Zeugniswert des liturgischen Gedenkens im Mittelalter* (Munich, 1984), 384–440, here 427.

REMEMBERING THE REFORMATION:
THE ROLE OF IMAGES

During the early seventeenth century, Reformation commemoration became increasingly important. This was due in part to the fact that the founding figures and events of the early evangelical movement had by this time passed from living memory. Above all, however, it was because this was a time of crisis for German Lutheranism. The 1617 jubilee was marked against the backdrop of the political and confessional tensions that led in 1618 to the outbreak of the Thirty Years' War: Bavaria's occupation of Donauwörth (1607), the formation of the Protestant Union and Catholic League (1608–09), and the Jülich-Cleves dispute (1610–14). In the churches of all members of the Protestant Union, 2 November 1617 was given over to prayers of thanksgiving for the Reformation. In Electoral Saxony, the desire of Wittenberg's elite theology professors to celebrate the 'first Lutheran century' was taken up with alacrity by Johann Georg I. The Elector maintained Saxony's political neutrality until 1620 (when he entered the war on the side of the Catholic Emperor), but he decreed a three-day celebration in 1617 'because the light of the sacred Gospel has shone brightly in our electorate and territory for a hundred years'.[9] Again in 1630, in the immediate aftermath of the 1629 Edict of Restitution, Johann Georg decreed a three-day celebration for the centennial of the Augsburg Confession, with bells, sermons, communion, prayers, and hymns. The 'Unaltered Confession' was to be read from Saxony's pulpits. It was to be made known to everyone, so that the people were incited to greater 'Christian steadfastness'.[10] The Saxon jubilees provided a model for those in other territories, though not all the Empire's Lutherans could celebrate in such splendid fashion: in Berlin, for example, the 100-year anniversary of the 1539 church ordinance and of the institution of evangelical communion was observed by Lutheran preachers not only in the face of military trauma—the city was occupied by Swedish troops in August of 1639—but also under the watchful eye of Brandenburg's Calvinist Elector.[11]

The 1617 and 1630 centennials awakened a widespread interest in the history of the Reformation, and generated not only copious writings but also commemorative medals, coins, and prints. Figure 6.1 shows, for example, an image commissioned in 1617 by the Ernestine Duke Johann Ernst of Sachsen-Eisenach for the Georgenkirche in Eisenach. Within an elaborate frame, crowned by Johann Ernst's coat of arms and by allegorical figures, two painted panels sit side-by-side. The left-hand one shows the handing over of the Augsburg Confession: representatives of the

---

[9] Quoted in Reiner Gross, *Geschichte Sachsens* (Leipzig, 2001), 95. See also Flügel, *Konfession und Jubiläum*; Wolfgang Flügel, 'Zeitkonstrukte im Reformationsjubiläum', in Winfried Müller (ed.), *Das historische Jubiläum. Genese, Ordnungsleistung und Inszenierungsgeschichte eines institutionellen Mechanismus* (Münster, 2004), 77–99; Hans-Jürgen Schönstädt, *Antichrist, Weltheilsgeschehen und Gottes Werkzeug. Römische Kirche, Reformation und Luther im Spiegel des Reformationsjubiläums 1617* (Wiesbaden, 1978), esp. 10–85; Angelika Marsch, *Bilder zur Augsburger Konfession und ihren Jubiläen* (Weißenhorn, 1980).

[10] Marsch, *Bilder*, 59 ff.

[11] Walter Delius, 'Berliner Reformationsjubiläum1639', *Jahrbuch für Berlin-Brandenburgische Kirchengeschichte*, 40 (1965), 86–136.

Fig. 6.1. Commemorative image for the Reformation Anniversary of 1617 from the parish church of St Georgen, Eisenach.

Credit: © SLUB/Deutsche Fotothek.

Lutheran estates kneel before Charles V. Behind this central group we see the interior of a church filled with small-scale representations of the ritual life of a Lutheran congregation, including not only communion, baptism, and preaching but also catechization, music-making, and marriage. The right-hand panel shows Luther and Hus distributing communion to three Saxon electors. The Eisenach painting was not the earliest to commemorate, against a backdrop of Lutheran church ritual, the events of 1530.[12] But such images were given a new impetus by the anniversaries of 1617 and 1630. In a print by the Saxon engraver Johann Dürr from 1630, which copies the Eisenach painting closely, the Saxon chancellor Dr Christian Beyer reads from the Augsburg Confession, open at the passage from St Paul that underpins Lutheran teaching on justification (Romans 3:28). To the right is a representation of communion, taking place before a table bearing biblical quotations and a list of Luther's writings on the Eucharist. Christ's foot emerges from beneath the table, trampling death, the devil, and the names of the Wittenberg

---

[12] Wolfgang Brückner, 'Die lutherische Gattung evangelischer Bekenntnisbilder und ihre ikonographischen Ableitungen der Gnade vermittelnden Erlösungs- und Sakramentslehre', in Büttner and Wimböck, *Das Bild als Autorität*, 303–41, here 305–7.

reformer's key opponents.[13] There were numerous other variations on this commemorative theme, images that presented the key events and figures in Lutheran history, and conveyed, in various ways, the central teachings of the church. As a genre, they offer a wonderful insight into seventeenth-century attempts to create a cohesive Lutheran confessional identity based around history, doctrine, and ritual.

THE COMMEMORATION OF THE DEAD

For a historian, images of the Augsburg Confession (*Bekenntnisbilder*) are seductive sources, purporting to offer a tidy summary of what made Lutherans Lutheran. But they are, of course, normative: they show what Lutherans should have believed and how they should have behaved. To get beyond this idealized version of seventeenth-century Lutheranism, we can turn to another commemorative genre, the epitaph. These 'true memorials', monuments to the dead, offer, it seems to me, a much richer insight into the pluralism of Lutheran commemorative culture with all its variations and instabilities.[14] The cult of the dead had, of course, shaped the visual culture and ritual life of the pre-Reformation church decisively. From Antiquity onwards, memorial images of many kinds had made the dead present amongst the living, testifying to their social and legal status and binding them into a system of religious *memoria*.[15] Medieval epitaphs reminded their viewers to pray for the souls of those they depicted, often incorporating written injunctions to 'ora pro me' or 'ora pro eo'. Wealthy patrons gave not only memorial images but also perpetual masses in order to guarantee a continuous cycle of prayer that would speed their soul's passage through purgatory. Here the Reformation undoubtedly brought about a profound transformation. With the abrogation of purgatory and of intercessory prayer the soteriological link between the living and dead was broken. The living could no longer aid the dead, who must now make their journey into the beyond alone. The living could also no longer themselves receive spiritual benefit from the commemorative practices that they performed.[16]

In theological terms, the change wrought by the Reformation was huge. Yet, the impulse to commemorate the dead was far too deeply ingrained to be dislodged by mere transformations in dogma. It was an aspect of religious culture that went much deeper than any confessional divide.[17] The Reformation certainly did not dampen patrons' desire to provide visual memorials for themselves and their families. Even though actual burials were gradually, from the late fifteenth century onwards, redirected from the vicinity of urban parish churches to cemeteries on the edges of towns, Lutheran churches were still full of epitaphs that, through their images and inscriptions, made the dead present amongst the living. Altarpieces and epitaphs even continued to depict the living and dead together, in order to

---

[13] Brückner, 'Die lutherische Gattung', 332.
[14] Pierre Nora, *Rethinking France*, vol. 1 (Chicago, 2001), XIX.
[15] Oexle, 'Memoria und Memorialbild'.
[16] For an overview see Gordon and Marshall (eds), *The Place of the Dead*, here 4.
[17] Oexle, 'Memoria und Memorialbild', 429; Boettcher, 'Von der Trägheit der Memoria', 68.

demonstrate continuity of lineage and as a reflection of affective bonds.[18] Despite extensive transformations in the liturgical commemoration of the dead, they remained visible within the church.[19] We must ask, however, how far the functions of these memorials to the dead changed as a result of the Reformation. The dead were certainly still present, but was their commemoration now directed, as a number of art-historical studies have suggested, entirely towards the world of the living, offering only a representative confession of faith?

In his 1594 *Adels-Spiegel*, Cyriacus Spangenberg, one of the most important of Luther's later pupils, wrote that epitaphs were intended 'not only to thank, honour and commemorate the dead' but also to incite others to imitate the virtues and honourable deeds of their forefathers.[20] Spangenberg's justifications were entirely traditional, and reflected the functions that memorials had performed since Antiquity. They were to honour and commemorate: 'Gedächtnis' here refers to the ability to make the absent present and to remember it well. They were to inspire others to virtue and to honourable deeds. They were also, of course, representations of political and religious power and legitimacy. Oliver Meys and Inga Brinkmann have undertaken detailed studies of the memorials constructed for Lutheran nobles during the sixteenth and seventeenth centuries, Meys focusing on territorial rulers and Brinkmann on both the *reichsunmittelbar* (immediate) and the *landsässig* (resident) nobility (those who had an imperial prince as their overlord). Both studies emphasize, entirely correctly, the importance of epitaphs for representation. Their presence instrumentalized church space for the purposes of lordly self-depiction.[21] Patrons' need for portrayal, for the legitimation of both secular and spiritual lord-ship, should not, however, lead us to conclude that these memorials fulfilled *only* social and political needs. As the case studies presented here will show, some Lutheran memorials chronicled emotional loss in extraordinary ways, and even more standard memorials offered individual consolation: trust in the redeeming power of Christ's sacrifice, and in the promise of bodily resurrection and reunion with loved ones in the hereafter.[22] Representation was, I will suggest, only part of the story.

The two families examined here were both members of Saxony's *landsässig* nobil-ity, a group whose history and contribution to the creation of Lutheran confes-sional culture has only recently started to receive the attention that it deserves. The von Einsiedel had their ancestral seat at Gnandstein near Leipzig; the von Schleinitz near Meißen. In both cases, memorials that span the period from the late Middle Ages to the seventeenth century survive, alongside at least some textual sources. The most interesting of the von Einsiedel memorials were located in the village churches in Gnandstein and Prießnitz, while the von Schleinitz effectively colon-ized Meißen's main parish church, St Afra, for their dynastic commemoration. In Gnandstein and Prießnitz, the von Einsiedel served as *Patronatsherren* (patrons):

[18] Oexle, 'Memoria und Memorialbild', 427–8.   [19] Dornheim, *Der Pfarrer als Arbeiter,* 50.
[20] Cyriacus Spangenberg, *Ander Teil des Adels-Spiegel* (Schmalkalden: Michel Schmück, 1594), 287. See Müller, 'Repräsentationen des Luthertums', 223.
[21] Brinkmann, *Grabdenkmäler*, 350.
[22] Dornheim, *Der Pfarrer als Arbeiter*, 54–5 gives some nice references from *Begräbnisliedern*.

they were responsible for appointing pastors and other church officials; they administered the church's finances and maintained its structure and appearance; they played a part in supervising the religious education of its congregation through visitations.[23] In return, they expected to be prayed for, to have a place of honour reserved for their participation in worship (usually a *Herrschaftsloge*) and to be buried alongside the other members of their dynasty inside the church.[24] Noble piety could therefore, as we shall see, play a decisive role in determining the appearance of local churches.

THE NOBILITY: THE VON EINSIEDEL

The von Einsiedel were amongst Saxony's most important noble families. From the late fourteenth century onwards they developed their territorial lordship around the castles of Gnandstein and Kohren. From the mid-fifteenth century onwards, they were closely linked to the court. Heinrich von Einsiedel (1435–1507) served both Duke Wilhelm III and Elector Ernst, and after the Leipzig Division of 1485 he became a key advisor at the Albertine court. The von Einsiedel, like most of their peers, had a long history of church patronage. In typical pre-Reformation fashion, Heinrich von Einsiedel constructed a castle chapel at the family's ancestral seat in Gnandstein, endowed it with three altars and chaplains to recite perpetual masses and commissioned three splendid carved altarpieces that still survive today. His eldest son, Haubold von Einsiedel (*c.*1462–1522), canon in Naumburg, restored the village church in Gnandstein where members of the family were buried.[25]

Haubold is known in the literature as 'the first Lutheran of his house'.[26] He spent the last four years of his life as advisor to Elector Friedrich III, serving him during the Wittenberg 'disturbances' of 1521–22.[27] While Haubold's Lutheranism was, like that of his patron Friedrich, at best incipient, the evangelical convictions of his two brothers, Heinrich Hildebrand and Heinrich Abraham, cannot be doubted. They were in personal contact with Luther, who famously wrote in a letter to Spalatin in 1541 that 'in this century the Einsiedels are a rare and unique light in the very confused darkness of the nobility'.[28] In keeping with evangelical teaching, Heinrich Hildebrand in particular devoted considerable attention to

---

[23] Schattkowsky, *Zwischen Rittergut, Residenz und Reich*, 139.

[24] Gotthard Kießling, *Der Herrschaftstand. Aspekte repräsentativer Gestaltung im evangelischen Kirchenbau* (Munich, 1995).

[25] Marius Winzeler and Janos Stekovics, *Burg und Kirche. Christliche Kunst in Gnandstein* (Halle an der Saale, 1994); Marius Winzeler, 'Burgkapelle, Patronatskirche, Familiengrablege – Tradition und Wandel der Adelsfrömmigkeit und ihres künstlerischen Ausdrucks im 16. und 17. Jahrhundert. Das Beispiel der Familie von Einsiedel', in Katrin Keller and Josef Matzerath (eds), *Geschichte des sächsischen Adels* (Cologne etc., 1997), 207–24, esp. 209–12. See also Sächsisches Staatsarchiv, *Die Familie von Einsiedel. Stand, Aufgaben und Perspektiven der Adelsforschung in Sachsen. Kolloquium des Sächsischen Staatsarchivs/Staatsarchiv Leipzig in Zusammenarbeit mit der Universität Leipzig 9. November 2005* (Leipzig, 2007).

[26] *Die Familie von Eindsiedel*, 75.

[27] Ibid., 90. Krentz, *Ritualwandel und Deutungshoheit*, 197 ff.

[28] Quoted in Winzeler, 'Burgkapelle', 214–15, n. 23.

charitable activities, founding a hospital and a fund for the support of local villa-gers.[29] Yet, the Reformation did not bring to an end the family's patronage of religious art. The Gnandstein village church contains a painted epitaph altar for Heinrich Hildebrand (d.1557), and a carved sandstone, marble and serpentine epitaph mounted on the wall for Johannes von Einsiedel (d.1582). In the castle chapel today is another epitaph for Magdalena von Einsiedel, unmarried *Hofmeisterin* (mistress of the court) to the Saxon Elector, though this was originally displayed in Altenburg where she died in 1592.[30]

As we have seen, the Reformation rewrote the rules that had underpinned the culture of late-medieval religious commemoration. Whereas Heinrich von Einsiedel had dedicated three-quarters of the value of his altar donations to funding perpetual masses, the evangelical epitaphs in Gnandstein had no such liturgical *memoria* associated with them.[31] Yet, to conclude, as the literature has tended to do, that such monuments were now directed 'entirely towards this world' is to underestimate their significance. All three of these epitaphs, like numerous other Lutheran examples from the second half of the sixteenth century, testify to the true, evangelical piety of the deceased; they also, however, through both their images and their inscriptions, express their donors' desire for consolation, and their hope for the salvation and eternal happiness of the members of the von Einsiedel family that they depict. Heinrich Hildebrand's epitaph altar has portraits of the deceased and his family in the predella. In the main field is the Resurrection, and above, in the apex, the Last Judgement. The whole gives visual expression to hope directed at the hereafter, at the believer's resurrection and entry into heaven. Johannes' epitaph, probably the work of the sculptor Christoph Walther II, depicts the deceased and his wife and daughter (its donor) kneeling in prayer before Christ's cross. Above is a depiction of Christ's baptism, a promise of the acceptance of sinful mankind by God made possible by the crucifixion. Magdalena's also focuses on the hope of resurrection and salvation, and a plaque beneath ends with a plea for God to grant her a 'joyful resurrection'.

This desire for consolation and hope for future happiness was visualized in much more interesting ways in the jewel in the crown of von Einsiedel commemorative patronage: Prießnitz village church (Plate 8). This tiny village church was extended and richly furnished by its patron Hans von Einsiedel in honour of his beloved wife Anna, who had died aged 34 in 1616. Anna was buried, in keeping with the traditions of noble patrons, in the crypt immediately beneath the altar alongside various other family members. Hans himself designed the church's rich visual and textual programme: he was, according to a report placed in the capsule on the church's tower in 1615, a 'God-fearing and learned man and an excellent theologian'.[32] He was certainly helped by his pastor, Georg Thryllitzsch, whose portrait appears on the church's altarpiece, but an inventory of Hans' possessions drawn up after his death in confirms his reputation for piety and learning: it

[29] Ibid., 215–16.   [30] Winzeler and Stekovics, *Burg und Kirche*, 24–5, 27, 79–80.
[31] Winzeler, 'Burgkapelle', 222.   [32] *Neue sächsische Kirchengalerie* 11, col. 951.

mentions, for example, two prayerbooks that he 'used daily', and lists numerous works of Protestant church history and theology.[33]

The church's altarpiece shows in its central, painted panel the Last Supper, with Christ's resurrection above.[34] To the left and right, flanked by Corinthian columns of imitation marble, we see Christ as Saviour and Moses. Beneath the donor and his family kneel in prayer, with painted scenes of the Annunciation and Birth of Christ to either side. The most unusual element of the altar is its predella, which bears a long inscription on its front and can be opened to reveal two paintings: the Sacrifice of Isaac and the Raising of Lazarus. The pulpit shows on its door the Fall of Man and Christ Teaching in the Temple, on its steps the Annunciation and Jacob's Ladder, and on its main body the resurrected Christ and the four evangelists. Hans would have looked down at the altar and pulpit from his *Herrschaftsloge*, adorned with more than 90 painted glass panels and decorated inside with scenes from Christ's life and Passion and outside with inscriptions.

Until its removal in 1840, the focal point of the church was a painted epitaph for Anna. On a wooden table, approximately 2.5 m long and 1 m wide, lay a double panel, now displayed on the wall of the church (Plate 9).[35] Inside this double panel is an angel, the name of the painter ('Johann de Perr Antwerp fecit') and an inscription composed by Hans.[36] The outside shows Christ holding the sleeping Anna on his lap, while angels crown her and bring flowers and a palm branch. According to the inscription on the altar's predella, Anna's last words were 'my heart is enclosed in Christ's heart', and these words adorn her neck on the epitaph. The iconography of this image is unusual, if not unique, though the sentiment that it visualizes is well documented. In his preface to a 1542 collection of burial hymns, Luther wrote that the coffin was nothing other than 'the lap of our Lord Christ', and some memorial texts, for example a poem for the Wittenberg citizen Georg Niemeck who died in 1561, made use of this image of rest in Christ's lap.[37] Above the horizontal painted panels was a cupola. The commemoration of Anna extended to two opening panels, probably intended to hang on the walls of the church (Plates 10 and 11). The first shows on its inside Anna as an exemplary Lutheran mother at prayer with her children, and her marriage blessed by Christ, and on its outside the Last Judgement. On the side of the saved we see Hans and Anna and a second couple, probably his or her parents. The second panel shows Anna at prayer, with an inscription emphasizing her love of God's Word. Opposite is a representation of her dead body, surrounded by angels, and outside is Jacob's Ladder.

[33] SStAL, RG Prießnitz, 20523, Nr. 192 (Inventar nach dem Tod des Hans (Johann) von Einsiedel).
[34] On the artist see Andreas Priever, 'Johann de Perre, die "Auferstehung Christi" und der Stein des Anstoßes. Eine Fallstudie zum Bildergebrauch in der lutherischen Orthodoxie', *Zeitschrift für Kunstgeschichte*, 70 (4) (2007), 513–44, especially 518–20.
[35] *Neue sächsische Kirchengalerie* 11, col. 949. The inscriptions are given in Hartmut Mai, 'Der Einfluß der Reformation auf Kirchenbau und kirchliche Kunst', in Junghans (ed.), *Das Jahrhundert der Reformation in Sachsen*, 167–8.
[36] On Johann de Perre see Gustav Wustmann, *Beiträge zur Geschichte der Malerei in Leipzig vom 15. bis zum 17. Jahhundert* (Leipzig, 1879), 57. He was also responsible for the altarpiece in the Nikolaikirche in Leipzig. See Schmidt, 'Die Innenausstattung', 229.
[37] Zerbe, 'Memorialkunst im Wandel', 123.

This church is, of course, a site for representation and display. The quality of the painting, the extensive use of gold leaf, the complex iconographical programme and above all the opening epitaph, wall panels and predella (for which there is no possible liturgical justification), give the whole ensemble the feel of a *Kunstkammer*. This was a place where Hans, as the church's patron, could display his taste and erudition.[38] This was in no sense, however, a 'secularized' memorial. We might think of it as the visual equivalent of a funeral sermon—we know that one was preached for Anna, although it seems that no copy survives.[39] Like a funeral sermon, the church presents the deceased as an example of good behaviour. Spangenberg's belief that epitaphs should incite others to imitate the virtues and honourable deeds of their forefathers finds visual and verbal expression here. The inscription on the altar's predella records that Anna was the mother of six children, whom she admonished to prayer and piety. One of the opening wall panels shows her at prayer with these children, while the other depicts her alone with a prayer book and another book, presumably a Bible. Hans' poem on her epitaph records that she loved and praised God, spoke often about his Word, and took pleasure in helping the poor and sick.[40] The iconographical programme of the church was also a demonstration of the true Lutheran piety of its patron. Not only did Hans choose the Last Supper for the central image of its altarpiece; he also commissioned a series of portraits of Lutheran pastors and theologians to adorn its wall.[41] Such portrait galleries sought to demonstrate that the local tradition of evangelical teaching was firmly tied to that of Wittenberg.[42]

The church also, like a funeral sermon, served to strengthen communal ties.[43] Its renovation offered Hans the opportunity to fulfil his duties as patron. An opening panel that hangs today in the choir area states that the building work was carried out to honour God and Anna, and to provide more space and greater comfort for the church's parishioners. The cost of 4686 *Gulden* was borne, according to the panel, in part by the inhabitants of Prießnitz and the surrounding villages (whose names and contributions the panel records), in part by the church, but mostly (4052 *Gulden*) by 'myself Hans von Einsiedel, lord [*Lehnherr*] here at the time, willingly and gladly... with the heartfelt wish that God will nurture, preserve and keep his... Word clear and pure in this church until the last day'. On the front of this panel are a number of inscriptions that suggest that such contributions will be rewarded: 2 Corinthians 9:7: 'God loves a cheerful giver'; Exodus 34:20: 'God said to Moses: no-one shall appear before me empty'; Sirach 17:22: 'The Lord keeps the service of men as a signet ring, and their good works as the apple of his

---

[38] Thank you to Dr. Ruth Slenczka and Vera Isaiasz for the discussions in Prießnitz in January 2011—very cold, but very worth it!

[39] SStAL, RG Prießnitz, 20523, Nr. 192 (Inventar nach dem Tod des Hans (Johann) von Einsiedel).

[40] 'Sie libt und lobte ihren Gott / Red früh und spat von seinem Wort / Negst Gott war ihres Hertze Freud / Erquicken arm und kranke Leut'.

[41] On the portraits see R. Steche (ed.), *Beschreibende Darstellung der älteren Bau- und Kunstdenkmäler des Königreichs Sachsen,* vol. 15, *Amtshauptmannschaft Borna* (Dresden, 1891), 98.

[42] Enke et al. (eds), *Cranach der Jüngere*, cat. nos. 3/35, 3/36.

[43] On funeral sermons see, for example, Anna Linton, *Poetry and Parental Bereavement in Early Modern Germany* (Oxford, 2008), 5–9.

eye'; and Exodus 36:3: 'Every morning the children of Israel brought their willing gifts to the work of the sanctuary, so that it could be done'.[44]

Above all, however, the Prießnitz church is about consolation and hope for the afterlife, about resurrection and reunion, and about Hans's very personal memory of his dead wife. The staging of the church, with its hidden panels, was intended to encourage intimacy and immediacy: its key images and texts can be fully appreciated only in close proximity, when revealed for contemplation by or for an individual viewer. Scholarly literature has asked how far Lutheran memorials were used for private piety—this one, we can say with certainty, was. The inscriptions that Hans composed give eloquent expression to his mourning. The text on the predella of the altarpiece, for example, records that the epitaph was erected by Hans for his 'most beloved wife . . . in loving and eternal commemoration and with due honour and heart-felt love, but with a very grieving and most afflicted heart'. Anna's death was accompanied by great grief, 'wehemut' and 'schweren herzeleit', above all on the part of her husband. The series of rhymed inscriptions on the gallery (*Herrschaftsloge*), which open with a plea for peace in the land so that schools and churches can flourish and God's Word be proclaimed, express Hans' grief and provide solace drawn from Scripture. Through the death of his beloved God has clothed Hans with fear and sorrow, for 'there is no suffering on earth that brings such sorrow as when one sees before one's eyes one's most dear spouse laid in the grave'. In his hour of need, Hans depended on the daily consolation sent to him by God and on his heart being refreshed by God's word. He (or Thryllitzsch) chose three biblical passages that promised that his grief would be assuaged, and that gave spiritual meaning to his suffering: Matt 5:4 ('Blessed are those who suffer, God will comfort them for eternity'); Luke 6:21 ('Blessed are those who weep here, they will laugh for ever and ever'); and Psalm 126:5 ('They who here sow with tears shall there go in eternal joy'). 'Rejoice, rejoice, you who are full of tears, because your God himself has spoken', concludes the series of inscriptions.

Anna's epitaph—the church's central image until its nineteenth-century dismantlement—emphasized the prospect of salvation and resurrection (Plate 9). 'I live and you shall also live' (John 14:19) promise two inscriptions, once centrally placed flanking Christ's mouth and one above Anna's shoulder. In the heavenly space framed by angels above, we read another affirmation: 'Anna von Einsiedel rejoice; your name is written in heaven and in the book of life'. These sentiments are echoed in Hans' poem, inscribed on the reverse of the panel: '[Anna] sleeps sweetly here in Christ's lap, He has saved her with His own blood'. The poem continues:

> No grave nor stone can contain her, for she keeps her faith in God. But Christ must soon return her to eternal life. Come soon and awaken her Son of God, place upon her the crown of honour. Transform her suffering into eternal joy and glory.

The hope for future happiness that Hans expresses here turns to a very confident assertion of its imminence in the depiction of Hans and Anna together on the side

---

[44] These inscriptions are reproduced in *Neue sächsische Kirchengalerie* 11, col. 945. On God rewarding donations see Heal, 'Zum Andenken'.

of the saved in the Last Judgement on the smaller wall panel (Plate 10). What better visual expression of evangelical *Heilsgewissheit*—the certainty of salvation—could there be? The inscription around this image reads: 'Hurry in, come soon Lord Jesus Christ, Your coming is my salvation, give back to me my dearest one, then we will sing our joyful songs'. Here, as elsewhere in the church, the interplay of text and image leaves us in no doubt as to the affective content of the Prießnitz ensemble. Hans' texts speak frequently of the heart, of fear, of suffering, of sorrow, of hope and consolation, of love, of tears, of pain and finally of laughter and joy. The church's images give visual expression not only to Hans' proper Lutheran beliefs but also to his heartfelt sorrow, to his quest for consolation and to his hope for future joy. It would be nice to be able to say that Prießnitz therefore enables us to access some of the visceral qualities of early modern memory: those associated with deep inward feeling rather than with the intellect. But of course this is not really true. Like a funeral sermon, this commemorative work is very far from spontaneous: it is formalized, public and carefully staged. It does, however, show us individual memory shaped by collectively held, in this case distinctly *Lutheran*, beliefs; it gives visual expression to very personal memories that are interwoven with a particular understanding of salvation history. Prießnitz's message can be compared with the death records contained in written family histories: there, at least from the later sixteenth century onwards, traditional intercessory prayers were replaced by requests for God's grace, for participation in the Resurrection and for the family's reunion in eternal joy.[45]

While Prießnitz is a deeply personal memorial, later von Einsidel patronage returns us to more standard themes. In Gnandstein's village church, Hildebrand III added in 1640 a series of nine life-sized relief sculptures of the von Einsiedel *Patronatsherren* and their wives to the choir area, flanking Heinrich Hildebrand's epitaph altar (Fig. 6.2). The series of sculptures began with a retrospective depiction of Hildebrand I (d. 1461), founder of the ancestral seat in Gnandstein, and was augmented up to 1756. Above each of the 1640 figures are Latin verses, composed by Hildebrand III, describing the virtues of the deceased, and the sculptures themselves are modelled on a series of ancestor portraits in the Gnandstein castle.[46] With their epitaph altar and their series of life-sized relief sculptures the von Einsiedel claimed the most prominent place in the church for dynastic commemoration. The choir area became a lesser version of more famous examples, such as the Wettin burial chapel in Freiberg Cathedral. Through its historicism the Gnandstein series of sculpted figures, like more the famous examples in Freiberg and elsewhere, sought to fix in its viewers' minds a story of virtuous and legitimate

---

[45] Andrea Kammeier-Nebel, 'Der Wandel des Totengedächtnisses in privaten Aufzeichnungen unter dem Einfluß der Reformation', in Klaus Arnold, Sabine Schmolinsky and Urs Martin Zahnd (eds), *Das dargestellte Ich. Studien zu Selbstzeugnissen des späten Mittelalters und der frühen Neuzeit* (Bocum, 1999), 93–116. See also Heide Wunder, '>Gewirkte Geschichte<: Gedenken und >Handarbeit<. Überlegungen zum Tradieren von Geschichte im Mittelalter und zu seinem Wandel am Beginn der Neuzeit', in Joachim Heinzle (ed.), *Modernes Mittelalter. Neue Bilder einer populären Epoche* (Frankfurt am Main and Leipzig, 1994), 324–54, especially 348–54 on the commemorative practices of Protestant women.

[46] *Die Familie von Einsiedel*, 90; Winzeler, 'Burgkapelle', 221.

Fig. 6.2. Memorials for Hildebrand von Einsiedel (d. 1461) and Heinrich von Einsiedel (d. 1507) from the Village Church in Gnandstein, *c.*1640.

Credit: © Deutsche Fotothek.

lordship, to express symbolic solidarity with past generations. Between 1688 and 1696 the Gnandstein interior was transformed further by Abraham von Einsiedel, through the addition not only of a new *Kanzelaltar* (combined pulpit and altar) but also of a gallery and balconies adorned with paintings depicting the story of salvation and the Lutheran sacraments.[47]

THE NOBILITY: THE VON SCHLEINITZ

The patronage of the von Einsiedel family shows the varied role that images could play in the cultures and practises of Lutheran commemoration: from the sixteenth-century wall epitaphs, which served as expressions of confessional identity but also expressed through their texts and images hope for a joyful resurrection, to Prießnitz, where the space of a village church was claimed in an extraordinary manner by its lordly patron for affective and deeply personal remembrance, to the historicizing memorials installed in Gnandstein from the 1640s onwards. My second case study, of the commemorative patronage of the von Schleinitz family in the church of St Afra in Meißen, explores the ways in which these themes played out in one much more important church between the fifteenth and mid-seventeenth centuries.

---

[47] Winzeler, *Burg und Kirche*, 29–30. The gallery paintings are based on Merian's 1627 *Bilderbibel*.

St Afra was, after the Cathedral, Meißen's second church. Until the Reformation (1539) it was a minster, staffed by Augustinian canons. Thereafter the cloister buildings were transformed into a school, and the church itself became Meißen's main parish church, responsible for the pastoral care of the inhabitants of both the castle and the town.[48] The von Schleinitz, whose territorial lordship had developed by the early-fifteenth century around Schleinitz, 13 kilometres west of Meißen, and nearby Leuben and Seerhausen, had a long-standing connection to the Afrakirche. In 1408, the margraves' *Hofmeister* (court master) Hugold (I) von Schleinitz auf Seershausen (d. 1422) added a burial chapel to its south aisle. And members of the von Schleinitz family continued to be buried there throughout the sixteenth century.[49]

Despite modifications made in the seventeenth and nineteenth centuries, which entailed the destruction of a number of late-medieval and Renaissance memorials, the chapel still offers a wonderful insight into the von Schleinitz's commemorative culture, stretching across the rupture of the Reformation. Five fifteenth-century carved stone memorials survive, four of which show members of the family clothed in armour, carrying swords and presenting prominent coats of arms (Hugold II d.1435, Johannes d.1463, Hans d.1476, Hugold III d.1490) and one of which shows Heinrich von Schleinitz (d.1449), imperial *Hofmeister*, kneeling in prayer with God the Father above. These memorials formed part of a complex of donation that also included vestments and other textiles bearing the von Schleinitz arms and the endowment of perpetual masses.[50] They seek to establish posthumous reputation and assert dynastic continuity and legitimacy. But they also, of course, concern themselves with salvation: Hans's and Heinrich's have inscriptions that end 'dem get [sic] gnade'; Hugold's pleads 'requiescat in pace O.P.E.'.[51] During the sixteenth century, members of the family commissioned further epitaphs from the best artists in the region, in particular Christoph Walther and his sons and Hans Köhler. These sixteenth-century memorials are more ambitious than their predecessors both in their design and iconographical content, and draw on the visual idioms of the Italian Renaissance. The epitaph of Wolfgang von Schleinitz (d.1523), attributed to Christoph Walther I and set within a Renaissance-style frame, shows the deceased as a corpse, with snakes curled around his body. That of Johannes (d.1526) shows him kneeling before a crucifix with a banderol reading 'miserere mei'. He holds a rosary in his hands, and the inscriptions above commend him to God.

The epitaphs of Michael (d.1553) and his brother Georg (d.1555) are the earliest Protestant memorials. Michael served as *Hofmarschall* (court administrator) to Elector Moritz, as *Amtmann* (district official) in Meißen and as *Berghauptmann*

[48] Friedrich Maximilian Oertel, *Das Münster der Augustiner Chorherren zu St Afra in Meißen* (Leipzig, 1843); Cornelius Gurlitt (ed.), *Beschreibende Darstellung der älteren Bau- und Kunstdenkmäler des Königreichs Sachsen*, vol. 39, *Meißen* (Dresden, 1917), 337–43.
[49] Hans-Jürgen Pohl, *Aus der Geschichte der Familie von Schleinitz—ein Beitrag zur sächsischen Landesgeschichte* (Oschatz, 2010), 44–9; Gurlitt (ed.), *Beschreibende Darstellung*, vol. 39, 379–88.
[50] Oertel, *Das Münster der Augustiner Chorherren*, 138–41.   [51] Ibid., 50.

(supervisor and electoral representative in mining matters) in Freiberg.[52] His epitaph shows him clad in armour and kneeling in prayer before the resurrected
Christ, who hovers on a cloud above his tomb, around which are four sleeping
figures. Behind is a castle, and on a banderol are inscribed the words: 'Christ's resurrection is my life'. In the triangle above is God the Father, holding an orb in his
left hand and making a blessing gesture with his right. Georg's epitaph, carved by
Christoph Walther II and erected according to its inscription by Georg's wife and
son, also shows him armour-clad and kneeling in prayer, this time before a crucifix
(Fig. 6.3). At the foot of the crucifix stand John the Baptist, Adam, and Eve.
Georg is presented framed by original sin: Adam and Eve before him, the tree of
knowledge of good and evil behind. But he, like the other figures in the scene,
looks to the crucified Christ, the source of his salvation. This message is reinforced
by the inscription above from John 1:29: 'See the lamb of God that carries the sins
of the world'.

Haubold von Schleinitz died in 1562, fighting for the Huguenots at the Battle
of Dreux, the first major military engagement of the French Wars of Religion. His
memorial was, according to its inscription, erected by his sorrowing parents, who
expressed the hope of being reunited with him in the afterlife. At the top of
Haubold's memorial is a depiction of the Last Judgement. In the main field,
Haubold stands, again clad in armour and with his hands clasped in prayer. In a
scene that clearly derives from Georg's epitaph, Adam, Eve, and John the Baptist
stand in prayer before a now-damaged crucifix. In the background is Jerusalem,
and in the foreground a depiction of the story of Moses and the Brazen Serpent, a
type for Christ's Crucifixion. The chapel's last epitaph, for Abraham von Schleinitz
who died in 1594, commended the deceased to God in the same words as its
fifteenth-century predecessors: 'Dem Gott Gnade'. It shows in its main field the
Baptism of Christ, with the Nativity above. Beneath relief figures of Abraham and
his family kneel before a crucifix, now lost. Behind Abraham are six daughters in
shrouds; opposite him are two girls, two women, and three children (the children
again in shrouds). Here, as in so many epitaphs, living and dead are presented
together. The epitaph's inscriptions emphasize its donors' trust in Christ and in the
resurrection: 'Jesus Christ himself bore our sins in his body on the cross'; 'I know
that my saviour lives and that he will awaken me from the earth'; 'Christ is my life
and death is my gain'; and 'We know that we have passed from death into life'.[53]

The story told by these monuments is, in many ways, one of continuity, of
patrons' ongoing desire to honour the dead, to present them as worthy and pious
individuals through both images and vernacular and Latin inscriptions, and to
celebrate noble lineage through coats of arms. The series of von Schleinitz family
memorials that survives from 1435 to 1594 substantiates the assertion that even
though there was a fundamental transformation in theology and liturgy, the
impulse to commemorate the dead was barely disturbed by the Reformation. The
change in the nature of the memorials certainly cannot be characterized as a shift

---

[52] *Geschichte des Schleinitzschen Geschlechts von einem Mitgliede des Geschlechts* (Berlin, 1897), 201.
[53] The texs are based upon 1 Peter 2:24, Job, 19:25, Phlippians 1:21, and 1 John 3:14.

Fig. 6.3. Christoph Walther II, Memorial for Georg von Schleinitz (d. 1555), from the Church of St Afra, Meißen.

Credit: Photo: author's own, with permission from the Ev.-Luth. Kirchengemeinde St Afra.

Plate 1. Andreas Schlüter, pulpit for the Marienkirche in Berlin, 1703

Credit: © Markus Hilbich, Berlin

Plate 2. Master MS, The Prophet Hosea, from *Biblia: Das ist, die gantze Heilige Schrifft deudsch* (Wittenberg: Lufft, 1534)

Credit: © Herzog August Bibliothek Wolfenbüttel, shelfmark Bibel-S. 4° 11a

Der Prophet Nahum.

I.

Es ist die Last vber Nine- ue / vnd die weissagung Nahum von Elkos.
Der HERR ist ein eiueriger Gott vnd ein Recher / Ja ein Recher ist der HERR / vnd ein zorniger man / Der HERR ist ein Recher wider seine Wi- dersacher/vn der es seinen feinden nicht vergessen wird / Der HERR ist gedül- tig vnd von grosser krafft/vnd leist ni- chts vngestrafft / Er ist der HERR/ des wege jnn wetter vnd vngestüme sind/vnd vnter seinen füssen dicke wol- cken/Der das meer schilt/vnd trenge macht/vnd alle wasser vertro- ckent. Basan vnd Carmel vnd was auff dem berge Libanon blühet/ mus für jm erschrecken/Die berge beben für jm/vnd die hügel zerge- ben/das erdrich zittert für jm/dazu der welt kreis / vnd alle die drin- nen wonen/Wer kan für seinem zorn stehen? vnd wer kan für seinem grim bleiben? Sein zorn brennet wie feur/vnd die felsen zerspringen für jm.
Der HERR ist gütig/vnd eine Feste zur zeit der not/vnd kennet die/so auff jn trawen/Wenn die flut vber her leufft/so macht ers mit der selbigen ein ende/Aber seine feinde verfolget er mit finsternis.
Was ists

(Wetter) Wie im roten meer/ Exo.14.

Plate 3. Master MS, The Prophet Nahum, from *Biblia: Das ist, die gantze Heilige Schrifft deudsch* (Wittenberg: Lufft, 1534)

Credit: © Herzog August Bibliothek Wolfenbüttel, shelfmark Bibel-S. 4° 11a

Plate 4. Michael Wolgemut, altarpiece for the Marienkirche in Zwickau, 1479

Credit: © Landesamt für Denkmalpflege Sachsen

Plate 6. Andreas Schulze, altarpiece from the village church in Kemmen (Lower Lusatia), 1649–52

Credit: Photo: author's own

Plate 5. Anon., epitaph for Johann von Kötteritz and his wife Caritas Distelmeyer, 1616

Credit: © Stiftung Stadtmuseum Berlin. Photo: Michael Setzpfandt, Berlin

Plate 7. Valentin Otte, altarpiece from the Church of St Afra, Meißen, 1653

Credit: Photo: author's own, with permission from the Ev.-Luth. Kirchengemeinde St. Afra.

Plate 8. Prießnitz (Eulatal), interior of the village church, refurbished 1616–17

Credit: Photo: author's own, with permission from the Ev.-Luth. Christuskirchgemeinde Prießnitz-Flößberg

Plate 9. Johann de Perre, epitaph for Anna von Einsiedel in the village church in Prießnitz (Eulatal), c.1616

Credit: Photo: author's own, with permission from the Ev.-Luth. Christuskirchgemeinde Prießnitz-Flößberg

Plate 10. Johann de Perre, opening commemorative panel for Anna von Einsiedel in the village church in Prießnitz (Eulatal), c.1616

Credit: Photo: author's own, with permission from the Ev.-Luth. Christuskirchgemeinde Prießnitz-Flößberg

Plate 11. Johann de Perre, opening commemorative panel for Anna von Einsiedel in the village church in Prießnitz (Eulatal), *c.*1616

Credit: Photo: author's own, with permission from the Ev.-Luth. Christuskirchgemeinde Prießnitz-Flößberg

Plate 12. Schwarzenberg, Georgenkirche, 1690–99

Credit: Photo: Jürgen Leonhardt

Plate 13. Schwarzenberg, ceiling of the Georgenkirche, completed 1729

Credit: Photo: Jürgen Leonhardt

Plate 15. Johann Christoph Feige, altarpiece from the Frauenkirche, Dresden, 1734–39

Credit: © SLUB/Deutsche Fotothek. Photo: Walter Möbius, 1930

Plate 14. George Heermann and Philipp Ernst John, altarpiece from the town church of St Peter and Paul, Görlitz, 1695

Credit: © Verlag Janos Stekovics, with permission from the Ev. Innenstadtgemeinde Görlitz

towards secularization, or as an increased focus on this world at the expense of the next. The request that God show the deceased mercy—'dem Got gnade'—appears, for example, in identical form in 1449, in 1476, in 1526, and in 1594, and if anything, the von Schleinitz memorials move in the opposite direction. Not only in their visual style but also in their spiritual content they increased in complexity over the course of the period. Those of the Catholics Wolfgang and Johannes already drew on the visual idioms of the Renaissance, but it was not until the epitaphs commissioned on behalf of the Lutherans Michael (d.1553) and Georg (d.1555) that complex iconographies and lengthy pious inscriptions became the norm. With their visual representations of the Fall, Crucifixion, and Resurrection and their biblical citations, the von Schleinitz epitaphs of the second half of the sixteenth century manifested their patrons' *Heilsgewissheit*, their trust in the redeeming power of Christ's sacrifice, and in the promise of bodily resurrection and reunion with their loved ones in the hereafter.

Three further monuments were financed, in part at least, by members of the von Schleinitz family during the mid-seventeenth century. The first was the high altar, discussed already in Chapter 5, for which Heinrich von Schleinitz auf Jahna provided a substantial donation (Plate 7).[54] The second was a memorial for Heinrich and his wife, which hangs in the choir of the church (1654–56) (Fig. 6.4).[55] The third was the church's pulpit, given in 1657 by Anna Felicitas von Schleinitz, widow of Hans Georg the Elder auf Graupzig (Fig. 6.5).[56] Between Abraham von Schleinitz's 1594 wall epitaph and the Otte creations of the 1650s the community had, of course, experienced the traumas of the Thirty Years' War. Abraham Werdemann's 1653 consecration sermon for the altar refers extensively to them. The pastor chose as his text the story of Gideon and the Midianites, a story that he found especially appropriate for his purposes because Gideon built an altar for the Lord to remember that he and the people of Israel had been promised 'peace and freedom from their enemies'. Werdemann's audience had, he said, suffered for much longer than the Israelites—not for seven, but for four times seven years— and had been beset by enemies as punishment for their sins. Moses had, Werdemann reminded them, built an altar after the Israelites' victory over Amalek (Exodus 17); the Ancients erected altars or 'Gedächtnis=Seule' (commemorative columns) after long and dangerous journeys; Gustav Adolf had built his Swedish column near Oppenheim at the point at which his troops crossed the Rhine in November 1631, 'for eternal fame'. Even heathens established peace altars when they defeated their enemies. The Meißen congregation should, therefore, erect an altar to mark 'the longed-for golden peace' in their land.[57]

Altar, epitaph, and pulpit are all by the sculptor Valentin Otte, and constitute, together, a very different type of commemorative project to the wall epitaphs displayed in the von Schleinitz burial chapel. The three pieces dominate the church's

---

[54] Werdemann, *Altar Afranum.*
[55] Gurlitt (ed.), *Beschreibende Darstellung*, vol. 39, 389–91.
[56] *Geschichte des Schleinitzschen Geschlechts*, 379–83, 647.
[57] Werdemann, *Altar Afranum*, B iir–Biiiv. On the 'Schwedensäule' see Matthäus Merian, *Theatrum Europaeum,* vol. 2 (Frankfurt am Main: Matthäus Merian, 1637), 492.

Fig. 6.4. Valentin Otte and Johann Richter, Memorial for Heinrich von Schleinitz (d. 1654), from the Church of St Afra, Meißen.

Credit: Photo: author's own, with permission from the Ev.-Luth. Kirchengemeinde St. Afra.

Fig. 6.5. Valentin Otte and Johann Richter, Puplit from the Church of St Afra, Meißen, 1657.

Credit: Photo: author's own, with permission from the Ev.-Luth. Kirchengemeinde St. Afra.

large Gothic interior. Although the altar is a communal rather than a dynastic memorial, the obvious visual parallels between it and the epitaph and pulpit bind the three together into one spectacular ensemble. The von Schleinitz thus effectively colonized the parish church's space; their commemorative patronage dominated its main ritual focal points, the pulpit and choir. Heinrich von Schleinitz auf Jahna, was, from 1640, a colonel in the Saxon Elector's army. He served during the Thirty Years' War, most famously defending the Saxon border against Imperial troops in Bohemia in 1632.[58] The choir epitaph shows Heinrich (d. 1654) and his two wives Elizabeth (d.1639) and Dorothea (d.1656) kneeling before a carved crucifix, behind which is a painted landscape. Above are Heinrich's helmet, gauntlets, armour, weapons, and military banners, and at the very top is a flaming cannon ball. The second tier of the elaborate composition shows allegorical representations of love and faith, and Jacob Wrestling with the Angel in between. This story, told in Genesis 32, was for Luther an example of the tenacity required of a believer: Jacob refused to let the angel, whom Luther identified as Christ, go until he received in return a blessing.[59] At the bottom inscriptions record the biographies of Heinrich and his wives, and two biblical quotations express their faith in the bodily resurrection (Job 19: 25–27, as on Abraham von Schleinitz's 1594 epitaph) and in Christ (John 11: 25).

The Afrakirche's pulpit, commissioned by Anna Felicitas von Schleinitz, is an extraordinary object. The fashioning of pulpits into memorials and epitaphs was by no means unusual. Just as medieval donors had given the objects required for the celebration of Mass, so Lutherans gave what was necessary for the preaching of God's Word.[60] Pulpits were also, of course, placed so that the whole congregation could see them, making them an ideal stage for representation. Sometimes, for example on the 1638 miner's pulpit from Freiberg Cathedral, donors included portraits of themselves, in this case in prayer before Christ's cross.[61] Usually, however, evangelists and scenes from Christ's Life and Passion were the dominant visual motifs. The presumptuousness of the Meißen pulpit is therefore remarkable. Where one would normally find Christ and his evangelists one finds instead members of the von Schleinitz family. During each sermon the congregation was confronted with carved and polychromed sculptures of Anna Felicitas, her husband Hans Georg (d. 1635) and their children, Hans Georg der Jüngere, Dietrich (d. 1614), Felicitas (d. 1649) and Anna Dorothea (d. 1652). Religious content is not entirely lacking: the pulpit's steps are adorned with reliefs of the Birth of Christ, the Crucifixion and the Resurrection, and the figure of Jonah and the Whale beneath the pulpit also refers to Christ's resurrection (Matthew 12: 39–40). Nonetheless, the pulpit is above all a family monument. Anna Felicitas' funeral sermon suggests, however, that the clergy did not see it as inappropriate. The

[58] *Geschichte des Schleinitzschen Geschlechts*, 228 ff.

[59] Jane E. Strohl, 'Luther's Eschatology' in Robert Kolb, Irene Dingel and Lubomir Batka (eds), *The Oxford Handbook of Martin Luther's Theology* (Oxford, 2014), 353–64, here 357.

[60] Peter Poscharsky, *Die Kanzel: Erscheinungsform im Protestantismus bis zum Ende des Barocks* (Gütersloh, 1963), 210.

[61] See Chapter 5.

widow was, according to pastor Christoph Jäger, 'compassionate and charitable' towards churches, schools and the clergy, as well as the poor and needy, and gave the 'valuable pulpit' in 1657, 'to honour and adorn this church and for the praise-worthy commemoration of her whole most noble kin'.[62] Here a noblewoman appears not only, as in Prießnitz, as a model of Lutheran virtue, but also as a bearer of dynastic memory.

BEYOND THE NOBILITY

Dynastic commemoration was especially important for the nobility, since their political legitimacy and authority depended in part upon demonstrating historical continuity. This dynastic commemoration took, as we have seen, a variety of forms, from the commissioning of formulaic epitaphs shaped by centuries-old traditions of representation to the construction of highly individualized memorials such as that dedicated to Anna von Einsiedel in Prießnitz. But the desire for commemoration and representation was not, of course, confined to members of the nobility. Wealthy merchants and artisans commissioned elaborate epitaphs, even if their commemorative patronage did not dominate church space as completely as that of noble patrons. Lutheran churches, just like their Catholic precursors, were also full of large- and small-scale objects that were given, according to their inscriptions and donation records, for the remembrance and commemoration of both individuals and families, from altarpieces, pulpits, and fonts to candle holders and liturgical vessels.[63] There is therefore a wealth of material that testifies to the role that burghers played in shaping Lutheran commemorative culture, but here I wish to focus on one particular example: the *Knappschaften* (miners' guilds) of the Erzgebirge, a region that, as we saw in Chapter 5, had a particularly rich tradition of sacred art. Here we turn, then, from dynastic to corporate commemorative cultures and practices.

Before the Reformation, commemoration and care for the dead had been one of the most important duties of the guilds. Guilds were responsible for the administration of proper burial rites for their members, and contributed to the salvation of their souls through endowing masses and making other donations to the church.[64] With the Reformation donation practices changed: endowments were redirected towards poor relief, and material objects were generally given not for the adornment of the church but for the furnishing of the rooms in which the guilds assembled. Moreover, the Reformation, with its emphasis on the individual's relationship with

[62] Christoph Jäger, *Rechtschaffener Christen Lust= und Freuden=Tempel Aus dem schönen Macht=Spruche Im 3. Joh. Also hat GOtt die Welt geliebt etc. Bey dem Volckreichen und Christ=Adelicher Leich=Bestattung Der weiland HochEdelgebornen und so Viel=Ehr= als Tugend begabten Gottfürchtigen Matron, Frauen Annen Felicitas…* (Bautzen: Christoph Baumann, 1666), 50. Anna Felicitas' 1666 will is in the HSStAD, 10548 Grundherrschaft Schelinitz, Nr. 64.

[63] See, for example, Jürgen Beyer, 'Stiftung, Plazierung und Funktion von Wand- und Kronleuchtern in lutherischen Kirchen', *Zeitschrift für Lübeckische Geschichte*, 92 (2012), 101–50. See also Heal, 'Zum Andenken'.

[64] Patrick Schmidt, *Wandelbare Traditionen—tradierter Wandel. Zünftische Erinnerungskultur in der Frühen Neuzeit* (Cologne, 2009), esp. 12.

God and on the church as a communal body, lessened the religious significance of the guilds. They became primarily secular organizations, and material culture, which had always played an important part in creating communal identity, reflected this: on guild seals craftsmen's tools replaced patron saints; on chests and cupboards religious motifs gave way to everyday scenes of artisan life.[65]

The Erzgebirge's *Knappschaften* continued, however, to fulfil some important religious functions: their members met in the prayer rooms of the *Zech-* and *Huthäuser* (the buildings in which the miners' tools were stored) to pray before the start of each mining shift; they participated in solemn processions and church services; they attended special sermons (*Bergpredigten*), usually four times per year; and they played key roles in the elaborate Christmas celebrations that were already, in the sixteenth century, characteristic of the region.[66] Their material culture was certainly not secularized. The Reformation of course broke the traditional link between guilds and their patron saints, who had often been described and depicted as craftsmen themselves: St Luke for the painters, for example, or St Eloi (himself a goldsmith) for the metal workers.[67] But here, as elsewhere, Christocentric piety provided an alternative. The pastor Christian Lehmann described an image, sadly no longer in existence, from his own church in Scheibenberg that had been commissioned in 1572 by Martin Rauch, *Bergmeister* (mining supervisor). It showed the Trinity: God the Father as the *Zehntner* (responsible for collecting the ruler's tax tribute) with Tubalcain, the inventor of metalworking according to Genesis; Christ as a *Schichtmeister* (in charge of the mine's accounts) with the *Bergmeister*; and the Holy Ghost as *Austeiler* (distributor).[68] Beside a depiction of miners consulting about where to dig, the image had a text: 'He who puts his trust in God, will not be abandoned in need' and 'Whoever trusts God builds well'.[69]

More generally, guilds' commemorative practices continued into the seventeenth and eighteenth centuries, despite the absence of the salvific imperative that had once motivated them. Written records contained in the guild books and the inscriptions on surviving artefacts such as chests and ceremonial cups show that guilds continued to commemorate individual members, as well as to record their own corporate histories. Historical continuity was important here: the acts of donation recorded in the *Zunftbücher* often cited the examples of the donors' ancestors, and included requests for their successors to give too.[70] A half-metre high rock crystal, jasper and gilded silver crucifix from Freiberg's town hall provides a nice example of such commitment to historical continuity (Fig. 6.6). The cross itself and its foot

[65] Wilfried Reininghaus, 'Sachgut und handwerkliche Gruppenkultur. Neue Fragen an die "Zunftaltertümer"', in Otto Gerhard Oexle and Andrea von Hülsen-Esch (eds), *Die Repräsentation der Gruppen. Texte—Bilder—Objekte* (Göttingen, 1998), 429–63, esp. 460.

[66] On the *Knappschaften* see Helmut Wilsdorf, *Zur Geschichte der Erzgebirgischen Bergbrüderschaften und Bergknappschaften* (Schneeberg, 1986). Hermann Löscher, 'Die erzgebirgischen Knappschaften vor und nach der Reformation', *Blätter für deutsche Landesgeschichte*, 92 (1956), 162–90.

[67] Reininghaus, 'Sachgut', 461–2.

[68] On the various mining officials see Löscher, 'Die erzgebirgischen Knappschaften', 166, 168.

[69] Schmidt-Brücken and Richter, *Der Erzgebirgschronist*, 118–19.

[70] Schmidt, *Wandelbare Traditionen*, 19, 98, 226. See also Reinighaus. 'Sachgut und handwerkliche Gruppenkultur', esp. 434.

Fig. 6.6. *Ratskruzifix* (crucifix of the town council), late fifteenth and late sixteenth centuries.

Credit: © Stadt- und Bergbaumuseum Freiberg.

date from the fifteenth or early sixteenth century, from the era of Freiberg's first flourishing as a silver-mining community. But the figure of Christ and the small figures in the trefoils at the end of each arm were added in the late-sixteenth century. These trefoil figures are not, as one would expect, the four evangelists, but four representatives of the local mining and metallurgy industry: a miner, a barrow carrier, a metalworker and a supervisor. The crucifix was restored in 1605–6 and again in 1643, this time at the behest of *Bürgermeister* Jonas Schönlebe, whose arms appear on its reverse. This pre-Reformation image clearly continued to fulfil both representative and religious roles: it served as an expression of professional pride and showed that the miners' work was carried out under God's protection.[71]

The continued importance of religious commemoration is demonstrated above all by the guilds' post-Reformation funerary rites. Masses and prayers for the dead ended, but the communal funeral procession retained its importance. Guild members still accompanied the body, and each guild still had its own ceremonial equipment: the bier, the pall and the *Sargschilde* (coffin shields), often bearing the

[71] See Heal, 'Seeing Christ'.

Fig. 6.7. Samuel Linse, *Auflegekruzifix* (crucifix to adorn miners' coffins), 1664.
Credit: © Stadt- und Bergbaumuseum Freiberg.

insignia of the guild to symbolize the corporate identity of its members even after
death. For the funeral procession images, in particular images of Christ, were key.
On his 'last shift', as it was known, a member of one of the Erzgebirge *Knappschaften*
was placed in a coffin adorned with a crucifix (the 'Auflegekruzifix') and with
shields often showing scenes from Christ's Passion.[72] Fellow members of the guild
accompanied the coffin and carried before it a processional cross, such as the one
given to Christian Lehmann's Scheibenberg church in 1628. Fig. 6.7 shows an
Auflegekruzifix from 1664, made by the Freiberg goldsmith Samuel Linse, paid for
by the metal workers' guild to honour its members.[73] The inscription, on the
reverse, lists the guild's office holders. At the foot of this *Auflegekreuz* is a depiction
of Christ carrying the cross and on either side we see miners at work: on the left
ore roasting and on the right another stage in the processing of silver ore. Such
images were, in the guilds' eyes, indispensable: in 1636, for example, Freiberg's
goldsmiths appealed to the city council for money because they needed to replace

[72] See Helmut Wilsdorf, *Die letzte Schicht: Bergmännische Grabgebräuche* (Schneeberg-Chemnitz,
1994).
[73] Manfred Bachmann, Harald Marx and Eberhard Wächtler (eds), *Der silberne Boden. Kunst und
Bergbau in Sachsen* (Leipzig, 1990), cat. no. 501.

the silver *Auflegekruzifix* that they had been forced to surrender to the imperial commander Mohr von Walde in 1632.[74] Images were as important, it seems, to the corporate as to the dynastic commemorative culture of Lutheran Germany.

REMEMBERING THE RRE-REFORMATION PAST: THE ROLE OF IMAGES

This chapter opened with a discussion of *Bekenntnisbilder*, of images representing the foundational figures and events of the Lutheran church. But of course the history of a Lutheran community—be it a confession, a region, a town, a congregation, a guild, or a family—did not start in 1517 or in 1530 or whenever a local Reformation was introduced. Lutheran history writing acknowledged this, telling the story of an apostolic church that had been submerged during the time of the papacy only to emerge triumphant at the Reformation thanks to the controlling hand of God. This story enabled churchmen and scholars to reclaim elements of the medieval past: Jan Hus featured, for example, as an early witness to the evangelical truth. Lutheran visual culture told, as we have seen, a much less tidy story. We can accept the Gnandstein village church as an expression of Lutheran confessional culture. By the seventeenth century many of Saxony's Lutheran churches looked, in at least some ways, like this, with new altars, fonts, pulpits, galleries and epitaphs, all dedicated to reinforcing evangelical teaching. But what about Gnandstein's castle chapel, with its splendid late-medieval retables? The chapel was no longer staffed by a chaplain and was no longer the site of daily masses and the castle's inhabitants now attended Sunday services in the village church. But the chapel was still used as a place for private prayer, and family services, including baptisms and funerals, were still conducted there.[75] This is, of course, just one example of Lutheranism's 'preserving power', of the extensive survival of pre-Reformation images in post-Reformation churches.

Lutheranism's preserving power can and has been explained in a number of ways: Lutherans wanted to display their religious moderation; images were matters of indifference to salvation; some could be reinterpreted to fit with evangelical teaching; some soon came to be valued as art. But the fact remains that iconoclasm was undoubtedly, from an evangelical perspective, a more sensible way of dealing with images, of ensuring that the new present was not contaminated by survivals from the rejected past. However we rationalize it, Lutheran willingness to keep old images stands very much at odds with what both many early modern observers thought, and what modern anthropologists and art historians think, about the psychological power of images.[76] The theological debates and confessional tensions of the sixteenth century provide a necessary but not sufficient explanation for the phenomenon: images, after all, never fell from favour as a result of the preaching

---

[74] StadtAFr, I Ba (Stadt Protocoll), 9a (1628–40), 646–7.
[75] Winzeler, *Burg und Kirche*, 44–5.
[76] See the excellent discussion in Bynum, 'Are Things "Indifferent"?'.

of God's Word, as Luther had hoped they would. The strong desire for continuity and the awareness of history revealed by the commemorative patronage examined in this chapter provide additional explanations for Lutheran defences of traditional images. In 1558, in the Palatinate, for example, Heidelberg's *Schultheiß* (the Elector's official) tried to enforce Elector Ottheinrich's 1557 mandate against images. Weinheim's noble *Stadtherr* (civic overlord) resisted, arguing that 'the church with its altars and images stood and remained for many years under my ancestors, and I do not wish to be the one who first robs and dishonours churches'.[77] In Zwickau in 1569, as we saw in Chapter 2, a Lutheran pastor's campaign to remove Michael Wolgemut's altar (Plate 4), and to replace it with something more fitting to a Lutheran context, was frustrated: the city council retained and restored the masterwork, partly because they could not afford a replacement, and partly because local guild-masters advised them that it should be kept and displayed 'for the adornment of the church and in honour of our dear forefathers'.

Plenty of medieval images *were* banished from Lutheran churches. But during the later sixteenth and seventeenth centuries those that had survived intact and *in situ* were often restored. In Görlitz's town church, for example, Pastor Bartholmaeus Scultetus embarked on a meticulously documented renovation of the church's medieval images. Two statues of St Peter and Paul, the church's patrons, were removed, repainted, and reinstalled with new inscriptions that reminded viewers of their histories: their donation and installation on St Bartholomew's Day 1430, and their renovation in 1595, on the Feast of the Dispersion of the Apostles, 'after 165 years, 10 months and 21 days'.[78] Such early *Denkmalpflege* (monument preservation) attracted negative comments from Calvinist observers. Simon Gedicke wrote that 'the Calvinists prattle further [of] how the old idols are newly coloured by us, renovated, repaired with red and white colours, [and] placed on the walls and altar'. The accusation was, he added, unjust, for the images that Lutherans restored were Christian images, not idols: 'we do not spend any coins for the renewal of idols'.[79]

Sometimes, however, Lutheran patrons not only restored medieval images but also reset them in new frames. Fig. 6.8, for example, shows the altarpiece from the village church in Schorbus (Lower Lusatia). The carved, winged shrine dates from around 1480–1500, and shows the *Anna Selbdritt* (St Anne with Mary and the Christ Child) surrounded by saints. The ensemble was put together in its current form in 1582 at the behest of Caspar von Zabeltitz auf Schorbus.[80] It was given a new Renaissance-style frame with paintings and inscriptions appropriate to Lutheran devotion. Here the church's gothic altar has been turned into a Lutheran

---

[77] Quoted in Rott, 'Kirchen- und Bildersturm', 240.

[78] Alfred Zobel, 'Beiträge zur Geschichte der Peterskirche in Görlitz in den Jahren 1498–1624', *Neues Lausitzisches Magazin*, 109 (1933), 98–141, here 106 ff. RatsAG, Varia 98 (B. Sculteti Kirchensachen von 1594 bis 1614); Christian Nitsche, *Beschreibung der berühmten und prächtigen Kirche zu SS. Petri und Pauli in Görlitz…* (Görlitz, 1725), C3. See also Hahn, 'Sensing Sacred Space', 119.

[79] Gedicke, *Calviniana Religio*, 520–1.

[80] I am very grateful to Pastor Robert Marnitz for showing me Schorbus and Leuthen. Georg Schmidt, *Die Familie von Zabeltitz* (Rathenow, 1888).

Fig. 6.8. Anon., altarpiece from the Village Church in Schorbus (Lower Lusatia), *c*.1480–1500 (*Anna Selbdritt* and saints) and 1582 (frame).

Credit: Photo: author's own, with permission from the Ev. Kirchengemeinden Cottbus-Süd und Leuthen-Schorbus.

memorial, an epitaph altar, bearing portraits of the donor and his family in prayer before Christ's cross.[81] Medieval images sometimes came to provide the focal points for very elaborate Lutheran decorative schemes. Fig. 6.9 shows, for example, the village church in Klępsk (Klemzig) near Sulechów (Züllichau) in Silesia (formerly part of the territory of the Margraves of Brandenburg), where at the behest of the church's patron, Gregor von Kalckreutt, a fifteenth-century altarpiece became, in the seventeenth century, the focal point of a complex iconographical programme incorporating the pulpit, font, galleries and ceiling of the

Fig. 6.9. The Village Church in Klępsk (Klemzig) near Sulechów in Silesia.
Credit: Photo: B. Bielinis-Kopeć.

[81] There are other examples of late-sixteenth and seventeenth century altars that incorporate gothic statues. See, for example, Gericke et al., *Brandenburgische Dorfkirchen*, 49, on Bredereiche; Kurt Reismann, *Die Kunstdenkmäler der Provinz Brandenburg*, vol. 5 (3), *Stadt und Landkreis Cottbus* (Berlin, 1938), 182 on Sielow, where there is an altar from around 1600 that shows in its central shrine Mary of Egypt, carried aloft by five angels. Its Lutheran frame has painted figures of saints Peter and Paul, a depiction of the Last Supper and two inscriptions. For a general discussion see Wolfgang Götze, 'Gotische Plastik in barocken Gehäuse', in Kunsthistorisches Institut, Karl-Marx-Universität Leipzig (ed.), *Festschrift Johannes Jahn zum XXII. November MCMLVII* (Leipzig, 1958), 187–93.

church.[82] The parish church in Kalbensteinberg in Franconia was restored by its patrons, members of a Nuremberg patrician family, the Rieter, between 1603 and 1613. That church is filled with *memoria*—most notably death shields (*Totenschilde*) and a series of historicizing paintings of the family's ancestors on the walls of the choir. Most interestingly, however, as part of the restoration campaign the church's late-gothic furnishings were returned from hiding and were augmented by new acquisitions, including a *Palmesel* (wooden donkey) and two Marian statues that were set in a new altar, commissioned by Hans Rieter.[83]

Michael Schmidt, in his study of historicism in the architecture of southern Germany, rightly sees this anachronistic refurbishment as an expression of Hans Rieter's commitment to his family's cultural inheritance.[84] Of course we should not assume that early modern observers necessarily shared our refined sense of images' temporality. Roman and Romanesque might, as Christopher Wood has suggested, have blended together in the minds of fifteenth- and sixteenth-century beholders.[85] The gothic past was, however, still accessible, and Lutherans certainly recognized images such as Wolgemut's Zwickau altar or the shrine of the Schorbus altar or the Kalbensteinberg *Palmesel* as anachronisms, out of time and out of spiritual place. While some zealous pastors, such as Johann Petrejus in Zwickau, campaigned against them, others, for example Stephan Holstein who helped design the iconographical programme in Klępsk, apparently did not. Their retention and restoration were acts of commemoration, and testify to images' role as bearers of collective memory. By the early eighteenth century such images were, as we will see in Chapter 9, being described as antiquities.

CONCLUSION

Images—from the 1547 Wittenberg Altar to portraits of Luther and *Bekenntnisbilder*—helped create both local and supra-regional Lutheran confessional identities. Here visual evidence, the depiction of foundational figures and events in the history of the church, tells a story that finds fairly easy parallels in textual sources such as sermons and confessional histories. But if we look more broadly, as a study of noble and guild commemorative practices invites us to do, we find that visual evidence also says something slightly different. What does it mean to speak of '*Lutheran* visual culture', when the focal point of a castle chapel or a parish church is a 'papist' altarpiece? Such images were parts of the pre-Reformation past that could not, at any meaningful *religious* level, be reclaimed.

---

[82] Jan Harasimowicz and Agnieszka Seidel, 'Die Bildaussattung der ehem. evang. Kirche zu Klępsk (Klemzig) in der Mark Brandenburg', in Klaus Raschok and Reiner Sörries (eds), *Geschichte des protestantischen Kirchenbaues: Festschrift für Peter Poscharsky zum 60. Geburtstag* (Erlangen, 1994), 289–99.

[83] Michael Schmidt, *Reverentia und Magnificentia. Historizität in der Architektur Süddeutschlands, Österreichs und Böhmens von 14. bis 17. Jahrhundert* (Regensburg, 1999), 166–8.

[84] Ibid.   [85] Wood, *Forgery*, 189.

The preservation of Michael Wolgemut's Zwickau altarpiece cannot, for example, be equated with a Lutheran chronicler invoking Jan Hus as a witness to truth in a time of darkness. Some Lutheran pastors discussed these images in ways that emphasized their admonitory value: they could be left in place, 'and thereby remind us of the wretched state of our ancestors under the papacy'.[86] But the examples presented in this chapter were not preserved because of their value as confessional polemic; rather, they were preserved because of the historical awareness of Lutheran patrons. The self-image and interests of these patrons could create splendid Lutheran ensembles, such as Prießnitz or the Gnandstein parish church, but also, it seems, splendid anomalies such as Schorbus, Klepsk, or Kalbensteinberg.

Patrons' desire for representation, for continuity and the legitimation of both secular and spiritual lordship, should not, however, lead us to conclude that these monuments fulfilled *only* political needs. The elaborate decorative programme of the village church in Prießnitz clearly chronicles emotional loss. But even more standard memorials, with their frequent visual and verbal references to the Crucifixion and Resurrection, offered individual consolation. The viewer was instructed to trust in the redeeming power of Christ's sacrifice, and was sustained with the promise of bodily resurrection and reunion with loved ones in the hereafter. It has become a commonplace of scholarship to say that the Reformation divided the community of the living and the dead, and of course it did, in many ways. But the heartfelt pleas expressed in Prießnitz's iconography, as well as in other commemorative genres, reflect Lutherans' ongoing desire for some kind of bridge across that divide. Lutheran memorials to the dead were about both representation and devotion, and this conjoining of politics and piety became even more marked during the age of the princely baroque, to which we will now turn.

---

[86] Lappe, *Inauguratio Renovati Altari*, A iii v.

PART III

THE MAGNIFICENT IMAGE

7

The Visual Culture of a Lutheran Court
Dresden, 1650–1700

In 1648, the Peace of Westphalia brought to an end the Thirty Years' War. On 24 October, the Treaty of Osnabrück (*Intrumentum Pacis Osnabrugense* or *IPO*) reformed the imperial constitution and imposed a lasting religious settlement on the Empire. It recognized the Reformed faith alongside Lutheranism, and prescribed Protestant–Catholic parity in key imperial institutions such as the *Reichskammergericht* (Imperial Cameral Court). The Edict of Restitution was suspended, and the *IPO* imposed a 'normal year' of 1 January 1624: the Protestant subjects of Catholic rulers and the Catholic subjects of Protestant rulers were henceforth guaranteed the rights that they had enjoyed at that time, a time before the extensive Catholic confiscations that had led up to the 1629 Edict. The *ius reformandi*—right of Reformation—of the 1555 Peace of Augsburg was, in effect, restricted: rulers who converted could no longer force their new faith on their subjects. Only the Habsburgs' hereditary lands were exempt (though their Protestant subjects in Silesia did receive protection). Throughout the Empire, adherents of a territory's official religion were guaranteed public rights of worship and sovereignty of the so-called *Amtshandlung*: baptism, marriage and burial. Others could worship either in private chapels or their homes.[1] At an international level the era of intense religious conflict was over, and the Empire's constitution now properly reflected its confessional composition. But confessional tension was by no means a thing of the past. Indeed the *IPO* provided a framework within which, in many areas, confessionalization became possible for the first time. Stability—and the political and cultural reconstruction that it permitted—encouraged the development of confessional principalities within which differences between Catholics and Protestants became entrenched.[2]

Recovery from the political and socio-economic traumas of the Thirty Years' War was a slow process. The war had, of course, brought destruction and impoverishment to many parts of the Empire. Overall, the Empire's population may have declined by around a third; individual areas suffered particularly acutely, including Brandenburg and parts of Saxony. With peace came the chance for renewal. The princes of Germany's larger territories—Brandenburg and Albertine Electoral

---

[1] See Joachim Whaley, *Germany and the Holy Roman Empire. Volume I: Maximilian I to the Peace of Westphalia, 1493–1648* (Oxford, 2013), 624–6.
[2] See Whaley, *Germany and the Holy Roman Empire*, vol. 2, 287; Lehmann, *Das Zeitalter des Absolutismus*, 59.

Saxony amongst them—sought to increase their political power and authority both through administrative, legal and military reform and through cultural magnificence. Not all succeeded to an equal degree: Brandenburg's rise under the Great Elector and his successors was, of course, exceptional. But throughout the Empire, princes' efforts resulted in the revival of court life. Even if many of Germany's rulers failed to fully realize their reforming ambitions, this was, without doubt, the age of absolutism and of the baroque prince. The court was his key tool: it served not only as the focus of his administration and government but also as a site for the display of power, a measure of the significance and reputation of his state. While burghers had played a crucial role in shaping the cultural life of sixteenth-century Germany, the reigns of patronage now lay firmly in the hands of the ruling nobility and only a few wealthy trading cities like Hamburg and Leipzig could really compete. Baroque princes spent lavishly on palaces, churches and other architectural projects, but also on more ephemeral means of display: opera, theatre, ballet and elaborate festivals. They sought, to an even greater extent than their Renaissance predecessors had done, to outdo each other in splendour.[3] In Dresden, for example, the tradition of princely patronage of art, architecture and festivals (largely tournaments) begun under Elector Moritz (r. 1547–1553) was expanded hugely by his successors. It reached its apogee under Friedrich August I (r. 1694–1733), who achieved royal status as King Augustus II (the Strong) of Poland (r. 1697–1706 and 1709–1733). Friedrich August not only maintained the festival traditions of his forefathers but also reshaped the residential city, above all through the work of his court architect Matthäus Daniel Pöppelmann.

'Baroque' is a designation that would have meant no more to contemporaries than 'absolutist', yet it provides a convenient shorthand for describing an era during which cultural production—architecture, sculpture, painting, music, theatre, and literature—was characterized by a desire to impress and overwhelm. Baroque art is ornate, theatrical, and dynamic. Artists sought an intensification of sensual effect, and architecture, sculpture, and painting often came together to achieve this, for example in the seminal works of Gianlorenzo Bernini (1598–1680).[4] But the baroque could also produce, as in the paintings of Rembrandt or the Passion music of Johann Sebastian Bach, a deep inwardness and highly affective piety. Baroque visual culture is still frequently associated with Catholicism.[5] The Catholic baroque employed, so the story goes, visual and liturgical splendour in the face of Protestant opposition to images and elaborate ceremony. In his detailed study of early modern renovations of Southern Germany's medieval churches, Meinrad von Engelberg recognizes the importance of the baroque in Electoral Saxony in particular, and acknowledges that some patrons saw no contradiction between 'exuberant early baroque forms' and their evangelical faith. Yet, Protestant orientation towards the Word made, he suggests, such adornment 'unnecessary and incidental'. Where

---

[3] See, for example, Rudolf Vierhaus, *Germany in the Age of Absolutism*, tr. Jonathan Knudsen (Cambridge, 1988), here 37. On absolutism as a 'form of rule that was more often striven for than realized, more asserted than practiced' see 113.

[4] See, for example, Genevieve Warwick, *Bernini: Art as Theatre* (Yale, 2012).

[5] See, for example, Vierhaus, *Germany*, 65; Lehmann, *Das Zeitalter*, 59.

stylistic updating occurred in evangelical churches, it was the result not of religious conviction but of the need to adapt space and meet patrons' profane desires for representation.[6]

Many of the greatest patrons and artists of the baroque were indeed Catholic. But in Germany, as measured commentators have observed, the style was readily adopted by Protestants.[7] And it served, this chapter will argue, the piety of these Protestant patrons as well as their desire for magnificence. In Dresden, for example, Elector Johann Georg II (r. 1656–80) not only spent vast sums on court festivals but also lavished extraordinary attention on the visual and musical culture of his castle chapel. Indeed, even the Reformed were unable to entirely resist the appeal of the baroque. Brandenburg's court became one of the most magnificent in Europe under Elector Friedrich III (r. 1688–1713), whose aspirations to royal status were realized when he was crowned 'King in Prussia' in an elaborate ritual in Königsberg in 1701.[8] Fig. 7.1 shows the interior of the Berlin Cathedral during the 1705 funeral ceremonies for his wife, Sophie Charlotte.[9] The queen's sarcophagus is framed by an elaborate baldachin and surrounded by angels: the contrast to the empty church described by Philip Hainhofer on his 1617 visit could not be greater. Clearly, the baroque held great allure for Germany's princes, whatever their confessional orientation.

BEAUTY AND CONNOISSEURSHIP

In order to understand Lutheran engagement with the splendours of the baroque, we need to return to the *Bilderbibeln* and illustrated texts examined in Chapter 4. Where, in Lutheran evaluations of images, did aesthetic appreciation—the pursuit of beauty—fit?[10] According to art history's 'secularization narrative', the sixteenth century marked the beginning of the era of art.[11] Hans Belting argued that during this period obsession with the image as aesthetic object superseded preoccupation with the sacred image, the image as a revelation of the divine. During the sixteenth century, he wrote, 'the cult of the work of art... replaces the cult of the holy image'.[12] This shift occurred in part because of the Italian Renaissance: the theories of painting developed from Leon Battista Alberti's *De Pictura* (1435) onwards and humanist interest in collecting. In Germany too, humanists such as Conrad Celtis (1459–1508) and Willibald Pirckheimer (1470–1530) sought through their

[6] Engelberg, *Renovatio Ecclesiae*, 162, 189–90, 214.

[7] Whaley, *Germany and the Holy Roman Empire*, vol. 2, 295.

[8] On the coronation see Christopher Clark, 'When culture meets power: the Prussian coronation of 1701', in Hamish Scott and Brendan Simms (eds), *Cultures of Power in Europe During the Long Eighteenth Century* (Cambridge, 2007), 14–35.

[9] Stiftung Preußische Schlösser und Gärten Berlin-Brandenburg, *Cranach und die Kunst der Renaissance*, 308.

[10] Ringshausen, *Von der Buchillustration*, 35 points out that Luther ignored some of the traditional justifications for the use of religious images, including beauty.

[11] Wood, *Forgery*, 77.

[12] Hans Belting, *Likeness and Presence: A History of the Image Before the Era of Art*, tr. Edmund Jephcott (Chicago and London, 1994), 16, 459, 470, 490.

Fig. 7.1. Johann Georg Wolfgang, *Castrum doloris* for Sophie Charlotte inside Berlin Cathedral, 1705.

Credit: © Stiftung Preußische Schlösser und Gärten Berlin-Brandenburg, GK II (10) 850. Photo: Daniel Lindner.

patronage of art and letters to demonstrate their—and their nation's—cultural superiority, while Albrecht Dürer reflected extensively on artistic theory. Yet, Germany, Belting suggests, also made another, more important contribution to the secularization process, thanks not to the Nuremberg intellectuals but to the icono-clastic evangelicals. Belting postulates a stark division between the empty walls of Reformed churches that 'symbolized a purified, desensualized religion that now put its trust in the word' and the 'crowded walls of the picture cabinets in private houses'. The Reformation accelerated the pace of change, negating images' reli-gious role and forcing them out of the ecclesiastical sphere and into the palace and home: 'Images, which had lost their function in the church, took on a new role in representing art'.[13]

This secularization narrative has been challenged on various grounds. It is too teleological: the 'victory of aesthetic judgement' emerged only after a long and complex struggle that was far from over even at the end of the sixteenth century.[14] Moreover, many images and artefacts that were valued highly by contemporaries—for example, portraits, medals, coins, and tombs—do not fit easily within its con-tours. Such objects invited 'neither devotional nor protoaesthetic attention', and must be understood rather as the bearers of collective memory.[15] Even as an account of the Reformation's engagement with religious images the narrative is inadequate, shaped too much by a German historiographical tradition that sees in the religious turmoil of the early sixteenth century the origins of secular modernity. Mainstream Lutheranism not only continued to recognize images' pedagogical value, but also, after an initial period of uncertainty, assigned them a renewed role in religious devotion, as we saw in Chapters 4 and 5. And aesthetic appeal was increasingly invoked as a justification for both the retention of old images and the production of new. The beauty of the visual, the appropriate adornment that images provided, had become, by the mid-seventeenth century, a standard part of Lutheran image discourse. The Reformation, in its Lutheran manifestation, did not, therefore, sep-arate piety from aestheticism; rather the two converged during the seventeenth century to provide a solid foundation for the flourishing of the baroque.

Lutherans of course condemned cult images, images that attracted idolatrous prayer and pilgrimage, but the belief that paintings and sculptures provided appropriate adornment for a place of worship helped justify their survival. Already in 1538 an English Catholic, Thomas Goldwell, wrote to his father that the 'heretics' (Lutherans) whom he encountered on his travels in Southern Germany had 'goodly churches full of images, which they regard as ornaments of the church and memorials'.[16] Nuremberg—one of the cities visited by Goldwell—was perhaps particularly precocious with regard to the emergence of a predominantly aesthetic mode of viewing, thanks to its exceptionally rich late-medieval artistic heritage. But from the mid-sixteenth century onwards such rhetoric can be found not only amongst lay defenders of images but also in the writings of pastors and theologians. As we saw in Chapter 2, Zwickau's citizens defended Michael Wolgemut's altar

---

[13] Ibid., 458.   [14] See Heal, *The Cult of the Virgin Mary*, 107.
[15] Wood, *Forgery*, 77.   [16] Quoted in Heal, *The Cult of the Virgin Mary*, 108.

(Plate 4) in 1569 on the grounds that it was 'for the adornment of the church and in honour of our dear forefathers'. And in 1574 the church ordinance for Schwarzburg, a Saxon dependency, which gave a fuller defence of images than any earlier Lutheran ordinance, stated that 'panels, biblical figures and paintings' could remain because the populace could be taught that they are 'only an external adornment and decorum, through which the people will be moved to greater piety'.[17]

Life-like images were, in general, regarded with suspicion by sixteenth-century Protestants. Even Lutherans feared verisimilitude: Martin Chemnitz, for example, lamented that 'the outstanding diligence of the artist moved the more ignorant to more zealous worship'.[18] But for the authors of some of the polemical, anti-Calvinist defences of images examined in Chapter 2, images' beauty, and the artistic skill of their creators, increased their spiritual value. In his *Ikonographia*, Arndt complained about the 'great quantity of images that fill all corners': 'one often finds old images, so large, monstrous, [and] badly formed, that they are very offensive to look upon'. Such images should, he wrote, be removed, for they served no purpose and had not been created by masters such as the 'the two [Old Testament] artists Bezaleel and Oholiab'.[19] Simon Gedicke, in his 1597 *Von Bildern vnd Altarn*, defended the 'beautiful, magnificent, historical images and paintings' of the Lutheran church, contrasting them to the 'superstitious, idolatrous, godless, shameful images' of the Catholics. He went on to praise 'the fine, artistic paintings of biblical histories from the Old and New Testaments'. When pious Christians see these, he argued, they feel because of them 'good thoughts and movement of the heart'.[20] Here, visual magnificence worked in the service of piety.

In 1619, Johann Valentin Andreae gave Christianopolis, his ideal Christian city, a 'very roomy studio for the visual arts, which are very greatly appreciated in this community'. Acknowledging evangelical concerns about the social cost of art, Andreae described Christianopolis' temple as a 'royally magnificent building in which opulence vies with art—which indeed cannot be reproached, since no-one in this community has to go without'. The walls were 'bright and elegant with beautiful paintings of religious subjects or scenes from stories in the Bible'. And in an explicit acknowledgement of the value of artistic genius, Andreae wrote, as we have seen, that the temple's crucifix was 'so skilfully carved as to move even the hardest of hearts'. Andreae concluded his description with an attack on the hypocrisy of iconophobes who cleansed churches by removing their 'decorative objects' into their own homes: 'I could not marvel enough at the art and beauty, particularly when I recall those who under pretext of religion despoil churches and do not forget the luxury of their own homes'.[21] Andreae was, himself, a keen collector. But he did not collect, as Belting's thesis implies, because he was an iconoclast. In Italy, Belting acknowledges, old and new ideas about images were synthesized: images

---

[17] Sehling EKO II, Sachsen und Thüringen 2, 136.
[18] Chemnitz, *Examination*, 63. See also Pamela Smith, *The Body of the Artisan: Art and Experience in the Scientific Revolution* (Chicago, 2004), 10.
[19] Arndt, *Ikonographia* (1597), 66. Exodus 31:1–6.
[20] Gedicke, *Von Bildern und Altarn*, A iii v—A iv r.
[21] Andreae, *Christianopolis*, ed. Thompson, 257–8.

were both 'receptacles of the holy' and 'expressions of art'.[22] Andreae achieved a Lutheran equivalent: images were aids to devotion but also aesthetic objects, to be appreciated for their visual magnificence and as evidence of the skill of their creators.

The prefaces to Lutheran *Bilderbibeln* (image Bibles) provide another insight into this Lutheran merging of piety and aestheticism. These *Bilderbibeln* were, as we saw in Chapter 4, intended partly to educate the laity and partly to serve as pattern books for artists. Virgil Solis' *Biblische Figuren des Alten vnd Newen Testaments* (*Biblical Figures of the Old and New Testaments*), printed for the first time in Frankfurt am Main in 1560, was seminal.[23] It contains a series of 102 illustrations from the Old Testament and 45 from the New, and was not a Bible with illustrations, but rather an image Bible, a work driven by its visual component. Each woodcut is accompanied by brief Latin and German poems. The illustrations in the *Biblische Figuren* were, Solis' preface suggested, suited for painters, goldsmiths and other 'lovers of this art', as well as for 'simple Christians who cannot read Scripture'. The preface recounts how, just as Bezaleel and Oholiab had decorated the Ark of the Covenant and Solomon's Temple, so the 'artistic designer [*Reisser*] and painter, Virgil Solis of Nuremberg, adorned the Bible, translated by the most learned Dr Martin Luther, with his art and made it better looking'. Solis was, the preface asserted, even more worthy of honour and fame than the great artists of Antiquity, because he had used his art 'to honour God and adorn his sacred Word'.[24] Solis' illustrations proved very popular: for the next 50 years they continued to be reproduced, in Catholic as well as in Protestant Bibles.[25]

After the success of Solis' *Biblische Figuren* more *Bilder-Bibeln* followed during the 1560s and 1570s. Tobias Stimmer's *Neue Künstliche Figuren* (*New Artful Figures*), printed in Basel in 1576, contains a series of 134 Old and 34 New Testament images presented in the form of emblems with mottos and biblical citations above, explanatory verses below, and elaborate surrounding frames. Its verses and lengthy preface were written by Johann Fischart (1546/47–1590), an evangelical satirist and polemicist. In the preface Fischart, described the historical use of images, emphasizing in particular patrons' constant quest for 'pleasure and delight'. Their patronage of art was, Fischart suggested, motivated by worldly concerns. From Antiquity to the Renaissance, princely rulers, urban polities, and private individuals had surrounded themselves with images, which they believed to be essential adornments. They had decorated 'cities, palaces, squares, town halls, and pleasure houses' to please viewers' eyes, quicken their hearts, and promote wisdom. Fischart was not opposed to such decoration. Art, like learning, was a sign of civilization: it had vanished under the Barbarians, and was now suppressed by the Turks. But amidst all of this magnificence we must not forget, he emphasized,

---

[22] Belting, *Likeness and Presence*, 458.
[23] See Reinitzer, *Biblia deutsch*, 240–3. On Solis's work, and the other products of the Feyerabend workshop, see Münch, *Geteiltes Leid*, 121–8.
[24] *Biblische Figuren*, A ii r.   [25] Schmidt, *Die Illustration*, 236–8.

art's main purpose: art, which was now of the highest quality, should be used 'for the Christian histories contained herein, which show the way to divine wisdom and reverence'.[26]

The culmination of this merging of piety and aestheticism was Matthäus Merian's *Icones Biblicae*, discussed in Chapter 4. In this album, Merian presented a series of engraved scriptural images 'for the use and pleasure of God-fearing people and those who understand art'. The preface opens with a lengthy discussion of the arts, in particular the 'free [or liberal] art of painting', which Merian describes as waxing and waning like the moon, from the glory of Ancient Rome, through the barbarous times of the Goths, Lombards and Huns, to a revival under Emperors Friedrich III and Maximilian I. The culmination of this revival was, of course, the work of the great German artists of the Renaissance: Dürer, Cranach and Holbein, who could legitimately, Merian wrote, be called 'the German Apelles, Zeuxis and Parrhasius'. A century later, however, in the midst of the Thirty Years' War, the arts were once more under threat. Confronted by this new barbarity, Merian presented his engravings based on Holy Scripture, 'so that this, as a true hieroglyphic work, may serve not only to please and delight, but may also, most importantly, stimulate the soul to godly reflection and to contemplation of the stories depicted'.[27] Here, again, a Lutheran defence of images' spiritual significance sits alongside aesthetic appreciation and, in this case, a history of German art that echoes the rhetoric of the sixteenth-century humanists.

The invocation of 'lovers of this art' (Solis), of 'those who understand art' (Merian) and of the magnificence of Renaissance princes (Fischart) takes us into the realm of connoisseurship and collecting. Princely *Kunstkammern*, containing works of art and other objects of particular value or interest, emerged at the courts of Central Europe during the 1550s and 1560s—precisely the time at which Solis and his successors were producing their richly illustrated *Bilderbibeln*. Patrons assembled sculptures, paintings, precious objects and, in the case of the *Kunstkammer*, man-made and natural curiosities (from scientific instruments and automata to stuffed animals), in order to demonstrate their wealth, taste, and erudition.[28] When religious images were moved into these collections they lost some, at least, of their spiritual significance.[29] But the *Bilderbibeln* and other illustrated Lutheran texts warn us against assuming that once images had become 'art', once they hung on the 'crowded walls' of 'picture cabinets' (Belting), they no longer had a religious function. A number of these texts refer, like those of Solis, Merian and Fischart, to art's significance as a means of creating social distinction, but contain this connoisseurship carefully within the contours of an on-going commitment to its religious

---

[26] *Neue Künstliche Figuren Biblischer Historien/grüntlich von Tobia Stimmer gerissen...*(Basel: Thomas Guarin, 1576), 'An den gönstigen Leser'. On Fischart see above, 113 and Münch, *Geteiltes Leid*, 133–4.

[27] Merian, *Icones Biblicæ*, A iii r ff. See Reinitzer, *Biblia deutsch*, cat. no. 156.

[28] Already in 1531 Hieronymus Rodler had addressed a treatise on perspective to 'Kunstliebhabern'. See Thomas DaCosta Kaufmann, *Court, Cloister, and City: The Art and Culture of Central Europe, 1450–1800* (Chicago, 1995), 168–9, 171.

[29] Stefan Laube, *Von der Reliquie zum Ding. Heiliger Ort—Wunderkammer—Museum* (Berlin, 2011).

use. In 1630, for example, Josua Wegelin (1604–40), preacher in Augsburg until his forced exile in the wake of the 1629 Edict of Restitution, produced *Der Gemahlte Jesus Christus* (*The Painted Jesus Christ*). In this account of the basic tenets of Lutheran faith, Wegelin drew on testimony from Scripture, from the church fathers and from Luther and other evangelical theologians, but also made extensive use of images and emblems. These he justified in ways that we have, by now, come to recognize as standard: they were for the benefit of simple folk. Wegelin also, however, spoke to the patron seeking to affirm his social status through his appreciation of art, writing that his images were created so that 'a learned and wise man' could also take pleasure in them. 'A simple man sees the image or the history', he stated. A knowledgeable man, however, 'sees further': he notices, alongside this, the art.[30]

The merging of piety and aestheticism was never an entirely unproblematic process. In 1679, Melchior Küsel, a pupil of Merian, produced the *Icones Biblicae Veteris et Novi Testamenti* (*Biblical Images of the Old and New Testament*), dedicated to the Wittelsbach Elector Max Emanuel and furnished with a preface by the Augsburg evangelical pastor Georg Laub (1626–86). This preface was addressed to 'art-loving' viewers and readers, and spoke with approval of the honour accorded to painting and the other arts by great lords and potentates. Laub warned, however, of the dangers of images', particularly beautiful images', misuse: 'the more artful and true a model that incites vice is, the more dangerous it also is'. Following the examples of Merian and Stimmer, Küsel had therefore produced these biblical images, which Laub described as 'a good masterwork'.[31] In 1702, Küsel's engravings were reused in a Bible produced in Nuremberg. The Bible's editor, Johann Christoph Meelführer, pastor in Schwobach, noted that its printer had adorned it with well-chosen engravings by Herr Küsel. Some might observe, he suggested, that on occasion more art than biblical story went into such engravings.[32] Yet, artists and patrons continued to value beautiful biblical images, as the success of the Augsburg engraver Johann Ulrich Krauss's *Historische Bilder Bibel*, first published in 1700, indicates. Krauss was himself a Protestant, but his work was calculated to appeal across confessional boundaries. In the fifth part, each of the four evangelists is presented in a 'Kunst-Saal', an art gallery adorned with paintings depicting scenes from his writings. Texts beneath reinforce the spiritual significance of the images. Under Matthew (Fig. 7.2), for example, we read: 'What can give to the eye and to the heart greater loveliness, desire and joy than such a beautiful room?'[33]

[30] Josua Wegelin, *Der Gemahlte Jesus Christus In Grund gelegt: das ist/Gründtliche Augenscheinliche Erklärung und Abbildung/deß Gesätzes und Evangelii Unterscheid* (Kempten: Kraus, 1630), Vorrede.
[31] Melchior Küsel, *Icones Biblicae Veteris et Novi Testamenti…* (Augsburg: Georg Laub, 1679), Vorrede. Reinitzer, *Biblia deutsch*, cat. no. 157.
[32] *Biblia, Das ist: Die gantze Heilige Schrifft/Alten vnd Neuen Testaments/Durch Herrn D. Martin Luthern verteutschet…auch mit 250. schönen Kupfer=Figuren eines berühmten Künstlers in Augsburg gezieret…* (Nuremberg: Johann Leonhard Buggel, Moritz Hagen, 1702), 'Vorrede' by Meelführer.
[33] Johann Ulrich Krauss, *Historische Bilder-Bibel* (Augsburg: Krauß, 1700), 113.

Fig. 7.2. Johann Ulrich Krauss, *Historische Bilder Bibel* (Augsburg: Krauß, 1700), Part V, p. 113.

Credit: © UB Augsburg, shelfmark 221/BU 4050 K91 B5-1-5.

THE DRESDEN COURT

Concern that images—especially beautiful images—might distract their viewers from the pure Word of God never entirely disappeared, but Lutheran 'image theology' nonetheless provided, it seems, plenty of space for the aesthetic appreciation of art. Artists used their talents to honour God, and the beauty of the images that they produced in general reinforced rather than negated their spiritual value. What better place to explore the interplay of piety and aestheticism, of devotion and spectacle, than Dresden, Germany's most magnificent Protestant court?[34] Here this interplay was particularly intricate because of the Saxon electors' Italianate cultural orientation. While Brandenburg often looked to the Reformed courts of the Netherlands for its artistic and architectural models, Saxony looked, during the sixteenth and seventeenth centuries, to the south. Its rulers presented themselves as modern princes, affirming their presence on the European stage by bringing objects, artists and styles from Italy to Dresden. This cultural transfer started under Moritz, the first Albertine Elector (r. 1547–53). Inspired by the architecture that he encountered during a 1550 trip to Northern Italy, Moritz rebuilt the castle, transforming Dresden's medieval fortress into a Renaissance palace. Moritz's successor, August (r. 1553–86), completed work on the castle, founded Dresden's *Kunstkammer* and presided over spectacular tournaments and other Renaissance festivities. Under August and Christian I (r. 1586–91), Dresden developed a particularly strong relationship with Florence. This was fostered at first by the Medici's interest in Saxon mining expertise. Then from the 1570s onwards the Albertine electors were actively courted by the Medici, who invoked Dresden as 'Florence on the Elbe' as part of their bid to have their status as grand dukes recognized at an international level. This political *rapprochement* encouraged the aesthetic adaptation of Florentine artistic models. In 1575, the Swiss Giovanni Maria Nosseni was installed as court sculptor in Dresden. Within one year of his arrival he had converted to Lutheranism and he spent the rest of his long career, to 1620, in the employment of the Saxon electors, presiding over the Italianization of Dresden.[35]

Yet, while Saxony' electors sought, through their cultural patronage, to imitate Italian princes, they also remained acutely aware of their status as supreme bishops of the territory that had given birth to the Protestant Reformation. Saxony remained, in general, loyal to the Emperor, prioritizing political considerations over religious

[34] For an overview of Lutheran castle chapels see Kathrin Ellwardt, *Evangelischer Kirchenbau in Deutschland* (Petersberg, 2008). On the legitimation of princely splendour in the seventeenth and eighteenth centuries see Ilrich Schütte, 'Das Fürstenschloß als »Pracht-Gebäude«', in Lutz Unbehaun (ed.), *Die Künste und das Schloß in der frühen Neuzeit* (Munich and Berlin, 1998), 15–29.
[35] See Barbara Marx, 'Künstlermigration und Kulturkonsum. Die Florentiner Kulturpolitik im 16. Jahrhundert und die Formierung Dresdens als Elbflorenz', in Bodo Guthmüller (ed.), *Deutschland und Italien in ihren wechselseitigen Beziehungen während der Renaissance* (Wiesbaden, 2000), 211–97; Barbara Marx (ed.), *Elbflorenz. Italienische Präsenz in Dresden 16.-19. Jahrhundert* (Dresden, 2000); Helen Watanabe-O'Kelly, *Court Culture in Early Modern Dresden* (Basingstoke, 2002). On Nosseni see Jürgen Müller, 'Giovanni Maria Nosseni and Art in Dresden, 1580–1620', in Syndram and Scherner (eds), *Princely Splendour*, 34–45.

solidarity within Germany. But the Albertine electors provided a symbolic focal point for the Protestant cause and during the second half of the seventeenth century were honoured as leaders of the *Corpus Evangelicorum,* the assembly of Protestant Estates within the Imperial Diet.[36] Dresden's court culture was decisively shaped not only by its recourse to Italian cultural idioms but also by its Protestantism. Moritz, for example, established in 1548 the *Churfürstliche Cantorey*, a court choir to perform sacred music, and his successors continued to foster Lutheran devotional music. From at least the reign of Elector August onwards, biblical drama played an important part in court celebrations and even tournaments—supreme expressions of secular power—often contained evangelical messages.[37] In the fields of art and architecture, the apogee of Nosseni's work for the Saxon electors was certainly their burial chapel in Freiberg in the Erzgebirge, a monumental dynastic project begun under August and brought to fruition under Christian I (Fig. 5.7). It was intended to demonstrate the position of the House of Wettin as a leading Protestant power. At its centre Moritz kneels before a crucifix on a splendid, free-standing tomb. Through the work of Nosseni and Carlo di Cesare, a pupil of Giambologna whom he summoned from Florence, the surrounding chapel was transformed into a magnificent space, filled with both political and religious symbolism. Around the walls are life-sized kneeling portraits of the Albertine dukes and electors, all facing towards an altar bearing a bronze crucifix by Carlo di Cesare. In the gloriously polychromed ceiling above, the resurrected Christ and Archangel Michael hover in judgement, surrounded by music-making angels.[38]

Saxony's electors were not the only European princes who sought to reconcile visual magnificence, inspired in general by the examples set by Europe's leading Catholic dynasties, with commitment to the evangelical faith. But their Lutheran confession enabled them to integrate images fully into courtly religious life in a way that Reformed Protestants could not. In 1587, Gabriel Kaltemarckt, a Dresden-based artist, addressed to Elector Christian I a proposal to establish a *Kunstkammer* with himself, Kaltemarckt, as resident art expert. Dresden's first *Kunstkammer* had been founded in 1560 by Elector August I, but contained relatively few art objects and pictures.[39] Kaltemarckt proposed removing the scientific instruments and tools that had formed the core of August's collection, and replacing them with statues, paintings, and *naturalia*—more conventional objects for a princely *Kunstkammer*. The preface to his *Thoughts on How a Kunstkammer Should be Formed* provides a wonderful insight into the Lutheran merging of piety and magnificence. Kaltemarckt emphasized that writing and painting were necessary to preserve the names and deeds of emperors, kings, and princes. He cited the example of the Medici in Florence, 'whom many regard as having ascended to princely, indeed almost to kingly majesty, more through collections of good books and through supporting the liberal arts of the burghers than through any other of their praiseworthy deeds'.

---

[36] Vötsch, *Kursachsen, das Reich und der mitteldeutschen Raum*, 45–64.
[37] Watanabe-O'Kelly, *Court Culture*.
[38] For a full discussion see Monika Meine-Schawe, *Die Grablege der Wettiner im Dom zu Freiberg. Die Umgestaltung des Domchores durch Giovanni Maria Nosseni 1585–1594* (Göttingen, 1989).
[39] Watanabe-O'Kelly, *Court Culture*, 71 ff.

Happily for Dresden's Elector, however, images not only guaranteed the immortal memory of their patrons but also promoted true, Lutheran piety. 'Music', Kaltemarckt wrote, 'through hearing, and the visual arts, through sight, arouse man to proper and honest joy and are nobly given and ordained by God'. Images may, in the past, have 'often been forced into the use of idolatry', but the 'true religion' could make proper use of them. Kaltemarckt identified a Lutheran middle way, between the pagans of Antiquity and the Catholics, both of whom venerated images, and the Calvinists and the Turks, with their iconoclastic cultures. He thanked God for having given Lutherans 'the ability to appreciate the right use of the visual arts'.[40]

The examples of Europe's great Renaissance princes—the Medici, Francis I, Henry VIII—and of the Empire's rulers—Emperors Maximilian I and II and the Ernestine Elector Johann Friedrich I—informed Kaltemarckt's *Thoughts*. Even cities— notably Venice, Antwerp, and Nuremberg—achieved fame, he wrote, through their arts. 'The best adornment and treasure of a prince and sovereign includes not only and above all orthodox religion, faithful subjects and sufficient money, but also his possession of magnificent munitions and military equipment, of a glorious library and book collection, of artful sculptures and paintings', Kaltemarckt concluded.[41] His prospective patron, Christian I, had already achieved fame for his armoury and library; only an art collection was now lacking. Kaltemarck's ideal for a proper *Kunstkammer* remained unrealized at the time of Christian I's death in 1591. And while Christian had, indeed, been a significant patron, completing the Dresden stables and commissioning a splendid gallery with life-sized portraits of his ances- tors and depictions of the tournaments of Elector August by Heinrich Göding, it seems unlikely that he would have approved of Kaltemarckt's views on religious imagery.[42] Christian was, as we have seen, no orthodox Lutheran. He showed a marked inclination towards Calvinism and revoked Saxony's traditional loyalty to the Emperor, supporting French Huguenots and striving (unsuccessfully) to found a German Union of Protestants.[43] Had he lived longer, it seems likely that Saxony's churches would have been stripped of their images. But after Christian's death, and the territory's return to the orthodox Lutheran fold, Kaltemarckt's 'right use of the visual arts'—a use that was both political and pious—flourished in Dresden.

Christian II (r. 1591–1611) and Johann Georg I (r. 1611–56) maintained the traditions of princely splendour instigated by their predecessors; indeed Christian II brought Saxony to the brink of bankruptcy through his extravagant spending. The Thirty Years' War was not, of course, a propitious time for cultural patronage, with troop movement and disease devastating large parts of the electorate during

---

[40] Barbara Gutfleisch and Joachim Menzhausen, '"How a Kunstkammer Should be Formed." Gabriel Kaltemarckt's advice to Christian I of Saxony on the formation of an art collection, 1587', *Journal of the History of Collections*, 1 (1) (1989), 3–32, esp. 8.

[41] Ibid., 10.

[42] DaCosta Kaufmann, *Court, Cloister and City*, 175; Watanabe-O'Kelly, *Court Culture*, 43.

[43] Thomas Klein, 'Politische oder kirchlich-religiöse Reform? – Die Regierung Christans I. 1586–1591', *Dresdner Hefte. Beiträge zur Kulturgeschichte*, 29 (1992), 5–91; On his artistic patronage see Joachim Menzhausen, 'Die Dresdner Kunst unter Christian I.', *Dresdner Hefte. Beiträge zur Kulturgeschichte*, 29 (1992), 51–6.

the 1630s and 1640s.[44] But under Johann Georg I, Dresden's *Kunstkammer* was eventually transformed, in part through the Elector's acquisition of Nosseni's collection of paintings and casts. The composer Heinrich Schütz, who had studied in Venice with Giovanni Gabrielli from 1609 to 1612, arrived in Dresden in 1615 and spent much of the rest of his career at the court. And Johann Georg I continued to work on Italian-inspired architectural projects, notably the *Lusthaus* or *Belvedere* on Dresden's ramparts.

Under Johann Georg II (r. 1656–80), Dresden's court culture was re-established after the traumas of the war. Johann Georg II's political record was undistinguished; he certainly lacked the political acumen of his Hohenzollern contemporary, Elector Friedrich Wilhelm (r. 1640–88), who during this period laid the foundations for Brandenburg's rise to greatness. But his court was truly splendid. In elaborate festivals, Johann Georg II presented himself (optimistically) as a warrior and hero, as Jason, as St George, and as Nimrod, the mighty Old Testament king. Dresden began to compete with the international festive culture of Vienna and Munich: there were not only tournaments and fireworks but also ballets, operas, and drama.[45] Above all, however, there was music. Music was the Elector's chief passion and here he showed himself to be 'a bold and venturesome spirit', introducing the most recent Italian sacred music into the heart of Lutheran Germany.[46] Johann Georg II brought castrati to Dresden, appointed court composers from Rome, and assembled a large and Italian-dominated *Hofkapelle* (the musical ensemble associated with the court). In its musical significance, as well as in its festival culture, his court rivalled the Emperor's and the Bavarian Elector's.[47] Moreover, thanks to his father's decision to return, in his 1652 will, to the principle of *Landesteilung* and to divide Albertine Saxony between his four sons, three other courts competed with Dresden's in their displays of princely magnificence: Sachsen-Weißenfels, Sachsen-Merseburg, and Sachsen-Zeitz.[48]

We should not, however, underestimate the tension created by the Albertine rulers' on-going interest in, and engagement with, the visual and musical culture of Catholic Italy. Their cultural positioning as baroque princes and champions of the Protestant cause was ambivalent: they looked to Italy, and were keen to learn and to imitate, but recognized the need to avoid contamination. When, in 1601–2, the future Johann Georg I undertook a 13-month journey to Italy, he travelled incognito. The young prince spent much of his time in Venice, but also travelled to Rome and as far as Naples, visiting many of Italy's most important

[44] Thomas Munck, 'Keeping up Appearances: Patronage of the Arts, City Prestige, and Princely Power in Northern Germany and Denmark 1600–1670', *German History*, 6 (3) (1988), 213–32, esp. 229–31.
[45] Watanabe-O'Kelly, *Court Culture*, 105, 130 ff.
[46] Mary Frandsen, *Crossing Confessional Boundaries: The Patronage of Italian Sacred Music in Seventeenth-Century Dresden* (New York and Oxford, 2006).
[47] On Munich see Alex Fisher, *Music, Piety, and Propaganda: The Soundscapes of Counter-Reformation Bavaria* (Oxford, 2014).
[48] Martina Schattkowsky (ed.), *Sachsen und seine Sekundogenituren: die Nebenlinien Weißenfels, Merseburg und Zeitz (1657–1746)* (Leipzig, 2010); R. Jacobsen (ed.), *Weissenfels als Ort literarischer und künstlerischer Kultur im Barockzeitalter* (Amsterdam and Atlanta, 1995).

centres of art and learning. His disguise obviated the need for a large entourage and for ceremonial receptions. In 1680, Anton Weck, Johann Georg II's archivist and secretary, reflected in his official history of Dresden that on this trip the future Johann Georg I had overcome, amongst other dangers, the 'contrary religion' of Italy.[49] When, as Electoral Prince, the future Johann Georg IV visited Italy in 1685–86 he did so openly, but instructions for his journey included the proviso that he must be accompanied by a pastor, who was charged with keeping him loyal to 'pure, uncorrupted evangelical teaching' through sermons and daily prayers.[50]

The accounts of these two princes' trips to Italy are frustratingly silent about what they, or their companions, thought of the Catholic visual culture that they encountered. We learn only, for example, that in Venice Johann Georg IV visited Palladio's San Giorgio Maggiore, 'which was valued because of the architecture and paintings', and that in Rome he saw, amongst other things, Il Gesù, the mother church of the Jesuit order. The diary of Friedrich August's 1687–89 journey to France, Spain and Italy gives a little more information. It praises, for example, the church at Philip II's residence of El Escorial, the adornment of which was, 'indescribable and inestimable in its artistry because of its costliness'. In Italy, too, the Germans admired 'magnificent' (*herrliche*) cloisters and 'splendid' (*prächtige*) churches, and in Milan Cathedral the prince was shown a statue with gold offerings piled before it, which was 'incomparable' in its artistry.[51] This appreciation of the visual culture of Catholicism was not unusual. During the Grand Tour both Lutherans and Calvinists frequently visited Rome, Loreto and other key religious sites, and their travel diaries generally describe their encounters with the great buildings, images, and relics of the Catholic cult in neutral or even positive terms.[52] Lutheran theologians warned against such encounters: in a 1683 tract addressed to Lutherans travelling to or living in 'papist' places, Johann Friedrich Mayer stated, for example, that Lutherans could not, in good conscience, visit Catholic churches, participate in Catholic ceremonies, or fall down before Catholic images and reliquaries.[53] In practice, however, it seems that such confessional concerns were outweighed by travellers' curiosity and aesthetic appreciation.

[49] Anton Weck, *Der Chur=Fürstlichen Sächsischen weitberuffenen Residentz= und Haupt=Vestung* (Nuremberg: Hoffmann, 1680), 142.

[50] Katrin Keller (ed.), *'Mein herr befindet sich gottlob gesund und wohl'. Sächsische Prinzen auf Reisen* (Leipzig, 1994), 26–7. See also Barbara Marx, 'Die Italienreise Herzog Johann Georgs von Sachsen (1601–1602) und der Besuch von Cosimo III. de' Medici (1668) in Dresden. Zur Kausalität von Grand Tour und Kulturtransfer', in Rainer Babel and Werner Paravicini (eds), *Grand Tour. Adeliges Reisen und Europäische Kultur vom 14. bis zum 18. Jahrhundert* (Ostfildern, 2005), 373–421.

[51] Ibid., 27 ff., 257 ff., 360.

[52] Antje Stannek, 'Konfessionalisierung des »Giro d'Italia«? Protestanten im Italien des 17. Jahrhunderts', *Beihefte der Francia*, 60 (2005), 555–68; see also Gerrit Verhoeven, 'Calvinist Pilgrimages and Popish Encounters: Religious Identity and Sacred Space on the Dutch Grand Tour (1598–1685)', *Journal of Social History*, 43 (3) (2010), 615–34; Roberto Zaugg, '"bey den Italiern recht sinnreiche Gedancken…gespürt". Joseph Furttenbach als kultureller Vermittler', in von Greyerz, Siebenhüner and Zaugg (eds), *Lebenslauff 1652–1664*, 25–43.

[53] Stannek, 'Konfessionalisierung', 558.

Although German Protestants could travel and could admire, the actual transfer of Italian artistic and musical styles to Germany had, as Michael Baxandall so compellingly showed, long caused unease.[54] With the entrenchment of confessional cultures, this unease not suprisingly increased. The new musical styles of the seventeenth century, pioneered in Italy by Giovanni Gabrieli, Carlo Gesualdo, and Claudio Monteverdi, and brought to Germany by Michael Praetorius, Johann Hermann Schein, Samuel Scheidt, and (above all) Heinrich Schütz, stood, for some, in opposition to the Lutheran traditions of lay congregational singing. Learned critics of this new church music asked whether its Italian style, with soloists, chorus, and instruments, directed attention to God or only to the music itself: in a much-quoted attack published in 1661 by the Rostock theologian Theophilus Grossgebauer, such music was described as a plot by the papacy to silence the Word of God. Its hearers, 'deafened through the sound of the organ and the brilliant, peculiar performance of music', could not praise God, but were merely 'stunned in amazement and tickled in the ears'.[55] In Dresden, criticism focused not on the style of the music promoted by the electors, but on the religious affiliations of the artists charged with performing it. Johann Georg II's inability (or unwillingness) to prevent his Catholic musicians from attending Mass was a thorn in the side of Dresden's Lutheran city council and consistory. The Elector's cultural activities thus reinforced suspicions generated by his political orientation.[56]

Whether through genuine conviction, or through a desire to assuage his subjects' fears, Johann Georg II did, however, go to considerable lengths to articulate his Lutheran identity. In 1661–62, he restored, as we shall see, Dresden's castle chapel, the heart of the city's Lutheran cult, and thereafter lavished extraordinary attention on its visual appearance as well as on its music and liturgy. Sometime during the 1660s he instituted the first annual commemoration of Reformation Day: a court diary for 1667 records the celebration of 'the evangelical festival of thanksgiving for the Gospel brought forth 150 years ago by the illustrious Dr Luther through divine illumination', and by 1668 the feast day was celebrated with what was, for Johann Georg, typical solemnity and splendour.[57] Johann Georg II also constructed a new chapel at his hunting lodge, Moritzburg, consecrated with elaborate ceremony in 1672.[58] And in a very public statement of Lutheran piety, the Elector installed a crucifix on the bridge across the Elbe, marking the safest place for ships to pass through. A bronze crucifix had, according to Anton Weck, been made for the site 50 years ago, but had been sold by the artist's heirs. Johann Georg replaced it, and gave it a Latin inscription that warned against superstitious adoration.[59]

---

[54] Michael Baxandall, *The Limewood Sculptors of Renaissance Germany* (New Haven and London, 1980).

[55] Herl, *Worship Wars*, 116 ff., 198.

[56] Frandsen, *Crossing Confessional Boundaries*, esp. 77, 86.

[57] SLUB Dresden, Msc. Dresd. K 80 DIARIVM 1665–6, fol. 113 v; SHStAD 10024 Geheimer Rat (Geheimes Archiv), Loc. 8681/7.

[58] Watanabe-O'Kelly, *Court Culture*, 19.

[59] Weck, *Der Chur=Fürstlichen Sächsischen weitberuffenen Residentz= und Haupt=Vestung*, 86–8.

THE CASTLE CHAPEL

Ostentatious piety was, we know, a constitutive part of the rule of the Empire's Catholic princes. The Habsburgs and the Wittelsbachs founded churches and cloisters, donated money and sacred objects, participated in pilgrimages and processions and promoted the Counter-Reformation cults of Mary and the Eucharist. Their political culture was profoundly shaped by their piety. Protestant princes could not, of course, engage in many of these public acts of faith, but, as the Dresden court shows, Saxony's Lutheran rulers found other ways to manifest their religious conviction: through music, drama, and festivals, and through the commissioning of monuments and memorials. This extravagant Protestant piety reached its apogee in Dresden's castle chapel, built between 1551 and 1555 during the redesign of the castle carried out by Electors Moritz and August.[60] The chapel was the focal point of the religious and musical life of the Albertine court. Here its members gathered for regular Sunday worship and to celebrate the feast-days of the Lutheran liturgical year, and here the baptisms, marriages, and funerals of members of the princely family were conducted in the presence of dignitaries from inside and outside the Empire. Here Saxony's court preachers, figures such as Polycarp Leyser the Elder, Matthias Hoe von Hoenegg, and, briefly, Philipp Jakob Spener preached.[61] And here musicians of European significance, most notably Heinrich Schütz, performed. The chapel retained its significance as a focal point for Lutheran worship and as the symbolic heart of Germany's Lutheran political culture until 1737, when, in the face of considerable resistance, the Catholic Friedrich August II moved services for the evangelical members of the court from the chapel to the nearby Sophienkirche in order to make space for new residential apartments.[62]

The chapel was almost completely destroyed, along with the rest of Dresden's castle, on 13 February 1945, but a rich array of textual and visual sources enable us to reconstruct in detail not only its original appearance and the transformations that it underwent during the its seventeenth-century restorations, but also its liturgical and musical culture. Under Elector August the chapel was furnished with a splendid stone altar. Its central reliefs were made from alabaster, and had been commissioned in the Netherlands in 1553–54. Within an Italianate frame of Corinthian columns, adorned with Wettin coats of arms, the altar showed four biblical scenes: Christ's Birth and Crucifixion, Moses with the Brazen Serpent and Pentecost. Above were depictions of the Fall and Expulsion, flanked by caryatids representing faith, charity, and hope. The altar's predella, showing the Last Supper, and the statues of John the Baptist and Moses at its sides were later additions.[63] The pulpit, dating from 1553, bore sculptures of the four evangelists, with Moses and the Brazen Serpent beneath. There was also a richly carved font, installed in

---

[60] Heinrich Magirius, *Die evangelische Schlosskapelle zu Dresden aus kunstgeschichtlicher Sicht* (Altenburg, 2009).
[61] Wolfgang Sommer, *Die lutherischen Hofprediger in Dresden: Grundzüge ihrer Geschichte und Verkündigung im Kurfürstentum Sachsen* (Stuttgart, 2006).
[62] StadtAD, B III 49.   [63] Magirius, *Die evangelische Schlosskapelle*, 68.

1558.[64] Of the chapel's other sixteenth-century furnishings, its tapestries were perhaps the most famous, first mentioned in a report on the baptism of Duke Alexander of Saxony on 28 February 1554, when the chapel was 'adorned with precious silk tapestries, enhanced with gold, on which the history of Christ's suffering or Passion is depicted'.[65] Inventories from 1565, 1589, and 1611 also mention the tapestries, one series 'of gold, silver and silk' and one series 'of an old Passion, silver and silk'. The ten tapestries from the 'old Passion' were, according to the 1589 inventory, 'very artistically made', and four from this series, created in Brussels in *c.*1522–28, survive today.[66]

In a poem of praise for the city of Dresden from 1591, Daniel Wintzenberger mentioned the chapel, in particular its tapestries that showed the whole Passion in 'silk, gold, silver and beautiful colours'.[67] Wintzenberger also mentioned the chapel's vaulted ceiling, which was 'artfully formed, with wondrously depicted snakes on it'. This ceiling was, according to Philip Hainhofer, who saw it during his 1629 trip to Dresden, full of snakes and evil spirits carved in stone, derived from the Apocalypse. The Archangel Michael and other angels fought them, holding the instruments of Christ's Passion. The decoration represented, Hainhofer wrote, Christ's triumph over sin, death, the devil, and hell, as well as the destruction of vice and eternal damnation, and was intended to encourage meditation on eternity.[68] The ceiling was clearly a very accomplished work. In 1680, Anton Weck wrote that it was 'so artful that many of those who understand architecture avow that . . . there are not many similar vaults to be seen'. Its dragons or snakes of carved sandstone and its angel holding the instruments of Christ's Passion were so brilliantly constructed that 'they seemed to float in the air'.[69]

In addition to the ceiling, Hainhofer admired in particular the Elector's glazed prayer room, constructed in 1568 by August I. Here, he recorded, 'hung many small panels depicting sacred stories and portraits, amongst them one by Albrecht Dürer's hand, and others by Lucas Cranach'. The windows were made of polished glass; the stove was made of silver. On the chapel's altar was, he wrote, 'a handsome crucifix', and in the sacristy were 'three beautiful chasubles', used by the chapel's clergy on high feast days: 'on one is the Birth of Christ, raised up high with pearls and precious stones, on two others . . . the Crucifixion of Christ, beautifully embroidered and formed'. To cover the altar during communion there was a black velvet cloth embroidered with the Resurrection. Alongside chalices and patens there were also silver candlesticks held by angels. In a chest was kept a Bible with engraved illustrations, printed on parchment in Wittenberg in 1588. Its binding was decorated with silver, and it was wrapped in black velvet. It was, according to Hainhofer,

---

[64] Ibid., 77–9.
[65] Ibid., 89. Uta Neidhardt, 'Gewirkte Passion. Vier Bildteppiche der Gemäldegalerie Alte Meister', *Dresdner Kunstblätter*, 48 (3) (2004), 153–65; Annegret Laabs, 'Burgundische Tapisserien am Dresdner Hof', *Dresdner Kunstblätter*, 48 (3) (2004), 166–73.
[66] Magirius, *Die evangelische Schlosskapelle*, 89–93.   [67] Ibid., 89 ff.
[68] Oscar Doering, *Des Augsburger Patriciers Philipp Hainhofer Reisen nach Innsbruck und Dresden* (Vienna, 1901), 203.
[69] Weck, *Der Chur=Fürstlichen Sächsischen weitberuffenen Residentz= und Haupt=Vestung*, 200.

'very beautifully illuminated', and had been given to the ministers of the church by Elector August.[70] The Bible was inscribed in the Elector's own hand with a wonderful statement of Lutheran identity:

> From my youth onwards I have professed my faith in the Holy Bible and the Augsburg Confession, and I propose also to die in the same with God's help and grace. Because I saw that in my court church there was a Calvinist Bible…I removed it, and myself put Dr Luther's version in its place.[71]

The chapel was renovated in 1602–04 under Christian II, then again in 1661–62 under Johann Georg II. This second restoration was carried out under the direction of architect Wolf Caspar von Klengel, who wrote that chapel should be 'most beautifully and well decorated with painting and stucco work'.[72] Fig. 7.3, David Conrad's engraved frontispiece from Christoph Bernhard's 1676 *Geistreiches Gesangbuch*, shows the chapel after it was completed. In the foreground, Heinrich Schütz stands surrounded by his *Kantorie*. Instrumentalists are seated in the singers' galleries above the altar, which, according to Weck rested on 'four red marble columns', the like of which could not—because of their colour and because they were carved from single pieces of marble—be found even in Rome.[73] The pulpit and ceiling survive from the original decoration campaign; the organ depicted here, with its painted wings, dates from 1612. The walls are painted to imitate marble. On the balconies are inscriptions and beyond them are panel paintings probably dating from the 1602–04 restoration campaign and showing scenes from the Old and New Testaments.

The altar positioned beneath the organ in Conrad's engraving was installed during the 1661–62 restoration. The chapel's original alabaster altarpiece was removed and sent to the castle chapel in Torgau, and von Klengel stated that its replacement should be 'surrounded most decoratively with the four oriental green marble columns in a modern style [*nach Moderner manier*]'.[74] These four green marble columns were carved from stone that had been brought back from the Holy Land by Duke Albrecht in 1476, and were therefore bearers of both sacred and dynastic memory. In Klengel's design for the altar, double Corinthian columns frame a bare panel of red marble. Beneath are the electoral and the Saxon arms, and above two angels worship before a gloriole of light. When the altar was installed, a black cross with a white figure of Christ stood in front of its central panel (Fig. 7.4). Unlike its sixteenth-century predecessor, Klengel's marble altarpiece told no stories, but provided a dramatic backdrop for this single sculpted crucifix. Its style was, as he wished, more 'modern'. But the difference between the 1553–54 altar and its

---

[70] Doering, *Des Augsburger Patriciers Philipp Hainhofer Reisen*, 202–3. On the antependium see Magirius, *Die evangelische Schlosskapelle*, 94.

[71] Weck, *Der Chur=Fürstlichen Sächsischen weitberuffenen Residentz= und Haupt=Vestung*, 202–3.

[72] HStAD, 10024 Geheimer Rat (Geheimes Archiv), Loc. 04452/02. On von Klengel see Günter Passavant, *Wolf Caspar von Klengel: Dresden 1630–1691; Reisen—Skizzen—Baukünstlerische Tätigkeiten* (Berlin, 2001).

[73] Weck, *Der Chur=Fürstlichen Sächsischen weitberuffenen Residentz= und Haupt=Vestung*, 202.

[74] HStAD, 10024 Geheimer Rat (Geheimes Archiv), Loc. 04452/02. See Passavant, *Wolf Caspar von Klengel*, 439.

Fig. 7.3. David Conrad, View of the Interior of the Castle Chapel in Dresden, frontispiece from Christoph Bernhard, *Geistreiches Gesang-Buch*…(Dresden: Paul August Hamann, 1676).

Credit: © Herzog August Bibliothek Wolfenbüttel, shelfmark H: S 379.4° Helmst.

1661–62 successor also reflects, in microcosm, the transformations in Lutheran Passion piety described in Chapter 5. While the sixteenth-century altar is narrative, telling in abbreviated form—through a number of small scenes—the story of salvation, Wolf Caspar von Klengel's is devotional, focusing all of its viewer's attention on the figure of the crucified Christ.[75]

As Philip Hainhofer's 1629 account suggests, it was not only the chapel's altar, pulpit and other fixed furnishings that created an impression of magnificence; it was also its rich collection of precious textiles and liturgical vessels.[76] A series of inventories covering the period 1588 to 1705 provide a wonderful glimpse into these 'costly items [*Pretiosa*], gold and silver cans [for communion wine] and

[75] See Magirius, *Die evangelische Schlosskapelle*, 74 on the plans and model for the altar.
[76] On Lutheran liturgical vessels see Johann Michael Fritz and Martin Brecht (eds), *Das evangelische Abendmahlsgerät in Deutschland: vom Mittelalter bis zum Ende des alten Reiches* (Leipzig, 2004). Also Birgit Ulricke Münch, 'The Lutheran Tradition', in Lee Palmer Wandel (ed.), *A Companion to the Eucharist in the Reformation* (Leiden, 2014), 399–422.

Fig. 7.4. Wolf Kaspar von Klengel, altarpiece from the Castle Chapel in Dresden, *c.*1661–62.
Credit: © Landesamt für Denkmalpflege Sachsen.

dishes, [and] vestments', and testify to the proliferation of visual splendour that occurred during the second half of the seventeenth century.[77] The first inventory, drawn up during the reign of Christian I, lists silver gilded chalices, patens, cans for holding communion wine, pyx (containers for storing the host) and candlesticks. Amongst the chapel's textiles were vestments embroidered with pearls, altar cloths and hangings for the pulpit. There was also 'a new crucifix to be used for communion'. The 1608 inventory includes additional objects given by Christian II and his wife, Hedwig of Denmark. By 1666, after Johann Georg II's redecoration campaign, the chapel's 'Pretiosen' were so numerous and so valuable that they were divided between the sacristy, where objects that were in frequent use were kept, and 'the vaulted chamber called *das Jungste Gericht* [the Last Judgement]', located behind the organ.[78] In the vaulted chamber were silver bowls for holding baptism water, chalices, patens, cans for communion wine and candlesticks. Three entries in the inventories can be identified with objects that survive today: a 'communion can on which is engraved Christ's Last Supper and Crucifixion and, on the lid, the arms of Electoral Saxony', and a baptismal bowl and its water-carrying can, partially gilded and bearing mother of pearl decoration.[79] There was also a splendid collection of textiles: vestments and hangings for the altar and pulpit. Amongst the vestments, for example, was a velvet chasuble fringed with gold and silver braid, 'on which Christ on the cross, four angels and the four evangelists are richly and artistically embroidered with gold, silver, pearls and coloured silk'. Another was made from black velvet and showed the Birth of Christ, 'very artistically and richly emboidered' with gold, pearls and coloured silk, and adorned with jewels.[80]

It is impossible to reconstruct when, exactly, all of these objects were donated to the chapel, but many were certainly commissioned by Johann Georg II himself. In a lovely indication of his desire for princely display, the 1666 inventory lists a silver gilded chalice, paten, and communion can that Johann Georg used in 1658 in Frankfurt am Main during the election and coronation of Emperor Leopold I.[81] Amongst the splendid objects donated by Johann Georg to the chapel was a solid gold chalice, decorated with enamel images showing 24 stories from the New Testament, the four evangelists, four church fathers, and the arms of Electoral Saxony. This chalice was adorned with 560 jewels of various sorts. Its accompanying paten bore enamel depictions of the Last Supper and the *Arma Christi*, and 33 jewels. A gold pyx was enamelled with 17 'sacred histories', the four cardinal virtues, eight angels and four angels' heads as well as the arms of Electoral Saxony. On its lid was a

---

[77] SHStAD, 10024 Geheimer Rat (Geheimes Archiv), Loc. 8687/2.

[78] This chamber was named after the paintings of the Last Judgement kept there: M. Fürstenau, 'Zur Geschichte des Tapetenwirkerei am Hofe zu Dresden', *Sachsengrün. Culturgeschichtliche Zeitschrift aus sämtlichen Landen Sächsischen Stammes*, 1 (1861), 199–200, here 200. In 1668 Cosimo de' Medici, son of the Grand Duke of Tuscany, visited the 'Jungste Gericht' on his tour of the castle. SHStAD, 10006 Oberhofmarschallamt, O IV Nr. 23 (15–18 March). On the 'daily use' of the objects in the sacristy see SHStAD, 10024 Geheimer Rat (Geheimes Archiv), Loc. 8687/2, 83r–83v (1692).

[79] SHStAD, 10024 Geheimer Rat (Geheimes Archiv), Loc. 8687/2, fol. 18v (no. 6), fol. 18r (no. 1); Magirius, *Die evangelische Schlosskapelle*, 100, no. 11, no. 10.

[80] SHStAD, 10024 Geheimer Rat (Geheimes Archiv), Loc. 8687/2, fol. 23r, no. 34, no. 32.

[81] Ibid., fol. 18r-v, no. 4.

crucifix, beneath which 343 jewels were to be found.[82] A golden can for communion wine that was made slightly later to accompany these was also adorned with enamelled stories from Scripture, the electoral arms and 950 jewels, including 23 sapphires and 61 diamonds.[83] The 1681 inventory remarked of this splendid object that it 'is studded with very many costly jewels that almost cannot be counted'.[84] Johann Georg II also donated a richly embroidered antependium that showed, in its centre, Christ's Resurrection surrounded by coats of arms, and in its corners the four evangelists.[85] The 1666 inventory listed a silver crucifix on a black base with a silver skull, and a large crucifix made of ivory, tortoiseshell, ebony, and silver. Another crucifix, this time large and silver with an enamel depiction of the Last Supper on its base, stood on the chapel's altar and had also been given, along with three silver gilded candlesticks, by Johann Georg II.[86]

The visual magnificence of Johann Georg II's castle chapel was remarkable. What more ostentatious act of piety could a Lutheran prince possibly engage in than the celebration of the Eucharist using solid gold, jewel-encrusted communion vessels at a baroque marble altar, covered with velvet hangings embroidered with silver and pearls on which stood an ivory, tortoiseshell, silver, and ebony crucifix? In Johann Georg II's chapel, however, such visual magnificence was deployed alongside music and ritual to create a feast for the eyes and ears that was intended not only to impress but also, like contemporary devotional texts, to intensify the individual believer's encounter with Christ. As testimony to his passionate interest in music the Elector left a unique record of the liturgical life of his court from 1660 onwards: a series of orders of worship contained within court diaries that record in great detail not only the musical works that were performed during church services but also the images and textiles that were used on particular feast days.[87] The court's liturgical year and its elaborate musical accompaniment have been investi-gated in detail by Mary Frandsen, and for the purposes of my study two key points emerge from her analysis. Firstly, the Gospel text appointed for a particular Sunday or feast day determined the theme not only of the sermon but also of the entire service, as Dresden's court composers presented 'musical realizations of texts appro-priate to the occasion'.[88] This was not just music, as Grossgebauer would have had it, intended to amaze its hearers and 'tickle' their ears; it was music to reinforce the scriptural message of the service. Secondly, the music imported to Saxony from around 1650 onwards provided not just a new, modern style but also new settings of texts, settings that responded to changes in Lutheran piety. The Roman composers Vincenzo Albrici and Giuseppe Peranda arrived in Dresden, Frandsen points out, 'just at a time when the type of textual material with which they were accustomed

---

[82] Ibid., fol. 20r–v, no. 25, no. 26.   [83] Ibid., fol. 34r–37r.

[84] Ibid., fol. 42r.   [85] Ibid., fol. 23v, no. 35.

[86] Ibid., 20v–21 r, no. 27/1, fol. 25v, no. 55, fol. 28r, no. 11. The ivory crucifix is described more fully in the 1681 inventory, ibid., fol. 47v–48r and illustrated in Magirius, *Die evangelische Schlosskapelle*, 75.

[87] I am hugely grateful to Mary Frandsen for her guidance on the court diaries. See Frandsen, *Crossing Confessional Boundaries*, esp. chapter 8.

[88] Ibid., 365.

to engage (and the musical style with which they engaged it) was uniquely suited to the new spirit of personal devotion that had developed in seventeenth-century Lutheranism'.[89]

Careful thematic integration—the desire to strengthen the spiritual significance of the service—shaped the chapel's visual appearance as well as its musical performances. For Johann Georg splendour was paramount, as his elaborate pre-service protocols for feast days demonstrate. The court diary for Christmas Day 1677, for example, records that bells were rung in the castle and in the city and weapons were fired before the service. Shawms played in the castle courtyard and the Elector's guards paraded. A display of secular power framed the spiritual observance of the holy day, the core of which consisted of a lengthy service with preaching, music and congregational singing.[90] In the chapel itself, visual splendour reinforced religious content: this was surely a perfect expression of Kaltemarckts' 'right use of the visual arts'. Christmas and Easter were the most important points in the liturgical year, and on these two festivals the chapel's magnificent tapestries were hung. At Christmas those chosen showed scenes from the life and Passion of Christ, including 'on the Elector's gallery, the Birth of Christ and the Three Kings'.[91] The richness of the tapestries was complemented by hangings on the pulpit and altar (the parament), by the celebrant's magnificent vestments and by red velvet chairs and cushions.

Seventeenth-century Lutheran churches, unlike the post-Tridentine Catholic church, did not prescribe a fixed cycle of liturgical colours, and the images on the vestments and parament rarely related directly to the feast-day being celebrated (at Christmas in 1678, for example, the pulpit was adorned with Christ amongst the Doctors, while the altar cloth showed the *Pietà*—Mary holding the crucified Christ on her lap).[92] But their use nonetheless contributed to the solemnity of the occasion. During Holy Week, for example, which was a period of ritual simplicity for the court, the altar and pulpit were hung with black velvet paraments fringed with gold and silver.[93] Then in the morning on Holy Saturday, the chapel was transformed by the hanging of the tapestries. Once again the tapestries were chosen to reinforce the festival's spiritual significance, depicting the story of Christ's Passion, from his prayer on the Mount of Olives to the Crucifixion:

> On the electoral gallery the *Ölberg* (Christ on the Mount of Olives), beneath the arch of the electress' ladies-in-waiting, how Christ was taken prisoner in the garden, under the next arch, how he was led before Caiaphas, next on the right-hand side of the pulpit the Flagellation, above the sacristy the Crowning [with thorns], above the church door, the *Ecce Homo*, beside it the Judgement and Handwashing of Pilate, then beneath the privy council's arch the Procession [to Calvary], next to it the Crucifixion, and beneath the electoral box, the Easter Lamb.[94]

---

[89] Ibid., 436.   [90] See ibid., 374–80 for a full account of the Christmas festivities.
[91] SLUB Dresden, Msc. Dresd. K 80 DIARIVM 1665–6. For an account of Christmas 1673 see SLUB Dresden, Msc. Dresd. K 117 Diarium 1673 (Advent 1672–July 1673).
[92] HStAD, 10006 Oberhofmarschallamt, N I Vol. 8, 'Beilage' (no folio numbers).
[93] Frandsen, *Crossing Confessional Boundaries*, 392–8.
[94] SLUB Dresden, Msc. Dresd. K 80 DIARIVM 1665–6, fol. 47v–48r; see Frandsen, *Crossing Confessional Boundaries*, 401–3.

Amongst the other feast days observed at court, two deserve particular mention as expressions of Johann Georg II's court Lutheranism. The first was the Elector's birthday, which was celebrated to enhance his personal image.[95] The second was Reformation Day (31 October), instituted, as we have seen, during the 1660s. In 1668, for example, in preparation for this feast day, the choir in the chapel was adorned with red velvet and woolen cloth, and the altar and pulpit with scarlet velvet paraments, richly embroidered with pearls, gold and silver. After the Elector had prayed and confessed the bells were rung. In the chapel, there was organ music and the 'German litany' was sung from the altar by the boys of the chapel choir (the court's Catholic musicians were rarely required to participate in this celebration of schism, for there were no sacred concertos or motets).[96] The senior court preacher, at this time Valentin Heerbrand, conducted the service, and administered communion from the Elector's solid gold, enameled, and bejewelled chalice, paten, pyx, and can. On the altar stood the ivory crucifix and gilded angel candlesticks.[97]

The material and musical culture of Elector Johann Georg II's court chapel provides a wonderful example of a Lutheran prince's 'deployment of cultural power'.[98] The Elector's musical patronage—his rejection of the older, Schützian idiom—reflected his belief that to support a more traditional Lutheran repertoire would damage his standing amongst his peers.[99] His redecoration of the chapel in 1661–62, and his subsequent lavish donations of precious furnishings for it, were products of his piety but also of his desire to project a suitably splendid public image. Such princely desire for representation 'in a modern style', as Wolf Caspar von Klengel had put it, of course outlasted Johann Georg II's reign. He was succeeded by his son, Johann Georg III (r. 1680–91) and grandson, Johann Georg IV (r. 1691–94). Under these two electors the musical culture of the castle chapel changed. Johann Georg III dismissed his father's Italian musicians and appointed Christoph Bernhard as *Kapellmeister*. Until his death in 1692 Bernhard presided over a reduced ensemble of German musicians. When Italian musicians reappeared in Dresden from 1685 onwards they did so primarily as composers of opera.[100] In 1687, Carlo Pallavicino staged his *Gerusalemme liberata* there, and the lead role was sung by Margherita Salicola, whom the Elector had himself heard in Venice and brought to Dresden.[101] This opera certainly impressed the visiting Ernestine Duke Friedrich I of Sachsen-Gotha-Altenburg considerably more than the castle chapel. While Friedrich's travel diary mentions only the pastors who preached in the chapel and Sophienkirche during his visit, it reports enthusiastically that at

[95] Ibid., 378, 411, 413. SLUB Dresden, Msc. Dresd. K 117 Diarium 1673, fol. 57r.

[96] Frandsen, *Crossing Confessional Boundaries*, 432–3.

[97] HStAD, 10006 Oberhofmarshallamt, O IV, Nr. 23, 31st October.

[98] Whaley, *Germany and the Holy Roman Empire*, vol. 2, 221.

[99] Mary Frandsen, 'Worship as Representation: The Italianate 'Hofkapelle' of Johann Georg II as an Instrument of Image Creation', in Barbara Marx (ed.), *Kunst und Repräsentation am Dresdner Hof* (Munich and Berlin, 2005).

[100] Frandsen, *Crossing Confessional Boundaries*, 70–1; 438–9.

[101] Watanabe-O'Kelly, *Court Culture in Dresden*, 189 ff., 192.

the opera 'the voices were altogether splendid and the decoration in the theatre sumptuous and not to be bettered'.[102]

Italian opera—a relatively novel art form north of the Alps—captured the attention of visiting dignitaries. But Dresden's liturgical life did retain its visual splendour. Court diaries from the period after 1680 are not nearly as rich in detail as those produced during Johann Georg II's reign, but they do afford occasional glimpses into the still-elaborate ceremony of the castle chapel. On New Year's Day 1693, for example, Johann Georg IV and his wife, Eleonore Erdmuthe Luise, received communion there. The diary includes a diagram that shows the exact positioning of the various members of the court, and records that the fabric hangings that had been there since Christmas were taken down and replaced with velvet.[103] With the conversion of Elector Friedrich August I in 1697, the main focus of the court's religious life shifted to the audience room, which was consecrated for Catholic use. But the court's evangelicals continued to use the chapel. In 1703, for example, Electress Christiane Eberhardine, known as Saxony's 'Betsäule' (pillar of prayer) for her resolute loyalty to the Lutheran church, received communion in the castle chapel, which was adorned with gold and silver paraments, with fabric hangings and with cushions for kneeling.[104] The chapel's inventories confirm that most of the rich furnishings donated under Johann Georg II and his predecessors survived into the eighteenth century. In 1682, Johann Georg III gave away some textiles that were no longer in use to the 'poor church in Raußlitz' (south-west of Meißen), and his successors also disposed of some superfluous objects.[105] But inventories from 1681, 1687, 1692, and 1705 indicate that the majority of the chapel's treasures, including Johann Georg II's solid gold communion vessels, survived, and that electors and their consorts continued to make new donations.[106]

In 1737, the castle chapel was finally stripped of its role as the focus of a magnificent, princely Lutheran cult. When Elector Friedrich August II transferred evangelical services to the Sophienkirche, he permitted his Lutheran courtiers to take with them the chapel's bells and vestments.[107] Inventories confirm that some, at least, of the chapel's textiles did end up in the Sophienkirche, as did its font and Wolf Caspar von Klengel's altar.[108] The Sophienkirche also had a magnificent high altar by Giovanni Nosseni, which had been donated in 1606 by Electress Sophia (widow of Christian I), as well as the epitaphs of Nosseni himself and many other eminent Dresden burghers. Evangelical services were conducted there in a visual

[102] SLUB Msc. Dresd. c.22. Miscellanae historica, Bl. 307.
[103] HStAD, 10006 Oberhofmarschallamt, N I Vol. 8, 138–9, 142. Johann Georg IV was the first of the Saxon electors to live openly with his mistress, Magdalena Sibylla von Neitschütz, who was rumoured to have been his half-sister.
[104] On Christiane Eberhardine see Siegfried Seifert, *Niedergang und Wiederaufstieg der Katholischen Kirche in Sachsen 1517–1773* (Leipzig, 1964), 137. HStAD, 10006 Oberhofmarschallamt, N I Vol. 8, 'Beilage' (no folio numbers), and fol. 161.
[105] HAStD, 10024 Geheimer Rat, Loc. 8687/2, fol. 22r.   [106] Ibid., fol. 137r–137v.
[107] StadtAD, Ratsarchiv B III 108 k, especially fol. 4v.
[108] Magirius, *Die evangelische Schlosskapelle*, 74; Robert Bruck, *Die Sophienkirche in Dresden. Ihre Geschichte und Ihre Kunstschätze* (Dresden, 1912), 23–4.

environment that was far from plain, but they certainly did not achieve the same level of magnificence as they had done at court. In Dresden, the era of princely Lutheranism was over, and to find the lasting and most splendid manifestation of Saxony's Lutheran baroque we must look not to the court, but to the city: to the Frauenkirche, examined in detail in Chapter 9.

CONCLUSION

During the early decades of the Reformation, theological discourse rarely cited the pursuit of beauty as a justification for the retention or continued production of religious images, even though it is clear that aesthetic appreciation played a part in determining their survival. From the later sixteenth century onwards, however, Lutheran discussions of images merged piety with aestheticism, and reconciled connoisseurship with an ongoing commitment to the religious use of art during the age of the *Kunstkammer*. It is almost too easy to disprove, by the second half of the seventeenth century, the thesis of Protestant opposition to images and elaborate liturgical ritual. Most spectacularly at the Dresden court of Elector Johann Georg II, but also, to a somewhat lesser extent, under his Lutheran predecessors and successors, sacred art, music and liturgy were readily employed in the service of princely magnificence. The German baroque was not a confessional style, a product of Counter-Reformation piety. Its beauty and artistry, its ability to impress and overwhelm, made it the ideal vehicle for the display of wealth and power. It was readily adopted by Lutherans, who understood well both its aesthetic and its spiritual appeal. Gabriel Kaltemarckt's 'right use of the visual arts', a use that demonstrated princely magnificence but also promoted true, Lutheran piety, found its perfect expression in Johann Georg II's magnificent castle chapel, with its rich decoration.

A vignette from the court at Weißenfels, from 1656 residence of the cadet branch of the Wettin dynasty founded by Johann Georg II's brother Augustus, shows just how fine the line between Lutheran and Catholic baroque could be. In 1675–82, Johann Heinrich Böhme the Younger installed a new altar in the castle church that was even more splendid than Wolf Caspar von Klengel's Dresden construction. The Weißenfels altar was a monumental structure, supported by life-sized carved angels and marble columns, and crowned by a gloriole of light with a sculpted Crucifixion above. At its centre was a pulpit: this was, originally, a *Kanzelaltar* (combined pulpit and altar), that provided a spectacular visual setting for the preaching of the Word of God. When, in 1746, the Saxe-Weißenfels cadet branch died out, and the territory returned to Saxony's now-Catholic electoral house, the altar remained in all its baroque splendour. Only one change was made: the pulpit was removed, and replaced by a marble relief of the Annunciation.[109] At one level the general inclination towards magnificence that produced the baroque

---

[109] Mario Titze, *Das barocke Schneeberg: Kunst und städtische Kultur des 17. und 18. Jahrhunderts in Sachsen* (Dresden, 2002), 101 ff. Ibid., *Barockskulptur im Herzogtum Sachsen-Weissenfels* (Halle, 2007).

suggests, perhaps, that there was no such thing as confessional visual culture by the later seventeenth century: both the Lutheran duke, who commissioned the Weißenfels altar, and the Catholic Elector, who inherited it, clearly valued its baroque aesthetic. But the Weißenfels story also suggests that beneath the pomp and splendour, beneath the veneer of precious metal, marble, gold and stucco that conjured up a vision of princely magnificence and heavenly glory, very real religious differences remained. These religious differences—and images' ongoing role as confessional markers—emerged especially clearly in the new confessional contexts of eighteenth-century Brandenburg and Saxony, and are examined in the final chapters of this book.

8

Protestant Aesthetics beyond the Court

Courts undoubtedly provided key focal points for Germany's spiritual and cultural life in around 1700: the Empire's princes offered, through their patronage, the best possible opportunities for musicians and artists. But baroque culture was not confined to princely courts or to the residences of the nobility. The desire for representation 'in a modern manner', as Dresden's court architect Wolf Caspar von Klengel had expressed it in 1661–2, was widespread, and shaped the visual culture of cities and towns throughout the Empire. In Dresden itself, and in many of the prosperous mining and mercantile towns of Electoral Saxony, churches were *barockisiert*: brought into line with an aesthetic inspired, in part, by knowledge of contemporary Italian models. In newly constructed churches such as the Trinitatskirche in Carlsfeld (1684–88) or the Georgenkirche in Schwarzenberg (1690–99), both in the Erzgebirge, Lutheran patrons showed their eagerness to adopt the visual idioms of the baroque. The Carlsfeld church (Fig. 8.1), commissioned by one of the most important mining entrepreneurs of the region, was designed by Wolf Caspar von Klengel, and is the oldest centrally planned, vaulted church in Saxony, an important precedent for Dresden's Frauenkirche. It also contains one of the region's oldest *Kanzelaltäre* (combined pulpit and altar), and the whole church is directed towards this central 'stage', where the preacher preached and the congregation encountered a monumental sculpted Crucifixion group. The Schwarzenberg church was financed by the local community, and provided an even more magnificent setting for Lutheran worship, from its elaborate ceiling to its richly adorned pulpit and nobles' gallery (Plate 12). Even if Lutheran patrons lacked the opportunity to build anew, they refurbished. In Görlitz, for example, the interior of the town church of St Peter and Paul was devastated by fire in 1691. By the end of the century, it had been filled with splendid images and furnishings given by members of the local elite, providing a visual environment that reflected not only the town's Lutheran piety but also its mercantile wealth.

Brandenburg's confessional situation was, of course, very different, and here baroque art and architecture were, in general, put to work in the service of princely splendour rather than evangelical piety. Elector Friedrich III (r. 1688–1713) was certainly no enemy of art and elaborate ritual, despite his Calvinism.[1] But the drive towards toleration (or at least co-existence) that had shaped Brandenburg's religious

---

[1] See, for example, Bernd Wolfgang Lindemann, 'Die Kunst in Berlin zu Zeiten Friedrichs, Kurfürst von Brandenburg und erster König in Polen', in Hans-Ulrich Kessler (ed.), *Andreas Schlüter und das barocke Berlin* (Berlin, 2014), 78–93.

Fig. 8.1. Johann Heinrich Böhme the Younger, Pulpit and Altar from the Trinitatiskirche in Carlsfeld (Erzgebirge), 1688.

Credit: Photo: author's own, with permission from the Kirchengemeinde Eibenstock-Carlsfeld.

history since the reign of the Great Elector placed the territory's Lutherans in a relatively weak position. By 1700 not only was Brandenburg's court and political establishment dominated by Calvinists; one third of Berlin's population was also made up of Huguenot refugees. The city's Lutheran churches were partially updated, but the new church building of the era was directed largely towards providing structures intended either for Reformed or simultaneous worship. Elector Friedrich III also welcomed Pietists: Philipp Jakob Spener, who had been dismissed from his post as court preacher in Dresden in 1691, and August Hermann Francke (1663–1727), who, with the Elector's support, founded the famous Halle orphanage. Like Arndt, Spener and some of his followers accorded images a positive role in the process of religious internalization and renewal. In Halle, however, Pietist objections to baroque splendour found full expression. Francke, for example, praised the appearance of his orphanage for its plain style, not lacking in good order or symmetry but without extraneous ornamentation of any kind. Here, finally, we have an explicit articulation of a Protestant aesthetic of plainness. Dominated by the Reformed and by Pietism, Brandenburg's religious climate was not favourable to a flourishing of Lutheran visual culture such as that seen in Saxony.

SAXON BAROQUE

During the second half of the seventeenth century—the time at which Elector Johann Georg II and his successors were presiding over a magnificent Lutheran cult at the Dresden court—the baroque spread throughout Saxony. Village churches were updated at the behest of their noble patrons, while parish churches in towns were given new, modern furnishings by local citizens.[2] A few examples from two particularly interesting regions—the prosperous silver-mining Erzgebirge and the confessionally mixed Oberlausitz—will suffice to illustrate the widespread appeal of the baroque. In 1676, Veit Hans Schnorr, a mining entrepreneur, established a smelting mill south of the Erzgebirge town of Eibenstock, close to the Bohemian border. Schnorr donated money for a church and school in 1682, and the community of Carslfeld developed under his patronage. The Trinitatiskirche was constructed between 1684 and 1688, according to plans drawn up by Wolff Caspar von Klengel (Fig. 8.1). In architectural terms, it is significant because of its centrally planned form and cupola, which provided important precedents for Dresden's Frauenkirche.[3]

The Trinitatiskirche's interior, a square space lined on three sides with galleries and pews, is ideally suited to Lutheran worship. All attention is directed towards the *Kanzelaltar*, one of the earliest and finest examples in Saxony. On the altar

[2] For examples see Fritz Löffler, *Die Stadtkirchen in Sachsen* (Berlin, 1973); Heinrich Magirius and Hartmut Mai, *Dorfkirchen in Sachsen* (Berlin, 1985).

[3] On Carlsfeld see Mario Titze, 'Vor 325 Jahren wurde der Grundstein zur Dreifaltigkeitskiche in Carlsfeld gelegt', *Erzgebirgische Heimatblätter* 31 (4) (2009), 11–14; Magirius and Mai, *Dorfkirchen in Sachsen*, 188. Sigfried Asche, *Drei Bildhauerfamilien an der Elbe* (Vienna, 1961), 111.

stands a life-sized Crucifixion group, carved, painted, and embellished with gold. A pulpit, supported by two palm trees, occupies the space behind Christ's cross, and above is an organ. This is a multi-media work: on the church's central stage, music, preaching and images combine to engage both the intellect and the senses, both the head and the heart. At the foot of Christ's cross, the lively figures of Mary, John, and two apostles engage the viewer and direct his or her attention upwards. Swirling drapery, in Mary's case used to wipe away tears, brings drama to the ensemble. Two kneeling angels support the pulpit and pray to the cross; saints Peter and Paul sit on its main body, and the resurrected Christ appears above. While the art-historian Sigfried Asche's description of the *Kanzelaltar* as a 'Protestant Cathedra Petri' is hyperbole, the work certainly owes a good deal to Roman models, both in its overall conception and in its detail.[4] Its creator, the Schneeberg-born artist Johann Heinrich Böhme the Younger, who had produced the Weißenfels altar discussed in Chapter 7, came from a family of sculptors and, according to the local chronicler Christian Meltzer, surpassed his father and grandfather, becoming a 'splendid artist' because of the trip that he made to Rome sometime shortly after 1683.[5]

Between 1690 and 1699, another splendid baroque church was built in Schwarzenberg, 30 km to the northeast. In 1555–58, Schwarzenberg's medieval castle, which guarded a river crossing on the route to Bohemia, had been converted into an electoral hunting lodge.[6] The ground for a new church building, one that properly reflected the aspirations of the towns' seventeenth-century inhabitants, was provided by Elector Johann Friedrich III and by the senior mining official Georg Balthasar Lehmann. It was not, however, the Elector or his officials who financed the new church, but the local community, through loans, collections, individual donations, and fines. Accounts for the entire construction survive, and give a valuable insight into the financial strains that the process placed on the resources of the town's council and inhabitants. The splendid, light-filled space was consecrated with great ceremony in 1699 (Plate 12). Its altar, Renaissance in style and showing the Last Supper with Abraham and Isaac and Christian virtues, was completed in 1699, and the church also had pews and galleries at this point. Its pulpit, a spectacular construction that projects out into the main space of the church, was completed only in 1704. The altar rail, adorned with representations of miners, dates from 1721. And the church's magnificent ceiling, showing the Hebrew tetragrammaton (JHWH) surrounded by gold rays of light, stucco angels and clouds, was finally finished only in 1729 after a long struggle to find the funds to 'bring the work to perfection' (Plate 13).[7] In 1729, the congregation also managed to pay, after a significant delay, for the sculpture of the Resurrected Christ, which links the Renaissance altar visually to the elaborate ceiling.[8] Schwarzenberg may be 'bäuerlicher Barock' (peasant baroque)—the workmanship here is certainly not

[4] Asche, *Drei Bildhauerfamilien*, 113.   [5] Quoted in ibid., 192.
[6] Dehio, *Handbuch der deutschen Kunstdenkmäler. Sachsen II,* 908.
[7] SStAC: 30016 Kreisamt Schwarzenberg Nr. 2289.
[8] Roswitha Brock, *Auf Fels gebaut. Die St. Georgenkirche zu Schwarzenberg im Erzgebirge* (Scheibenberg, 1999), 33.

of the same quality as Böhme's in Carlsfeld—but the overall effect is nonetheless astonishing: in this small mining town a Lutheran community came together to represent itself and its faith in a modern and truly magnificent manner.

The parish church of St Peter and Paul in Görlitz provides an excellent example of 'bürgerlicher Barock', of visual splendour sponsored by the citizens of this prosperous trading town on the Neisse, the river that marked the border between Upper Lusatia and Silesia. The gothic building dates from the fifteenth century. Görlitz was the earliest of the Lusatian towns to turn to the Reformation (1525), and its council minutes provide some wonderful glimpses into a Lutheran congregation's relationship with its medieval church.[9] From 1502 onwards, the council enjoyed unlimited rights of patronage over the church, not only appointing its minsters but also making decisions concerning its appearance. We have heard already, in Chapter 5, the story of this church's crucifix, removed twice during the second half of the sixteenth century by members of the Catholic nobility and replaced twice by local Lutherans. During the second half of the seventeenth century, the council was called upon to resolve a number of issues concerning other furnishings. In 1660, it turned down a request to hang a new picture in the church, because there were already enough images there. In 1663, it approved a request to dismantle the wing of an old altar, because the congregant whose pew was located near it wished to see and hear the preacher better. In 1666, the executioner Lorentz Straßburger asked permission to have a red velvet altar cloth made for the church, 'because of a terrible fall with a horse, during which God saved his life'. The council refused permission, however, 'because of his person': commemoration and representation on the altar of the church was not appropriate for such a man. If the executioner wished to donate for pious purposes he should, the council determined, give money, which would be put to appropriate use by the church's administrators.[10]

In 1691, the interior of the town church was destroyed by fire.[11] It was rapidly rebuilt, and reconsecrated in 1696. No longer cluttered by medieval remnants—by an excess of pictures and by old altars that obstructed access to the pulpit—the empty church now offered Görlitz's citizens an opportunity to present themselves in a truly 'modern manner', as wealthy and stylistically sophisticated Lutherans. The first object commissioned was the pulpit, the gift of August Kober, a Leipzig merchant who had been born in Görlitz. In 1691, Kober gave 400 *Thaler* for the

---

[9] Ernst-Heinz Lemper, 'Görlitz und die Oberlausitz im Jahrhundert der Reformation' in Erich Donner (ed.), *Europa in der Frühen Neuzeit. Festschrift für Günter Mühlpfordt*, vol. 1 (Weimar, 1997), 281–300; Alfred Zobel, *Die Anfänge der Reformation in Görlitz und der Preußischen Oberlausitz*, 2nd ed. (Görlitz, 1925); Stefan Laube, 'Glaube, Macht und Anschauung in Görlitz zwischen Reformation, Barock und Pietismus', in Ulrich Rosseaux, Wolfgang Flügel and Veit Damm (eds), *Zeitrhythmen und performative Akte in der städtischen Erinnerungs- und Repräsentationskultur zwischen Früher Neuzeit und Gegenwart* (Dresden, 2005), 11–35. On the church see Stefan Bürger and Marius Winzeler, *Die Stadtkirche St. Peter und Paul in Görlitz* (Dössel, 2006); Nitsche, *Beschreibung*.

[10] RatsAG, Varia 133, fol. 68v, fol. 78r, fol. 94r. On executioners see Kathy Stuart, *Defiled Trades and Social Outcasts: Honour and Ritual Pollution in Early Modern Germany* (Cambridge, 1999), chapter 3.

[11] Nitsche, *Beschreibung*, chapter 8, with a wonderful account of 'Gottes sonderlich-wunderbare Erhaltung' of an image of Christ and an illustrated Bible.

pulpit, which was, according to its inscription, to honour his 'patriae dulcissimæ'. The pulpit is supported by an angel and shows the four Evangelists on its sandstone body. The wooden canopy has various Old and New Testament figures carrying texts relating to the proclamation of God's Word. It provided a magnificent focal point for the Lutheran liturgy; it was also, however, a memorial, as the initial stipulations accompanying Kober's gift made absolutely clear. Like many of the images that we encountered in Chapter 6, Kober's pulpit was intended to commemorate both an individual and a dynasty. The wealthy merchant gave his money under three conditions: that his arms would be displayed on the pulpit; that his family would receive a suitable pew as compensation; and, most interestingly, that after his death each year on the feast-day of St Augustine (28 August) one or two burial hymns would be sung in the church as an act of remembrance. Although the request for a liturgical commemoration on the day of the donor's patron saint was undoubtedly unusual, the council was willing to acquiesce. When Kober died the pulpit was not yet finished, and the council turned to his heirs to finance its completion, in particular its splendid white and gold painting. The council promised, in return, that they and their successors would be bound to give thanks in memory of Kober in front of the 'magnificent monument'. In 1698, they confirmed that Kober's wish for an annual commemoration would be fulfilled.[12]

Görlitz's town church was also given a splendid council pew in 1694–95, adorned with a monumental coat of arms supported by allegorical figures of abundance bearing a cornucopia and justice wielding a sword. In total, the church's new pews provided 3,180 seats, allocated, of course, in ways that reflected the social hierarchies of the local community. The altar was financed by Margaretha Summer, and was donated, according to its inscription, to honour God at the instruction of her dead husband, the mayor and merchant Andreas Summer (Plate 14). It was the work of Georg Heermann, who described himself on its reverse as 'architect and sculptor of Dresden' and also worked on the church's splendid organ. Heerman provided a preliminary model, and a detailed contract was drawn up that described the altar's architectural structure, its iconography, and the materials from which it was to be built. The completed work is around 16 metres high, and dominates the choir area, providing a monumental focal point for the gothic church. As the eighteenth-century author Christian Nitsche put it, when one enters the church's main doors, the altarpiece 'strikes the eyes very well and splendidly'. It is constructed of grey, pink, and white imitation marble, its columns described by Nitsche as 'artistic . . . made in the Italian manner from plaster in the form of marble'. In these columns, Nitsche added, 'the master proves his art, especially to those who understand'.[13] At the altarpiece's centre are two paintings by Philipp Ernst John of Christ's burial and ascension. In a typically baroque moment of theatrical illusion, Christ rises towards a gloriole of light bearing the word Jehovah, described in the altar's contract as 'a *Gloria* of natural illumination falling in [to the church]'.[14]

---

[12] RatsAG, Akten Rep I, fol. 80, no. 66.
[13] Nitsche, *Beschreibung*, n.p. (chapter 9).
[14] Asche, *Drei Bildhauerfamilien*, 195–6.

Above the Resurrection, which has no upper frame, sunlight falls 'at certain hours' from the choir windows onto the back of the copper gloriole, and is then reflected onto the figure of Christ, 'which at such times is very beautiful to see'.[15] Sculpted figures add to the drama: two angels beneath draw the viewer's attention to the instruments of Christ's Passion, and above are representations of the evangelists and of charity and hope. The altar is a wonderful Saxon translation of the spirit and energy of the Roman high baroque.

Amongst the church's other baroque furnishings were three pews for private confession, which remained a duty for Saxon Lutherans in accordance with the 1580 church ordinance.[16] All three were given by local patrons, and bear life-sized sculpted figures that speak to the themes of confession and repentance. The most magnificent was donated in 1717 by two brothers, Gottfried and Johann George Pauli (Fig. 8.2). Görlitz's sub-deacon would have heard confession here, flanked by Mary Magdalene and the Apostle Peter. An inscription (no longer visible) beneath Mary reminded the viewer that 'your faith has helped you' (Luke 7:50). Peter is accompanied by a cockerel, a symbol of his betrayal of Christ, and another inscription emphasized sorrow and penitence: 'and he went out and wept bitterly' (Matthew 26:75). The church's magnificent organ was consecrated in 1703, and its fame apparently reached Tsar Peter I, who commissioned a copy of it for St Petersburg. Its technical complexity and visual magnificence did not, however, appeal to all: J. S. Bach described it as 'a horse's organ...for it is a horse-like work to play up there', while Johann Andreas Silbermann complained in 1741 that it looked to him 'like a building made of fireworks, hung about with many pin wheels and suns'.[17]

The church also received numerous other less monumental donations: chandeliers, epitaphs (even though there were no new burials here), and liturgical vessels and textiles. The church's medieval vessels and textiles survived the 1691 fire: in 1717, for the Reformation's 200th anniversary, the church's clergy wore their medieval vestments, though new ones were given in the following decades. On high feast days the pillar against which the pulpit stood was adorned with a red velvet cloth, embroidered with gold and silver. Donated in 1711, it had been made by the Ursulines in Breslau: it was a rare example, therefore, of Catholic cloister work intended for an evangelical church. Such visual splendour was appropriate given the solemnity of Görlitz's baroque liturgy, which included, for example, the singing of Latin hymns and the use of a bell to mark the consecration during communion as well as the elaboration of the town's Holy Sepulchre cult. Görlitz was famous during this period for its goldsmiths' work, and this specialism was reflected in the church's rich collection of communion cans, chalices, pyxes, and candlesticks. An elaborate Easter candlestick donated by the heirs of Johann Jacob Lichtner, who owned the estate of Deutsch-Ossig, survives today and gives an idea of the former richness of the church's collection.[18] Made by a local goldsmith it shows

---

[15] Nitsche, *Beschreibung*, n.p. (chapter 9); Bürger and Winzeler, *Die Stadtkirche,* 116–17.

[16] Ibid., 117.   [17] Ibid., 119–20.

[18] Ibid., 131–5. Evelin Wetter, 'Der Kronstädter Paramentenschatz. Altkirchliche Messgewänder in nachreformatorischer Nutzung', *Acta Historiae Artium*, 45 (2004), 257–315, here 269. On the Holy Sepulchre see Chapter 5.

Fig. 8.2. Confessional of the sub-deacon from the town church of St Peter and Paul, Görlitz, 1717.

Credit: © Verlag Janos Stekovics, with permission from the Ev. Innenstadtgemeinde Görlitz.

Moses with the Tablets, the Brazen Serpent, angels holding the instruments of the Passion, Christ in Prayer on the Mount of Olives, the Last Supper and Christ's Burial. The collection also included an ivory crucifix commissioned at the same time as the altar, and a stylistically related small sculpture of *Christus in der Rast*. Examples of this popular late-medieval devotional theme survived, as we saw in Chapter 5, in a number of Saxon churches, but it is rare to find newly commissioned evangelical versions.

Görlitz's town church may be highly unusual in the completeness of the survival of its baroque furnishings, and in the richness of the textual documentation relating to them. But other churches, both in Görlitz and in the surrounding area, also testify to the Lutheran love of baroque splendour. In 1713, Görlitz's Dreifaltigkeitskirche, which had recently been reconsecrated, acquired a spectacular new altar by Kapsar Gottlob von Rodewitz, a pupil of Bathasar Permoser (Fig. 8.3). Four monumental columns support a triumphal arch with angels, rays of light, garlands, and a depiction of the Trinity. In the main field is a sculpted depiction of Christ in Prayer on the Mount of Olives, and to either side are life-sized figures of Moses and John the Baptist, representing the Law and Gospel. Kapsar Gottlob von Rodewitz also worked in the village church at nearby Deutsch Ossig, providing it with a spectacular *Kanzelaltar* and a sculpted angel used at baptisms (a *Taufengel*). The baroque and rococo ensemble created by Rodewitz and his successors was so spectacular that when, in the 1980s, Deutsch Ossig was emptied and destroyed to make way for open-cast mining, the church was dismantled and rebuilt meticulously in Görlitz-Königshufen.[19] The village church in Kittlitz, near Löbau, contains perhaps the most remarkable example of Saxon baroque (Fig. 8.4). In this splendid light-filled village church, built between 1749 and 1775 at the behest of Heinrich Adolf von Gersdorff and Karl Gotthelf von Hundt, an altar bearing a crucifix framed by columns stands beneath a monumental ciborium.[20] Four tall Corinthian columns support arches bearing flowers, leaves and a gloriole, directing all attention towards the altar. Karl Gotthelf von Hundt (1722–76), the church's main patron, came from a Silesian evangelical family. He attended university in Leipzig, but in the early 1740s, during his Grand Tour, converted secretly to Catholicism in Paris.[21] It is impossible to know how much his extraordinary commission owed to his Catholicism and to his knowledge of Gianlorenzo Bernini's magnificent baldachin in St Peter's in Rome (1623–34), but whatever its origin the ciborium remained in Kittlitz's Lutheran village church as powerful testimony to the cross-confessional allure of the baroque.

---

[19] Ricarda Kube and Cornelia Wendt, 'Deutsch Ossig. Das Schicksal eines Dorfes im Braunkohleabbaugebiet', in Landesamt für Denkmalpflege Sachsen, *Denkmalpflege in Sachsen 1894–1994. Erster Teil* (Weimar, 1997), 271–73. See also Landesamt für Denkmalpflege Sachsen (ed.), *Von Deutsch-Ossig nach Görlitz-Königshufen. Die Rettung einer Dorfkirche* (Dresden, 1998). On the altar in the Dreifaltigkeitskirche in Görlitz see Magirius, *Die Dresdner Frauenkirche*, 252–4.

[20] On Kittlitz see Cornelius Gurlitt (ed.), *Beschreibende Darstellung der älteren Bau- und Kunstdenkmäler des Königreichs Sachsen*, vol. 34, *Amtshauptmannschaft Löbau* (Dresden, 1910), 242–55; Vorstände der Ev.-Luth. Kirchengemeinden Kittlitz und Nostitz, *Die Evangelisch-Lutherischen Kirchengemeinden Kittlitz und Nostitz* (Bautzen, 2006), esp. 49 ff.

[21] On conversions during the Grand Tour see Stannek, 'Konfessionalisierung des »Giro d'Italia«?', 564–5.

Fig. 8.3. Caspar Gottlob von Rodewitz, altarpiece of the Dreifaltigkeitskirche, Görlitz, 1715.

Credit: Photo: author's own, with permission from the Ev. Innenstadtgemeinde Görlitz.

BRANDENBURG-PRUSSIA

Of course the appeal of the baroque was not confined to Saxony. Berlin-Cölln was transformed into a baroque residential city under Elector Friedrich III. Friedrich III, who was crowned 'King in Prussia' with great ceremony in Königsberg in 1701, maintained a splendid court, and placed great emphasis on ritual and on the

Fig. 8.4. Altar and Ciborium from the Village Church in Kittlitz near Löbau, completed 1768.

Credit: Photo: author's own, with permission from the Ev.-Luth. Kirchgemeinde Kittlitz-Nostitz.

arts. In 1696, he founded the *Akademie der Künste* (Academy of Arts); during his reign the *Zeughaus* (arsenal), the *Stadtschloß* (city palace) and the Charlottenburg palace complex were built. Friedrich III's successor, the 'soldier king' Friedrich Wilhelm I (r. 1713–40), reacted against the extravagance of his father's court and directed the majority of his state revenues to military expenditure, but Berlin-Cölln's cityscape had, by that time, been decisively shaped by the work of baroque architects and sculptors, amongst them Johann Friedrich Eosander von Göthe and Andreas Schlüter. At Berlin's court in the late seventeenth and early eighteenth centuries, as at Dresden's during the same period, desire for representation in a 'modern style' was key.

Berlin's Nikolaikirche and Marienkirche—churches that, as we saw in Chapter 3, had formed important focal points for Lutheran confessional identity since the conversion of the Hohenzollern electors—were also partially modernized during this time. *Altes und Neues Berlin* (*Old and New Berlin*), a detailed description of the history of the city written by Johann Christoph Müller and Georg Gottfried Küster and published in 1737, provides a partial account of this modernization. In 1680, the Nikolaikirche, which had been depicted in all its medieval splendour on the 1616 epitaph for Johann von Kötteritz and Caritas Distelmeyer (Plate 5), acquired a new pulpit that was financed by a legacy from Johann Beer. Müller and Küster remarked that the pulpit 'lacked nothing in [its] decoration'. The sculpted work was, they wrote, admired above all, and the pulpit also had 'gilding in gold and silver, beautiful colours and the like'. In 1715, the church underwent a thorough renovation: its old altar and stone sacrament house were removed, its galleries were replaced by new ones 'beautifully decorated' with oil paint and gold gilding, and it was given 'a splendid new altar'.[22]

Müller and Küster's description of this new altar provides a good insight into evangelical admiration for the baroque. They praised its pure, Italianate design, saying that it was a pleasing variation of true Roman design. Its columns, pilasters, pedestals, and the rest of its architectural structure were made from beautifully coloured marble, and in the whole work there was nothing of the 'old gothic carpenter's and woodturner's adornment', such as side panels, 'unnecessary and incorrectly placed festoons, childish baubles, nonsense stories, and other often vexing decoration found on most of Germany's altars'. As well as praising the altar's modern appearance, Müller and Küster also wrote eloquently of its imagery. Its paintings were by Samuel Theodor Gericke, rector and professor at the *Akademie der Künste*. They showed scenes from the life and Passion of Christ. Müller and Küster praised in particular the pathos of the main image, which showed Christ in the Garden of Gethsemane, 'the hardest and most important' station of the Passion. Christ was depicted, they wrote, 'laden with the innumerable great and

---

[22] Müller and Küster, *Altes und Neues Berlin*, 236, 239. Friedrich Nicolai reported that behind the altar of the church there was a 'schätzbare Sammlung alter Gemälde aus dem sechszehnten Jahrhunderte auf Holtz gemalt, welche vorher an der Grabmälern verschiedener Familien der Kirche zerstreuet gewesen': Friedrich Nicolai, *Beschreibung der Königlichen Residenzstädte Berlin und Potsdam* . . . 3rd ed. (Berlin, 1786), 853.

heavy sins of the whole human race'.[23] The altar was crowned by a gloriole and statues of the virtues.

Despite Müller and Küster's harsh condemnation of gothic altars, plenty remained in local Lutheran churches. The old altar from the Nikolaikirche, which had showed the Virgin and Child with saints, was sold to the parish church in nearby Teltow. The Teltow congregation was not pleased to find, when it arrived, that it would require extensive and costly renovation to make it presentable.[24] In Berlin's Marienkirche, the old Marian altar, 'a work built in Roman-Catholic times', was restored in 1694. In this case, Müller and Küster acknowledged the workmanship that had gone into it, even if they did not approve its style: 'this altar cost the sculptors and carpenters... great effort and work, and they did not stint on the gold'.[25] The Marienkirche also, however, acquired a magnificent new pulpit carved by Andreas Schlüter (Plate 1). Schlüter, one of the greatest sculptors and architects of the Central European baroque, had arrived in Berlin in 1694 to serve as Friedrich III's court sculptor. He worked, at the Elector's behest, on the rebuilding and decoration of the *Stadtschloß* on the northern bank of the Spree, and on the bronze equestrian statue of the Great Elector that stood (until 1943) on the bridge leading to it.[26]

The pulpit in the Marienkirche, a truly magnificent monument, was financed in part by a legacy from Anna Maria Lehmanns, widow of the electoral official Georg Friedrich Fehr, in part by her son, and in part by Schlüter himself. It was consecrated in 1703 and stood originally on the north side of the nave.[27] In a wonderful visual conceit, it appears to float on volutes held by life-sized sculpted angels, though four sandstone columns cleverly inserted into a gap cut in church's medieval pillars in fact bear its weight. Its main body is covered in alabaster, and bears a relief sculpture of John the Baptist preaching. The canopy is crowned with cherubs, clouds and rays of light. The pulpit references the traditional Lutheran iconography of the Law and Gospel: angels on the canopy hold Moses's tablets and a book inscribed with John 1:17, 'For the law was given through Moses; grace and truth came through Jesus Christ'. Yet, its dramatic style clearly owes everything to Schlüter's knowledge of the Italian high baroque, in particular of Bernini's *Cathedra Petri* in St Peter's, which he encountered during his 1696 journey to Rome.[28] Bernini's masterpiece presents the relic thought to be St Peter's throne, held aloft on volutes by sculpted bronze figures of four doctors of the church. Above is a gloriole with rays of light, clouds and angels. Schlüter transferred some, at least, of the drama and splendour of this key image of the Catholic

---

[23] Müller and Küster, *Altes und Neues Berlin*, 238–9.

[24] Ibid., 239; EKLAB, Repositur I, 1423–1945, 122 Inventarium der Nikolaikirche I 1575–1812.

[25] Müller and Küster, *Fortgesetzes Altes und Neues Berlin*, (Berlin, 1752), 463; see also Nicolai, *Beschreibung*, 857–6 ('in derselben [the library] siehet man auch die Heiligenbilder und Zierrathen des vorigen alten Altars').

[26] Kessler (ed.), *Andreas Schlüter*.

[27] Claire Guinomet, 'Die Kanzel in der Berliner Marienkirche', in Kessler (ed.), *Andreas Schlüter*, 344–57.

[28] Ibid., 349. See also Regina Deckers, 'Andreas Schlüter in Danzig und Polen', in Kessler (ed.), *Andreas Schlüter*, 20–31, here 28.

Counter-Reformation to a Protestant context, using it to glorify the site at which God's Word was preached.

According to Müller and Küster, there was no altar anywhere else in the Electorate of Brandenburg that could compare to the one installed in the Nikolaikirche in 1715, on account of its 'artistic structure, beautiful paintings, sculpture, and other decoration'.[29] This was, perhaps, true: in general, Brandenburg's town and village churches were not as magnificently *barockisiert* as Saxony's. The Mark's Lutheran patrons did, however, sometimes at least, seek representation in a 'modern manner'. They commissioned new altars that, like Wolf Caspar von Klengel's in Dresden's castle chapel, presented lonely crucifixes for devout contemplation, and they occasionally adopted Italianate visual idioms.[30] The medieval Marienkirche in Treuenbrietzen, near Postdam, contains, for example, a scaled-down copy of Schlüter's Marienkirche pulpit, attributed to F. Ziegler (1737).[31] This church's altar, installed in *c.*1730–40, shows a sculpted crucifix before a painted depiction of Golgotha, with carved figures of Moses and John the Baptist at the sides and the Brazen Serpent above. The whole is crowned by a gloriole. In Markau, to the west of Berlin, Henning Caspar von Bredow and his wife Gottliebe Dorothee (née Hünicke) built a new village church in 1712. Their son, who served as an officer in Friedrich II's army during the Seven Years' War, installed a splendid altar, pulpit, baptism angel, and gallery in 1758–63 (Fig. 8.5).[32] The altar, dated 1758, is adorned with sculptures of the four evangelists, the Trinity and allegorical figures, all notable for their movement and drama: St John's eagle, for example, perches at the base of a column, its wing outstretched as if preparing for flight. In the centre is a painting of the scene at Gethsemane. Such ensembles harnessed art's illusionistic powers, using both painting and sculpture to stimulate viewers to immerse themselves in the key moments of Christ's Passion.

In Berlin, the Marienkirche eventually received a new altar to complement Schlüter's magnificent pulpit (Fig. 8.6). Like the Nikolaikirche's 1715 altar, it replaced an old (gothic) work, which had been, according to Provost Johann Ulrich Christian Köppen, 'adorned with many un-edifying figures'.[33] The new altar, consecrated in 1762, fitted not only with the aesthetic but also with the religious sensibilities of the period. Its monumental frame was designed by the architect Andreas Krüger, and the whole was financed by members of the congregation. Its paintings a gift from the painter Bernhard Rode, a local parishioner. Rode's work owed more to the Enlightenment than to the Counter-Reformation and baroque: after a journey to Paris, Rome, and Venice the artist had established, in 1754, a drawing academy in Berlin. Although he worked in a variety of media and

---

[29] Müller and Küster, *Altes und Neues Berlin*, 237.

[30] See, for example, Nauen (1708), in Badstübner, *Stadtkirchen der Mark Brandenburg*, 192, 113 (1708). Bardenitz (1721) and Briesen (1701), in Gericke and Wendland, *Brandenburgische Dorfkirchen*, 142, 43 and 143, 51.

[31] Dehio, *Brandenburg*, 1062. On this church see also Badstübner, *Stadtkirchen*, 205, 142.

[32] Dehio, *Brandenburg*, 642.

[33] Johann Ulrich Christian Köppen, *Die Freude der Gläubigen bey den Altaren Gottes…* (Berlin: Rellstab, 1762), 10.

Fig. 8.5. Altarpiece from the Village Church in Markau near Berlin, 1758.
Credit: © Bildarchiv Monheim GmbH / Alamy Stock Photo.

illustrated various themes, history painting became his particular speciality.[34] In 1783, he was appointed director of Berlin's *Akademie der Künste* by Friedrich II.

Rode's paintings for the Marienkirche altar show three scenes: in the centre the Descent from the Cross; on the left Christ in Prayer on the Mount of Olives; and on the right Thomas placing his hand in the risen Christ's wound. In his 1762

---

[34] Dorothee Ritter, 'Rode, Christian Bernhard', in *Neue Deutsche Biographie*, vol. 21 (2003), 690–1.

Fig. 8.6. Bernhard Rode, altarpiece for the Church of St Marien, Berlin, 1762.
Credit: © Ev. Kirchengemeinde St. Petri - St. Marien Berlin.

consecration sermon, Köppen invoked standard Lutheran defences of altars. He also, however, referred to the altar's local context, asking God to bless the Prussian King, and to give peace to Europe, which, during the Seven Years' War, was 'almost entirely burned by the flames of war'. In a typical Lutheran formulation, Köppen asked for God's blessing on the altar's donors: 'reward them in a paternal manner, and let their harvest both here and there be great'. He gave a detailed description of its appearance, mentioning, for example, the angel in the left-hand scene 'who covers his face, turning away from the suffering saviour'. He emphasized that the altar was 'not for empty adornment, and not for vain pomp', but rather 'to awaken piety and for the livelier stirring of human souls to the veneration of [God's] name'.[35]

The Marienkirche altar is monumental, but looks austere when compared to the Schlüter pulpit or the exuberant sculpted and gilded altarpiece in Dresden's Frauenkirche (Plates 1, 15). The colour scheme of the Rode paintings and of their frames is muted: predominantly grey and brown. The composition of the central panel, in particular the depiction of the figure bearing the weight of Christ's body, suggests that Rode knew Peter Paul Rubens's famous Antwerp *Descent from the Cross*, which had been frequently reproduced in both painting and print. The overall impression, however, is one of pathos not drama: Rubens's visual innovations are here presented in simplified and subdued form. Christ's body, light against a

---

[35] Köppen, *Die Freude*, 11, 13–14.

dark background, draws the viewer's eye from everywhere in the church. Köppen praised the Berlin altar for its sobriety and ability to evoke an emotional response, emphasizing several times during his sermon that it had no 'empty and superfluous adornment'. Its creators had, he wrote, applied gliding with moderation, to avoid the danger of a 'too-sumptuous brilliance that hits the eye and dissipates, rather than promotes, devotion'. Moreover, they chose the paintings and figures carefully, and tried to arrange the whole altar so that the Christian who wished to improve himself would not lack for stirring sentiment 'to raise his soul from the visible [world] to the invisible'.[36]

Köppen's preached and printed account of Rode's work in the Marienkirche owed something at least to a Pietist-inspired rejection of baroque magnificence. Köppen had studied at the university in Halle, and in 1717–18 had travelled through Franconia and Swabia with August Hermann Francke, founder of Halle's Pietist orphanage. In 1725, he served briefly as preacher in Berlin's *Regiment Gendarmes*, but spent most of his career as a deacon, provost and preacher in Lutheran churches: first in Salzwedel in Brandenburg's Altmark, then from 1728 at Berlin's Nikolaikirche.[37] His qualified endorsement of baroque splendour, his concern that visual magnificence might distract from true piety, must, as his career suggests, be understood in the context of Brandenburg-Prussia's particular confessional environment.

By the early eighteenth century, this confessional environment had been profoundly shaped by successive electors' policies of religious toleration. Brandenburg's Lutherans had, of course, been living in the shadow of a Calvinist court since 1614. The electorate recovered from the traumas of the Thirty Years' War thanks to the efforts of a series of exceptionally talented rulers, but religious toleration, or at least enforced co-existence, was important to that recovery. Friedrich Wilhelm, the Great Elector (r. 1640–88), laid the foundations for Brandenburg's eventual rise to power though his military and administrative reforms. He also, in 1661 and 1685, encouraged Reformed Protestants from the Netherlands and France to settle in the electorate, and welcomed the presence of smaller groups of religious exiles: Socinians, Jews, and Waldensians. This toleration generated opposition from the territory's orthodox Lutherans. But the Huguenots in particular, many of whom were highly skilled artisans, helped transform Brandenburg's economy. By 1700, there were 6,000–7,000 Huguenots in Berlin alone, making up about one third of the city's population.[38]

The new churches built in and around the city during the late seventeenth and early eighteenth centuries reflected this culturally mixed environment. Some were intended for French-speaking Reformed congregations: the church in

---

[36] Ibid., 15.

[37] This biographical information is taken from the digital databank of the Franckesche Stiftung zu Halle (Saale), accessed 3/9/2016.

[38] Lehmann, *Das Zeitalter des Absolutismus*, 84 ff. Whaley, *Germany and the Holy Roman Empire*, vol. 2, 266. Iselin Gundermann, 'Verordnete Eintracht: Lutheraner und Reformierte in Berlin-Brandenburg (1613–1740)', *Herbergen der Christenheit. Jahrbuch für deutsche Kirchengeschichte* 28/29 (2004/2005), 141–55. See also Barabara Dölemeyer, *Die Hugenotten* (Stuttgart, 2006), chapter 4.

Dorotheenstadt, for example, where Huguenots worshipped from 1688. Some were used by German-speaking Calvinists, most notably the Parochialkirche in the city centre, built between 1695 and 1703.[39] Some were *Simultankirchen*, shared between French and German and Reformed and Lutheran: the Garnisonskirche, for example, built between 1701 and 1703, and the church in Friedrichswerde begun in 1700. As this chronology suggests, it was above all Friedrich III who transformed Berlin's ecclesiastical landscape, constructing new churches throughout the city, including the Französische Kirche and the Neue Kirche (for German Reformed Protestants) on the Gendarmenmarkt.[40] Although, after the destruction and chaos of 1940–45, the appearance of these churches cannot be reconstructed in great detail, eighteenth-century accounts provide enough information to suggest that Berlin's Reformed churches, unlike the Lutheran Marienkirche and Nikolaikirche, were largely bare. The Parochialkirche, for example, contained nothing 'notable' except for two epitaphs, and the Dorotheenstadt church was also adorned only with memorials. In the Garnisonskirche, there was an elaborate organ, and the writer and bookseller Friedrich Nicolai also commented on the flags and standards captured during Frederick the Great's Silesian Wars and on four large paintings by Bernhard Rode of 'Prussian heroes'.[41] In his discussion of liturgy, Nicolai pointed towards a lingering Lutheran attachment to traditional forms of worship. The Reformed, he observed, exercised their religion 'very simply, without many ceremonies', and the Lutherans accommodated themselves to this simplicity in the churches that they shared 'except for a few small details'. In the Nikolaikirche, however, preachers still used white surplices and lit candles during the celebration of communion.[42]

PIETISM

In Berlin, Lutheran visual culture and ritual practice were shaped by close encounters with Calvinism. Both within and beyond the residential city, Brandenburg's religious landscape was also, however, profoundly influenced by its electors' acceptance of Pietism. Here, as elsewhere, Pietism ultimately gave much clearer contours to the movement for religious reform that we encountered in Chapters 4 and 5.[43] Philipp Jakob Spener (1635–1705), Pietism's founding father, spent time in both Dresden and Berlin, and his experiences in those two cities highlight the very real differences between the evangelical confessional cultures of Saxony and Brandenburg.

[39] Müller and Küster, *Altes und Neues Berlin*, 192–201.
[40] Johannes Wallmann, 'Philipp Jakob Spener in Berlin 1691–1705', *Zeitschrift für Theologie und Kirche* 84 (1987), 58–85, reprinted in ibid., *Theologie und Frömmigkeit im Zeitalter des Barock. Gesammelte Aufsätze* (Tübingen, 1995), 295–324.
[41] Nicolai, *Beschreibung*, 860–1; 923–4; 861. [42] Ibid., 611–2.
[43] For overviews see Martin Brecht, Klaus Deppermann, Ulrich Gäbler and Hartmut Lehmann (eds), *Geschichte des Pietismus*, vol. 1, *Der Pietismus von siebzehnten bis zum frühen achtzehnten Jahrhundert* (Göttingen, 1993); Johannes Wallmann, *Der Pietismus* (Göttingen, 1990); Johannes Wallmann, *Gesammelte Aufsätze: Teil 2, Pietismus-Studien* (Tübingen, 2008); Douglas Shantz (ed.), *A Companion to German Pietism* (Leiden, 2014).

Spener had served, from 1666 to 1685, as senior minister of the pastors' assembly in Frankfurt am Main. Here he established the first *Collegium Pietatis*, a small group that met together for Bible reading, prayer and discussion of sermons. In 1675, he published his *Pia Desideria*. This key text began as a preface to an edition of Arndt's *Evangelienpostille* and laid out Spener's recommendations for reforming the church and deepening individual piety, calling for a better-trained clergy and a more intensive *praxis pietatis*. In 1686, Spener was called to Dresden to serve as senior court preacher, member of the upper consistory, and confessor to Elector Johann Georg III and his wife. The court congregation was under his care, and he preached regularly in the richly decorated castle chapel. The challenge of implementing his pastoral ideas in a baroque court, combined with the unrest caused by Pietist 'conventicles' in Leipzig, proved too much, however. Spener became increasingly isolated, and in 1691 left for Berlin where he found refuge as provost of the Nikolaikirche.[44]

Spener's career in Brandenburg was by no means trouble free. He was willing to accept the co-existence of confessions but continued to understand himself as a Lutheran and opposed the (ultimately unsuccessful) attempts of Ernst Jablonski, Friedrich III's court preacher, to form a union of Protestants. He also became involved in the so-called *Beichtstuhlstreit* (Dispute about Confessionals), opposing the Elector's 1698 attempt to abolish compulsory private confession before communion, a hallmark of Lutheranism in Brandenburg. Yet, Spener made a lasting impact on the religious culture of the territory: with his help the University of Halle was founded in 1694 with August Hermann Francke amongst its first professors.[45]

For Friedrich III and his successors, Pietism promised to bridge the gap between Lutherans and Calvinists, and to diminish the political influence of Brandenburg's orthodox Lutheran church and Territorial Estates. Here there developed a 'partnership between Pietism and the absolutist state,' a partnership that meant that, for a while at least, Pietism became the dominant orthodoxy in Brandenburg-Prussia.[46] The educational and economic activities of Francke and his fellow Pietists in Halle also helped to establish Hohenzollern control over the former Archbishopric of Magdeburg, which had passed to the dynasty after the death of its administrator, August of Saxe-Weißenfels, in 1680. In Halle, against a confessionally mixed backdrop of Lutherans and Reformed (many of them exiles from the Palatinate), Francke established his schools and orphanage, with its printing press and pharmacy. The great pedagogical enterprise that became the *Franckesche Stiftungen* stimulated local manufacture and

---

[44] On Spener see Martin Brecht, 'Philipp Jakob Spener, sein Programm und dessen Auswirkungen', in Brecht et al. (eds), *Geschichte des Pietismus* vol. 1, 279–390; Wallmann, 'Philipp Jakob Spener in Berlin'.

[45] Ibid. See also Marianne Taatz-Jacobi, *Erwünschte Harmonie: Die Gründung der Friedrichs-Universität Halle als Instrument brandenburg-preußicher Konfessionspolitik—Motive, Verfahren, Mythos (1680–1713)* (Berlin, 2014).

[46] Mary Fulbrook, *Piety and Politics: Religion and the Rise of Absolutism in England, Württemberg and Prussia* (Cambridge, 1983), 159, 169. Whaley, *Germany and the Holy Roman Empire*, vol. 2, 312.

trade, and came to dominate the city. It and the university supplied Pietist-trained men to fill influential offices in church and state, as well as preachers for the Prussian military.[47]

The traditional scholarly orthodoxy that saw Pietism as opposed to, or at least indifferent to, art has undergone revision in recent decades. The rejection of earthly splendour—of the elaborate visual and musical culture of the baroque—in favour of proper focus on the divine was, of course, constitutive of the movement as a whole. This does not mean, however, that Pietism made no contribution to music, literature, art, and architecture.[48] Pietism was no more monolithic than Lutheranism, but in its Halle form—of most relevance to us here—it produced its own traditions of hymnody, of spiritual poetry, of portraiture, and of church architecture.[49] Francke's foundation even, under his son, Gotthilf August, built up a splendid collection of images and objects intended for teaching, the *Kunst-* and *Naturalienkammer*.[50]

In the visual realm, we can see already in the career of Spener himself a certain tension between the rejection of visual magnificence and a Lutheran awareness of images' ability to appeal to both the intellect and the emotions. In Frankfurt, where a predominantly Lutheran population co-existed with Reformed and other minorities, Spener was forced to confront the image question on a number of occasions. In 1672, for example, he defended a painting by Matthäus Merian the Younger intended for the altar of the city's Barfüßerkirche, which had attracted criticism because it depicted Christ's bodily resurrection in a manner thought to reflect Calvinist rather than orthodox Lutheran teaching on the Eucharist.[51] In general, Spener opted for a cautious endorsement of images, on both educational and aesthetic grounds. In a letter of 1678, he wrote that it would be useful to have engravings in school, so that the histories that they depicted would be imprinted more deeply in pupils' memories.[52] His 1689 *Kurtze Catechismuspredigten* (*Short Catechism Sermons*) Spener reflected that it was acceptable to have images in church 'for commemoration, remembrance and adornment', but that it was idolatry when 'one honours God in them, falls down before them and prays to the images, with the view that God much prefers to hear such prayer, and is prayed to through and

[47] Martin Brecht, 'August Hermann Francke und der Hallesche Pietismus', in Brecht et al. (eds), *Geschichte des Pietismus,* vol. 1, 440–540.

[48] See Thomas Müller-Bahlke, 'Der Hallesche Pietismus und die Kunst. Bemerkungen zu einem alten Vorurteil', in Rainer Lächele (ed.), *Das Echo Halles. Kulturelle Wirkungen des Piestimus* (Tübingen, 2001), 243–69. See also Sdzuj, *Adiaphorie und Kunst*.

[49] Jan Harasimowicz, 'Der Beitrag des hallischen Pietismus zur Kulturgeschichte Pommerns im 18. Jahrhundert', in Johannes Wallmann und Udo Sträter (eds), *Halle und Osteuropa: zur europäischen Ausstrahlung des hallischen Pietismus* (Tübingen, 1998), 173–210; ibid., 'Architektur und Kunst', in Brecht et al. (eds), *Geschichte des Pietimsus. Band 4: Glaubenswelt und Lebenswelten* (Göttingen, 2004), 456–85.

[50] Max Kunze (ed.), *Kunst und Aufklärung im 18. Jahrhundert. Kunstausbildung der Akademien; Kunstvermittlung der Fürsten; Kunstsammlung der Universität* (Ruhpolding, 2005), 321–32.

[51] Andreas Previer, 'Die "causa" Merian. Streit im Chor der Frankfurter Barfüßerkirche', in Andrea Bendlage (ed.), *Recht und Verhalten in vormodernen Gesellschaften* (Bielefeld, 2008), 233–53.

[52] Ringshausen, *Von der Buchillustration*, 82. Philipp Jakob Spener, *Consilia et Iudicia Theologicæ Latina. Opus Posthumum Ex eiusdem Litteris 1709. Partes 1–2* (reprint, Hildesheim and New York, 1989), 60.

in images'.[53] He was suspicious, however, not only of anything that smacked of idolatry but also of excessive expenditure on art and architecture. In 1685, he wrote, in a reflection on church building that was published in 1701, that churches were useful as places of assembly, and should be provided for the convenience of the congregation. Where money was in short supply, however, it should be used for more important things: to pay preachers and school teachers, and to look after the poor. Moreover, eye-catching churches belonged, Spener wrote, not to 'us' (the Lutherans) but to those who loved pomp and splendour in their religion. We know, he wrote, that true service to the New Testament is internal rather than external. All that is required externally is 'cleanliness, purity and good order'. Beyond this, over-abundance hinders rather than promotes piety.[54]

The emphasis on order and simplicity became, as we shall see, a hallmark of Halle Pietism. But Spener himself also drew on the visual traditions of Arndt's earlier movement for the renewal of piety. Fig. 8.7, a 1683 engraving by Johann Ulrich Krauss, shows the interior of the Katharinenkirche in Frankfurt during Spener's incumbency. Its layout, with the pulpit located in the middle of the long nave and galleries opposite it, suited it to evangelical preaching services, but it was richly decorated, in particular with paintings on its galleries and ceiling. These paintings had been installed at Spener's suggestion after the church was rebuilt in 1678–81. The ceiling paintings showed biblical scenes, and were removed in 1778 as part of a restoration campaign. The gallery paintings survived, however. On the upper gallery were emblems, taken from the 1679 illustrated edition of Arndt's *True Christianity*, and biblical images, many derived from Matthäus Merian the Elder's engravings. On the lower gallery were further scenes from the Old and New Testaments. Heinrich Müller's 1670 *Geistlicher Danck-Altar*, which describes the birth of Christ in the heart of the believer, also provided models for several allegorical images. Together the images formed a carefully chosen visual sermon, emphasizing repentance and spiritual renewal.[55] A particularly lovely emblem from the upper gallery depicts, for example, the penitent Peter with the thrice-crowing cockerel on the left (Matthew 26:75), and on the right onions symbolizing tears of repentance. Frankfurt's Katharinenkirche shows Spener's willingness, in keeping with the traditions of authors such as Arndt and Müller, to use images in order to activate and intensify religious feeling, to encourage the *Verinnerlichung* (internalization or intensification) that was central to his programme of piety.

In Halle itself, however, Francke's orphanage—the prototypical Pietist foundation—looked very different indeed. In his preaching and writing Francke moved away from the verbal images, emblems, and stories used in the devotional works of authors such as Christian Scriver. He emphasized clarity, writing, for

---

[53] Philipp Jakob Spener, *Schriften, Band II.2. Kurtze Catechismuspredigten 1689* (reprint, Hildesheim and New York, 1982), 34.

[54] Philipp Jakob Spener, *Theologische Bedencken… Anderer Theil… 1701* (reprint, Hildesheim and New York, 1999), 178–81. See also Paul Grünberg, *Philipp Jakob Spener*, vol. 2, *Spener als praktischer Theologe und kirchlicher Reformer* (Göttingen, 1905), 131.

[55] Joachim Proescholdt (ed.), *St. Katharinen zu Frankfurt am Main* (Frankfurt am Main, 1981), esp. Maria Lilek-Schirmer, 'Die Emporengemälde: eine Bilderpredigt', 164–88.

Fig. 8.7. Johann Ulrich Krauss, Interior of the Katharinenkirche, Frankfurt am Main, 1683.
Credit: © Historisches Museum Frankfurt. Photo: Horst Ziegenfusz.

example, in the preface to his 1693 *Glauchisches Gedenck-Büchlein* (*Little Memorial Book of Glaucha*) that he sought 'neither high words nor erudition' but rather strove after great simplicity.[56] The visual idiom that he favoured was equally simple: the orphanage is impressive in its scale, but sober and ascetic in comparison to Spener's Katharinenkirche. Francke's attitude to images, like Spener's, was not entirely straightforward. He certainly recognized their pedagogical value. In his 1698 *Von der Erziehung der Töchter* (*On the Education of Daughters*), a translation and adaptation of a tract by the French bishop François Fénelon, Francke reproduced without criticism the suggestion that engravings or paintings of sacred stories could be used alongside oral instruction.[57] 'For general use engravings are adequate, but if one is in the pleasant position of being able to show children good paintings, one should not miss this; for the effect of the colours, and with this the life-sized figures, will excite the imagination of the children much more actively'.[58] What was acceptable in domestic instruction was not, however, necessarily to be condoned in school rooms. In 1702, Francke criticized a Gotha territorial ordinance that had advocated the use of images to help children learn Scripture. Such images could, he warned, do more harm than good, introducing false ideas to impressionable minds. The ordinances for Halle's schools contain plenty of references to the use of objects and images in the teaching of history and geography, but not in religious instruction. Francke advocated the use of Johannes Buno's historical images, but not his *Bilder-Bibel*: the catechism and teaching of the Bible must be entirely about the text, its recitation, explanation and application.[59]

Francke's most substantial reflection on the visual is contained in his 1709 *Segensvolle Fußstapfen* (*Blessed Footsteps*), a 'masterpiece of publicity and propaganda' produced to defend and promote his new orphanage.[60] The *Fußstapfen* present a full account of the creation and use of the Halle establishment, and discusses in detail the appearance of its most important building, the orphanage. Impressive in its scale, the four-storey orphanage has a classical façade adorned with a tympanum bearing a painted relief sculpture of two eagles and the sun, with an inscription from Isaiah 40:31 beneath.[61] Georg Heinrich Neubauer, Francke's colleague at Halle, wrote in 1714 that in the impressive buildings many people recognized and praised God's handiwork. Francke answered accusations that it was too costly by emphasizing that it was constructed of simple material in a modest style. He argued that a 'costly building means one that is made from costly materials, such as marble, carved stones etc., and in an artful and extravagant manner'. A 'costly building'

[56] August Hermann Francke, *Glauchisches Gedenck-Büchlein/Oder Einfältiger Unterricht Für die Christliche Gemeinde zu Glauche an Halle…* (Halle: Würdig, 1693), Vorrede.

[57] Ringshausen, *Von der Buchillustration,* 83.

[58] François de Salignac de La Mothe Fénelon, *Von der Erziehung der Töchter…* (Halle: Fritzsch, 1698), 86–7, from chapter 6, 'Vom Brauche der Historien bey den Kindern'.

[59] Ringshausen, *Von der Buchillustration*, 82, 86.

[60] Fulbrook, *Piety and Politics,* 157; August Hermann Francke, *Segensvolle Fußstapfen* ed. Michael Wele (Gießen, 1994).

[61] Mette Birkedal Bruun et al., 'Withdrawal and Engagement in the Long Seventeenth Century: Four Case Studies', *Journal of Early Modern Christianity*, 1 (2) (2014), 249–343, here 297–303.

would be adorned with typically baroque ornamentation: 'windows cut artistically from stone, plinths for statues, garlands of fruit and all kinds of sculpture and carving'. The orphanage, by contrast, was constructed of cheap stone, and there was so little artistic work to be found upon it that anyone who was knowledgeable about buildings would think that its architect was a fool. Both inside and outside the building avoided, Francke claimed, everything that served only 'for adornment and appearance'. Despite this rejection of magnificence, the orphanage had, Francke noted, been given 'a fine appearance, because in it good order and symmetry were observed'.[62]

CONCLUSION

This chapter has juxtaposed the visual culture of late seventeenth- and early eighteenth-century Electoral Saxony—in particular of the borderland regions of the Erzgebirge and Upper Lusatia—with that of Brandenburg during the same period. In the former, the Lutheran baroque flourished. Wherever finances permitted, nobles and townsfolk rebuilt, or at least redecorated, local churches, employing visual magnificence in the service of both representation and piety. Artists such as Johann Heinrich Böhme the Younger and Kapsar Gottlob von Rodewitz were valued for their ability to reproduce something, at least, of the splendour and drama of the Italian baroque. In Berlin too, Andreas Schlüter produced in his Marienkirche pulpit a monument to the cross-confessional allure of the work of Gianlorenzo Bernini in particular. In Berlin, Johann Christoph Müller and Georg Gottfried Küster celebrated in 1737 the ornamentation, the gilding and the bright colours of the new altar in the Lutheran Nikolaikirche: these subjects of the Prussian king were no enemies of magnificence and splendour. The comparison between Electoral Saxony and Brandenburg shows, however, that there was no pre-determined path from the Wittenberg of Luther's lifetime to the flourishing of the Lutheran baroque. It drives home, once again, the importance of local context for shaping confessional culture.

In Brandenburg, Lutheran culture was shaped by the presence of Calvinists, both local and foreign, and by the growth of Pietism. While the former were, in general, enemies of religious art, the latter were not. In the service of practicality, Francke promoted an aesthetic of simplicity that has come to be seen as indicative of the Pietist movement as a whole. Yet, Francke, like Spener and many of his followers, recognized the role that images could play in stimulating the imagination, for good as well as for ill. If we return to Köppen's 1762 consecration sermon for the altar in Berlin's Marienkirche, the preacher's Pietist-inspired reservations about visual magnificence are immediately apparent (Fig. 8.6). Köppen warns against 'empty adornment' and 'vain pomp', and praises the moderation with which gilding has been applied to the altar. Yet, the altar, and its images, served an important

---

[62] Holger Zaunstöck (ed.), *Gebaute Utopien. Franckes Schulstadt in der Geschichte europäische Stadtentwürfe* (Halle, 2010), 116, 128–30.

purpose: the 'awakening of piety'. This 'awakening' was achieved partly through iconography, through the choice of two highly emotive Passion scenes: Christ in Prayer on the Mount of Olives and the Descent from the Cross. It was achieved also through the painter's art. In the Gethsemane scene, for example, the angel who covers his face and turns it away from the suffering Christ provides the viewer with a model of sorrowful response. Even where, as in Brandenburg, the local confessional climate was not conducive to a flourishing of Lutheran culture, the emphasis on inner renewal that Pietism's exponents shared with Arndt's earlier devotional movement shaped eighteenth-century Lutheran religious life, and guaranteed images an important place within it.

9

Art and Identity after the 'Confessional Age'

By the early eighteenth century, baroque visual culture was well established in both Electoral Saxony and Brandenburg. It flourished most spectacularly at court, but its appeal was widespread, extending well beyond the residential cities of Dresden and Berlin-Cölln. Not only princes but also nobles and wealthy burghers sought representation in a modern manner, and chose, in many cases, to bestow their patronage on artists familiar with the visual idioms of the Italian baroque. This was also the age of the *Kunstkammer* during which the collection and presentation of 'artful sculptures and paintings', as Dresden's Gabriel Kaltemarckt had put it in 1587, constituted an important part of proper princely magnificence. Some of the splendid treasures listed in the inventories of Dresden's seventeenth-century castle chapel were quite clearly on the path to *Musealisierung*, to becoming museum exhibits: they were kept in a vault and shown to visiting dignitaries, and were eventually subsumed into Friedrich August I's treasure chamber, the *Grünes Gewölbe*. When we think of splendid baroque courts, or when we look at the engravings from Johann Ulrich Krauss's widely received 1705 *Historische Bilder Bibel* showing the evangelists seated in elaborate art galleries (Fig. 7.2), surely we must conclude that the age of the confessional image was over? Here art is about power and about pleasure. Yet, as we have seen, religious images did not lose their spiritual significance as they moved from churches to the 'crowded walls of picture cabinets'. Orthodox Lutherans, and even Pietist writers too, continued to recognize images' role in stimulating the spiritual imagination. Recourse to the models provided by Bernini and Rubens was inspired not only by contemporary fashion but also by the desire of Lutheran patrons and artists to intensify viewers' affective encounters with images of the Passion.

Where, then, amidst all of this magnificence, do we locate the dividing line between Lutheran and Catholic visual culture? Sometimes iconography provides an easy answer: whereas Bernini had used his skill to elevate St Peter's throne, Andreas Schlüter used his to celebrate the preaching of God's Word (Plate 1). Yet, many iconographies were common to both Lutheranism and Catholicism. An altarpiece depicting a scene from Christ's Passion could adorn a church of either confession, as Bernhard Rode's adaptation of Rubens's Antwerp *Descent from the Cross* for Berlin's Marienkirche demonstrates (Fig. 8.6). This chapter will suggest that even though the stylistic allure of the baroque and the spiritual importance of Passion piety cut across confessional boundaries, Lutherans remained acutely aware of the dangers of papist idolatry. Indeed, in eighteenth-century Electoral

Saxony the image question was given a new lease of life by religious and political changes both within the territory and beyond.

At the level of imperial politics, the period after 1648 witnessed the gradual increase of Habsburg power, and the emergence of Austria as an important player on the international stage. In Hungary and Bohemia, the Habsburgs, exempted from the restrictions placed on princes of the Empire by the *IPO*, pursued policies of re-catholicization.[1] Within the Empire, the Palatinate returned to Catholicism under the Pfalz-Neuburg branch of the Wittelsbach family in 1685, while Bavaria remained a stronghold of the Counter-Reformation. In Electoral Saxony, the Lutheran Territorial Estates had already, under Johann Georg II, feared that their Elector might convert to Catholicism. In 1697, Elector Friedrich August I, who had inherited the title from his brother Johann Georg IV in 1694, did just that in order to win election to the Polish throne. The Catholic orientation of Saxony's Wettin electors was confirmed by the conversion of the crown prince, the future Friedrich August II, secretly in 1712 and publicly in 1717, and by his subsequent marriage to a Habsburg, Archduchess Maria Josepha.[2] Saxony retained its leader-ship of the *Corpus Evangelicorum* in the face of competition from both Hesse and Brandenburg-Prussia, but Friedrich August handed over its business to still-evangelical members of the Wettin dynasty.[3]

Although in Electoral Saxony, as elsewhere in the Empire, Protestants were protected from forced re-catholicization by the terms of the *IPO*, Lutherans undoubtedly felt under threat. In Dresden in particular, confessional tensions ran high: in 1726 they reached a climax when the killing of an evangelical clergyman by a soldier who had recently converted from Catholicism to Lutheranism pro-voked two days of rioting.[4] In such circumstances, it is perhaps scarcely surprising that images retained—or regained—their inflammatory potential. This chapter will examine conflicts over images in two areas: firstly, the borderland region of Upper Lusatia, where Catholics and Lutherans had long co-existed but where Habsburg re-catholicization in neighbouring Bohemia created particular tensions; secondly, in Dresden itself, where local Lutherans came face-to-face with the renewal of Catholic devotional life. Ultimately, however, Dresden's Lutheran citi-zens responded not by rejecting baroque splendour, but by embracing it in order to produce the Frauenkirche. This magnificent monument must be understood not only within the broad chronological framework outlined in the previous chap-ters of this book, but also within the immediate context of eighteenth-century Dresden, where Lutherans burghers sought to defend their confessional identity against a Catholic court.

---

[1] See in particular Howard Louthan, *Converting Bohemia: Force and Persuasion in the Catholic Reformation* (Cambridge, 2009).

[2] Seifert, *Niedergang und Wiederaufstieg*, 148–53.

[3] Vötsch, *Kursachsen, das Reich und der Mitteldeutsche Raum*, esp. 45–169.

[4] Mathis Leibetseder, *Die Hostie im Hals: eine 'schröckliche' Bluttat und der Dresdner Tumult des Jahres 1726* (Konstanz, 2009).

UPPER LUSATIA

As we saw in Chapter 8, Upper Lusatia had some magnificent baroque monuments: in Görlitz local citizens commissioned splendid images and church furnishings (Plate 14 and Fig. 8.2) and village churches were rebuilt and redecorated at the behest of their noble patrons (Fig. 8.4). The territory may have been of marginal importance in political terms, sandwiched between Electoral Saxony, to which it was subject from 1635, and Silesia and Bohemia.[5] But its confessional history is fascinating. The Reformation had established itself early in the mercantile cities of the medieval 'Sechsstädtebund' (Lusatian League) and amongst the nobility: Görlitz's churches testify, for example, to both the prosperity and strong confessional identity of that town's Lutheran burghers. But Catholic institutions—most notably the cloisters of Marienstern and Marienthaler—also survived. Their rights were protected until 1635 by the territory's Habsburg overlords and were subsequently guaranteed by the Saxon electors in accordance with the terms of the Peace of Prague.[6] In Bautzen, where the Cathedral Chapter remained in place, Lutherans and Catholics shared the cathedral space from 1543 in an early, if not always harmonious, example of *Simultaneum*.[7] Moreover, Upper Lusatia had no strong territorial church to impose uniformity in Protestant doctrine and practice. As a result, its evangelical religious culture was characterized by variety: Martin Moller (1547–1606), the exponent of medieval mysticism whom we encountered in Chapter 5, spent part of his career in Görlitz, where the spiritualist Jakob Böhme (1575–1624) was also born and worked. The high point of the territory's religious pluralism was the foundation, in the 1720s, of the Herrnhut community of Moravian exiles by Count Nikolaus Ludwig von Zinzendorf.

In such a complex confessional environment, where did the line between legitimate Lutheran image use and Catholic idolatry lie? The liturgical commemoration requested by August Kober when he donated a new pulpit to Görlitz's town church in 1691 was apparently acceptable, as was the rich adornment of this and other Lutheran churches. In Bautzen, however, where the Catholic Cathedral Chapter continued to exercise certain jurisdictional rights over a predominantly Lutheran population, images caused friction. There is plenty of evidence of peaceful co-existence in Upper Lusatia: in 1678, for example, the superintendent of Bischofswerda reported that in Göda near Bautzen it seemed 'as if Lutheran and Papist were one and the same'.[8] The region's inhabitants, both Lutheran and Catholic,

---

[5] See Manfred Rudersdorf, 'Die Oberlausitz, die Habsburger und das Reich im 16. und 17. Jahrhundert', in Joachim Bahlcke (ed.), *Die Oberlausitz im frühneuzeitlichen Mitteleuropa: Beziehungen—Strukturen—Prozesse* (Stuttgart, 2007), 19–35; Joachim Bahlcke and Volker Dudeck (eds), *Welt—Macht—Geist. Das Haus Habsburg und die Oberlausitz 1526–1635* (Zittau, 2002).

[6] Karlheinz Blaschke and Siegfried Seifert, 'Reformation und Konfessionalisierung in der Oberlausitz', in Bahlcke and Dudeck (eds), *Welt—Macht—Geist*, 121–7.

[7] Siegfried Seifert, 'Das Domstift St. Petri in Bautzen—ein Überblick', in Steffen Gärtner, Volker Hänsel and Gunter Oettel (eds), *Via Sacra. Oberlausitz—Schlesien—Böhmen* (Görlitz and Zittau, 2007), 55–67.

[8] Alexander Schunka, *Gäste, die bleiben: Zuwanderer in Kursachsen und der Oberlausitz im 17. und frühen 18. Jahrhundert* (Hamburg, 2006), 350.

were, however, determined to resist 'Neuerungen', religious innovations that might lead to forced conversions.

In 1688, for example, Bautzen's Lutheran magistrates interrogated five witnesses about a 'so-called Marian pillar' that had been erected by Dean Brückner on the road to Belschwitz, a village just south of Bautzen.[9] All five witnesses denied any knowledge of a column showing the Virgin Mary, but attested that Brückner had indeed put up a pillar bearing a crucifix the previous year. The community at Belschwitz was, the witnesses stated, entirely evangelical. In a complaint addressed to the Elector, Bautzen's magistrates argued that Brückner's erection of what they now described as a 'sacred pillar' on the public road that belonged to the Elector was a religious innovation. Brückner had also, they stated, compelled local Lutherans to bury their dead with 'papist ceremonies' in Mönchswalde, part of the territory belonging to Bautzen's Cathedral Chapter. The magistrates acknowledged that similar columns existed in some of the territory's cloisters, but argued that there they presented no danger because they had been there since 'time immemorial'. Brückner's suspected plan 'to erect and set up new pillars in Lutheran villages' was, however, unacceptable. It was, they feared, part of a campaign to change the villages' confessional allegiance.

Ten years later a Catholic community in Radibor, ten kilometres north of Bautzen, was on the receiving end of an equivalent campaign. Radibor had been bought in 1685 by Hans Julius von Burkersroda. After his death in 1690 his widow, Katharina Elizabeth (née von Nostitz), came into conflict with the community, which refused her the dues that it owed.[10] Katharina Elizabeth had also, it seems, sought to impose her own Lutheran faith on the inhabitants of this Catholic village. In 1698, Bautzen's Cathedral Chapter appealed to the local district administrator to discipline her because she had torn down a 'crucifix and image of our Saviour'. Religious innovations were, the chapter complained, forbidden to Catholics, and should therefore also be forbidden to adherents of the Augsburg Confession: the crucifix must be reinstalled, and Radibor's pastor must refrain from trying to convert the local Catholics to Lutheranism.[11]

In both of these cases, images served as confessional markers: in 1688, one was imposed as part of an attempt to make Lutherans Catholic, and, in 1698, another was removed as part of an attempt to make Catholics Lutheran. There was, it seems, some confusion about what the Belschwitz 'sacred pillar' depicted, but it probably, like the Radibor image, showed the Crucifixion. In most contexts, Lutherans defended crucifixes vehemently; indeed, in Görlitz's town church the congregation twice replaced life-sized crucifixes that had been appropriated by Catholic nobles.[12] Context was, these Upper Lusatian cases suggest, all-important: there was nothing wrong with the images themselves, but their imposition or removal could not be tolerated if it was perceived as an innovation contravening

---

[9] CWB Zittau, A 242/11 Urkunden 1675–1700, fol. 195–6.
[10] Walther von Boetticher, *Geschichte des Oberlausitzischen Adels und seiner Güter 1635–1815*, 4 vols. (Görlitz, 1912–23), vol. I, 230–1.
[11] CWB Zittau, A 242/11 Urkunden 1675–1700, fol. 318.   [12] See above, Chapter 5.

the confessional settlement enshrined in the 1635 Peace of Prague. These late seventeenth-century disputes in Bautzen foreshadowed, as we shall see, conflicts that occurred in bi-confessional Dresden during the 1720s.

One final case from Upper Lusatia suggests again that the dividing line between Lutheran and Catholic visual culture, between legitimate image and illegitimate idol, was determined as much by context as by subject matter. Upper Lusatia was a territory that was not only confessionally mixed itself, but that also received, during the seventeenth and early eighteenth centuries, a large number of exiles and migrants from neighbouring Habsburg territories. Some came as Protestant refugees, in flight from Habsburg re-catholicization. Others came as Catholics, willing to convert in pursuit of a better life in the 'mother land of Lutheranism'. In general, exiles and converts were integrated into Lutheran confessional culture.[13] There remained, however, confessional boundaries that, at least from the perspective of the Lutheran clergy, could not be transgressed. The idolatrous worship of images was one of those boundaries.

In Zittau, a member of the Lusatian League located to the south west of Görlitz on the Bohemian border, the pastor Martin Grünwald (1664–1716) was responsible for guiding and assessing exiles who wished to convert to Lutheranism. In the course of his work, he assembled a scrapbook of texts and images that he entitled *Collectanae papisticae idololatriae (Spolia Aegypti)* (*Collections of Papist Idolatry (the Spoils of Egypt)*).[14] Grünwald, who described himself as 'collector of papist idols', directed the reader's attention to a polemical tract by the Württemberg theologian Andreas Osiander the Younger entitled *Papa non Papa*, first published in 1599. In Osiander's tract, the Lutheran position on the invocation of saints (chapter 25) and on images and idolatry (chapter 26) is laid out in full.[15] Grünwald's own collection opens with a series of 'Revocations=Puncte', questions to be addressed to the convert to ensure that he or she has abandoned the Roman church and will henceforth recognize the evangelical church as the true church that follows the teaching of Christ and the apostles. These 'Puncte' are followed by Grünwald's collection of 'papistica'—printed images and prayers collected from Catholics— which are interspersed with testimonials concerning individual conversions.

The 'papistica' are, in many ways, fairly predictable. They consist of small, often hand-coloured images of, and prayers to, Christ, the Virgin Mary, and saints (Fig. 9.1). Many of them were clearly distributed either by the Jesuits or by particular confraternities. Some depict pilgrimage images, most of which were located, not surprisingly given Zittau's setting, in Bohemia and Silesia. One shows, for example, the Virgin of Rosenthal, a Marian statue in Upper Lusatia promoted by the Jesuits that attracted the particular scorn of the local Lutheran pastor Abraham Frenzel (1656–1740).[16] A number of images are indulgenced: one, for example, purports to reproduce exactly the footprint of the Virgin Mary, while another

---

[13] Schunka, *Gäste, die bleiben*, 328, 350.   [14] CWB Zittau, A 44 a.

[15] Andreas Osiander, *Papa non papa: hoc est, Pape et papicolarum de praecipuis christianae doctrinae partibus…* (Tübingen: Georg Gruppenbach, 1599).

[16] CWB Zittau, A 25 Collectanea Lusatica Abrahami Frenzelii.

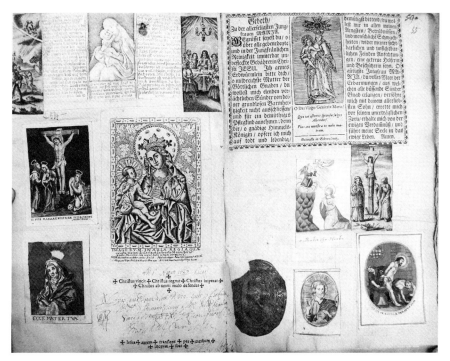

Fig. 9.1. Martin Grünwald, a page from *Collectanae papisticae idololatriae (Spolia Aegypti)*, *c.*1716.

Credit: Photo: author's own, Christian-Weise-Bibliothek Zittau, Wissenschaftlicher und Heimatgeschichtlicher Altbestand, Mscr. A 44 a.

shows a wound of Christ and promises a seven-year indulgence each time it is kissed by a devotee. There are also, however, images of the *Ecce Homo* and of the instruments of Christ's Passion, both of which were, by this time, established parts of the Lutheran visual repertoire. In Grünwald's collection, however, their origins and immediate context have led to them being named as idols. For Grünwald the confiscation of such idols was part of conversion, the process by which a Catholic could be integrated into the Lutheran church.[17] The subsequent collection and display of the idols was perhaps intended, like hand-written civic chronicles of the period, for the edification of local magistrates or church officials. For a Lutheran audience the *Collectanae papisticae idololatriae* served to reinforce confessional consciousness, marking a clear boundary between 'them' and 'us': 'you see here' Grünwald wrote on its title page, 'the idols that the Roman people honour'.

---

[17] On conversion see Ute Lotz-Heumann, Jan-Friedrich Mißfelder and Matthias Pohlig (eds), *Konversion und Konfession in der Frühen Neuzeit* (Gütersloh, 2007); Duane Corpis, *Crossing the Boundaries of Belief: Geographies of Religious Conversion in Southern Germany, 1648–1800* (Charlottesville, 2014).

EIGHTEENTH-CENTURY DRESDEN

From 1697 Electoral Saxony, the cradle of the Reformation and the territory that had, by the later seventeenth century, defined itself as the foremost protector of Lutheranism in the Empire, was ruled by a Catholic.[18] Not only in Saxony's Lusatian borderlands but throughout the territory adherents of the Augsburg Confession now operated in a complex religious environment. Dresden itself was subjected to what has been described as 'secondary biconfessionalism'. Thanks to the provisions of the *IPO* and of the Elector's mandates guaranteeing the religious status quo there was no risk of forced conversion, and Catholics did not enjoy legal parity with Protestants: they could not become citizens, and were not entitled to buy property in the city.[19] At first, Catholic worship was restricted to the Elector and his courtiers, and attempts were made to limit the visibility of the Roman church and its rituals. From 1699 Catholic masses were celebrated in the audience room of the Dresden castle and in the chapel at nearby Schloß Moritzburg, while evangelicals, amongst them Electress Christiane Eberhardine, retained the use of Dresden's castle chapel.[20] During Sweden's 1706–07 occupation of Saxony, the survival of Catholicism even seemed in doubt. But after Sweden's withdrawal and Friedrich August's recovery of the Polish crown Saxony's Catholic church was strengthened significantly.[21]

In 1708, Dresden's opera house was converted into a Catholic *Hofkirche* (court church), and placed under the charge of the Jesuits. Alert to the potential for confessional conflict, the king issued a decree stating that the *Hofkirche*'s preachers should not use sharp words against the Protestants and that Protestants, for their part, must show respect for the services conducted there. At the same time, however, he permitted freedom of worship to Catholics.[22] In 1712, the 16-year-old crown prince, who had been brought up in the evangelical faith by Christiane Eberhardine and whose loyalty to the Augsburg Confession the Elector had guaranteed to his Territorial Estates, was sent by his father to Italy and persuaded to convert to Catholicism. In 1717, this conversion was made public, when Mass was celebrated for him during a trip to Vienna, and in 1719 he married the Habsburg Archduchess Maria Josepha.[23]

Dresden's evangelicals felt increasingly under threat. The city's Lutheran clergy, led from 1709 by Superintendent Valentin Ernst Löscher (1673–1749), struggled to defend their exclusive right to perform key religious ceremonies—baptism,

---

[18] On Friedrich August I's conversion see Seifert, *Niedergang und Wiederaufstieg*, 122 ff.

[19] Ulrich Rosseaux, 'Das bedrohte Zion: Lutheraner und Katholiken in Dresden nach der Konversion Augusts des Starken (1697–1751)', in Lotz-Heumann et al. (eds), *Konversion und Konfession*, 212–35. See also Dagmar Freist, 'Religionssicherheiten und Gefahren für das "Seelenheil". Religiös-politische Befindlichkeiten in Kursachsen seit dem Übertritt Augusts des Starken zum Katholizismus', in Ulrich Rosseaux und Gerhard Poppe (eds), *Konfession und Konflikt. Religiöse Pluralisierung in Sachsen im 18. und 19. Jahrhundert* (Münster, 2012), 35–53.

[20] Seifert, *Niedergang und Wiederaufstieg*, 136.   [21] Rosseaux, 'Das bedrohte Zion', 216 ff.

[22] Seifert, *Niedergang und Wiederaufstieg*, 142–8; Freist, 'Religionssicherheiten', 41.

[23] Seifert, *Niedergang und Wiederaufstieg*, 137 ff. and 148–53.

marriage and burial.[24] With the 1719 Wettin–Habsburg marriage alliance, the Catholic presence at court was strengthened significantly, and more Catholics were drawn to the city as a whole. By the 1720s confessional tensions were very high. They reached their apogee in 1726, when the killing of an evangelical clergyman by a soldier who had recently converted from Catholicism provoked two days of violence. On 21 May, Hermann Joachim Hahn, deacon at the Kreuzkirche, was murdered by Franz Laubler, whose conversion to Lutheranism he had overseen three years previously. It is not clear whether Laubler had, in fact, renounced his new, Lutheran faith, but the rumour that a local evangelical pastor had been killed by a Catholic spread quickly through the city. In an already tense environment, it provoked a riot that could be stopped only by substantial military intervention by the city's evangelical *Gouverneur*. The subsequent investigations uncovered a clear feeling that, as the city's gold- and silversmiths' guild put it, the riot had happened because 'here the multitude of Catholics prevail'. From his residence in Warsaw, the king published a mandate punishing the ringleaders and demanding compensation for local Catholics, which did little to improve confessional relations in Dresden. As the most recent study of these events has demonstrated, they remained part of the collective consciousness, commemorated in broadsheets and medals for decades to come.[25]

Conflicts about the right to perform religious ceremonies and about mixed marriages and burials constituted the core of Lutheran–Catholic discord, but church space and its use was another highly inflammatory issue. As the news of the future Friedrich August II's conversion spread, a polemical tract asked the Elector to protect 'the freedom of the evangelical religion' in accordance with the imperial constitution, and to guarantee, amongst other things, to leave the Evangelical Estate free and strong, 'especially in the so-called castle chapel', in accordance with the 'normal year' (1 January 1624) prescribed by the *IPO*.[26] The chapel, which the tract demanded remain in evangelical hands, was, as we saw in Chapter 7, a key site of Lutheran identity. Although Friedrich August made no overt move, during his reign, to appropriate it for Catholic use, he did make one significant change to its appearance. Under Johann Georg II and his two successors its iconographic programme had been scriptural and Christocentric: there were no images of non-biblical saints, and the Virgin Mary appeared only in narrative scenes on the tapestries, on an altar cloth showing the *Pietà*, and on a cope.[27] In 1666–67, we find the first mention of a red velvet altar cloth showing her clothed in the sun, that is, as the Woman of the Apocalypse. This altar cloth was kept in the vault,

[24] Rosseaux, 'Das bedrohte Zion', 219–22; Freist, 'Religionssicherheiten', 41–2; Seifert, *Niedergang und Wiederaufstieg*, 155–7.

[25] Leibetseder, *Die Hostie im Hals*; see also Rosseaux, 'Das bedrohte Zion', 224–7.

[26] Friedrich Förster (ed.), *Die Höfe und Cabinette Europas im achtzehnten Jahrhundert*, vol. 3 (Potsdam, 1839), 250–4, here 254. See Christoph Münchow, '»… damit das Werk zu vollkommen Stand gebracht werde«. Valentin Ernst Löscher und der Bau der Frauenkirche', *Die Dresdner Frauenkirche*, 5 (1999), 133–42, here 136; Vötsch, *Kursachsen*, 108–119, esp. 118, n. 384.

[27] SHStAD, 10006 Oberhofmarschallamt, N I Vol. 8, 'Beilage' (no folio numbers), 1678; SHStAD, 10024 Geheimer Rat, Loc. 8687/2, fol. 55r (1687), fol. 63v (1692).

according to the 1681 and 1705 inventories.[28] A document from 1715, however, records that this cloth was moved from the vault into the church for 'daily use' on the altar at the behest of the King.[29] Friedrich August brought the altar cloth showing the Woman of the Apocalypse out from its hiding place and designated it for daily use, placing a reminder of Mary's Immaculate Conception at the very heart of this evangelical liturgical space.

When, in 1737, his son Friedrich August II finally moved services for the Lutheran members of the court from the chapel to the nearby Sophienkirche, the reaction was predictably hostile. With memories of the 1726 riots in mind, the city's magistrates made careful provision for avoiding unrest during the transfer, though they failed to prevent verbal attacks: notices appeared on walls and doors criticizing the King's action.[30] Löscher preached the final sermon, which was, according to its published text, listened to amidst many tears. The text for the day, the parable of the good shepherd (John 10: 1–11), offered the Lutheran stalwart an opportunity to warn his hearers of the dangers of false teaching and 'impure worship', and to admonish them to 'remain faithful in the true service of God', so that changing circumstances could not harm them.[31]

There was a gradual confessionalization of Dresden's public space.[32] While evangelicals retained, until 1737, the use of the castle chapel, the growing Catholic congregation attended daily Mass and, on Sundays and feast-days, a splendid solemn Mass with preaching and music, in the *Hofkirche*.[33] This former opera house was the main focus of Catholic life in the city until the completion of Gaetano Chiaveri's elegant new church in 1751.[34] An inventory from 1718 provides an insight into its visual splendour.[35] Some of the objects listed could have served equally well in the Lutheran castle chapel: silver crucifixes and candlesticks, precious chalices and patens, elaborate altar cloths and vestments. Many, however, testify to the particularities of the Catholic cult. There were monstrances to display the consecrated host, including one that was 'gilded over and over' and adorned with emeralds, diamonds and rubies. It bore images of Melchidezek, the Old Testament king and high priest (Genesis 14), and of the imperial crown, and should perhaps be seen as a riposte to the solid gold and bejeweled communion vessels donated to the castle chapel by Johann Georg II. In the Catholic *Hofkirche*,

---

[28] SHStAD, 10024 Geheimer Rat, Loc. 8687/2, fol. 38v, fol. 45v (1681), fol. 141v (1705).

[29] SHStAD, 10024 Geheimer Rat, Loc. 8687/2, fol. 145r.

[30] SHStAD, 11254, Gouvernement Dresden Loc. 14630/10. See Seifert, *Niedergang und Wiederaufstieg*, 160.

[31] Valentin Ernst Löscher, *Letzte Predigt, Welche … In der Königl. und Churfl. Säschsichen Schloß-Capelle in Dreßden… mit grosser Bewegung gehalten, und unter vielen Thränen angehöret worden* (Dresden, 1737), 28–9.

[32] Freist, 'Religionssicherheiten', 46.   [33] Seifert, 144.

[34] Ulrich Rosseaux, 'Der Kampf der Steine. Die Frauenkirche und die katholische Hofkirche in Dresden', in Rosseaux and Poppe (eds), *Konfession und Konflikte,* 153–63, here 160–2. On the exterior, which was adorned with 78 monumental statues of saints, see Friedrich August Forwerck, *Geschichte und Beschreibung der königlichen katholischen Hof- und Pfarrkirche zu Dresden* (Dresden, 1851), esp. 57–66; Siegfried Seifert, 'Das Bildprogramm der katholischen Hofkirche in Dresden, Kathedrale des Bistums Dresden-Meissen', in Menzhausen (ed.), *Ecclesia Triumphans Dresdensis*, 15–20.

[35] SLUB Dresden, Msc. Dresd. K26, S.00145–00151, 'Inventarium'.

there were baldachins to place over the monstrances, containers for incense and for chrism, and a relic of the 'redeeming cross' enclosed in gold and crystal and adorned with rubies and diamonds. There was a Holy Sepulchre, 'made at great expense', and there were paintings, many given by the king himself. On the church's main, 'royal altar' was a painted altarpiece showing the Virgin and Child with Joseph and John the Baptist, and on the two side altars were paintings of the Immaculate Conception and of St Joseph. Through the choice of subject matter for its altarpieces, and through its celebration of saints, relics and the consecrated host, the interior of the *Hofkirche* provided a strong visual affirmation of the Counter-Reformation Catholic cult.

Yet, Dresden's particular confessional context imposed limits on this visual affirmation of Counter-Reformation Catholicism. Catholics could not, as they did elsewhere, process openly with their images and relics. The masses and other rituals performed both in the converted opera house and in Chiaveri's purpose-built *Hofkirche* had to remain within the confines of the building, in accordance with provisions put in place under Friedrich August.[36] In Dresden, even the Jesuits, usually great promoters of visual piety, had to adapt to an environment that required circumspection. In 1726, a report by a fellow Catholic criticized their activity, suggesting that they were not well suited to work in land where people of different confessions lived together, and that the men chosen for the Saxon mission and for Dresden's royal chapel by the Bohemian Province of the Society of Jesus were not always appropriate.[37] The report, which reached the Sacred Congregation de Propaganda Fide in Rome, argued that although the Jesuits of course had to perform services with proper magnificence in order to promote piety amongst the populace, they should 'omit all those adornments and petty decorations, which transform the royal chapel into a village church and only offer the Protestants material to mock our supposedly superstitious ceremonies'. On 18 May 1726 the Jesuit Superior General Michelangelo Tamburini responded, writing to the senior royal chaplain in Dresden to draw his attention to the need to reconcile the establishment and advancement of religion with the interests of the king and public peace. The Jesuits should, Tamburini wrote, avoid all invective, sharpness, and cutting and ironic expressions in their preaching and catechizing. They should also 'exercise great circumspection regarding the display of images suitable for the [Catholic] cult', abstaining from anything that could give their religious opponents cause for contempt.[38]

Tamburini and the author of the initial 1726 report were correct to think that the image question retained its divisive potential. Dresden's evangelicals, like those in the confessionally mixed Upper Lusatia, were indeed sensitive to the confessional connotations of publicly displayed religious images, as two cases from the 1720s suggest. The first concerns the relief sculpture of the Dance of Death that had been commissioned in 1534 for Duke Georg's castle (Fig. 9.2). In 1721, this sculpture was transferred, at the behest of the king, to the part of the city north of the river,

[36] Rosseaux, 'Das bedrohte Zion', 234.   [37] Seifert, *Niedergang und Wiederaufstieg*, 157–9.
[38] SHStAD, 10026 Geheimes Kabinett, Loc. 553/4 Die katholischen Kapellen zu Dresden und Leipzig und deren Versorgung durch die Jesuiten 1709–26.

Fig. 9.2. Dance of Death, Dreikönigskirche Dresden, 1534.
Credit: © SLUB/Deutsche Fotothek.

where Pastor Paul Christian Hilscher (1666–1730) wished to install it on the exterior of the Dreikönigskirche's sacristy, facing the churchyard. Hilscher had, by 1721, a well-established interest in religious images.[39] Amongst the numerous texts that he had published on various aspects of biblical and ecclesiastical history was a 1689 discussion of the various errors introduced by artists into illustrations of the Nativity.[40] Here and in his other writings Hilscher showed himself to be particularly alert to the dangers of idolatry and superstition. His 1721 discussion of Dresden's ecclesiastical history contains, for example, a section discussing the survival of problematic pre-Reformation objects and practices, in which images feature prominently. Hilscher complained about crucifixes and 'Marter-Seulen' (columns bearing depictions of Christ being crucified or flagellated) that remained the focus of idolatry after the Reformation, citing various examples in and around Dresden. These were, however, 'kept today by us evangelicals without superstitious veneration, simply for devout remembrance of the suffering and death of Jesus Christ'. The crucifix installed on the bridge over the Elbe by Johann Georg II served the same purpose, he argued: its inscription by the then senior court preacher Martin Geier negated any suspicion that Dresden's citizens continued to favour 'papist image worship'.[41]

Hilscher recognized a popular proclivity for 'superstitious' stories and practices relating to images. He reported, for example, that there was a legend amongst the people that blood had been seen flowing from the crucifix on the bridge over the Elbe. The event almost came to be seen as a miracle, but thanks to 'more accurate investigation' the red-coloured dampness was found to have natural causes. He also recalled that before the Dreikönigskirche was damaged by fire in 1685, there had been a statue of the Virgin and Child on its altar that was richly adorned on high feat days. It was not only the custom, he complained, to put a small white shirt on

[39] On Hilscher see Julius August Wagemann, 'Hilscher, Paul Christian', in *Allgemeine Deutsche Biographie*, vol. 12, (1980), 431.

[40] *Errores pictorum circa nativitatem Christi*, subsequently published in German as 'Curiöse Gedancken Von den Fehlern der Mahler Bey Abbildung der Geburt Christi', in *Deliciarum: das ist: Annehmliche u. rare Discurse von mancherley nützlichen u. curiosen* (Dresden, 1703–4).

[41] Paul Christian Hilscher, *Etwas Zu der Kirchen-Historie in Alt-Dreßden, Von der Reformation an biß auff das andere Jubilæum* (Dresden and Leipzig: Joh. Christoph Mieths sel. Erben, 1721), 51 ff., 58.

the wooden Christ Child and a crown on its head, 'but also to adorn the carved Mother of God most splendidly, and by doing this to imagine doing her a special service'.[42] He lamented that elsewhere, above all in the villages where there were still 'papist altars', such practices remained common. There, young women in particular thought it a 'particular devotion' to decorate the little figures of Christ at their own cost. Such examples proved, he believed, that the effort expended over a period of almost 200 years had not been adequate 'to remove the papacy fully from people's hearts'. It was therefore very necessary, he warned, 'even now to take care everywhere that the remaining roots of such evil do not germinate anew'.[43]

Yet, Hilscher was convinced of the value of the pre-Reformation relief of the Dance of Death. He had already in 1705, published a description of it. It was, he wrote, one of Dresden's 'local antiquities', and was worthy of study 'not only in itself, but also on account of the beautiful work, remarked upon by those learned in art'.[44] His detailed account compared the Dresden example with others, including those in Basel, Annaberg and Leipzig. The image's main message was, he wrote: 'You must die!' The purpose of the entire work was to bring these words 'through the eyes into the hearts of mankind'.[45] His correspondence with the city council shows, however, that in the context of eighteenth-century Dresden the image's papist connotations could not be ignored.[46] Hilscher had to convince the council not only that the site was a suitable one, but also that their concerns about the image's iconography were unfounded. Could a sculpted relief that showed the pope leading the most eminent people in the world be displayed on a Protestant church without scandal? The sculpture might be very precious, but the proposed location was not ideal, above all 'in the present crisis'. In response to the suggestion that the image might create a scandal by giving the appearance that they wished, in an evangelical church, to give precedence to the pope because he lead the Dance of Death, Hischer argued (not unreasonably) that it was no great honour to depict the pope as the kind of person who led all his followers 'out of the world into the pit'.[47] Eventually, the sculpture was transferred to the graveyard, and, as Hilscher had suggested, given an inscription to clarify its significance: 'There is no difference here, we must all die!' In the same year, a brief tract was published that included a print of the dancing figures, and fixed their Lutheran interpretation. It was addressed especially to children: each child should, it stated, remember on seeing this ancient and edifying monument that 'death is already holding him by the hand', and will eventually dance with him out into the world.[48]

---

[42] Ibid., 60–1.   [43] Ibid., 65.

[44] Paul Christian Hilscher, *Beschreibung des sogenannten Todtentanzes… Wie selbiger An unterschiedlichen Orten/Sonderlich an Hertzog Georgens Schlosse in Dreßden/Als ein curiöses Denck-Mahl Menschlicher Sterbligkeit zu finden…* (Dresden, 1718), Vorrede. See Marius Winzeler (ed.), *Dresdner Totentanz. Das Relief in der Dreikönigskirche Dresden* (Halle an der Saale, 2001), especially 18–21 on the sculpture's eighteenth-century restoration and colouring.

[45] Hilscher, *Beschreibung*, 118.

[46] StadtAD, 21. Ratsarchiv 1370–c.1940, B II 11, fol. 1–15.

[47] StadtAD, 21. Ratsarchiv 1370–c.1940, B II 11, fol. 5r–5v, fol. 8 ff.

[48] *Kurtze Nachricht von dem Gottes=Acker zu Alt=Dreßden befindlichen Todten=Tantze…* (1721). Copy preserved in StadtAD, 21. Ratsarchiv 1370–c.1940, B II 11.

In 1724, the public display of Catholic images once again caused unease. This time the case focused on a house in Dresden that belonged to the excise councillor Johann Albrecht Gerren and that was occupied by a Catholic courtier, Franciscus Josephus Hoffmann. Hoffmann had, according to the local *Viertelsmeister* (representative of the citizenry), bought Gerren's house, which, as a Catholic, he was not permitted to do.[49] Moreover, he had, through his decoration of its exterior, provided an opportunity for a 'religious cult', which would, the *Viertelsmeister* feared, offend his neighbours.[50] Once again Pastor Hilscher played a role, this time reporting on Hoffmann's decorative scheme to the magistrates. The magistrates were presented with a number of sketches that summarized this decorative scheme: beneath an inscription with Hoffmann's name and the date of his restoration of the house was a niche, which was intended to house an image. In this niche, instead of an image there was now a vase. Beneath this vase were the words: 'S. Joh: Hassil ora'. Gerren was asked to remove this 'suspicious-seeming flower vase' with its inscription and name, which might refer to a saint, and the case was sent to the city council for resolution. According to rumour, Hoffmann had wished, the council heard, to have a statue of St John Nepomuk installed in the niche. When he was prevented from doing this, he placed a vase there instead of the saint, but let the inscription remain. This inscription caused some puzzlement to Dresden's Lutherans, but Löscher provided an explanation that confirmed the gossip concerning Hoffmann's intentions: 'in Bohemian, the word Hassil means one who protects against fire, and is supposedly an attribute of the said John Nepomuk'.[51]

The Hoffmann case was, according to Löscher, 'offensive and dangerous'.[52] Several times the records refer to gossip and rumour—tales were clearly circulating concerning Hoffmann's infringements of the jealously guarded rights of local Lutherans. Part of the problem was, of course, Hoffmann's purchase of the house and his public declaration of ownership. But the magistrates were also worried by the incongruous combination of a flower vase and an invocation of a saint that adorned its exterior. While a number of Dresden's buildings still bore statues of the Virgin Mary, Nepomuk was the archetypal Counter-Reformation saint, famed as a defender of orthodoxy against Protestant error. His was a very current cult: his beatification process had begun in 1715, and in 1719 his body had been exhumed from its tomb in St Vitus's Cathedral in Prague, revealing an intact piece of flesh, said to be his tongue. Devotion to Nepomuk's tongue, which was preserved in a newly built church at Zelená Hora, was promoted through printed images and prayers, examples of which were preserved in Grünwald's Zittau *Collectanae papisticae idololatriae*.[53] Dresden's Catholic Elector was amongst those pushing, at the behest of Emperor Charles VI, for Nepomuk's canonization, achieved finally in

---

[49] StadtAD, 21. Ratsarchiv 1370–*c*.1940, B I 13; SHStAD, 11254, Gouvernement Dresden, Loc. 14626/01, fol. 7r–15r.

[50] SHStAD, 11254, Gouvernement Dresden, Loc. 14626/01, fol. 7r–7v.

[51] SHStAD, 11254, Gouvernement Dresden, Loc. 14626/01, fol. 8r–14r. See also StadtAD, 21. Ratsarchiv 1370–*c*.1940, B I 13.

[52] SHStAD, 11254, Gouvernement Dresden, Loc. 14626/01, fol. 14r.

[53] See Chapter 8.

1729. It is scarcely surprising, therefore, that the rumour that a Catholic courtier wished to depict Nepomuk on the exterior of his house caused consternation amongst Dresden's Lutheran magistrates. Eventually both the vase and the inscription were removed.

DRESDEN'S FRAUENKIRCHE

In early-eighteenth-century Dresden, confessional tensions coalesced around the ecclesiastical rites of Lutheran pastors, but also around church space, ritual and images: control of the castle chapel; the appearance and use of the *Hofkirche*; the public display of 'papist' pictures such as the Dance of Death a statue of St John Nepomuk. Yet, Dresden's Lutherans did not, in this mixed environment, react by rejecting visual magnificence. Instead, they used architecture and images to assert their own confessional identity. Fig. 9.3 shows an engraving by Anna Maria Werner of the interior of Dresden's Dreikönigskirche on 2 November 1717, at the end of a three-day celebration of the 200th anniversary of the Reformation. The church is filled with fashionably dressed Dresdeners, and the preacher stands before them at a centrally placed lectern. Behind is a magnificent baroque altar. The Dreikönigskirche had been badly damaged by fire in 1685, and rebuilt and refurbished, just like Görlitz's town church, by members of the local community.[54] Its monumental new altarpiece showed Moses and the Brazen Serpent framed by marble columns and crowned with a gloriole. In Werner's print, a crucifix stands on the altar. The church's new pulpit bore on its canopy a sculpted personification of faith holding in one hand a crucifix and in the other a book inscribed with Romans 10: 17, a text that reminded the congregation, in the midst of all this visual splendour, of the importance of hearing: 'Faith comes from hearing, and hearing from the Word of God'. The text beneath Werner's print leaves the viewer in do doubt as to the triumphalist connotations of the festivities that it depicts: 'GOD crowns the Gospel with palms when the papacy wishes to whither or mock it'.

The Dreikönigkirche's impressive interior survived only until 1732, when the church was destroyed to make way for a wide new street.[55] By 1717 the city's Kreuzkirche was also, however, in need of refurbishment. This church, located on the other side of the Elbe near Dresden's Altmarkt, had functioned since the Reformation as the *Hauptkirche*: it was here that Dresden's superintendent served as pastor, and it was here that the city's parishioners brought their children to be baptized.[56] In 1717, Dresden's city council petitioned Elector Friedrich August concerning its furnishings. Not surprisingly, given Dresden's growing population,

---

[54] Cornelius Gurlitt (ed.), *Beschreibende Darstellung der älteren Bau- und Kunstdenkmäler des Königreichs Sachsen,* vols. 21–23, *Stadt Dresden* (Dresden, 1903), 127–31.

[55] The church was reconstructed by Georg Bähr according to plans by Pöppelmann. It was consecrated in 1739, and had a monumental high altar showing the Wise and Foolish Virgins. Gurlitt (ed.), *Beschreibende Darstellung,* vols. 21–23, 133–9.

[56] Ibid., 1–29; Friedrich Hermann Löscher, *Die Kreuzkirche und ihre geschichtliche Bedeutung für die Stadt Dresden* (Berlin, 1999), 129 ff.

Fig. 9.3. Anna Maria Werner, View of the Interior of the Dreikönigskirche, Dresden, 1717.
Credit: © SLUB/Deutsche Fotothek.

the church's congregation had increased, necessitating, the council argued, a widening of its altar gates. To achieve this the font needed to be moved. This font, a work by Hans Walter from 1569, was, in any case according to the council 'very large and misshapen in the old style'.[57] The Lutheran magistrates hoped, therefore, that the Elector would give them a new font like the one at the Dreikönigskirche, made from beautiful marble for the adornment of the church. The church's altar, from 1573, certainly survived intact and *in situ* until the building was destroyed in the Prussian bombardment of 1760. It is not clear whether the council's 1717 request for a new and suitably ornate font was granted.

---

[57] StadtAD, 2.1.2 Ratsarchiv B II 10, Ansuchen und Vertröstungen wegen eines neuen Marmor-Taufsteins in die Kreuzkirche. On the sixteenth-century pulpit see Gurlitt (ed.), *Beschreibende Darstellung*, vols. 21–23, 21.

The anniversary celebrations of 1717 provided an opportunity for Dresden's Lutherans to assert their confessional identity. At the Kreuzkirche the then super-intendent, Valentin Ernst Löscher, orchestrated suitably splendid festivities.[58] Löscher, who had served prior to 1709 in Wittenberg, in Jüterborg near Berlin and Delitzsch near Leipzig, was one of the last great representatives of Lutheran Orthodoxy, a man who certainly deserves to be described as an architect of confessional culture. His career and copious writings were shaped by his desire to defend Lutheranism against all threats: against the Reformed, and the attempts during the late seventeenth and early eighteenth centuries to achieve a union of Protestant churches in Brandenburg-Prussia; against Pietism; against Catholicism and Dresden's absolutist ruler; and against the religious 'indifference' of the early Enlightenment philosophers such as Christian Thomasius and Christian Wolff.[59] In 1717, Löscher started to publish a multi-volume defence of the Lutheran anniversary. This work was dedicated to the 'refutation in particular of those opponents who speak against the joy of our jubilee'. Its anti-Catholic polemic includes a lengthy condemnation of idolatrous practices such as pilgrimage, the clothing of Marian statues, and the veneration of saints (with St John Nepomuk singled out for mention).[60]

It was against this backdrop of confessional competition that plans for the new Frauenkirche took shape. The Frauenkirche has become, since its reconstruction in 1993–2005, a monument to German re-unification, and every aspect of its history has been documented in meticulous detail.[61] Some recapitulation is required, however, as the church represents the high point of the Lutheran baroque, as well as the end point of this study. By the early eighteenth-century Dresden's medieval Frauenkirche was in need of replacement. It had lost its status as the city's main church at the Reformation, but continued to provide services for the villages nearby. Now, however, its congregation had outgrown it, and the area in which it was located—the Neuer Markt—was being developed into a prestigious living quarter for nobles and wealthy burghers. Amidst splendid burghers' houses and nobles' palaces the medieval church looked out of place.[62] In 1714, the Elector ordered the destruction of the Marienkirche's graveyard, which contained memorials to many prominent local families, as part of his plan to build a new guard house. In response, Löscher, never one to shy away from a confrontation, preached

---

[58] Löscher, *Die Kreuzkirche*, 131.

[59] Klaus Petzold, *Der unterlegen Sieger. Valentin Ernst Löscher im absolutischen Sachsen* (Leipzig, 2001); Martin Greschat, 'Valentin Ernst Löscher in Dresden', *Die Dresdner Frauenkirche* 5 (1999), 125–31; Münchow, '»… damit das Werk zu vollkommen Stand gebracht werde«', 133–42.

[60] Valentin Ernst Löscher, *Römisch-Catholische Discurse, vom Evangel. Lutherischen Jubel-Jahr* (Leipzig, 1717–20), Vorbericht, A 4 r, 594 ff., 605 ff.

[61] See, for example, Magirius, *Die Dresdner Frauenkirche*. Stefan Laube, 'Konfessionelle Hybridität zwischen Reformation, Barock und Aufklärung. Komplementärer Kirchenbau in Kurfürstentum Sachsen', in S. Wegmann and G. Wimböck (eds), *Konfessionen im Kirchenraum: Dimensionen des Sakralraums in der frühen Neuzeit* (Korb, 2007), 195–213, here 205–9.

[62] Magirius, *Die Dresdner Frauenkirche*, 21–5. See Siegfried Hoyer, 'Bürgerkultur einer Residenzstadt – Dresden im 18. Jahrhundert' in Wilhelm Rausch (ed.), *Städtische Kultur in die Barockzeit* (Linz an der Donau, 1982), 105–16.

a sermon that fuelled Lutheran discontent.[63] Calls for a new church were given urgency, therefore, not only by the inadequacies of the existing building, but also by the confessional tensions of the 1710s and 1720s. Planning started in earnest in 1722, when the Elector appointed a building commission that included Löscher, as a representative of the Upper Consistory, and Dresden's mayor. The architect George Bähr was entrusted with the design of the new church.

Negotiations concerning the new church were lengthy, not least because of the difficulties of financing the project. In 1724, Löscher responded to Bähr's initial plans, which he considered too costly, by telling the building committee that for him the 'capacity and splendour of the church was distasteful'. Representatives of the city council responded by invoking the Elector, stating that because his majesty was so pleased by splendid buildings, they wished to present him with a plan that was suited to his Dresden residence.[64] Tension between the exigencies of civic finance and Friedrich August's desire for a sufficiently magnificent structure continued. In 1725, the Elector's senior architect, Johann Christoph Knöffel, produced alternative plans, which modified the church's exterior appearance to fit better with the redevelopment of the city.[65] In May 1726, the anti-Catholic riots, and the concomitant need to avoid additional tension between Dresden's courtly and civic authorities, provided the final impetus for the project. On 26 June, Dresden's *Gouverneur*, Count August Christoph von Wackerbarth, approved Bähr's final plans, which incorporated elements of Knöffel's revisions. The foundation stone for the new church was laid on 26 August, though it was still unclear how the building was to be financed. The Elector offered little more than reductions on taxation and customs duties on the raw materials needed for its construction; beyond this, special collections in the Kreuzkirche, donations from noble patrons (including the electress), a lottery, the sale of burial sites in the crypt and eventually, in 1732, the forced appropriation of money gathered by Löscher to help the Salzburg refugees, were all needed to bring the project to fruition.[66]

Although Dresden's Catholic court certainly played an important part in its conception, the Frauenkirche must be understood, ultimately, as an assertion of Lutheran self-consciousness. The laying of its foundation stone by Gottlob Hiernoymus von Leipziger, president of the Upper Consistory, took place, according to contemporary reports, before an audience of 10,000. The ceremonies that accompanied it were reported on in detail by Johann Andreas Rothe, in an account published shortly afterwards.[67] They lasted all day, beginning with the gathering together of the civic militia, and with a solemn procession of Dresden's civic and courtly officials, clergy and guilds to the old church, where Löscher preached a

[63] Ibid., 28–31.
[64] Hans-Joachim Kuke, *Die Frauenkirche in Dresden. »Ein Sankt Peter der wahren evangelischen Religion«*, (Worms, 1996), 30.
[65] Magirius, *Die Dresdner Frauenkirche*, 201 ff.
[66] Ibid., 197 ff.; Greschat, 'Valentin Ernst Löscher in Dresden', 130.
[67] Johann Andreas Rothe, *Kurtzer, doch zuverläßlicher Bericht von den Solennitaeten, welche bey beschehener Legung des Grund-Steins Zu der Neuen Frauen-Kirche in Dreßden... vorgegangen, und observiert worden...* (Dresden, 1726). See also Leibetseder, *Die Hostie im Hals*, 7 ff.

sermon. After the service in the old church the procession continued, accompanied by drums and trumpets, to the site of the new building. The foundation stone was laid during a carefully staged ceremony, with prayers and with music that was praised by Rothe for its 'magnificence and splendour'.[68] The civic official Paul Christian Schröter gave a speech, in which he thanked the Elector for having permitted, in accordance with his 'repeatedly given and most dear religious assurances', the construction of the new church.[69] The foundation stone itself contained a copy of the Augsburg Confession, a commemorative medal, and an account of the unrest of May 1726.[70] While Rothe's description of pious Christians shedding tears of joy both during the service and during the laying of the stone was probably a rhetorical exaggeration, there can be no doubt that this was indeed a deeply significant moment for Dresden's Lutherans.[71]

The church took 17 years to complete: it was not until 1743 that both its interior and exterior decoration were fully finished, and a cross and capsule containing documents commemorating its construction were placed on top of its cupola.[72] In 1734, however, Löscher preached a consecration sermon for the new building and declared that it was ready for use as a burial site.[73] The inside of the church's cupola was not yet cleaned and painted, its altar and confessionals were not ready, and the council feared the danger posed by remaining scaffolding.[74] Löscher's haste was the result, in part at least, of the fact that Saxony's new Elector, August III, was about to return to Dresden from his residence in Cracow. His commitment to the religious assurances offered by his father was yet to be proven, and Löscher sought to avoid the danger of *Simultaneum*—of the new church being used for Catholic as well as Lutheran services—by asserting continuity of use. To qualify for protection under the *IPO*, the Frauenkirche had to have been the site of regular Lutheran services since 1 January 1624. The old church had been destroyed in 1727, but services had, the council claimed, been temporarily transferred to other sites—the Sophienkirche and the little chapel beside the orphanage at the Pirnaisches Tor—rather than interrupted.[75] Nonetheless, Löscher was determined to bring the new church into use as soon as possible.

Löscher's consecration sermon provides a wonderful insight into the value he placed on the Frauenkirche, the expense and splendour of which had initially, as we have seen, caused him unease. His central theme was the importance of hearing and of preaching. His sermon opened, like many Lutheran consecration sermons, with a discussion of Solomon's Temple, which was, he argued, not just 'for sacrifice and prayer' but also for teaching: 'although in that magnificent Temple upon entering

---

[68] Rothe, *Kurtzer, doch zuverläßlicher Bericht*, 33.   [69] Ibid., 27.
[70] Ibid., 25; Magirius, *Die Dresdner Frauenkirche*, 35. On the laying of foundation stones see Dornheim, *Der Pfarrer als Arbeiter*, 203–36.
[71] Rothe, *Kurtzer, doch zuverläßlicher Bericht*, 34.
[72] Magirius, *Die Dresdner Frauenkirche*, 105 ff.
[73] Valentin Ernst Löscher, *Evangelische Predigt von unterschiedlichen Hören der göttlichen Rede, so zu erst in der neu-erbauten Frauen=Kirche Domin. Sexagesima 1734. Als dieselbe zum Gottesdienst der Nothdurft nach fertig war, Gehalten Worden* (Dresden, 1734).
[74] Münchow, '»… damit das Werk zu vollkommen Stand gebracht werde«', 141.
[75] Ibid., 140 ff.

the sanctuary one saw more than one heard, nonetheless chambers were built...in which teachers instructed the people'. Hearing was, for Löscher, the correct way to approach God, but it must be hearing not only with the 'bodily ears' but also with 'the spiritual ear, which lets one hear like a disciple, so that the Word presses into the heart through hearing'. In a passage that was perhaps intended as a direct castigation of Dresden's Catholics, who were at that time still worshipping in a consecrated opera house, Löscher stated that churches should not be 'theatres, to which one goes to see vain representations and great processions'. Rather, they are 'auditoria, where we gather to hear God's word and receive the holy sacraments; they are houses for teaching and hearing'.[76]

Using the Gospel text for the day, which told the Parable of the Sower (Luke 8: 4–5), Löscher emphasized the importance not only of hearing but also of responding properly to God's Word. He cited Johann Arndt, and spoke of the need for spiritual life to be transformed, so that 'it lays down living roots'.[77] He went on to criticize those who did not attend church for months on end, and who claimed that they had 'no space for listening to the divine Word, and thus wished to read in a spiritual book at home'. In response, Löscher argued that hearing was commanded so often and so clearly in Scripture 'that the meetings at which God's Word is taught and preached should not be abandoned'.[78] In an age during which Lutheran Orthodoxy was under threat from both Pietist separatism and early Enlightenment religious 'indifference', Löscher emphasized the importance of places of assembly, of sermons and of the theologians who preserved God's teaching. It was, he wrote, 'frightful foolishness' to hold, with today's *Raisonneurs*, that sermons are unnecessary, to write publicly that they do not edify their hearers, and to suggest 'that one can be properly enlightened and improved through reading good books', especially the 'new philosophical writings'.[79]

Löscher had relatively little to say about visual magnificence. For him, the splendour of God was to be found above all in the preaching of the Word and in the distribution of the sacraments.[80] His sermon did, however, acknowledge that churches were usually taller than other houses or had towers, as an indication 'that they are dedicated to the service of Him who lives above'. Löscher may have had reservations about the cost of the Frauenkirche, but for him towering Protestant churches were no paradox.[81] They might, he acknowledged, be called a 'Tower of Babel' by the 'false enthusiasts and mockers of our time'. But temples were spaces that God gave in order to commemorate his name. God was pleased by humble and plain churches, but it was not against his wishes when worldly authorities made such buildings somewhat higher, and decorated them appropriately. The contrast with Francke's 1709 condemnation of buildings constructed 'in an artful and extravagant manner' is immediately apparent. Löscher told his congregation that when they saw a church, especially a new church, they should think of such buildings as 'spiritual granaries, in which priests' lips preserve knowledge'.[82] He went on: 'as often as we see a church standing out amongst other buildings, so we

---

[76] Löscher, *Evangelische Predigt von unterschiedlichen Hören der göttlichen Rede*, 2, 4.
[77] Ibid., 16.   [78] Ibid., 26–7.   [79] Ibid., 28–9.   [80] Ibid., 30.
[81] Terpstra, *Religious Refugees*, 284.   [82] Malachi 2:7.

should think: here the Word of the Lord has its home, here the noble treasure is preserved, and at once sigh from our hearts: Lord keep us steadfast in Your Word'.[83] Church buildings were sites for admonition and exhortation, for assembling with fellow evangelicals, for prayer and piety, and, finally, for burial.[84]

The Frauenkirche did indeed stand out. Thanks to its splendid cupola it dominated Dresden's skyline until the completion of Gaetano Charivari's Catholic *Hofkirche* in 1751 (Fig. 9.4). It was from this cupola that Goethe looked out over the 'wretched ruins' of Dresden's centre eight years after the Prussian bombardment of 1760.[85] It led eighteenth-century commentators to compare the Frauenkirche to St Peter's in Rome: in his 1777 topographical description of Dresden Benjamin Gottfried Weinart, for example, wrote of it as the 'most magnificent temple in Saxony, the true likeness of the famous Church of St Peter in Rome'.[86] The interior of the Frauenkirche was centrally planned, like the Trinitatiskirche in Carlsfeld in the Erzgebirge, which Bähr knew.[87] With its pews and galleries it provided seating for 3,500. It was, as Löscher suggested, an auditorium, designed for hearing God's Word and seeing the administration of his sacraments. At first, preaching took place from the lectern located in front of the altar. There the preacher was highly visible but not, unfortunately, audible. Another pulpit, this time with a sounding board, had to be installed, located on the pillar to the left of the choir area.[88]

The design of the Frauenkirche seems to reflect, in some ways, the theoretical writings of the Pietist-influenced architect Leonhard Christoph Sturm, which were well known at the time.[89] Sturm emphasized, for example, the central importance of the pulpit, writing that all the congregation wish 'not only to hear the preacher clearly, but also to see him, for which the orderly division of seats is necessary'.[90] Sturm proposed, however, a form of Protestant church building that was clearly different from that of Catholics. He rejected the traditional cross-shape of medieval churches, and viewed cupolas as clear signs of 'papist churches', even though he admired the ingenuity that went into their construction.[91] Sturm, who was strongly influenced by Pietism and eventually converted to Calvinism, also advocated simplicity and frugality, for religion required 'more purity than splendour'.[92] Juxtaposing his theoretical reflections with the completed Frauenkirche certainly belies any notion of a uniform Protestant aesthetic or visual culture. The interior

[83] 'Erhalt uns, Herr, bei deinem Wort': the reference is to a hymn written by Luther in 1541.
[84] Löscher, *Evangelische Predigt von unterschiedlichen Hören der göttlichen Rede*, 31–4.
[85] Wolfgang Paul (ed.), *Dresden in alten und neuen Reisebeschreibungen* (Düsseldorf, 1990), 28–9.
[86] Kuke, *Die Frauenkirche in Dresden*, 64.   [87] Magirius, *Die Dresdner Frauenkirche*, 186–7.
[88] Though as Kuke points out, for those on the parterre, events at altar were not visible: Kuke, *Die Frauenkirche in Dresden*, 79.
[89] Christoph Leonhard Sturm, *Architectonisches Bedencken von Protestantischer Kleinen Kirchen Figure und Einrichtung* (Hamburg, 1712); ibid., *Vollständige Anweisung alle Arten von Kirchen wohl anzugeben* (Augsburg, 1718).
[90] Quoted in Magirius, *Die Dresdner Frauenkirche*, 182.
[91] See Jan Harasimowicz, 'Christoph Leonhard Sturm: Von der Erfahrung beim Umbau der Schelfkirche in Schwerin zur Entstehung einer pietistisch inspirierten Architekturtheorie', in Christian Soboth and Udo Sträter (eds), *»Aus Gottes Wort und eigener Erfahrung gezeiget«. Erfahrung—— Glauben, Erkennen und Handeln im Pietismus* (Wiesbaden, 2012), 599–621, esp. 621.
[92] Quoted in Kuke, *Die Frauenkirche in Dresden*, 78.

Fig. 9.4. View of the Frauenkirche, Dresden.
Credit: © SLUB/Deutsche Fotothek. Photo: Walter Möbius, 1934.

of the Frauenkirche's cupola, for example, was decorated with paintings of the
evangelists and virtues by Giovanni Battista Grone, who had been born in Venice
but resided, from 1719, in Dresden. Grone remained Catholic, and was eventually,
in 1740, appointed as 'theatrical painter and architect' to the court.[93] The visual
focal point of the church was its magnificent sculpted altarpiece, designed by

---

[93] Fritz Löffler, 'Grone, Johann Baptist', in *Neue Deutsche Biographie*, vol. 7 (1966), 126 f.

Johann Christian Feige, a local Saxon artist.[94] Above the altar was an organ, on either side were confessionals, and behind was a communion gallery, which enabled congregants to walk after receiving the host on the north side to receive the wine on the south.[95] This was a church that was carefully designed for the Lutheran liturgy, but that certainly did not eschew 'splendour' in favour of 'purity'.

The Frauenkirche's carved altarpiece is clearly, like the rest of the church, a statement of Lutheran confessional identity: an inscription immediately above the altar records a vow made by the senate and the people of Dresden to Christ as intercessor.[96] Sculpted figures flank the altarpiece's main scene: Moses and Aaron, with the apostles Paul and Peter beside them (Plate 14). The pairing of Moses with the High Priest Aaron appears in illustrated Bibles, where they stand beside the Ark of the Covenant in the Temple of Solomon.[97] Their presence may, therefore, refer, as Löscher's sermon did, to the church as the Temple of Solomon. On an altarpiece installed in 1712 in the Wolfgangskirche in Schneeberg (Erzgebirge) the pairing also showed, according to a local chronicler, 'how things go well in a city, when Moses and Aaron are united, and the worldly and spiritual estates live together in peace and agreement with each other'.[98] This was a message that was of as much relevance to Dresden's Lutherans as to Schneeberg's, living under the rule of a Catholic prince. The apostle Paul was an obvious choice for any Lutheran audience, while Peter may have been included because of his work baptizing (Acts 8) or because he was particularly venerated in the old Frauenkirche.[99] Festoons of corn and grapes—references to the eucharistic elements of the bread and wine—hang down from the gloriole at the top of the altarpiece. The central scene depicts Christ in the Garden of Gethsemane, an iconography that, like the *Ecce Homo*, had become popular amongst Lutheran patrons during the seventeenth century.[100] This choice of image was rooted in Lutheran—especially Saxon—Passion piety of the period: in the sermons, prayers, spiritual meditations and music that invoked Christ's suffering to move the hearts and minds of individual believers.[101] In the

[94] Joachim Menzhausen, 'Der Altar der Dresdner Frauenkirche und der Bildhauer Johann Christian Feige d. Ä.', *Die Dresdner Frauenkirche*, 4 (1988), 135–63; Heinrich Magirius, 'Die Gloriole des Altars der Dresdner Frauenkirche als Zeichen der Theophanie', *Die Dresdner Frauenkirche*, 7 (2001), 221–9.

[95] On the church's liturgical setting see Magirius, *Die Dresdner Frauenkirche*, 242–8. See also C. Wetzel, 'Das kirchliche Leben an der Frauenkirche zu Dresden von ihrer Weihe bis zu ihrer Zerstörung 1945. 1. Teil', *Die Dresdner Frauenkirche*, 7 (2001), 113–35.

[96] Magirius, *Die Dresdner Frauenkirche*, 100.

[97] Titze, *Das Barocke Schneeberg*, 87–8.

[98] Christian Meltzer, *Historia Schneebergensis Renovata. Das ist: Erneuerte Stadt= und berg=Chronica Der im Ober=Ertz=Gebürge des belobten Meißens gelegenen Wohl-löbl. Freyen Berg=Stadt Schneeberg* (Schneeberg, 1716), 89. On Schneeberg see Bridget Heal, 'Lutheran Baroque: The Afterlife of a Reformation Altarpiece', in Bridget Heal and Joseph Koerner (eds), *Art and Religious Reform in Early Modern Europe*, special issue of *Art History*, 40 (2) (April 2017), 358–79.

[99] Magirius, *Die Dresdner Frauenkirche*, 254 ff.

[100] On the *Ecce Homo* see Walter Hentschel, *Dresdner Bildhauer des 16. und 17. Jahhunderts* (Weimar, 1966), 82–3; Magirius, *Die Dresdner Frauenkirche*, 31.

[101] Christoph Münchow, '»Die Historie von Christo am Ölberge«. Das Bildrelief des Altars der Dresdner Frauenkirche und die evangelische Passionsfrömmigkeit', *Die Dresdner Frauenkirche* 8 (2002), 111–25; Magirius, *Die Dresdner Frauenkirche*, 250, 252–4. The von Rodewitz altar in Görlitz's Dreifaltigkeitskiche altar is a precedent. See above, Chapter 8.

Frauenkirche altarpiece Christ, in his distress, provides an example of prayer. He is consoled by an angel who, according to the Gospel of Luke (22:43), appeared to strengthen him. Above, from the altarpiece's gloriole, the eye of God watches over the Dresden congregation, and the ensemble is crowned with an inscription: 'S. D. G.', 'Soli Deo Gloria' (Glory to God Alone).

CONCLUSION

The process of *Barockiseirung*, whether accomplished through the construction of new churches or the refurbishment of old ones, entailed the adoption of Italian visual idioms. Either through their own travels or through their engagement with prints and other copies of Italian models, German artists learned to employ characteristically baroque techniques: the dramatic juxtaposition of painting and sculpture; the theatrical manipulation of space; the use of precious materials such as marble and gold and of particular visual devices such as monumental columns and glorioles of light. Artists and patrons delighted in the splendour of the baroque, in the visual accomplishments of the seventeenth-century Italian manner of building. The baroque was, however, about more than just the desire to impress and overwhelm. Unlike Feige's altar for Dresden's Frauenkirche, the high altar of Berlin's Marienkirche (Fig. 8.6), described so eloquently in Johann Ulrich Christian Köppen's 1762 consecration sermon, does not revel in an excess of decoration. Indeed, Köppen celebrated the Berlin altar's modesty and austerity, the fact that it was not *too* magnificent. But both the Dresden and the Berlin altars sought an intensification of devotion, an 'awakening of piety' that was just as much a part of baroque visual culture as ornate marble and gold. The desire for representation 'in a modern manner' was certainly one driving force behind the *Barockisierung* of Lutheran churches. But the desire to intensify individual piety, to create an affective response in the viewer was another, as the frequent inclusion of emotive scenes from Christ's Passion—the *Ölberg*, the Crucifixion, and the Deposition—shows.

The final section of this book has documented, in a variety of contexts, this Lutheran merging of piety and aestheticism, of devotion and magnificence. It has shown the extent to which the stylistic appeal of the baroque and the spiritual significance of Passion piety cut across confessional boundaries. In Saxony, however, those confessional boundaries did not weaken as a result. Indeed, faced with a Catholic prince and court, and with a growing Catholic population in Dresden itself, Saxony's Lutherans defended their confessional identity vehemently. Images, and their proper use, remained one of the ways in which confessional boundaries were defined, as examples of conflict from both the borderland area of Upper Lusatia and Dresden show. In both areas, it was, not surprisingly, above all the clergy who policed those boundaries. In Zittau, Pastor Martin Grünwald, with his *Collectanae papisticae idololatriae*, provides a wonderful example: he confiscated and collected 'papist' images as he integrated Catholic migrants into the Lutheran church. In Dresden, Paul Christian Hilscher, pastor at the Dreikönigskirche, played an important role in defending a medieval Dance of Death sculpture, but also in condemning 'superstitious' image use and in reporting to the city's Lutheran magistrates on a Catholic sculpture of St John Nepomuk. Valentin Ernst Löscher was an avid defender of Lutheran confessional interests, warning in his sermons and his publications of the threat posed not only by Catholicism but also by separatism and religious indifference. Such men do indeed deserve to be described as the architects of confessional culture. Yet, their plans, just like George Bähr's plans for the Frauenkirche, were shaped by forces beyond their control, by the realities of religious life in the age of princely absolutism.

Conclusion

For Lutherans, the Word has always had a 'culture shaping significance'. During the early modern period, Lutheran religious life was built around the spoken and printed word: around the sermon; around the use of catechisms, prayer books and hymnals; and around Luther's translation of the Bible. The book has therefore been understood, not surprisingly, as the most 'profound symbol' of Lutheran confessionalism.[1] By the seventeenth century, Bibles, hymn books, and devotional texts had become, for German Protestants, 'not only a companion for every day, but also a guardian, a sanctuary, and thereby a part of their own identity'.[2] Yet, Lutheranism was not only a religion of the Word. Ritual was also central to Lutheran religious identity: pastors and theologians as well as laymen and women vehemently defended particular forms of communion and baptism.[3] The same was true of images, which over the course of the sixteenth century became ever more deeply embedded in Lutheran confessional consciousness. Lutherans had, as the 1568 revised church ordinance for the Duchy of Prussia put it, to distinguish themselves from the 'intolerable Calvinists and false enthusiasts...who think that one cannot be evangelical unless one destroys all paintings, tears down all images, and abolishes all ceremonies'.[4] But images were more than just symbols of confessional delineation: they were also necessary parts of religious experience. Lutheran emphasis on hearing God's Word did not lead to a negation of the significance of the sense of sight. This was no zero-sum game: the disciplined use of all the senses, but in particular of both hearing and seeing, provided access to the divine. The verbal did not triumph over the visual, and to foreground the word while forgetting the image is to misrepresent the nature of early modern Lutheran piety.

The seeds of the confession's rich and varied visual traditions were sown by Luther himself during the 1520s and 1530s. Luther's shift from an initial rejection of images to a sustained, if not overly enthusiastic, endorsement of them was driven, like so much of his teaching, by events. Iconoclasm has featured in this account of Lutheran visual culture only as a voice offstage. We cannot, however, deny its importance. It was the iconoclasm of the 'Schwärmer' (fanatics) and the Calvinists that encouraged Luther during the early decades of the Reformation, and his successors during the second half of the sixteenth century, to defend images.

---

[1] Thomas Kaufmann, 'What Is Lutheran Confessional Culture?', in Per Ingesman (ed.), *Religion as an Agent of Change: Crusades—Reformation—Pietism* (Leiden, 2016), 127–48, here 132, 134.

[2] François, 'Das religiöse Buch', 221.   [3] Nischan, *Lutherans and Calvinists*.

[4] Sehling EKO IV, Preussen, Polen, Pommern, 73. See Heal, 'Kirchenordnungen', 170–1.

Images were, for them, matters of Christian freedom and signs of moderation in the face of radical threat. For Luther, however, they were not just markers of religious allegiance. Images—both internal (spiritual) and external (physical)—helped Christians to understand and experience faith. Images and visible signs, such as the Eucharist, helped make the Word accessible to frail human understanding. Images were also useful aids in the struggle to disseminate God's message. Scripture did not, the reformers quickly discovered, speak for itself. Proclaiming the Gospel required the multiplication of media: the use of words, the use of music, and the use of images. The illustration of Bibles and catechisms, from the lively and engaging illustrations for Luther's *Small Catechism* to the sophisticated visual exegesis of the woodcuts in Hans Lufft's 1534 complete Bible, made Scripture and the basic tenets of the faith more immediately accessible and appealing to all.

If Luther sowed the seeds of a rich visual culture, then some fell on barren and some on fertile ground. By the mid-sixteenth century it was clear that the territorial divisions within the Holy Roman Empire would shape Lutheran confessional culture in decisive ways. In some Lutheran areas, pastors and theologians responded to the crisis that followed the reformer's death and the 1548 Augsburg Interim by campaigning against ceremonies and images. The removal of altarpieces and other 'papist' images became, in Ernestine Saxony in particular, a way of demonstrating loyalty to the Gnesio-Lutheran cause, of distinguishing the territory's church from that of its 'adiaphorist' neighbour, Albertine (Electoral) Saxony. In general, however, the rise of Calvinism—with its attendant iconoclasm—both within the Empire and beyond, encouraged adherents of the Wittenberg Reformation to defend images. For a relatively brief but crucially important period, images, alongside ritual, became a litmus test of confessional allegiance, not only for pastors and theologians but also for the laity. In Electoral Saxony, for example, after a brief encounter with Calvinism under Christian I, members of the lesser nobility demonstrated their loyalty to the Unaltered Augsburg Confession and to a Lutheran understanding of communion by commissioning altarpieces adorned with the Last Supper or with Christ on the Cross. In Berlin in 1615, members of the city's largely Lutheran population rioted in response to Regent Johann Georg's iconoclasm and an inflammatory sermon by the Elector's court preacher. 'The Cathedral is destroyed, soon they will come and destroy our churches too', warned one rebellious tailor.[5]

By the early seventeenth century, however, images were much more than just confessional markers, as Johann Arndt's writings show. *Ikonographia* was Arndt's response to the 1596 iconoclasm in Anhalt, and the formulations that it and other polemical tracts of the period contain on internal and external images, on images' affective power, marked a crucial turning point in Lutheran image theology. The conviction, incipient already in Luther's writings, that images were a necessary part of *Einbildung*—of the process by which God's Word was impressed upon human hearts—was now articulated with new clarity and vigour. On the basis of a rich mixture of sources, both ancient and modern, Catholic and Protestant, Arndt and his contemporaries emphasized images' ability to move the heart and soul: 'what

---

[5] See above, Chapter 3.

one sees truly goes also to the heart'.[6] The work of the artist could therefore complement that of the preacher. Nowhere was this message more important than in relation to Passion piety. New types of Passion meditation emerged from the pens of theologians and of laymen and women. These emphasized, as medieval commentaries had done, physical suffering and compassion. In the visual sphere, iconographies such as the *Arma Christi*, the *Ecce Homo* and Christ in the Garden of Gethsemane returned to church furnishings as well as to book illustration. It was, however, the crucifix that became the most important and widely disseminated Lutheran devotional image. The pious house father described in Christian Scriver's 1675–96 *Seelenschatz*, weeping with his Bible, prayer book and crucifix, provides the most wonderful example of this new type of Lutheran religious practice.[7]

During the seventeenth century the flourishing of Lutheran visual culture was fostered not only by transformations in Lutheran piety but also by patrons' need for representation. This need was not, of course, confession-specific: princes, nobles and prosperous burghers of every faith sought appropriate forms of representation for themselves, their dynasties and the corporate bodies to which they belonged. Yet, the Lutheran belief in 'the right use of the visual arts', as Gabriel Kaltemarckt had put it in 1586, allowed patrons to make extensive use of religious imagery in their commemorative practices.[8] This was as true for miners in the Erzgebirge, who laid silver crucifixes on their brothers' coffins during their 'last shifts', as it was for Elector Johann Georg II of Saxony, leader of the Empire's *Corpus Evangelicorum*. Johann Georg II's castle chapel, with its magnificent images, textiles and treasures, epitomizes the Lutheran 'right use of the visual arts'. The castle chapel belonged to the age of the *Kunstkammer*: the age during which princely patrons sought to achieve fame through their collections of 'artful sculptures and paintings'.[9] Yet, here, as in the Italianate musical repertoire that Johann Georg II promoted, aestheticism and piety merged. When the Elector's servants decorated his chapel with tapestries showing scenes from Christ's life at Christmas and from the Passion at Easter, and when his court musicians performed settings of texts appropriate to these feast days, the result was a synthesis of sights and sounds that was intended not only to impress but also to intensify the worshipper's encounter with Christ.

It is easy enough to identify a coherent core to Lutheran iconography: it comprised portraits and allegories, alongside scriptural images that from the mid-seventeenth century onwards focused increasingly strongly on Christ's Passion. It is much harder to identify a distinctively Lutheran aesthetic. Lutheran churches often preserved gothic images, and in the seventeenth century many were reset in renaissance or baroque frames. The 'simple' and often inscription-laden paintings and prints produced by the Cranach workshop represent a particular moment in the history of Lutheran art: throughout the sixteenth century they defined Lutheran visual culture in Saxony and beyond. Ultimately, however, developments unrelated to religion—patrons' desire for representation in a 'modern manner'—encouraged

---

[6] Arndt, *Ikonographia (1597)*, 63.   [7] See above, 136–7.
[8] Gutfleisch and Menzhausen, '"How a Kunstkammer Should Be Formed"', 8.
[9] Ibid., 10.

the adoption of new visual idioms.[10] Lutheran churches of the later seventeenth and eighteenth centuries, from Johann Georg II's magnificent castle chapel to the richly decorated parish churches of the Erzgebirge and Upper Lusatia and Dresden's Frauenkirche, challenge the age-old association of Protestantism with an aesthetic of plainness. The Lutheran baroque was not, of course, a universal phenomenon. But in Saxony, the 'motherland' of the Reformation, it was widespread. Even in neighbouring Brandenburg, where Lutheran self-representation was held in check by the presence of a Calvinist court and a powerful Pietist movement, the Italian baroque was welcomed, as Andreas Schlüter's pulpit for Berlin's Marienkirche shows (Plate 1).

In art, as in music, stylistic shifts were not driven purely by aesthetic concerns. Kaufmann suggests that while the texts of the works of J. S. Bach were the product of Lutheran confessional culture, the music—their 'means of articulation'—was not. Bach's music, he suggests, 'unfolds into a sound world that leaves all confessional boundaries behind'.[11] Yet, for sacred music, as for sacred art, is it really possible to separate out content from style? The musical forms adopted by Bach, and by earlier Lutheran composers, were suited to the devotional needs of their time. In the visual sphere, at a time at which Lutherans wished, thanks to the changes in piety fostered by Arndt and his successors, to use images not only to teach and commemorate but also to move the heart and soul, the art of the Italian baroque offered an appropriate set of tools. The juxtaposition of painting and sculpture (Fig. 8.5), the manipulation of space (Fig. 8.1) and the dramatic use of light (Plate 14) all heightened not only the splendour but also the emotional impact of the religious image. If we are to speak at all of a 'Lutheran visual culture', we must at least recognize, therefore, that it was not a static and unchanging phenomenon, but rather responded to the needs—both religious and secular—of its time. As incongruous as it might seem to us, in the light of scholarly narratives that equate bare churches with evangelical faith and the Reformation with a cultural break from the Roman world, seventeenth-century Lutherans recognized not only the magnificence but also the devotional potential of the baroque. Artists such as Andreas Schlüter were able to serve as cultural mediators, adapting visual formulae devised by Bernini to the needs of Protestant patrons.

What can we say, finally, of the people who created these rich Lutheran visual cultures? What of the individuals and groups whose identities—Lutheran and other—the images illustrated in this study expressed? Theologians certainly deserve to be termed the 'architects' of Lutheran confessional culture. Amongst them were great household names: Luther himself, of course, but also Johann Arndt, Protestantism's most successful devotional writer.[12] There were also many lesser figures who composed polemical defences of images or devotional works advocating their use: Simon Gedicke, with his 1597 *Von Bildern vnd Altarn*, or Johannes

---

[10] See above, Chapters 7 and 8.

[11] Kaufmann, 'What is Lutheran Confessional Culture?', 143.

[12] Brecht, 'Johann Arndt und das Wahre Christentum', in Brecht et al. (eds), *Geschichte des Pietismus*, vol. 1, 130–50, here 149–50.

Saubert, author of the 1629 *Icones Precantium*. And there were the local pastors who policed, on a day-to-day basis, the confessional boundaries that images helped to define: Johann Petrejus campaigning against the Wolgemut altarpiece in Zwickau, for example, or Martin Grünwald with his *Collectanae papisticae idololatriae* in Zittau.[13] Even in the normative prescriptions of the great theologians, however, the laity played a decisive role: it was above all for the sake of 'simple folk' that images were retained and used in instruction. They worked, the reformers recognized, in ways that theological arguments could not. Pastoral concern for the 'common man' was clearly one of the driving motors behind Lutheran visual culture, from Luther's 1529 illustrated prayer book onwards.

While the laity tend to appear in this theological discourse as 'simple folk' in need of instruction, or as the weak in faith who might be alienated by the trauma of iconoclasm, in practice they were certainly not merely passive recipients of the plans of the theologian-architects. The appearance of Lutheran churches was shaped, for example, not only by theology and liturgy—by the need to focus attention on the pulpit and altar—but also by the desire for commemoration, a traditional concern that was scarcely interrupted by the doctrinal changes introduced during the Reformation. Lutheran churches were full of epitaphs and commemorative donations. Some, like the pulpit in the town church in Görlitz that was linked to an annual liturgical celebration of its donor, or that in St Afra in Meißen that showed Anna Felicitas von Schleinitz and her family (Fig. 6.5), were presumptuous in the extreme, claiming communal religious space for dynastic representation. The nobility, driven by their awareness of history and by their desire to represent and legitimate their lordship, created some particularly remarkable 'Lutheran' visual ensembles (Fig. 6.9), but the citizens who defended Wolgemut's altarpiece in Zwickau and the members of the Erzgebirge miners' guilds also showed a strong awareness of images' role in preserving memory.[14] And while art-historical literature tends to emphasize the emergence of confessionally specific visual traditions—of iconographies that reinforced confessional discipline—the images commissioned by Lutheran patrons in fact fulfilled a great variety of needs, from demonstrating religious and political loyalty (Fig. 3.2) to narrating and assuaging grief (Plates 6 and 9).[15] Lutherans commissioned such works not because they were, as Calvinists suggested, 'half papists' and 'idolaters', but because they had a particular understanding of their own confessional identity, an understanding in which images—from simple woodcuts to magnificent church interiors—played a key role.

[13] See above, Chapters 2 and 9.   [14] See above, Chapter 6.
[15] See, for example, Harasimowicz, *Kunst als Glaubensbekenntnis*; Müller, 'Repräsentationen des Luthertums'; Thomas Packeiser, 'Zum Austausch von Konfessionalisierungs Forschung und Kunstgeschichte', *Archiv für Reformationsgeschichte* 93 (2002), 317–38; Andreas Priever, 'Johann de Perre, die "Auferstehung Christi" und der Stein des Anstoßes. Eine Fallstudie zum Bildergebrauch in der lutherischen Orthodoxie', *Zeitschrift für Kunstgeschichte*, 70 (4) (2007), 513–44.

Bibliography

PRINTED PRIMARY SOURCES

Amman, Jost, *Neuwe Biblische Figuren: Künstlich vnd artig greissen, durch den sinn vnd kunstreichen auch weitberühmte[n] Jost Amman, von Zürych, mit schönen Teutschen Reimen* (Frankfurt am Main: Sigmund Feyerabend, 1571).

Andreae, Jacob, *Colloquium Mompelgartense…Auß dem Latein Verdeutscht* (Tübingen: Georg Gruppenbach, 1587).

Andreae, Johann Valentin, *Christianopolis*, ed. Edward H. Thompson (Dordrecht: Kluwer, 1999).

Arndt, Johann, *Paradies=Gärtlein, Voller Christlicher Tugenden, Wie solche, Zur Ubung des wahren Christenthums, Durch Andächtige, lehrhaffte und trostreiche Gebete in die Seele zu pflantzen* (Leipzig: Johann Samuel Heins, 1753).

Arndt, Johann, *True Christianity*, tr. Peter Erb (London: SPCK, 1979).

Arndt, Johann, *Ikonographia (1597). Kritisch herausgegeben, kommentiert und mit einem Nachwort versehen von Johann Anselm Steiger* (Hildesheim etc.: Georg Olms, 2014).

Arnold, Georg, *Chronicon Annæbergense continuatum…biss uffs 1658. Jahr nach Christi Geburth* (Annaberg: Hasper, 1812; reprint Stuttgart: von Elterlein, 1992).

Beyer, Hartmann, *Historien Bibel. Das ist/Alle vornemste Historien aller bücher des Alten Testaments/auß dem Text der Bibel gezogen* (Frankfurt: Chr. Egen, 1555).

Biblia, das ist/die gantze Heilige Schrifft Alten und Neuen Testaments/Deutsch/D. Martin Luthers/Sampt D. Hütteri Summarien/der Biblischen Bücher und Capitel richtiger Eintheilung… (Wittenberg: Balth. Christ. Wust, 1670).

Biblia, Das ist: Die gantze Heilige Schrifft/Alten und Neuen Testaments/Durch Herrn D. Martin Luthern verteutschet…auch mit 250. Schönen Kupfer=Figuren eines berühmten Künstlers in Augspurg geziert… (Nuremberg: Johann Leonhard Buggel, Moritz Hagen, 1702).

Buno, Johannes, *Bilder Bibel* (Hamburg: Lichtenstein, 1680).

Chemnitz, Martin, *Examination of the Council of Trent,* part 4, tr. Fred Kramer (St Louis: Concordia, 1986).

Conovius, Peter, *Bescheidentliche Abfertigunge eines Tractateins Georgii Gottfrieden Berlinensis, Theologiae Studiosi. Die Ausmusterung der Bilder/So wol Die Abschaffung des Exorcismi Betreffend* (Wittenberg: Georg Kelner, 1615).

Evenius, Sigismund, *Christliche Gottselige Bilder Schule* (Jena: J. Reiffenberger, 1636).

'Extract schreibens sub dato Cöln an der Sprew den 13. aprilis a. 1615', *Forschungen zur Brandenburgischen und Preußischen Geschichte*, 9 (1) (1896), 18–21.

Fénelon, François de Salignac de La Mothe, *Von der Erziehung der Töchter,* tr. and ed. August Hermann Francke (Halle: Fritzsch, 1698).

Fortgesetzte Sammlung von Alten und Neuen Theologischen Sachen, Büchern, Uhrkunden, Controversien, Veränderungen, Anmerckungen, Vorschlägen, u. d. g. zur geheiligten Ubung in beliebigem Beytrag ertheilet von Einigen Dienern des Göttlichen Wortes (Leipzig: Braun, 1728).

Francke, August Hermann, *Glauchisches Gedenck-Büchlein/Oder Einfältiger Unterricht Für die Christliche Gemeinde zu Glauche an Halle* (Halle: Würdig, 1693).

Francke, August Hermann, *Segensvolle Fußstapfen*, ed. Michael Wele (Gießen, 1994).

Furttenbach, Joseph, *KirchenGebäw: Der Erste Theil* (Augsburg: Schultes, 1649).

Furttenbach, Joseph, *Lebenslauff 1652–1664*, ed. Kaspar von Greyerz, Kim Siebenhüner, and Roberto Zaugg (Cologne etc.: Böhlau, 2013).

Garth, Helwig, *Christliche/Evangelische Altar=Weyhe* (Freiberg: Hoffman, 1611).

Gedicke, Simon, *Von Bildern vnd Altarn/In den Euangelischen Kirchen Augspurgischer Confession* (Magdeburg: Johann Francke, 1597).

Gedicke, Simon, *Calviniana oder Calvinisterey/So fälschlich die Reformirte Religion genennet wird* (Leipzig: Abraham Lamberg, 1615).

Gedicke, Simon, *Encaenia Sacra, oder christliche Predigt bey Renovatio oder Ernewerung der großen herrlichen Dom Kirche zu Meissen* (Freiberg: Melchior Hoffmann, 1616).

Gerhard, Johann, *Erklärung der Historien des Leidens vnnd Sterbens vnsers Herrn Christi Jesu nach den vier Evangelisten* (Jena: Tobias Steinmann, 1611).

Greiffenberg, Catharina Regina von, *Meditations on the Incarnation, Passion, and Death of Jesus Christ*, ed. and tr. Lynne Tatlock (Chicago: University of Chicago Press, 2009).

Grimmelshausen, Johann Jakob Christoffel von, *The Adventures of Simplicissimus*, tr. Mike Mitchell (Sawtry, Cambs.: Dedalus,1999).

Harsdörffer, Georg Philipp, *Frauenzimmer Gesprechspiele*, parts IV and VI (Nuremberg: Endter, 1643, 1646).

Hering, Daniel Heinrich, *Historische Nachricht von dem ersten Anfang der Evangelisch-Reformirten Kirche in Brandenburg und Preußen* (Halle: Johann Jacob Curt, 1778).

Hilscher, Paul Christian, 'Curiöse Gedancken Von den Fehlern der Mahler Bey Abbildung der Geburt Christi', in *Deliciarum Manipulus: das ist: Annehmliche u. rare Discurse von mancherley nützlichen u. curiosen Dingen* (Dresden, 1703–04).

Hilscher, Paul Christian, *Beschreibung des sogenannten Todtentanzes… Wie selbiger An unter-schiedlichen Orten/Sonderlich an Hertzog Georgens Schlosse in Dreßden/Als ein curiöses Denck-Mahl Menschlicher Sterbligkeit zu finden* (Dresden: Mieth, 1718).

Hilscher, Paul Christian, *Etwas Zu der Kirchen-Historie in Alt-Dreßden, Von der Reformation an biß auff das andere Jubilæum* (Dresden and Leipzig: Joh. Christoph Mieths sel. Erben, 1721).

Hilscher, Paul Christian, *Kurtze Nachricht von dem Gottes=Acker zu Alt=Dreßden befindli-chen Todten=Tantze* (Dresden: Mieth, 1721).

Jäger, Christoph, *Rechtschaffener Christen Lust= und Freuden=Tempel Aus dem schönen Macht=Spruche Im 3. Joh. Also hat GOtt die Welt geliebt etc. Bey dem Volckreicher und Christ=Adelicher Leich=Bestattung Der weiland HochEdelgebornen und so Viel=Ehr= als Tugend begabten Gottfürchtigen Matron, Frauen Annen Felicitas…* (Bautzen: Christoph Baumann, 1666).

Köppen, Johann Ulrich Christian, *Die Freude der Gläubigen bey den Altaren Gottes* (Berlin: Rellstab, 1762).

Krauss, Johann Ulrich, *Historische Bilder-Bibel* (Augsburg: Krauss, 1705).

Küsel, Melchior, *Icones Biblicae Veteris Et Novi Testamenti* (Augsburg: Georg Laub, 1679).

Lappe, Nicodemus, *Inauguratio Renocati Altari Arnstadiensis* (n. p., 1642).

Lindener, Johannes, *Christliche Leichpredigt von dem letzten Wort… Bey Leichbestattung des Dietrich von Grünraden auff Seyffersdorf u. Widerode* (Dresden: Stöckel, 1603).

Löscher, Valentin Ernst, *Römisch-Catholische Discurse, vom Evangel. Lutherischen Jubel-Jahr* (Leipzig: Braun, 1717–20).

Löscher, Valentin Ernst, *Evangelische Predigt von unterschiedlichen Hören der göttlichen Rede, so zu erst in der neu-erbauten Frauen=Kirche Domin. Sexagesima 1734. Als dieselbe zum Gottesdienst der Nothdurft nach fertig war, Gehalten Worden* (Dresden: Robring, 1734).

Löscher, Valentin Ernst, *Letzte Predigt, Welche Am 3. Pfingst-Feyer-Tage 1737…gehalten* (Dresden, 1737).

Luther, Martin, *Enchiridion. Der kleyn Catechismus für die gemeyne Pfarrherren vnnd Predigern. Auffs new zugericht. Marti. Luther* (Nuremberg: Christoff Gutknecht, 1547; reprint Nuremberg: Medien & Kultur, 1980).

Luther, Martin, *Enchiridion. Der Kleine Catechismus des Hocherleuchten vnd Geistreichen Mannes D. Martini Lutheri…Fein richtig vnd ördentlich zusammen gezogen/vnd mit den allerschönsten/herrlichten vnd besten Sprüchen der heiligen Göttlichen Schrifft also gezieret/geschmücket vnd erwiesen…Durch Petrum Victorium Pfarrern zu Kyritz* (Leipzig: Michael Lantsenberger, 1591).

Mangrum, Bryan and Giuseppe Scavizzi (eds), *A Reformation Debate: Karlstadt, Emser, and Eck on Sacred Images. Three Treatises in Translation* (Ottawa: Dovehouse, 1991).

Mann, Thomas, *Buddenbrooks*, tr. H. T. Lowe-Porter (London: Vintage, 1924).

Mathesius, Johann, *Sarepta oder Bergpostill Sampt der Joachimßthalischen kurtzen Chronicken* (Nuremberg: Neuber, 1564; reprint Prague: Národní Technické Muzeum, 1975).

Mattsperger, Melchior, *Geistliche Herzens=Einbildungen* (Augsburg: Bodenehr, 1685).

Mehlhausen, Joachim (ed.), *Das Augsburger Interim von 1548. Nach den Reichstagsakten deutsch und lateinisch* (Neukirchen-Vluyn: Neukirchender Verl., 1970).

Meltzer, Christian, *Historia Schneebergensis Renovata. Das ist: Erneuerte Stadt= und berg=Chronica Der im Ober=Ertz=Gebürge des belobten Meißens gelegenen Wohl-löbl. Freyen Berg=Stadt Schneeberg* (Schneeberg: Fuld, 1716).

Merian, Matthäus, *Icones Biblicæ Præcipuas Sacræ Scripturæ Historias eleganter & graphice repræsentantes* (Frankfurt am Main: De Bry, 1625).

Merian, Matthäus, *Theatrum Europaeum*, vol. 2 (Frankfurt am Main: Matthäus Merian, 1637).

Möller, Andreas, *Theatrum Freibergense Chronicum. Beschreibung der alten löblichen BergHauptStadt Freyberg in Meissen…* (Freiberg: Georg Beuther, 1653).

Moller, Martin, *Soliloquia de passion Iesu Christi* (Görlitz: Fritsch, 1590).

Müller, Johann Christoph and Georg Gottfried Küster, *Altes und Neues Berlin. Das ist: vollständige Nachricht von der Stadt Berlin, derselben Erbauen, Lage, Kirchen…Erster Theil* (Berlin: Johann Peter Schmid, 1737).

Müller, Johann Christoph and Georg Gottfried Küster, *Fortgesetzes Altes und Neues Berlin* (Berlin: Johann Peter Schmid, 1752).

Nicolai, Friedrich, *Beschreibung der Königlichen Residenzstädte Berlin und Potsdam*, 3rd ed. (Berlin: Nicolai, 1786).

Nitsche, Christian, *Beschreibung der berühmten und prächtigen Kirche zu SS. Petri und Pauli in Görlitz* (Görlitz: Laurentius, 1725).

Olearius, Johannes, *Geistliche Singe-Kunst, und ordentlich verfassetes vollständiges Gesang-Buch* (Leipzig: Caspar Linitius, 1671).

Osiander, Andreas, *Papa non papa: hoc est, Pape et papicolarum de praecipuis christianae doctrinae partibus* (Tübingen: Georg Gruppenbach, 1599).

Parneman, Christianus, *Consecrationum Quaternio, Das ist/Vierfache Einweyhung* (Wittenberg: Hartmann, 1663).

Petrejus, Johannes, *Warnung und Vermanung: Das man an das Vnauffhörliche Schreien der Flacianer…sich nicht keren* (Wittenberg: Seitz, Peter d. J., 1571).

Prasch, Johann Ludwig, *Emblematischer Catechismus/Oder Geist= und Sinnreiche Gedancken. Uber die Hauptstücke Christlicher Lehrer* (Nuremberg: Johann Andreæ Endters Söhne, 1683).

Rothe, Johann Andreas, *Kurtzer, doch zuverläßlicher Bericht von den Solennitaeten, welche bey beschehener Legung des Grund-Steins Zu der Neuen Frauen-Kirche in Dreßden…vorgegangen, und observiert worden* (Dresden: Robring, 1726).

Saubert, Johannes, *Icones precantium: das ist: Christliche Figuren, zur Gebetstund angesehen* (Nuremberg: Endter, 1629, 1637).

Schönfeld, Gregor, *Historischer Bericht der Newlichen Monats Augusti zugetragenen Marpurgischen Kirchen Händel* (Marburg: Hutwelcker, 1605).

Scriver, Christian, *Seelen=Schatz…* (Leipzig: Johann Melchior Süstermann and Christoph Seidel, 1698).

Scriver, Christian, *Das Blut=rünstige Bild Jesu Christi des Gecreutzigten…* (Magdeburg: Müller, 1728).

Solis, Virgil, *Biblische Figuren des Alten und Newen Testaments/gantz künstlich gerissen. Durch den weitberümpten Vergilium Solis zu Nürnberg* (Frankfurt am Main: David Zöpfel, Johann Rasch, Sigmund Feyerabend, 1560).

Spangenberg, Cyriacus, *Ander Teil des Adels-Spiegel* (Schmalkalden: Michel Schmück, 1594).

Spener, Philipp Jakob, *Schriften*, vol. II.2, *Kurtze Catechismuspredigten 1689* (reprint Hildesheim and New York: Olms, 1982).

Spener, Philipp Jakob, *Consilia et Iudicia Theologicæ Latina. Opus Posthumum Ex eiusdem Litteris 1709. Partes 1–2* (reprint Hildesheim and New York: Olms, 1989).

Spener, Philipp Jakob, *Theologische Bedencken…Anderer Theil…1701* (reprint Hildesheim and New York: Olms, 1999).

Stimmer, Tobias and Johann Fischart, *Neue Künstliche Figuren Biblischer Historien/grüntlich von Tobia Stimmer gerissen: Vnd zu Gotsförchtiger ergetzung andächtiger hertzen/mit artigen Reimen begriffen* (Basel: Thomas Guarin, 1576).

Streuber, Peter, *Einweyhung der New erbawten Schloßkirchen zu Sora* (Sora, 1593).

Suevus, Sigismund, *Geistliche Wallfarth oder Pilgerschafft zum heiligen Grabe* (Görlitz: Fritsch, 1573).

Taurer, Abraham, *Hochnothwendigster Bericht/Wider den newen Bildstürmerischen Carlstadtischen Geist in Fürstenthumb Anhald* (Eisleben: Urban Gaubisch, 1597).

Walther, Christoph, *Bericht von vnterschied der biblien vnd anderer des Ehrnwirdigen vnd seligen Herrn Doct. Martini Lutheri Bücher/so zu Wittemberg vnd an andern enden gedruckt werden/dem Christlichen leser zu nutz. Durch Christoffel Walther/des Herrn Hans Lufffts Corrector* (Wittenberg: Lufft, 1563).

Weck, Anton, *Der Chur=Fürstlichen Sächsischen weitberuffenen Residentz= und Haupt=Vestung* (Nuremberg: Hoffmann, 1680).

Wegelin, Josua, *Der Gemahlte Jesus Christus In Grund gelegt: das ist/Gründtliche Augenscheinliche Erklärung und Abbildung/deß Gesätzes und Evangelii Unterscheid* (Kempten: Kraus, 1630).

Werdemann, Abraham, *Altar Afranum, Oder Schrifftmessige Einweihungs-Predigt des Neuen Altars/Welcher Anno 1653, den 18. Maij in der Kirchen zu S. Afra in Meissen gesetzt: und folgendes Tages…mit Christlichen Ceremonien dem Herrn des Friedens feyerlich geheiliget worden* (Dresden: Bergen, 1653).

Wilhelm, Lorenz, *Descriptio Urbis Cyneæ. Das ist Warhafftige vnd Eigendliche Beschreibung/ der vhralten Stadt Zwickau…Von Laurentio Wilhelmo Obern Cantori alhier* (Zwickau: Melchior Göpner, 1633).

Willich, Peter, *Leichbegängnis vnd Ehren=predigt/bey der Begrebnis des weyland Edlen/ Gestrengen/Ehrnvehsten vnd Hochgelehrten Herrn IOACHIMI von Beust/Auff Planitz.* (Leipzig: Schnelboltz, 1597).

Zedler, Johann Heinrich, *Grosses vollständiges Universallexikon alle Wissenschaften und Künste*, 64 vols. (Leipzig: Zedler, 1731–54) [online at www.zedler-lexikon.de].

Zeidler, Johann Gottfried, *Johann Gottfried Zeidlers Neu=ausgefertigte Bilder=Bibel/darinnen Die denckwürdigsten Historien Heiliger Schrifft in vielen anmuthigen und künstlichen Biblischen Figuren vorgestellet* (Magdeburg: Johann Daniel Müller, 1701).

Zörler, Johann, *Zwo Leichpredigten Uber den vnuerhofften Tödlichen…abgang der beyden Christlichen…Eheleut, des…Otto von Diskaw…und auch der…Ursulae* (Eisleben: Hornigk, 1599).

SECONDARY SOURCES

Aikin, Judith P., *A Ruler's Consort in Early Modern Germany: Aemilia Juliana of Schwarzburg-Rudolstadt* (Farnham: Ashgate, 2014).

Alexander, Dorothy and Walter L. Strauss, *The German Single-Leaf Woodcut, 1600–1700*, vol. 1 (New York: Abaris Books, 1977).

Algazi, Gadi, 'Forget Memory: Some Critical Remarks on Memory, Forgetting and History', in Sebastian Scholz, Gerald Schwedler, and Kai-Michael Sprenger (eds), *Damnatio in Memoria: Deformation und Gegenkonstruktionen in der Geschichte* (Vienna, Cologne and Weimar: Böhlau, 2014), 25–34.

Althaus, Paul, *Forschungen zu evangelischen Gebetsliteratur* (Hildesheim: Olms, 1966).

Anders, I. and M. Winzeler (eds), *Lausitzer Jerusalem. 500 Jahre Heiliges Grab zu Görlitz*, exh. cat. (Görlitz and Zittau: Oettel, 2005).

Anttila, Miikka, *Luther's Theology of Music: Spiritual Beauty and Pleasure* (Berlin: De Gruyter, 2013).

Armborst-Weihs, Kerstin and Judith Becker (eds), *Toleranz und Identität: Geschichtsschreibung und Geschichtsbewusstsein zwischen religiösem Anspruch und historischer Erfahrung* (Göttingen: Vandenhoeck & Ruprecht, 2010).

Armbruster, Jörg, *Luthers Bibelvorreden. Studien zu ihrer Theologie* (Stuttgart: Deutsche Bibelgesellschaft, 2005).

Arnold, Jochen, '"… eine Regiererin des menschlichen Herzen"—ein Versuch zu Martin Luthers Theologie der Musik', in Jochen M. Arnold, Konrad Küster, and Hans Otte (eds), *Singen, Beten, Musizieren. Theologische Grundlagen der Kirchenmusik in Nord- und Mitteldeutschland zwischen Reformation und Pietismus (1530–1750)* (Göttingen: Vandenhoeck & Ruprecht, 2014), 13–34.

Asche, Matthias and Anton Schindling (eds), *Das Strafgericht Gottes: Kriegserfahrungen und Religion im Heiligen Römischen Reich Deutscher Nation im Zeitalter des Dreißigjährigen Krieges* (Münster: Aschendorff, 2001).

Asche, Sigfried, *Drei Bildhauerfamilien an der Elbe* (Vienna: Rohrer, 1961).

Axmacher, Elke, *Praxis Evangeliorum. Theologie und Frömmigkeit bei Martin Moller (1547–1606)* (Göttingen: Vandenhoeck & Ruprecht, 1989).

Axmacher, Elke, *'Aus Liebe will mein Heyland sterben'. Untersuchungen zum Wandel des Passionsverständnisses im frühen 18. Jahrhundert*, 2nd ed. (Stuttgart: Carus-Verl., 2001).

Axmacher, Elke, *Johann Arndt und Paul Gerhardt. Studien zur Theologie, Frömmigkeit und geistlichen Dichtung des 17. Jahrhunderts* (Tübingen and Basel: Francke, 2001).

Bachmann, Manfred, Harald Marx, and Eberhard Wächtler (eds), *Der silberne Boden. Kunst und Bergbau in Sachsen* (Leipzig: Edition Leipzig, 1990).

Badstübner, Ernst, *Stadtkirchen der Mark Brandenburg* (Berlin: Evang. Verl.-Anst., 1982).

Bahlcke, Joachim and Volker Dudeck (eds), *Welt–Macht–Geist. Das Haus Habsburg und die Oberlausitz 1526–1635* (Zittau: Oettel, 2002).

Bangerter-Schmid, Eva-Maria, *Erbauliche illustrierte Flugblätter aus den Jahren 1570–1670* (Frankfurt am Main: Lang, 1986).

Bannasch, Bettina, 'Von der "Tunckelheit" der Bilder. Das Emblem als Gegenstand der Meditation bei Harsdörffer', in Gerhard Kurz (ed.), *Meditation und Erinnerung in der Frühen Neuzeit* (Göttingen: Vandenhoeck & Ruprecht, 2000), 307–25.

Baxandall, Michael, *The Limewood Sculptors of Renaissance Germany* (New Haven and London: Yale University Press, 1980).

Becken, J., 'Die Epitaphien Distelmeyer-Kötteritzsch in der Nikolaikirche Berlin-Mitte', *Jahrbuch Stiftung Stadtmuseum Berlin*, 10 (2004/5), 73–95.

Beeskow, Angela, *St. Trinitatis in Finsterwalde, Grosse Baudenkmäler 485* (Munich and Berlin: Dt. Kunstverl., 1993).

Belting, Hans, *Likeness and Presence: A History of the Image Before the Era of Art*, tr. Edmund Jephcott (Chicago and London: University of Chicago Press, 1994).

Beyer, Jürgen, 'Stiftung, Plazierung und Funktion von Wand- und Kronleuchtern in lutherischen Kirchen', *Zeitschrift für Lübeckische Geschichte*, 92 (2012), 101–50.

Beyer, Michael, 'Übersetzer', in Volker Leppin and Gury Schneider-Ludorff (eds), *Das Luther-Lexikon* (Regensburg: Bückle und Böhm, 2014), 709–11.

Blaschke, Karlheinz and Siegfried Seifert, 'Reformation und Konfessionalisierung in der Oberlausitz', in Joachim Bahlcke and Volker Dudeck (eds), *Welt–Macht–Geist. Das Haus Habsburg und die Oberlausitz 1526–1635* (Zittau: Oettel, 2002).

Bode, Gerhard, 'Instruction of the Christian Faith by Lutherans after Luther', in *Lutheran Ecclesiastical Culture, 1550–1675* (Leiden and Boston: Brill, 2008), 159–204.

Boettcher, Susan, 'Von der Trägheit der Memoria. Cranachs Lutheraltarbilder im Zusammenhang der evangelischen Luther-Memoria im späten 16. Jahrhundert', in Joachim Eibach and Marcus Sandl (eds), *Protestantische Identität und Erinnerung: von der Reformation bis zur Bürgerrechtsbewegung in der DDR* (Göttingen: Vandenhoeck & Ruprecht, 2003), 47–69.

Boetticher, Walther von, *Geschichte des Oberlausitzischen Adels und seiner Güter 1635–1815*, 4 vols. (Görlitz: Oberlausitzische Gesellsch. d. Wiss., 1912–23).

Böhnisch, F., *Andreas Schultze—ein Niederlausitzer Bildhauer des 17. Jahrhunderts* (Cottbus: Niederlausitzer Arbeitskreis für Regionale Forschung, 1984).

Bornkamm, Heinrich, *Luther und das Alte Testament* (Tübingen: Mohr, 1948).

Boyd Brown, Christopher, 'Devotional Life in Hymns, Liturgy, Music, and Prayer', in Robert Kolb (ed.), *Lutheran Ecclesiastical Culture, 1550–1675* (Leiden and Boston: Brill, 2008), 205–58.

Brady, Thomas A. Jr., *German Histories in the Age of Reformations, 1400–1650* (Cambridge: CUP, 2009).

Braw, Christian, *Bücher im Staube. Die Theologie Johann Arndts in ihrem Verhältnis zur Mystic* (Leiden: Brill, 1986).

Brecht, Martin, *Martin Luther. Shaping and Defining the Reformation, 1521–1532*, tr. James Schaaf (Minneapolis: Fortress Press, 1990).

Brecht, Martin, 'August Hermann Francke und der Hallesche Pietismus', in Martin Brecht, Klaus Deppermann, Ulrich Gäbler, and Hartmut Lehmann (eds), *Geschichte des Pietismus*, vol. 1, *Der Pietismus von siebzehnten bis zum frühen achtzehnten Jahrhundert* (Göttingen: Vandenhoeck & Ruprecht, 1993), 440–540.

Brecht, Martin, 'Johann Arndt und das Wahre Christentum', in Martin Brecht, Klaus Deppermann, Ulrich Gäbler, and Hartmut Lehmann (eds), *Geschichte des Pietismus*, vol. 1, *Der Pietismus von siebzehnten bis zum frühen achtzehnten Jahrhundert* (Göttingen: Vandenhoeck & Ruprecht, 1993), 130–50.

Brecht, Martin, 'Philipp Jakob Spener, sein Programm und dessen Auswirkungen', in Martin Brecht, Klaus Deppermann, Ulrich Gäbler, and Hartmut Lehmann (eds), *Geschichte des Pietismus*, vol. 1, *Der Pietismus von siebzehnten bis zum frühen achtzehnten Jahrhundert* (Göttingen: Vandenhoeck & Ruprecht, 1993), 279–390.

Brecht, Martin, 'Ein "Gastmahl" an Predigten. Christian Scrivers Seelenschatz (1675–1692)', *Pietismus und Neuzeit*, 28 (2002), 72–117.

Brecht, Martin, Klaus Deppermann, Ulrich Gäbler, and Hartmut Lehmann (eds), *Geschichte des Pietismus*, vol. 1, *Der Pietismus von siebzehnten bis zum frühen achtzehnten Jahrhundert* (Göttingen: Vandenhoeck & Ruprecht, 1993).

Bremer, Ludolf, *Sigismund Evenius (1585/89–1639). Ein Pädagoge des 17. Jahrhunderts* (Cologne and Vienna: Böhlau, 2001).

Brinkmann, Bodo, 'The Smile of the Madonna: Lucas Cranach, a Serial Painter', in Bodo Brinkmann (ed.), *Cranach*, exh. cat. (London: Royal Academy of Arts, 2007), 17–27.

Brinkmann, Inga, *Grabdenkmäler, Grablegen und Begräbniswesen des lutherischen Adels: adelige Funeralrepräsentation im Spannungsfeld von Kontinuität und Wandel im 16. und beginnenden 17. Jahrhundert* (Berlin: Dt. Kunstverl., 2010).

Brock, Roswitha, *Auf Fels gebaut. Die St. Georgenkirche zu Schwarzenberg im Erzgebirge* (Scheibenberg: H-und-F Verlag, 1999).

Brubaker, Rogers and Frederick Cooper, 'Beyond Identity', *Theory and Society*, 29 (1) (2000), 1–47.

Bruck, Robert, *Die Sophienkirche in Dresden. Ihre Geschichte und Ihre Kunstschätze* (Dresden: H. von Keller, 1912).

Brückner, Wolfgang, 'Die lutherische Gattung evangelischer Bekenntnisbilder und ihre ikonographischen Ableitungen der Gnade vermittelnden Erlösungs- und Sakramentslehre', in Frank Büttner and Gabriele Wimböck (eds), *Das Bild als Autorität. Die normierende Kraft des Bildes* (Münster: Aschendorff, 2004), 303–41.

Bruun, Mette Birkedal, Sven Rune Havsteen, Kristian Mejrup, Eelco Nagelsmit, and Lars Nørgaard, 'Withdrawal and Engagement in the Long Seventeenth Century: Four Case Studies', *Journal of Early Modern Christianity*, 1 (2) (2014), 249–343.

Bulisch, J. and F. C. Ilgner, 'Der Tanzende Zwingli. Zwei lutherische Spottbilder auf das Abendmahl der Reformierten', *Das Münster: Zeitschrift für christliche Kunst und Kunstwissenschaft*, 1 (1999), 66–74.

Bürger, Stefan and Marius Winzeler, *Die Stadtkirche St. Peter und Paul in Görlitz* (Dössel: Skekovics, 2006).

Burnett, Amy Nelson, *Karlstadt and the Origins of the Eucharistic Controversy: A Study in the Circulation of Ideas* (New York and Oxford: OUP, 2011).

Butzer, Günter, 'Rhetorik der Meditation. Martin Mollers "Soliloqvia de Passione Iesu Christi" und die Tradition der *eloquentia sacra*', in Gerhard Kurz (ed.), *Meditation und Erinnerung in der Frühen Neuzeit* (Göttingen: Vandenhoeck & Ruprecht, 2000), 57–78.

Bynum, Caroline Walker, 'Are Things 'Indifferent'? How Objects Change Our Understanding of Religious History', *German History*, 34 (1) (2016), 88–112.

Campenhausen, H. von, 'Die Bilderfrage in der Reformation', *Zeitschrift für Kirchengeschichte*, 68 (1957), 96–128.

Cante, Marcus (ed.), *Denkmaltopographie Bundesrepublik Deutschland. Denkmale in Brandenburg*, vol. 1/1, *Stadt Brandenburg an der Havel*, part 1 (Worms am Rhein: Werner, 1994).

Chazelle, Celia, 'Pictures, Books, and the Illiterate: Pope Gregory I's Letters to Serenus of Marseille', *Word and Image*, 6 (1990), 138–53.

Christ, Martin, 'The Town Chronicle of Johannes Hass: History Writing and Divine Intervention in the Early Sixteenth Century', *German History* 35 (1) (2017), 1–20.

Christensen, Carl, 'The Reformation of Bible Illustration: Genesis Woodcuts in Wittenberg, 1523–1534', *Archiv für Reformationsgeschichte*, 90 (1990), 103–29.

Clark, Christopher, 'When Culture Meets Power: The Prussian Coronation of 1701', in Hamish Scott and Brendan Simms (eds), *Cultures of Power in Europe During the Long Eighteenth Century* (Cambridge: CUP, 2007), 14–35.

Clark, Stuart, *Vanities of the Eye: Vision in Early Modern European Culture* (Oxford: OUP, 2007).

Cohrs, Ferdinand, *Vierhundert Jahre Luthers Kleiner Katechismus. Kurze Geschichte seiner Entstehung und seines Gebrauchs* (Langensalza: H. Beyer und Söhne, 1929).

Corpis, Duane, *Crossing the Boundaries of Belief: Geographies of Religious Conversion in Southern Germany, 1648–1800* (Charlottesville: University of Virginia Press, 2014).

Decker, Bernhard, *Das Ende des mittelalterlichen Kultbildes und die Plastik Hans Leinbergers* (Bamberg: Lehrstuhl für Kunstgeschichte, 1985).

Deckers, Regina, 'Andreas Schlüter in Danzig und Polen', in Hans-Ulrich Kessler (ed.), *Andreas Schlüter und das barocke Berlin*, exh. cat. (Berlin: Hirmer, 2014), 20–31.

Dehio, Georg, *Handbuch der Deutschen Kunstdenkmäler. Sachsen II, Regierungsbezirke Leipzig und Chemnitz*, (Munich: Deutscher Kunstverlag, 1998).

Dehio, Georg, *Handbuch der Deutschen Kunstdenkmäler: Brandenburg* (Munich: Deutscher Kunstverlag, 2000).

Dehio, Georg, *Handbuch der Deutschen Kunstdenkmäler. Sachsen-Anhalt I, Regierungsbezirk Magdeburg* (Munich and Berlin: Deutscher Kunstverlag, 2002).

Deiters, Maria, 'Individuum – Gemeinde – Raum. Zur nachreformatorischen Ausstattungen von St. Marien und St. Nikolai in Berlin', in Evelin Wetter (ed.), *Formierung des konfessionellen Raumes in Ostmitteleuropa* (Stuttgart: Steiner, 2008), 41–56.

Delius, H. U., 'Johann Christoph Beckmann's handschriftliche "Brandenburgische Kirchengeschichte" ', *Jahrbuch für Berlin-Brandenburgische Kirchengeschichte*, 47 (1972), 71–91.

Delius, Walter, 'Berliner Reformationsjubiläum 1639', *Jahrbuch für Berlin-Brandenburgische Kirchengeschichte*, 40 (1965), 86–136.

Dingel, Irene, 'Ablehnung und Aneignung. Die Bewertung der Autorität Martin Luthers in den Auseinandersetzungen um die Konkordienformel', *Zeitschrift für Kirchengeschichte*, 105 (1994), 35–57.

Dingel, Irene, *Concordia controversa. Die öffentlichen Diskussionen um das lutherische Konkordienwerk am Ende des 16. Jahrhunderts* (Gütersloh: Gütersloher Verl.-Haus, 1996).

Dingel, Irene, ' "Daß wir Gott in keiner Weise verbilden". Die Bilderfrage zwischen Calvinismus und Luthertum' in Andreas Wagner, Volker Hörner and Günter Geisthardt (eds), *Gott im Wort—Gott im Bild: Bilderlosigkeit als Bedingung des Monotheismus?* (Neukirchen-Vluyn: Neukirchener, 2005), 97–111.

Dingel, Irene, 'The Culture of Conflict in the Controversies Leading to the Formula of Concord (1548–1580)', in Robert Kolb (ed.), *Lutheran Ecclesiastical Culture, 1550–1675* (Leiden and Boston: Brill, 2008), 15–64.

Dingel, Irene, *Die Debatte um die Wittenberger Abendmahlslehre und Christologie (1570–1574)* (Göttingen: Vandenhoeck & Ruprecht, 2008).

Doering, Oscar, *Das Augsburger Patriciers Philipp Hainhofer Reisen nach Innsbruck und Dresden* (Vienna: Graeser, 1901).

Dölemeyer, Barabara, *Die Hugenotten* (Stuttgart: Kohlhammer Verlag, 2006).

Dornheim, Stefan, *Der Pfarrer als Arbeiter am Gedächtnis. Lutherische Erinnerungskultur in der Frühen Neuzeit zwischen Religion und sozialer Kohäsion* (Leipzig: Leipziger Univ-Verl., 2013).

Dülberg, Angelica, 'Wand- und Deckenmalereien vom 15. bis zum ausgehenden 17. Jahrhundert in Freiberger Bürgerhäusern', in Yves Hoffmann and Uwe Richter (eds), *Denkmale in Sachsen. Stadt Freiberg. Beiträge*, vol. 3 (Freiberg: Werbung und Verl., 2004), 828–68.

Dürr, Renate, *Politische Kultur in der Frühen Neuzeit: Kirchenräume in Hildesheimer Stadt- und Landgemeinde, 1550–1750* (Gütersloh: Gütersloher Verl.-Haus, 2006).

Dürr, Renate, 'Laienprophetien. Zur Emotionalisierung politischer Phantasien im 17. Jahrhundert', in Claudia Jarzebowski and Anne Kwaschik (eds), *Performing Emotions. Interdisziplinäre Perspektiven auf das Verhältnis von Politik und Emotion in der Frühen Neuzeit und in der Moderne* (Göttingen: Vandenhoeck & Ruprecht, 2013), 17–41.

Ehrenpreis, Stefan, 'Teaching Religion in Early Modern Europe: Catechisms, Emblems and Local Traditions', in Heinz Schilling and István György Tóth (eds), *Cultural Exchange in Early Modern Europe*, vol. 1, *Religion and Cultural Exchange in Europe, 1400–1700* (Cambridge: CUP, 2006), 256–73.

Eibach, Joachim and Marcus Sandl, *Protestantische Identität und Erinnerung: von der Reformation bis zur Bürgerrechtsbewegung in der DDR* (Göttingen: Vandenhoeck & Ruprecht, 2003).

Eichenberger, Walter and Henning Wendland, *Deutsche Bibeln vor Luther: die Buchkunst der achtzehn deutschen Bibeln zwischen 1466 und 1522*, 2nd ed. (Hamburg: Wittig, 1977).

Eire, Carlos, *War Against the Idols: The Reformation of Worship from Erasmus to Calvin* (Cambridge: CUP, 1986).

Ellwardt, Kathrin, *Evangelischer Kirchenbau in Deutschland* (Petersberg: Imhof, 2008).

Elze, Martin, 'Das Verständnis der Passion Jesu im ausgehenden Mittelalter und bei Luther', in Heinz Liebing and Klaus Scholder (eds), *Geist und Geschichte der Reformation. Festgabe Hanns Rückert zum 65. Geburtstag* (Berlin: De Gruyter, 1966), 127–51.

Engelberg, Meinrad von, *Renovatio Ecclesiae: Die 'Barockisierung' mittelalterlicher Kirchen* (Petersberg: Imhof, 2005).

Enke, Roland, Katja Schneider, and Jutta Strehe (eds), *Lucas Cranach der Jüngere— Entdeckung eines Meisters*, exh. cat. (Munich: Hirmer, 2015).

Erll, Astrid, *Memory in Culture*, tr. Sara Young (Basingstoke: Palgrave Macmillan, 2011).

Fincham, Kenneth and Nicholas Tyacke, *Altars Restored: The Changing Face of English Religious Worship, 1547–c.1700* (Oxford: OUP, 2007).

Finney, Paul Corby (ed.), *Seeing Beyond the Word: Visual Arts and the Calvinist Tradition* (Grand Rapids: W. B. Eerdmans, 1999).

Fisher, Alex, *Music, Piety, and Propaganda: The Soundscapes of Counter-Reformation Bavaria* (Oxford: OUP, 2014).

Fleck, Niels, *Fürstliche Repräsentation im Sakralraum. Die Schlosskirchen der thüringisch-ernestinischen Residenzen im 17. und beginnenden 18. Jahrhundert* (Munich: Deutscher Kunstverlag, 2015).

Flood, John, *Poets Laureate in the Holy Roman Empire. A Bio-bibliographical Handbook*, vol. 4: S-Z (Berlin and New York: De Gruyter, 2006).

Flügel, Wolfgang, 'Zeitkonstrukte im Reformationsjubiläum', in Winfried Müller (ed.), *Das historische Jubiläum. Genese, Ordnungsleistung und Inszenierungsgeschichte eines institutionellen Mechanismus* (Münster: Aschendorff, 2004), 77–99.

Flügel, Wolfgang, *Konfession und Jubiläum: zur Institutionalisierung der lutherischen Gedenkkultur in Sachsen 1617–1830* (Leipzig: Leipziger Univ.-Verl., 2005).

Förster, Friedrich (ed.), *Die Höfe und Cabinette Europa's im achtzehnten Jahrhundert*, vol. 3 (Potsdam: Riegel, 1839).

Forster, Marc, *Catholic Revival in the Age of the Baroque: Religious Identity in Southwest Germany, 1550–1750* (Cambridge: CUP, 2001).

'Forum: Memory before Modernity: Cultures and Practices in Early Modern Germany', *German History*, 33 (1) (2015), 100–22.

'Forum: Religious History beyond Confessionalization', *German History*, 32 (4) (2014), 579–98.

Forwerck, Friedrich August, *Geschichte und Beschreibung der königlichen katholischen Hof- und Pfarrkirche zu Dresden* (Dresden: Janssen, 1851).

François, Etienne, 'Das religiöse Buch als Nothelfer, Familienreliquie und Identitätssymbol im protestantischen Deutschland der Frühneuzeit (17.–19. Jahrhunderts)', in Ursula Brunold-Bigler and Hermann Bausinger (eds), *Hören Sagen Lesen Lernen. Bausteine zu einer Geschichte der kommunikativen Kultur* (Bern etc.: Lang, 1995), 219–30.

Frandsen, Mary, 'Worship as Representation: The Italianate 'Hofkapelle' of Johann Georg II as an Instrument of Image Creation', in Barbara Marx (ed.), *Kunst und Repräsentation am Dresdner Hof* (Munich and Berlin: Deutscher Kunstverlag, 2005), 198–216.

Frandsen, Mary, *Crossing Confessional Boundaries: The Patronage of Italian Sacred Music in Seventeenth-Century Dresden* (New York and Oxford: OUP, 2006).

Freist, Dagmar, 'Religionssicherheiten und Gefahren für das "Seelenheil". Religiös-politische Befindlichkeiten in Kursachsen seit dem Übertritt Augusts des Starken zum Katholizismus', in Ulrich Rosseaux and Gerhard Poppe (eds), *Konfession und Konflikt. Religiöse Pluralisierung in Sachsen im 18. und 19. Jahrhundert* (Münster: Aschendorff, 2012), 35–53.

Friedrich, Karin, *Brandenburg-Prussia, 1466–1806: The Rise of a Composite State* (Basingstoke: Palgrave Macmillan, 2012).

Friedrich, Markus, 'Das Hör-Reich und das Sehe-Reich. Zur Bewertung des Sehens bei Luther und im frühneuzeitlichen Protestantismus', in Gabriele Wimböck, Karin Leonhard, and Markus Friedrich (eds), *Evidentia. Reichweiten visueller Wahrnehmung in der Frühen Neuzeit* (Berlin: Lit-Verl., 2007), 453–82.

Fritz, Johann Michael (ed.), *Die bewahrende Kraft des Luthertums* (Regensburg: Schnell & Steiner, 1997).

Fritz, Johann Michael and Martin Brecht (eds), *Das evangelische Abendmahlsgerät in Deutschland: vom Mittelalter bis zum Ende des alten Reiches* (Leipzig: Evang. Verl.-Anst., 2004).

Fuchs, Thomas, 'Reformation, Tradition und Geschichte. Erinnerungsstrategien der reformatorischen Bewegung', in Joachim Eibach and Marcus Sandl (eds), *Protestantische Identität und Erinnerung. Von der Reformation bis zur Bürgerrechtsbewegung in der DDR* (Göttingen: Vandenhoeck & Ruprecht, 2003), 71–89.

Fulbrook, Mary, *Piety and Politics: Religion and the Rise of Absolutism in England, Württemberg and Prussia* (Cambridge: CUP, 1983).

Fürstenau, M., 'Zur Geschichte des Tapetenwirkerei am Hofe zu Dresden', *Sachsengrün. Culturgeschichtliche Zeitschrift aus sämtlichen Landen Sächsischen Stammes*, 1 (1861), 199–200.

Fuss, Ulrike Valerie, *Matthaeus Merian der Ältere. Von der lieblichen Landschaft zum Kriegsschauplatz—Landsschaft als Kulisse des 30 jährigen Krieges* (Frankfurt am Main: Lang, 2000).

Gaşior, Agnieszka, 'Der Reliquienschatz eines protestantischen Landesherren. Joachim II. von Brandenburg und Hedwig von Polen in Berlin', in Evelin Wetter (ed.), *Formierung des konfessionellen Raumes in Ostmitteleuropa* (Stuttgart: Steiner, 2008), 237–50.

Gassen, Richard, 'Die Leien Bibel des Straßburger Druckers Wendelin Rihel. Kunst, Religion, Pädagogik und Buchdruck in der Reformation', *Memminger Geschichtsblätter* (1983/84), 5–271.

Geiger, Erika, *Nikolaus Ludwig Graf von Zinzendorf*, 4th ed. (Holzgerlingen: SCM Hänssler, 2009).

Gericke, Wolfgang, Heinrich-Volker Schlieff, and Winfried Wendland, *Brandenburgische Dorfkirchen* (Berlin: Evangelische Verlangsanstalt, 1975).

Geschichte des Schleinitzschen Geschlechts von einem Mitgliede des Geschlechts (Berlin, 1897).

Goecke, Theodor, *Die Kunstdenkmäler der Provinz Brandenburg*, vol. 6/2, *Stadt Frankfurt a. O.* (Berlin: Vossische Buchh., 1912).

Goecke, Theodor, *Die Kunstdenkmäler der Provinz Brandenburg*, vol. 5/1, *Luckau* (Berlin: Vossische Buchh., 1917).

Goeters, J. F. Gerhard, 'Genesis, Formen und Hauptthemen des reformierten Bekenntnisses in Deutschland', in Heinz Schilling (ed.), *Die reformierte Konfessionalisierung. Das Problem der 'zweiten Reformation'* (Gütersloh: Gütersloher Verlagshaus Mohn, 1986), 44–59.

Gordon, Bruce (ed.), *Protestant History and Identity in Sixteenth-Century Europe* (Aldershot: Ashgate, 1998).

Gordon, Bruce and Peter Marshall (eds), *The Place of the Dead in Late Medieval and Early Modern Europe* (Cambridge: CUP, 2000).

Götz, Joh. B., *Die erste Einführung des Kalvinismus in der Oberpfalz 1559–1576* (Münster: Aschendorff, 1933).

Götze, Wolfgang, 'Gotische Plastik in barocken Gehäuse', in Kunsthistorisches Institut, Karl-Marx-Universität Leipzig (ed.), *Festschrift Johannes Jahn zum XXII. November MCMLVII* (Leipzig: Seemann, 1958), 187–93.

Graff, P., *Geschichte der Auflösung der alten gottesdienstlichen Formen in der evangelischen Kirche Deutschlands bis zum Eintritt der Aufklärung und des Rationalismus* (Göttingen: Vandenhoeck & Ruprecht, 1921).

Greschat, Martin, 'Valentin Ernst Löscher in Dresden', *Die Dresdner Frauenkirche*, 5 (1999), 125–31.

Greyerz, Kaspar von, Manfred Jakubowski-Tiessen, Thomas Kaufmann and Hartmut Lehmann, (eds), *Interkonfessionalität–Transkonfessionalität–binnenkonferrionelle Pluralität* (Gütersloh: Gütersloher Verl.-Haus, 2003).

Gross, Reiner, *Geschichte Sachsens* (Leipzig: Ed. Leipzig, 2001).

Grün, H., 'Die kirchliche Beerdigung im 16. Jahrhundert', *Theologische Studien und Kritiken*, 105 (2) (1933), 138–209.

Grünberg, Paul, *Philipp Jakob Spener*, vol. 2, *Spener als praktischer Theologe und kirchlicher Reformer* (Göttingen: Vandenhoeck & Ruprecht, 1905).

Grüneisen, Ernst, 'Grundlegendes für die Bilder in Luthers Katechismen', *Luther=Jahrbuch*, 20 (1938), 1–44.

Guinomet, Claire, 'Die Kanzel in der Berliner Marienkirche', in Hans-Ulrich Kessler (ed.), *Andreas Schlüter und das barocke Berlin*, exh. cat. (Berlin: Hirmer, 2014), 344–57.

Gundermann, Iselin, 'Verordnete Eintracht: Lutheraner und Reformierte in Berlin-Brandenburg (1613–1740)', *Herbergen der Christenheit. Jahrbuch für deutsche Kirchengeschichte*, 28/29 (2004/05), 141–55.

Gurlitt, Cornelius (ed.), *Beschreibende Darstellung der älteren Bau- und Kunstdenkmäler des Königreichs Sachsen*, vol. 17, *Stadt Leipzig (I. Theil)* (Dresden: Meinhold, 1895).

Gurlitt, Cornelius (ed.), *Beschreibende Darstellung der älteren Bau- und Kunstdenkmäler des Königreichs Sachsen*, vols. 21–23, *Stadt Dresden* (Dresden: Meinhold, 1903).

Gurlitt, Cornelius (ed.), *Beschreibende Darstellung der älteren Bau- und Kunstdenkmäler des Königreichs Sachsen*, vol. 26, *Amtshauptmannschaft Dresden-Neustadt* (Dresden: Meinhold, 1904).

Gurlitt, Cornelius (ed.), *Beschreibende Darstellung der älteren Bau- und Kunstdenkmäler des Königreichs Sachsen*, vol. 34, *Amtshauptmannschaft Löbau* (Dresden: Meinhold, 1910).

Gurlitt, Cornelius (ed.), *Beschreibende Darstellung der älteren Bau- und Kunstdenkmäler des Königreichs Sachsen*, vol. 39, *Meißen* (Dresden: Meinhold, 1917).

Gutfleisch, Barbara and Joachim Menzhausen, 'How a Kunstkammer Should be Formed'. Gabriel Kaltemarckt's advice to Christian I of Saxony on the formation of an art collection, 1587', *Journal of the History of Collections*, 1 (1) (1989), 3–32.

Haebler, H. C. von, *Das Bild in der evangelischen Kirche* (Berlin: Evang. Verl.-Anst., 1957).

Hahn, Philip, 'Sensing Sacred Space: Ulm Minster, the Reformation, and Parishioners' Sensory Perception, *c.*1470 to 1640', *Archiv für Reformationsgeschichte*, 105 (2014), 55–91.

Hallenkamp-Lumpe, J., 'Das Bekenntnis am Kachelofen? Überlegungen zu den sogenannten "Reformationskacheln"', in Carola Jäggi and Jörn Staecker (eds), *Archäologie der Reformation. Studien zu den Auswirkungen des Konfessionswechsels auf die materielle Kultur* (Berlin: De Gruyter, 2007), 323–43.

Hamling, Tara, *Decorating the 'Godly' Household: Religious Art in Post-Reformation Britain* (New Haven and London: Yale University Press, 2010).

Harasimowicz, Jan, *Kunst als Glaubensbekenntnis: Beiträge zur Kunst- und Kulturgeschichte der Reformationszeit* (Baden-Baden: Koerner, 1996).

Harasimowicz, Jan, 'Der Beitrag des hallischen Pietismus zur Kulturgeschichte Pommerns im 18. Jahrhundert', in Johannes Wallmann and Udo Sträter (eds), *Halle und Osteuropa: zur europäischen Ausstrahlung des hallischen Pietismus* (Tübingen: Neimeyer-Verl., 1998), 173–210.

Harasimowicz, Jan, 'Architektur und Kunst', in Martin Brecht, Klaus Deppermann, Ulrich Gäbler, and Hartmut Lehmann (eds), *Geschichte des Pietismus*, vol. 4, *Glaubenswelt und Lebenswelten* (Göttingen: Vandenhoeck & Ruprecht, 2004), 456–85.

Harasimowicz, Jan, 'Christoph Leonhard Sturm: Von der Erfahrung beim Umbau der Schelfkirche in Schwerin zur Entstehung einer pietistisch inspirierten Architekturtheorie', in Christian Soboth and Udo Sträter (eds), *'Aus Gottes Wort und eigener Erfahrung gezeiget'. Erfahrung—Glauben, Erkennen und Handeln im Pietismus* (Wiesbaden: Harrassowitz, 2012), 599–621.

Harasimowicz, Jan and Agnieszka Seidel, 'Die Bildausstattung der ehem. evang. Kirche zu Klepsk (Klemzig) in der Mark Brandenburg', in Klaus Raschok and Reiner Sörries (eds), *Geschichte des protestantischen Kirchenbaues: Festschrift für Peter Poscharsky zum 60. Geburtstag* (Erlangen: Junge, 1994), 289–99.

Haskell, Francis, 'Visual Sources and The Embarrassment of Riches', *Past and Present*, 120 (1) (1988), 216–26.

Havsteen, Sven Rune, 'Das "Music-Büchlein" (1631) von Christopher Frick', in Jochen M. Arnold, Konrad Küster, and Hans Otte (eds), *Singen, Beten, Musizieren. Theologische Grundlagen der Kirchenmusik in Nord- und Mitteldeutschland zwischen Reformation und Pietismus (1530–1750)* (Göttingen: Vandenhoeck & Ruprecht, 2014), 53–74.

'Die Hauptkirche zu St. Marien in Zwickau', in *Neue Sächsische Kirchengalerie* (Leipzig, 1902), cols 71–106.

Heal, Bridget, *The Cult of the Virgin Mary in Early Modern Germany: Protestant and Catholic Piety, 1500–1648* (Cambridge: CUP, 2007).

Heal, Bridget, '"Better Papist than Calvinist": Art and Identity in Later Lutheran Germany', *German History*, 29 (4) (2011), 584–609.

Heal, Bridget, '"Zum Andenken und zur Ehre Gottes": Kunst und Frömmigkeit im frühneuzeitlichen Luthertum', *Archiv für Reformationsgeschichte*, 104 (2013), 185–210.

Heal, Bridget, 'Seeing Christ: Visual Piety in Saxony's Erzgebirge', in Jeffrey Chipps Smith (ed.), *Visual Acuity and the Arts of Communication in Early Modern Germany* (Farnham: Ashgate, 2014).

Heal, Bridget, 'Kirchenordnungen und das Weiterbestehen religiöser Kunstwerke in lutherischen Kirchen', in Sabine Arend and Gerald Dörner (eds), *Ordnungen für die*

Kirche—Wirkungen auf die Welt. Evangelische Kirchenordnungen des 16. Jahrhunderts (Tübingen: Mohr Siebeck, 2015), 157–74.

Heal, Bridget, 'Lutheran Baroque: The Afterlife of a Reformation Altarpiece', in Bridget Heal and Joseph Koerner (eds), *Art and Religious Reform in Early Modern Europe*, special issue of *Art History*, 40 (2) (April 2017), 358–79.

Heal, Bridget, 'Reformationsbilder in der Kunst der Aufklärung', in Wolf-Friedrich Schäufele and Christoph Strohm (eds), *Das Bild der Reformation in der Aufklärung* (Gütersloh: Gütersloher Verl.-Haus, forthcoming).

Hecht, Christian, *Katholische Bildertheologie im Zeitalter von Gegenreformation und Barock: Studien zu Traktaten von Johannes Molanus, Gabriele Paleotti und anderen Autoren* (Berlin: Gebr. Mann, 1997; 2nd ed. Berlin, 2012).

Heerdegen, Arno, 'Geschichte der allgemeinen Kirchen Visitation in den ernestinischen Landen im Jahre 1554/55, nach Akten des Sachsen-Ernestinischen Gesamt-Archivs in Weimar', *Zeitschrift des Vereins für Thüringische Geschichte und Altertumskunde*, N. F. 6. Supplementheft (Jena, 1914).

Hennen, Insa Christiane, 'Die Wittenberger Stadtkirche: bauliche Situation und Wandel der Ausstattung', in Jan Harasimowicz and Bettina Seyderhelm (eds), *Cranachs Kirche: Begleitbuch zur Landesausstellung Sachsen-Anhalt Cranach der Jüngere* (Markkleeberg: Sax-Verl., 2015), 21–6.

Hentschel, Walter, *Dresdner Bildhauer des 16. und 17. Jahhunderts* (Weimar: Böhlau, 1966).

Herl, Joseph, *Worship Wars in Early Lutheranism: Choir, Congregation, and Three Centuries of Conflict* (Oxford: OUP, 2004).

Herrmann, Johannes, 'Beobachtungen zur Kontinuität von Frömmigkeit. Leipziger Land vor und nach der Reformation', in Gerhard Graf (ed.), *Vestigia Pietatis. Studien zur Geschichte der Frömmigkeit in Thüringen und Sachsen* (Leipzig: Evang. Verl.-Anst., 2000), 61–76.

Herrmann, Rudolf, 'Die Generalvisitationen in den Ernestinischen Landen zur Zeit der Lehrstreitigkeiten des 16. Jahrhunderts (1554/55, 1562, 1569/70, 1573)', *Zeitschrift des Vereins für Thüringische Geschichte und Altertumskunde*, N. F. 22 (1915), 75–156.

Herrmann, Rudolf, *Thüringische Kirchengeschichte*, vol. 2 (Weimar: Böhlau, 1947; reprint Waltrop, 2000).

Hildebrand, M. T. W., *Historische Nachrichten über die Kirchen der Stadt Zwickau* (Zwickau: König, 1819).

Honée, Eugène, 'Image and Imagination in the Medieval Culture of Prayer: A Historical Perspective', in H. van Os (ed.), *The Art of Devotion in the Late Middle Ages in Europe, 1300–1500* (Princeton: Princeton University Press, 1994), 157–74.

Hoyer, Siegfried, 'Bürgerkultur einer Residenzstadt – Dresden im 18. Jahrhundert' in Wilhelm Rausch (ed.), *Städtische Kultur in die Barockzeit* (Linz an der Donau: Österr. Arbeitskreis für Stadtgeschichtsforschung, 1982), 105–16.

Hruby, Ingrid, '1636. Sigismund Evenius: Christliche / Gottselige Bilder Schule', in Theodor Brüggemann (ed.), *Handbuch zur Kinder- und Jugendliteratur. Von 1570 bis 1750* (Stuttgart: Metzler, 1991), cols 145–56.

Hund, Johannes, *Das Wort ward Fleisch: eine systematisch-theologische Untersuchung zur Debatte um die Wittenberger Christologie und Abendmahlslehre in den Jahren 1567 bis 1574* (Göttingen: Vandenhoeck & Ruprecht, 2006).

Irwin, Joyce, *Neither Voice nor Heart Alone. German Lutheran Theology of Music in the Age of the Baroque* (New York: P. Lang, 1993).

Jacobsen, R. (ed.), *Weissenfels als Ort literarischer und künstlerischer Kultur im Barockzeitalter* (Amsterdam and Atlanta: Rodopi, 1995).

Jaser, Nadine, 'Fugute idola! Reformierte Bildentfernungen in Anhalt', in Norbert Michels (ed.), *Cranach in Anhalt: Vom alten zum neuen Glauben,* exh. cat. (Petersberg: Imhof, 2015), 77–84.

Johne, Renate, *Reformatorisches Gedankengut in der St. Gotthardtkirche zu Brandenburg an der Havel: Die Epitaphien* (Berlin: R. Johne, 2008).

Kammeier-Nebel, Andrea, 'Der Wandel des Totengedächtnisses in Privaten Aufzeichnungen unter dem Einfluß der Reformation', in Klaus Arnold, Sabine Schmolinsky, and Urs Martin Zahnd (eds), *Das dargestellte Ich. Studien zu Selbstzeugnissen des späten Mittelalters und der frühen Neuzeit* (Bochum: Winkler, 1999), 93–116.

Karant-Nunn, Susan, *Zwickau in Transition, 1500–1547: The Reformation as an Agent of Change* (Columbus: Ohio State University Press, 1987).

Karant-Nunn, Susan, *The Reformation of Feeling: Shaping the Religious Emotions in Early Modern Germany* (Oxford: OUP, 2010).

Kaufmann, Thomas, *Der dreißigjähriger Krieg und Westfälischer Frieden: Kirchengeschichtliche zur lutherischen Konfessionskultur* (Tübingen: Mohr Siebeck, 1998).

Kaufmann, Thomas, *Das Ende der Reformation: Magdeburgs 'Herrgotts Kanzelei' (1548–1551/2)* (Tübingen: Mohr Siebeck, 2003).

Kaufmann, Thomas, *Konfession und Kultur: Lutherischer Protestantismus in der zweiten Hälfte des Reformationsjahrhunderts* (Tübingen: Mohr Siebeck, 2006).

Kaufmann, Thomas, 'Die Sinn- und Leiblichkeit der Heilsaneignung im späten Mittelalter und in der Reformation', in Johanna Harberer and Berndt Hamm (eds), *Medialität, Unmittelbarkeit, Präsenz: Die Nähe des Heils im Verständis der Reformation* (Tübingen: Mohr Siebeck, 2012), 11–44.

Kaufmann, Thomas, 'What is Lutheran Confessional Culture?', in Per Ingesman (ed.), *Religion as an Agent of Change: Crusades—Reformation—Pietism* (Leiden: Brill, 2016), 127–48.

Kaufmann, Thomas DaCosta, *Court, Cloister, and City: The Art and Culture of Central Europe, 1450–1800* (Chicago: University of Chicago Press, 1995).

Keller, Katrin (ed.), *'Mein herr befindet sich gottlob gesund und wohl'. Sächsische Prinzen auf Reisen* (Leipzig: Leipziger Univ.-Verl., 1994).

Keuchen, Marion, *Bild-Konzeptionen in Bilder- und Kinderbibeln: die historische Anfänge und ihre Wiederentdeckung in der Gegenwart* (Göttingen: Vandenhoeck & Ruprecht, 2016).

Kießling, Gotthard, *Der Herrschaftsstand. Aspekte repräsentativer Gestaltung im evangelischen Kirchenbau* (Munich: Scaneg, 1995).

Klein, Thomas, *Der Kampf um die zweite Reformation in Kursachsen, 1586–1591* (Cologne and Graz: Böhlau, 1962).

Klein, Thomas, 'Politische oder kirchlich-religiöse Reform? – Die Regierung Christans I. 1586–1591', *Dresdner Hefte. Beiträge zur Kulturgeschichte,* 29 (1992), 5–91.

Knebel, K., 'Die Freiberger Goldschmiedeinnung, ihre Mester und deren Werke', *Mitteilungen des Freiberger Altertumsvereins,* 31 (1894), 1–116.

Koch, Eduard Emil, *Geschichte des Kirchenlieds und Kirchengesangs mit besonderer Rücksicht auf Württemberg. Zweiter Teil. Die Lieder und Weisen* (Stuttgart: Chr. Belser, 1847).

Koch, Ernst, 'Die Beseitigung der "abgöttischen Bilder" und ihre Folgen im ernestinischen Thüringen', in Hans-Jörg Nieden and Marcel Nieden (eds), *Praxis Pietatis: Beiträge zu Theologie und Frömmigkeit in der Frühen Neuzeit: Wolfgang Sommer zum 60. Geburtstag* (Stuttgart: Kohlhammer, 1999), 225–41.

Koch, Ernst, 'Ausbau, Gefährdung und Festigung der lutherischen Landeskirche von 1553 bis 1601', in Helmar Junghans (ed.), *Das Jahrhundert der Reformation in Sachsen,* 2nd ed. (Leipzig: Evang. Verl.-Anst., 2005), 191–218.

Koch, Ernst, 'Passion und Affekte in der lutherischen Erbauungsliteratur des 17. Jahrhunderts', in Johann Anselm Steiger (ed.), *Passion, Affekt und Leidenschaft in der frühen Neuzeit* (Wiesbaden: Harrassowitz, 2005), 509–18.

Koch, Ernst, 'Der Ausbruch des adiaphoristischen Streits und seine Folgewirkung', in Irene Dingel and Günther Wartenberg (eds), *Politik und Bekenntnis. Die Reaktion auf das Interim von 1548* (Leipzig: Evang. Verl.-Anst., 2007), 179–90.

Koepplin, Dieter, 'Kommet her zu mir alle. Das tröstliche Bild des Gekreuzigten nach dem Verständnis Luthers', in Kurt Löscher (ed.), *Martin Luther und die Reformation in Deutschland. Vorträge zur Ausstellung im Germanischen Nationalmusuem Nürnberg 1983* (Schweinfurt: Weppert, 1983), 153–99.

Koepplin, Dieter, 'Lutherische Glaubensbilder' in Gerhard Bott (ed), *Martin Luther und die Reformation in Deutschland. Vorträge zur Ausstellung im Germanischen Nationalmusuem Nürnberg 1983* (Schweinfurt: Weppert, 1983), 352–63.

Koepplin, Dieter and Tilman Falk, *Lukas Cranach: Gemälde, Zeichnungen, Druckgraphik*, 2 vols., exh. cat. (Basel and Stuttgart: Birkhäuser, 1974).

Koerner, Joseph, *The Moment of Self-Portraiture in German Renaissance Art* (Chicago: University of Chicago Press, 1993).

Koerner, Joseph, 'The Icon as Iconoclash', in Bruno Latour and Peter Weibel (eds), *Iconoclash: Beyond the Image Wars in Science, Religion, and Art*, exh. Cat. (Karlsruhe and Cambridge MA: MIT Press, 2002), 164–213.

Koerner, Joseph, *The Reformation of the Image* (London: Reaktion, 2004).

Kolb, Robert, *Luther's Heirs Define his Legacy: Studies on Lutheran Confessionalization* (Aldershot: Variorum, 1996).

Kolb, Robert, 'Passionsmeditation. Luthers und Melanchthons Schüler predigen und beten die Passion', in Michael Beyer and Günther Wartenberg (eds), *Humanismus und Wittenberger Reformation: Festgabe anläßlich des 500. Geburtstages des Praeceptor Germaniae Philipp Melanchthon am 16. Februar 1997* (Leipzig: Evang. Verl.-Anst., 1996), 267–93.

Kolb, Robert (ed.), *Lutheran Ecclesiastical Culture, 1550–1675* (Leiden and Boston: Brill, 2008).

Kolb, Robert and Timothy Wengert (eds), *The Book of Concord. The Confessions of the Evangelical Lutheran Church,* (Minneapolis: Fortress Press, 2000).

Krause, Gerhard, *Studien zu Luthers Auslegung der Kleinen Propheten* (Tübingen: Mohr, 1962).

Kreidt, Ulrich, '1684/92. Melchior Mattsperger: Geistliche Herzens = Einbildungen', in Theodor Brüggemann (ed.), *Handbuch zur Kinder- und Jugendliteratur. Von 1570 bis 1750* (Stuttgart: Metzler, 1991), cols 171–90.

Krentz, Natalie, *Ritualwandel und Deutungshoheit: Die Frühe Reformation in der Residenzstadt Wittenberg (1500–1533)* (Tübingen: Mohr Siebeck, 2014).

Krusenstjern, Benigna von, 'Seliges Sterben und böser Tod: Tod und Sterben in der Zeit des Dreißigjährigen Krieges', in Benigna von Krusenstjern and Hans Medick (eds), *Zwischen Alltag und Katastrophe. Der Dreißigjährige Krieg aus der Nähe* (Göttingen: Vandenhoeck & Ruprecht, 1999), 469–96.

Kube, Ricarda and Cornelia Wendt, 'Deutsch Ossig. Das Schicksal eines Dorfes im Braunkohleabbaugebiet', in Landesamt für Denkmalpflege Sachsen (ed.), *Denkmalpflege in Sachsen 1894–1994*, vol. 1 (Weimar: Böhlau, 1997), 271–3.

Kuke, Hans-Joachim, *Die Frauenkirche in Dresden. 'Ein Sankt Peter der wahren evangelischen Religion'* (Worms: Werner, 1996).

Kümmel, B., *Der Ikonoklast als Kunstliebhaber: Studien zu Landgraf Moritz von Hessen-Kassel (1592–1627)* (Marburg: Jonas-Verlag, 1996).

Kunze, Jens, 'Friesen, Carl von (zu Kauern, später zu Rötha)', in Institut für Sächsische Geschichte und Volkskunde e.V. (ed.), *Sächsische Biografie* (Dresden: ISGV), http://www.isgv.de/saebi/ [accessed 18.10.2013].

Kunze, Jens, 'Friesen, Heinrich d. Ä. Freiherr von (zu Rötha)', in Institut für Sächsische Geschichte und Volkskunde e.V. (ed.), *Sächsische Biografie* (Dresden: ISGV), http://www.isgv.de/saebi/ [accessed 18.10.2013].

Kunze, Max (ed.), *Kunst und Aufklärung im 18. Jahrhundert. Kunstausbildung der Akademien; Kunstvermittlung der Fürsten; Kunstsammlung der Universität*, exh. cat. (Ruhpolding: Rutzen, 2005).

Laabs, Annegret, 'Burgundische Tapisserien am Dresdner Hof', *Dresdner Kunstblätter*, 48 (3) (2004), 166–73.

Landesamt für Denkmalpflege Sachsen (ed.), *Von Deutsch-Ossig nach Görlitz-Königshufen. Die Rettung einer Dorfkirche* (Dresden: Sandstein Kommunkation, 1998).

Landesamt für Denkmalpflege Sachsen (ed.), *Der Zwickauer Wolgemut-Altar: Beiträge zu Geschichte, Ikonographie, Autorschaft und Restaurierung* (Görlitz and Zittau: Oettel, 2008).

Langer, Otto, 'Der Kampf des Pfarrers Joh. Petrejus gegen den Wohlgemutschen Altar in der Marienkirche', *Mitteilungen des Altertumsvereins für Zwickau und Umgebung*, 11 (1914), 31–49.

Langer, Otto, 'Über drei Kunstwerke der Marienkirche zu Zwickau: den Altar, die Beweinung Christi und das heilige Grab', *Mitteilungen des Altertumsvereins für Zwickau und Umgegend*, 12 (1919), 75–101.

Laube, Stefan, *Das Lutherhaus Wittenberg. Eine Museumsgeschichte* (Leipzig: Evang. Verl.-Anst., 2003).

Laube, Stefan, 'Glaube, Macht und Anschauung in Görlitz zwischen Reformation, Barock und Pietismus', in Ulrich Rosseaux, Wolfgang Flügel, and Veit Damm (eds), *Zeitrhythmen und performative Akte in der städtischen Erinnerungs- und Repräsentationskultur zwischen Früher Neuzeit und Gegenwart* (Dresden: Thelem, 2005), 11–35.

Laube, Stefan, 'Konfessionelle Hybridität zwischen Reformation, Barock und Aufklärung. Komplementärer Kirchenbau in Kurfürstentum Sachsen', in Susanne Wegmann and Gabrielle Wimböck (eds), *Konfessionen im Kirchenraum: Dimensionen des Sakralraums in der frühen Neuzeit* (Korb: Didymos-Verl., 2007), 195–215.

Laube, Stefan, *Von der Reliquie zum Ding. Heiliger Ort—Wunderkammer—Museum* (Berlin: Akad.-Verl., 2011).

Lechner, Elmar, *Pädagogik und Kulturkritik in der deutschen Frühaufklärung: Johann Gottfried Zeidler (1655–1711). Zehn Thesen und Edition einiger seiner autobiographischen, pädagogischen und historischen sowie aphoristischen Schriften* (Frankfurt am Main: Lang, 2008).

Lehmann, Hartmut, *Das Zeitalter des Absolutismus. Gottesgnadentum und Kriegsnot* (Stuttgart etc.: Kohlhammer, 1980).

Lehmann, Hartmut, 'Europäisches Christentum im Zeichen der Krise', in Hartmut Lehmann and Anne-Charlott Trepp (eds), *Im Zeichen der Krise. Religiosität im Europa des 17. Jahrhunderts* (Göttingen: Vandenhoeck & Ruprecht, 1999), 9–15.

Lehmann, Nadine, 'Reformierte Bildersturm und Herrschaftsrepräsentation: Der Umgang mit fürstlichen Grabmälern während der obrigkeitlichen Bildentfernung im Zuge der Zweiten Reformation', in Anna-Maria Blank, Vera Isaiasz, and Nadine Lehmann (eds), *Bild—Macht—UnOrdnung. Visuelle Repräsentationen zwischen Stabilität und Konflikt* (Frankfurt am Main: Campus-Verl., 2011), 165–93.

Leibetseder, Mathis, *Die Hostie im Hals: eine 'schröckliche' Bluttat und der Dresdner Tumult des Jahres 1726* (Konstanz: UVK-Verl.-Ges., 2009).

Lemper, Ernst-Heinz, 'Görlitz und die Oberlausitz im Jahrhundert der Reformation', in Erich Donner (ed.), *Europa in der Frühen Neuzeit. Festschrift für Günter Mühlpfordt*, vol. 1 (Weimar: Böhlau, 1997), 281–300.

Lentes, Thomas, 'Auf der Suche nach dem Ort des Gedächtnisses. Thesen zur Umwertung der symbolischen Formen in Abendmahlslehre, Bildtheorie und Bildandacht des 14. bis 16. Jahrhunderts', in Klaus Krüger and Alessandro Nova (eds), *Imagination und Wirklichkeit. Zum Verhältnis von mentalen und realen Bildern und der Kunst der frühen Neuzeit* (Mainz: von Zabern, 2000), 21–46.

Lentes, Thomas, 'Zwischen Adiaphora und Artefakt. Bildbestreibung in der Reformation', in R. Hoeps (ed.), *Handbuch der Bildtheologie*, vol. 1, *Bild-Konflikte* (Paderborn: Schöningh, 2007), 213–40.

Leppin, Volker and Ulrich A. Wien (eds), *Konfessionsbildung und Konfessionskultur in Siebenbürgen in der frühen Neuzeit* (Stuttgart: Steiner, 2005).

Leppin, Volker, 'Kirchenausstattungen in territorialen Kirchenordnungen bis 1548', in Sabine Arend and Gerald Dörner (eds), *Ordnungen für die Kirche—Wirkungen auf die Welt. Evangelische Kirchenordnungen des 16. Jahrhunderts* (Tübingen: Mohr Siebeck, 2015), 137–55.

Lieske, R., *Protestantische Frömmigkeit im Spiegel der kirchlichen Kunst des Herzogtums Württemberg* (Munich: Deutscher Kunstverlag, 1973).

Lilek-Schirmer, Maria, 'Die Emporengemälde: eine Bilderpredigt', in Joachim Proescholdt (ed.), *St. Katharinen zu Frankfurt am Main* (Frankfurt am Main: Kramer, 1981), 164–88.

Lindberg, David, *Theories of Vision from Al-Kindi to Kepler* (Chicago: University of Chicago Press, 1976).

Lindemann, Bernd Wolfgang, 'Die Kunst in Berlin zu Zeiten Friedrichs, Kurfürst von Brandenburg und erster König in Polen', in Hans-Ulrich Kessler (ed.), *Andreas Schlüter und das barocke Berlin* (Berlin: Hirmer, 2014), 78–93.

Linton, Anna, *Poetry and Parental Bereavement in Early Modern Germany* (Oxford: OUP, 2008).

Litz, Gudrun, *Die reformatorische Bilderfrage in den schwäbischen Reichsstädten* (Tübingen: Mohr Siebeck, 2007).

Löffler, Fritz, *Die Stadtkirchen in Sachsen* (Berlin: Evangelische Verlagsanstalt, 1973).

Löscher, Friedrich Hermann, *Die Kreuzkirche und ihre geschichtliche Bedeutung für die Stadt Dresden* (Berlin: Altis-Verl., 1999).

Löscher, Hermann, 'Die erzgebirgischen Knappschaften vor und nach der Reformation', *Blätter für deutsche Landesgeschichte*, 92 (1956), 162–90.

Lotz-Heumann, Ute, Jan-Friedrich Mißfelder, and Matthias Pohlig (eds), *Konversion und Konfession in der Frühen Neuzeit* (Gütersloh: Gütersloher Verl.-Haus, 2007).

Louthan, Howard, *Converting Bohemia: Force and Persuasion in the Catholic Reformation* (Cambridge: CUP, 2009).

Lund, Eric, '*modus docendi mysticus*. The Interpretation of the Bible in Johann Arndt's Postilla', in Torbjörn Johansson, Robert Kolb and Johann Anselm Steiger (eds), *Hermeneutica Sacra. Studien zur Auslegung der heiligen Schrift im 16. und 17. Jahrhundert/ Studies of the Interpretation of Scripture in the Sixteenth and Seventeenth Centuries* (Berlin: De Gruyter, 2010), 223–45.

Mager, Inge, 'Johann Arndts Bildfrömmigkeit', in Udo Sträter (ed.), *Pietas in der lutherischen Orthodoxie* (Wittenberg: Ed. Hans Lufft, 1998), 41–60.

Mager, Inge, 'Weshalb hat Martin Luther kein Passionslied geschrieben?', in Johann Anselm Steiger (ed.), *Passion, Affekt und Leidenschaft in der frühen Neuzeit*, vol. 1 (Wiesbaden: Harrassowitz, 2005), 405–22.

Magirius, Heinrich, *Der Dom zu Freiberg* (Leipzig: Koehler und Amelang, 1986).

Magirius, Heinrich, 'Die Werke der Freiberger Bildhauerfamilie Ditterich und die lutherische Altarkunst in Obersachsen zwischen 1550 und 1650', in Hans-Herbert Möller (ed.), *Die Hauptkirche Beatae Mariae Virginis in Wolfenbüttel* (Hamlyn: Niemeyer, 1987), 169–78.

Magirius, Heinrich, 'Die Gloriole des Altars der Dresdner Frauenkirche als Zeichen der Theophanie', *Die Dresdner Frauenkirche*, 7 (2001), 221–9.

Magirius, Heinrich, *Die Dresdner Frauenkirche von George Bähr: Entstehung und Bedeutung* (Berlin: Dt. Verl. für Kunstwiss., 2005).

Magirius, Heinrich, *Die evangelische Schlosskapelle zu Dresden aus kunstgeschichtlicher Sicht* (Altenburg: Kamprad, 2009).

Magirius, Heinrich and Hartmut Mai, *Dorfkirchen in Sachsen* (Berlin: Evangelische Verlagsanstalt, 1985).

Mahlmann, Theodor, 'Stein gewordene Christologie. Balthasar Mentzer und der Altar der Lutherischen Pfarrkirche St. Marien', in Hans-Joachim Kunst and Eckart Glockzin (eds), *Kirche Zwischen Schloß und Markt. Die Lutherische Pfarrkirche St. Marien zu Marburg* (Marburg: Evang. Pfarramt, 1997), 70–104.

Mai, Hartmut, 'Der Einfluß der Reformation auf Kirchenbau und kirchliche Kunst', in Helmar Junghans (ed.), *Das Jahrhundert der Reformation in Sachsen*, 2nd ed. (Leipzig: Evang. Verl.-Anst., 2005), 167–8.

Marsch, Angelika, *Bilder zur Augsburger Konfession und ihren Jubiläen* (Weißenhorn: Konrad, 1980).

Martin, Peter, *Martin Luther und die Bilder zur Apokalypse* (Hamburg: Wittig, 1983).

Marx, Barbara (ed.), *Elbflorenz. Italienische Präsenz in Dresden 16.–19. Jahrhundert* (Dresden: Verl. der Kunst, 2000).

Marx, Barbara, 'Künstlermigration und Kulturkonsum. Die Florentiner Kulturpolitik im 16. Jahrhundert und die Formierung Dresdens als Elbflorenz', in Bodo Guthmüller (ed.), *Deutschland und Italien in ihren wechselseitigen Beziehungen während der Renaissance* (Wiesbaden: Harrassowitz, 2000), 211–97.

Marx, Barbara, 'Die Italienreise Herzog Johann Georgs von Sachsen (1601–1602) und der Besuch von Cosimo III. de' Medici (1668) in Dresden. Zur Kausalität von Grand Tour und Kulturtransfer', in Rainer Babel and Werner Paravicini (eds), *Grand Tour. Adeliges Reisen und Europäische Kultur vom 14. bis zum 18. Jahrhundert* (Ostfildern: Thorbecke, 2005), 373–421.

Mayes, D., *Communal Christianity: The Life and Loss of a Peasant Vision in Early Modern Germany* (Boston and Leiden: Brill, 2004).

Mehlhausen, Joachim, 'Der Streit um die Adiaphora', in Martin Brecht and Reinhard Schwarz (eds), *Bekenntnis und Einheit der Kirche. Studien zum Konkordienbuch* (Stuttgart: Calwer Verlag, 1980), 105–28.

Meine-Schawe, Monika, *Die Grablege der Wettiner im Dom zu Freiberg. Die Umgestaltung des Domchores durch Giovanni Maria Nosseni 1585–1594* (Göttingen: Vandenhoeck & Ruprecht, 1989).

Meller, Harald (ed.), *Fundsache Luther. Archäologen auf den Spuren des Reformators*, exh. cat. (Stuttgart: Theiss, 2009).

Menk, Gerhard, 'Landgraf Moritz und die Rolle Marburgs bei der Einführung der "Verbesserungspunkte"', in Hans-Joachim Kunst and Eckart Glockzin (eds), *Kirche Zwischen Schloß und Markt. Die Lutherische Pfarrkirche St. Marien zu Marburg* (Marburg: Evang. Pfarramt, 1997), 48–57.

Menzhausen, Joachim, 'Der Altar der Dresdner Frauenkirche und der Bildhauer Johann Christian Feige d. Ä.', *Die Dresdner Frauenkirche*, 4 (1988), 135–63.

Menzhausen, Joachim, 'Die Dresdner Kunst unter Christian I.', *Dresdner Hefte. Beiträge zur Kulturgeschichte*, 29 (1992), 51–6.

Menzhausen, Joachim (ed.), *Ecclesia Triumphans Dresdensis*, exh. cat. (Vienna: Ed. Tusch, 1988).

Meys, Oliver, *Memoria und Bekenntnis: die Grabdenkmäler evangelischer Landesherren im Heiligen Römischen Reich Deutscher Nation im Zeitalter der Konfessionalisierung* (Regensburg: Schnell & Steiner, 2009).

Michalski, Sergiusz, 'Bild, Spiegelbild, Figura, Repraesentatio: Ikonitätsbegriffe im Spannungsfeld zwischen Bilderfrage und Abendmahlskontroverse', *Annuarium historiae conciliorum*, 20 (1988), 458–88.

Michalski, Sergiusz, *The Reformation and the Visual Arts. The Protestant Image Question in Western and Eastern Europe* (London: Routledge, 1993).

Michalski, Sergiusz, 'Die lutherisch-katholisch-reformierte Rivalität im Bereich der Bildenden Kunst im Gebiet von Danzig um 1600', in J. Bahlcke and A. Stromeyer (eds), *Konfessionalisierung in Ostmitteleuropa* (Stuttgart: Steiner, 1999), 267–87.

Michalski, Sergiusz, 'Die Ausbreitung des reformatorischen Bildersturms 1521–1537', in Cécile Dupeaux, Peter Jezler, and Jean Wirth (eds), *Bildersturm. Wahnsinn oder Gottes Wille?*, exh. cat. (Munich: Fink, 2000).

Michel, Stefan, 'Bibel', in Volker Leppin and Gury Schneider-Ludorff (eds), *Das Luther-Lexikon* (Regensburg: Bückle und Böhm, 2014), 108–12.

Michels, Norbert (ed.), *Cranach in Anhalt: vom alten zum neuen Glauben*, exh. cat. (Petersberg: Imhof, 2015).

Michels, Norbert, 'Einführung', in ibid. (ed.), *Cranach in Anhalt: vom alten zum neuen Glauben*, exh. cat. (Petersberg: Imhoff, 2015), 13–16.

Mochizuki, Mia, *The Netherlandish Image after Iconoclasm, 1566–1672: Material Religion in the Dutch Golden Age* (Aldershot: Ashgate, 2008).

Moeller, Bernd, 'Annaberg als Stadt der Reformation', in Harald Marx and Cecilie Holberg (eds), *Glaube und Macht: Sachsen in Europa der Reformationszeit. Aufsätze* (Dresden: Standstein, 2004), 103–11.

Mühlen, Karl-Heinz zur, 'Die Affektenlehre im Spätmittelalter und in der Reformationszeit', *Archiv für Begriffsgeschichte*, 35 (1992), 93–114.

Mühlen, Karl-Heinz zur, *Reformatorische Prägungen: Studien zur Theologie Martin Luthers und zur Reformationszeit* (Göttingen: Vandenhoeck & Ruprecht, 2011).

Müller, H., *Seelsorge und Tröstung. Christian Scriver (1629–1693)* (Waltrop: Spenner, 2005).

Müller, Jürgen, 'Giovanni Maria Nosseni and Art in Dresden, 1580–1620', in Dirk Syndram and Antje Scherner (eds), *Princely Splendour: The Dresden Court 1580–1620*, exh. cat. (Milan: Electa, 2004).

Müller, Nikolaus, *Der Dom zu Berlin* (Berlin: Schwetschke, 1906).

Müller, Siegfried, 'Repräsentationen des Luthertums – Disziplinierung und konfessionelle Kultur in Bildern', *Zeitschrift für Historische Forschung*, 29 (2002), 215–55.

Müller-Bahlke, Thomas, 'Der Hallesche Pietismus und die Kunst. Bemerkungen zu einem alten Vorurteil', in Rainer Lächele (ed.), *Das Echo Halles. Kulturelle Wirkungen des Piestimus* (Tübingen: Bibliotheca-Academica-Verl., 2001), 243–69.

Münch, Birgit Ulrike, *Geteiltes Leid: Die Passion Christi in Bildern und Texten der Konfessionalisierung* (Regensburg: Schnell & Steiner, 2009).

Münch, Birgit Ulrike, 'The Lutheran Tradition', in Lee Palmer Wandel (ed.), *A Companion to the Eucharist in the Reformation* (Leiden: Brill, 2014), 399–422.

Münchow, Christoph, ' "…damit das Werk zu vollkommen Stand gebracht werde". Valentin Ernst Löscher und der Bau der Frauenkirche', *Die Dresdner Frauenkirche*, 5 (1999), 133–42.

Münchow, Christoph, ' "Die Historie von Christo am Ölberge". Das Bildrelief des Altars der Dresdner Frauenkirche und die evangelische Passionsfrömmigkeit', *Die Dresdner Frauenkirche*, 8 (2002), 111–25.

Munck, Thomas, 'Keeping up Appearances: Patronage of the Arts, City Prestige, and Princely Power in Northern Germany and Denmark 1600–1670', *German History*, 6 (3) (1988), 213–32.

Müsch, Irmgard, *Geheiligte Naturwissenschaft. Die Kupfer-Bibel des Johann Jakob Scheuchzer* (Göttingen: Vandenhoeck & Ruprecht, 2000).

Neidhardt, Uta, 'Gewirkte Passion. Vier Bildteppiche der Gemäldegalerie Alte Meister', *Dresdner Kunstblätter*, 48 (3) (2004), 153–65.

Newmark, Catherine, *Passion—Affekt—Gefühl. Philosophische Theorien der Emotionen zwischen Aristoteles und Kant* (Hamburg: Meiner, 2008).

Nischan, Bodo, *Prince, People, and Confession: the Second Reformation in Brandenburg* (Philadelphia: University of Pennsylvania Press, 1994).

Nischan, Bodo, *Lutherans and Calvinists in the Age of Confessionalism* (Aldershot: Ashgate, 1999).

Nora, Pierre, *Rethinking France*, vol. 1 (Chicago: University of Chicago Press, 2001).

Oertel, Friedrich Maximilian, *Das Münster der Augustiner Chorherren zu St Afra in Meißen* (Leipzig: Reclam, 1843).

Oexle, Otto Gerhard, 'Memoria und Memorialbild', in Karl Schmid and Joachim Wollasch (eds), *Memoria. Der geschichtliche Zeugniswert des liturgischen Gedenkens im Mittelalter* (Munich: Fink, 1984), 384–440.

Packeiser, Thomas, 'Zum Austausch von Konfessionalisierungs Forschung und Kunstgeschichte', *Archiv für Reformationsgeschichte*, 93 (2002), 317–38.

Packeiser, Thomas, 'Umschlagende Fülle als Autorität des Einen: Abundanz, Inversion und Zentrierung in den Tafelaltären Heinrich Füllmaurers', in Frank Büttner and Gabriele Wimböck (eds), *Das Bild als Autorität. Die normierende Kraft des Bildes* (Münster: Aschendorff, 2004), 401–45.

Pahncke, Karl, 'Abraham Scultetus in Berlin', *Forschungen zur Brandenburgischen und Preußischen Geschichte*, 23 (1910), 35–53.

'Die Parochie Planitz', in *Neue Sächsische Kirchengalerie: Die Ephorie Zwickau* (Leipzig, 1902), cols 162–200.

Passavant, Günter, *Wolf Caspar von Klengel: Dresden 1630–1691; Reisen—Skizzen—Baukünstlerische Tätigkeiten* (Berlin: Dt. Kunstverl., 2001).

Paul, Wolfgang (ed.), *Dresden in alten und neuen Reisebeschreibungen* (Düsseldorf: Droste, 1990).

Peil, Dietmar, *Zur 'angewandten Emblematik' in protestantischen Erbauungsbüchern. Dilherr–Arndt–Francisci–Scriver* (Heidelberg: Winter, 1978).

Pettegree, Andrew, *Brand Luther: 1517, Printing, and the Making of the Reformation* (New York: Penguin Books, 2015).

Petzold, Klaus, *Der unterlegen Sieger. Valentin Ernst Löscher im absolutischen Sachsen* (Leipzig: Evang. Verl.-Anst., 2001).

Pietsch, Andreas and Barbara Stollberg-Rilinger, (eds), *Konfessionelle Ambiguität. Uneindeutigkeit und Verstellung als religiöse Praxis in der Frühen Neuzeit* (Gütersloh: Gütersloher Verl.-Haus, 2013).

Pohl, Hans-Jürgen, *Aus der Geschichte der Familie von Schleinitz—ein Beitrag zur sächsischen Landesgeschichte* (Oschatz: Schmidt, 2010).

Pohlig, Matthias, *Zwischen Gelehrsamkeit und konfessioneller Identitätsstiftung: Lutherische Kirchen- und Universalgeschichtsschreibung 1546–1617* (Tübingen: Mohr Siebeck, 2007).

Poscharsky, Peter, *Die Kanzel: Erscheinungsform im Protestantismus bis zum Ende des Barocks* (Gütersloh: Gütersloher Verl.-Haus, 1963).

Poscharsky, Peter, 'Das lutherische Bildprogramm', in ibid, *Die Bilder in den lutherischen Kirchen. Ikonographische Studien* (Munich: Scaneg, 1998), 21–34.

Poscharsky, Peter, 'Ikonographische Beobachtungen an lutherischen Altarretabeln in Sachsen bis zum Ende des Barock', in Jens Bulisch (ed.), *Kirchliche Kunst in Sachsen: Festgabe für Hartmut Mai zum 65. Geburtstag* (Beucha: Sax.-Verl., 2002), 111–28.

Priever, Andreas, 'Johann de Perre, die "Auferstehung Christi" und der Stein des Anstoßes. Eine Fallstudie zum Bildergebrauch in der lutherischen Orthodoxie', *Zeitschrift für Kunstgeschichte*, 70 (4) (2007), 513–44.

Previer, Andreas, 'Die 'causa' Merian. Streit im Chor der Frankfurter Barfüßerkirche', in Andrea Bendlage (ed.), *Recht und Verhalten in vormodernen Gesellschaften* (Bielefeld: Verl. für Regionalgeschichte, 2008), 233–53.

Proescholdt, Joachim (ed.), *St. Katharinen zu Frankfurt am Main* (Frankfurt am Main: Kramer, 1981).

Rau, Susanne, *Geschichte und Konfession: städtische Geschichtsschreibung und Erinnerungskultur im Zeitalter von Reformation und Konfessionalisierung in Bremen, Breslau, Hamburg und Köln* (Hamburg: Dölling und Galitz, 2002).

Reents, Christine and Christoph Melchior, *Die Geschichte der Kinder- und Schulbibel. Evangelisch–katholisch–jüdisch* (Göttingen: Vandenhoeck & Ruprecht, 2011).

Reininghaus, Wilfried, 'Sachgut und handwerkliche Gruppenkultur. Neue Fragen an die "Zunftaltertümer"', in Otto Gerhard Oexle and Andrea von Hülsen-Esch (eds), *Die Repräsentation der Gruppen. Texte–Bilder–Objekte* (Göttingen: Vandenhoeck & Ruprecht, 1998), 429–63.

Reinitzer, Heimo, *Biblia deutsch: Luthers Bibelübersetzung und ihre Tradition*, exh. cat. (Wolfenbüttel: Herzog August Bibliothek and Hamburg: Wittig, 1983).

Reinitzer, Heimo, 'Leserspuren in Bibeln', *Wolfenbütteler Beiträge: aus den Schätzen der Herzog August Bibliothek*, 13 (2005), 149–52.

Reinitzer, Heimo, *Gesetz und Evangelium: über ein reformatorisches Bildthema, seine Tradition, Funktion und Wirkungsgeschichte*, 2 vols. (Hamburg: Christians, 2006).

Reiß, Ansgar and Sabine Witt (eds), *Calvinismus. Die Reformierten in Deutschland und Europa*, exh. cat. (Berlin and Dresden: Sandstein, 2009).

Reißmann, Kurt (ed.), *Die Kunstdenkmäler der Provinz Brandenburg*, vol. 5/3, *Stadt- und Landkreis Cottbus* (Berlin: Dt. Kunstverlag, 1938).

Reu, Johann Michael, *Quellen zur Geschichte des kirchlichen Unterrichts in der evangelischen Kirche Deutschlands zwischen 1530 und 1600* (Gütersloh: Gütersloher Verl.-Haus, 1904–35).

Ringshausen, Gerhard, *Von der Buchillustration zum Unterrichtsmedium: Der Weg des Bildes in die Schule dargestellt am Beispiel des Religionsunterrichtes* (Weinheim and Basel: Beltz, 1976).

Ritter, Dorothee, 'Rode, Christian Bernhard', in *Neue Deutsche Biographie* (Munich), vol. 21 (2003), 690–1.

Rittgers, Ronald K., 'Mystical Union and Spiritual Desire in Late Reformation Devotion: The Case of Martin Moller's *The Great Mystery* (1595)', *Reformation & Renaissance Review*, 17 (3) (2015), 214–29.

Rodekamp, Volker (ed.), *Leipzig Original: Stadtgeschichte vom Mittelalter bis zur Völkerschlacht* (Altenburg: Verl. DZA, 2006).

Roeck, Bernd, *Eine Stadt in Krieg und Frieden: Studien zur Geschichte der Reichsstadt Augsburg zwischen Kalenderstreit und Parität* (Göttingen: Vandenhoeck & Ruprecht, 1989).

Roeck, Bernd, 'Der Dreißigjährige Krieg und die Menschen im Reich. Überlegungen zu den Formen psychischer Krisenbewältigung in der ersten Hälfte des 17. Jahrhunderts', in Bernhard R. Kroener and Ralf Pröve (eds), *Krieg und Frieden. Militär und Gesellschaft in der Frühen Neuzeit* (Paderborn etc.: Schöningh, 1996), 265–79.

Roper, Lyndal, *Martin Luther: Renegade and Prophet* (London: Bodley Head, 2016).

Rosseaux, Ulrich, 'Das bedrohte Zion: Lutheraner und Katholiken in Dresden nach der Konversion Augusts des Starken (1697–1751)', in Ute Lotz-Heumann, Jan-Friedrich Mißfelder, and Matthias Pohlig (eds), *Konversion und Konfession in der Frühen Neuzeit* (Gütersloh: Gütersloher Verl.-Haus, 2007), 212–35.

Rosseaux, Ulrich, 'Der Kampf der Steine. Die Frauenkirche und die katholische Hofkirche in Dresden', in Ulrich Rosseaux and Gerhard Poppe (eds), *Konfession und Konflikt. Religiöse Pluralisierung in Sachsen im 18. und 19. Jahrhundert* (Münster: Aschendorff, 2012), 153–63.

Roth, Fritz, *Christian Lehmanns Leben und Werke und seine Stellung zum Aberglauben* (Marburg: Gärtner, 1933).

Rott, Hans, 'Kirchen- und Bildersturm bei der Einführung der Reformation in der Pfalz', *Neues Archiv für die Geschichte der Stadt Heidelberg und der rheinischen Pfalz*, 6 (1905), 229–54.

Rudersdorf, Manfred, 'Die Oberlausitz, die Habsburger und das Reich im 16. und 17. Jahrhunder', in Joachim Bahlcke (ed.), *Die Oberlausitz im frühneuzeitlichen Mitteleuropa: Beziehungen–Strukturen–Prozesse* (Stuttgart: Steiner, 2007), 19–35.

Rudersdorf, Manfred and Anton Schindling, 'Kurbrandenburg', in Anton Schindling and Walter Ziegler (eds), *Die Territorien des Reichs im Zeitalter der Reformation und Konfessionalisierung,* vol. 2, *Der Nordosten* (Münster: Aschendorff, 1991), 34–66.

Ruschke, Johannes, *Paul Gerhardt und der Berliner Kirchenstreit. Eine Untersuchung der konfessionellen Auseinandersetzung über die kurfürstliche verordnete 'mutua tolerantia'* (Tübingen: Mohr Siebeck, 2012).

Sandner, Ingo, *Spätgotische Tafelmalerei in Sachsen* (Dresden: Verl. der Kunst, 1993).

Schade, Karl, *Andachtsbild. Die Geschichte eines kunsthistorischen Begriffs* (Weimar: Verl. und Datenbank für Geisteswiss., 1996).

Schattkowsky, Martina, *Zwischen Rittergut, Residenz und Reich: die Lebenswelt des kursächsischen Landadligen Christoph von Loß auf Schleinitz (1574–1620)* (Leipzig: Leipziger Univ.-Verl., 2007).

Schattkowsky, Martina (ed.), *Sachsen und seine Sekundogenituren: die Nebenlinien Weißenfels, Merseburg und Zeitz (1657–1746)* (Leipzig: Leipziger Univ.-Verl., 2010).

Schauerte, Thomas, 'Die Luther-Bibel des Hans Ulrich Krafft', *Wolfenbütteler Beiträge: aus den Schätzen der Herzog August Bibliothek*, 13 (2005), 256–307.

Schilling, Heinz, *Religion, Political Culture and the Emergence of Early Modern Society* (Leiden: Brill, 1992).

Schlie, Heike, 'Blut und Farbe. Sakramentale Dimensionen der frühneuzeitlichen Bild- und Kunsttheorie', in Stefanie Ertz, Heike Schlie and Daniel Weidner (eds), *Sakramentale Repräsentation. Substanz, Zeichen und Präsenz in der Frühen Neuzeit* (Munich: Fink, 2012), 51–80.

Schmidt, Frank, 'Die Innenausstattung der Nikolaikirche im Wandel der Jahrhundert', in Armin Kohle (ed.), *St. Nikolai zu Leipzig. 850 Jahre Kirche in der Stadt* (Petersberg: Imhof, 2015), 222–34.

Schmidt, Georg, *Die Familie von Zabeltitz* (Rathenow: Max Babenzien, 1888).

Schmidt, Michael, *Reverentia und Magnificentia. Historizität in der Architektur Süddeutschlands, Österreichs und Böhmens von 14. bis 17. Jahrhundert* (Regensburg: Schnell & Steiner, 1999).

Schmidt, Patrick, *Wandelbare Traditionen—tradierter Wandel. Zünftsche Erinnerungskultur in der Frühen Neuzeit* (Cologne: Böhlau, 2009).

Schmidt, Ph., *Die Illustration der Lutherbibel, 1522–1700. Ein Stück abendländische Kultur- und Kirchengeschichte* (Basel: F. Reinhardt, 1962).

Schmidt-Brücken, Stephan and Karsten Richter, *Der Erzgebirgschronist Christian Lehmann: Leben und Werk* (Marienberg: Dr. und Verl.-Ges. Marienberg, 2011).

Schneider, Hans, *Der fremde Arndt. Studien zu Leben, Werk und Wirkung Johann Arndts (1555–1621)* (Göttingen: Vandenhoeck & Ruprecht, 2006).

Schönstädt, Jürgen, *Antichrist, Weltheilsgeschehen und Gottes Werkzeug. Römische Kirche, Reformation und Luther im Spiegel des Reformationsjubiläums 1617* (Wiesbaden: Steiner, 1978), esp. 10–85.

Schöntube, Ulrich, 'Transkonfessionalität und Konfessionskonformität am Beispiel literarischer Quellen von Emporenbilderzyklen der Region des Kurfürstentums Brandenburg', in Thomas Kaufmann, Anselm Schubert and Kaspar von Greyerz (eds), *Frühneuzeitliche Konfessionskulturen* (Gütersloh: Gütersloher Verl.-Haus, 2008), 347–74.

Schorn-Schütte, Luise, *Das Interim 1548/50. Herrschaftskrise und Glaubenskonflikt* (Gütersloh: Gütersloher Verl.-Haus, 2005).

Schulze, Ingrid, *Lucas Cranach d. J. und die protestantische Bildkunst in Sachsen und Thüringen: Frömmigkeit, Theologie, Fürstenreform* (Bucha nr. Jena: Quartus-Verl., 2004).

Schunka, Alexander, *Gäste, die bleiben: Zuwanderer in Kursachsen und der Oberlausitz im 17. und frühen 18. Jahrhundert* (Hamburg: Lit.-Verl., 2006).

Schütte, Ilrich, 'Das Fürstenschloß als »Pracht-Gebäude«', in Lutz Unbehaun (ed.), *Die Künste und das Schloß in der frühen Neuzeit* (Munich and Berlin: Dt. Kunstverlag, 1998), 15–29.

Schwarz, Martin, *Martin Luther: Lehrer der christlichen Religion* (Tübingen: Mohr Siebeck, 2015).

Schwerhoff, Gerd, *Zungen wie Schwerter: Blasphemie in alteuropäischen Gesellschaften 1200– 1650* (Konstanz: UVK-Verl.-Ges., 2005).

Scribner, R. W., 'Popular Piety and Modes of Visual Perception in Late-Medieval and Reformation Germany', *Journal of Religious History*, 15 (4) (1989), 448–69.

Scribner, R. W., *For the Sake of Simple Folk: Popular Propaganda for the German Reformation*, 2nd ed. (Oxford: OUP, 1994).

Sdzuj, Reimund, *Adiaphorie und Kunst: Studien zur Genealogie ästhetischen Denkens* (Tübingen: Niemeyer, 2005).

Seifert, Siegfried, *Niedergang und Wiederaufstieg der Katholischen Kirche in Sachsen 1517– 1773* (Leipzig: St. Benno-Verl., 1964).

Seifert, Siegfried, 'Das Domstift St. Petri in Bautzen – ein Überblick', in Steffen Gärtner, Volker Hänsel, and Gunter Oettel (eds), *Via Sacra. Oberlausitz–Schlesien–Böhmen* (Görlitz and Zittau: Oettel, 2007), 55–67.

Seifert, Siegfried, 'Das Bildprogramm der katholischen Hofkirche in Dresden, Kathedrale des Bistums Dresden-Meissen', in Menzhausen, ed., *Ecclesia Triumphans Dresdensis* (Vienna: Ed. Tusch, 1988), 15–20.

Shantz, Douglas (ed.), *A Companion to German Pietism* (Leiden: Brill, 2014).

Sheehan, Jonathan, *The Enlightenment Bible: Translation, Scholarship, Culture* (Princeton: Princeton University Press, 2005).

Slenczka, Ruth, 'Cranach der Jüngere im Dienst der Reformation', in Roland Enke, Katja Schneider, and Jutta Strehe (eds), *Lucas Cranach der Jüngere—Entdeckung eines Meisters*, exh. cat. (Munich: Hirmer, 2015), 124–37.

Smith, Pamela, *The Body of the Artisan: Art and Experience in the Scientific Revolution* (Chicago: University of Chicago Press, 2004).

Smolinsky, Herbert, 'Albertinisches Sachsen', in Anton Schindling and Walter Ziegler (eds), *Die Territorien des Reichs im Zeitalter der Reformation und Konfessionalisierung*, vol. 2, *Der Nordosten* (Münster: Aschendorff, 1991), 8–32.

Soboth, Christian, 'Tränen des Auges, Tränen des Herzens. Anatomien des Weinens in Pietismus, Aufklärung und Empfindsamkeit', in Jürgen Helm and Karin Stukenbrock (eds), *Anatomie. Sektionen einer medizinischen Wissenschaft im 18. Jahrhundert* (Stuttgart: Steiner, , 2003), 293–315.

Sobotka, Bruno and Jürgen Strauss, *Burgen Schlösser Gutshäuser in Sachsen-Anhalt* (Stuttgart: Theiss, 1994).

Sobotta, Julia, 'Die Kirche der verhinderten Reichsstadt. Eine Untersuching zur Geschichte der Kirchen in Zwickau im Mittelalter' (unpublished PhD, University of Leipzig, 2009).

Sommer, Wolfgang, *Die lutherischen Hofprediger in Dresden: Grundzüge ihrer Geschichte und Verkündigung im Kurfürstentum Sachsen* (Stuttgart: Steiner, 2006).

Spicer, Andrew, *Lutheran Churches in Early Modern Europe* (Farnham: Ashgate, 2012).

Stannek, Antje, 'Konfessionalisierung des "Giro d'Italia"? Protestanten im Italien des 17. Jahrhunderts', *Beihefte der Francia*, 60 (2005), 555–68.

Steche, Richard (ed.), *Beschreibende Darstellung der älteren Bau- und Kunstdenkmäler des Königreichs Sachsen*, vol. 12, *Amtshauptmannschaft Zwickau* (Dresden: Meinhold, 1889).

Steche, Richard (ed.), *Beschreibende Darstellung der älteren Bau- und Kunstdenkmäler des Königreichs Sachsen*, vol. 15, *Amtshauptmannschaft Borna* (Dresden: Meinhold, 1891).

Steiger, Johann Anselm, *Johann Gerhard (1582–1637). Studien zu Theologie und Frömmigkeit des Kirchenvaters der lutherischen Orthodoxie* (Stuttgart: Frommann-Holzboog, 1997).

Steiger, Johann Anselm, 'Zorn Gottes, Leiden Christi und die Affekte der Passionsbetrachtung bei Luther und im Luthertum des 17. Jahrhunderts', in ibid. (ed.), *Passion, Affekt und Leidenschaft in der frühen Neuzeit* (Wiesbaden: Harrassowitz, 2005), 179–202.

Steiger, Johann Anselm, 'Christus Pictor. Der Gekreuzigte auf Golgatha als Bilder schaffendes Bild. Zur Entzifferung der Kreuzigungserzählung bei Luther und im barocken Luthertum sowie deren medientheoretischen Implikationen', in Johann Anselm Steiger and Ulrich Heinen (eds), *Golgatha in den Konfessionen und Medien der Frühen Neuzeit* (Berlin and New York: De Gruyter, 2010), 93–127.

Steinmüller, Paul, 'Das Bekenntnis Joachims II', *Forschungen zur Brandenburgischen und Preußischen Geschichte*, 17 (1) (1904), 237–46.

Stiftung Preußische Schlösser und Gärten Berlin-Brandenburg, *Cranach und die Kunst der Renaissance unter den Hohenzollern. Kirche, Hof und Stadtkultur*, exh. cat. (Berlin: Dt. Kunstverl., 2009).

Stirm, Margarete, *Die Bilderfrage in der Reformation* (Gütersloh: Gütersloher Verl.-Haus, 1977).

Stolt, Birgit, *Martin Luthers Rhetorik des Herzens* (Tübingen: Mohr Siebeck, 2014).

Strasser, Gerhard and Mara Wade, *Die Domänen des Emblems: Außerliterarische Anwendungen der Emblematik* (Wiesbaden: Harrassowitz, 2004).

Strasser, Gerhard F., *Emblematik und Mnemonik der Frühen Neuzeit im Zusammenspiel: Johannes Buno und Johann Justus Winckelmann* (Wiesbaden: Harrassowitz, 2000).

Sträter, Udo, *Meditation und Kirchenreform in der lutherischen Kirche des 17. Jahrhunderts* (Tübingen: Mohr, 1995).

Sträter, Udo, '"Wie bringen wir den Kopff in das Hertz?" Meditation in der Lutherischen Kirche des 17. Jahhunderts', in Gerhard Kurz (ed.), *Meditation und Erinnerung in der Frühen Neuzeit* (Göttingen: Vandenhoeck & Ruprecht, 2000), 11–35.

Strohmaier-Wiederanders, Gerline, '"Vera Euangely doctrina" im Bild: Evangelische Bildprogramme auf Altar und Grabbildern in St. Gotthard, Brandenburg', in Katharina Gaede (ed.), *Spuren in der Vergangenheit—Begegnungen in der Gegenwart. Glauben, Lehren und Leben in orthodoxen, altorientalischen und evangelischen Kirchen* (Berlin: K. Gaede, 1999), 147–53.

Strohmaier-Wiederanders, Gerlinde, 'Beobachtungen zur protestantischen Ikonographie an Altar- und Kanzelgestaltungen in Kirchen der Mark Brandenburg vom 16. bis zum 18. Jahrhundert', in Tatjana Bartsch and Jörg Meiner (eds), *Kunst: Kontext: Geschichte. Festgabe für Hubert Faensen zum 75. Geburtstag* (Berlin: Lukas-Verl., 2003), 156–77.

Stuart, Kathy, *Defiled Trades and Social Outcasts: Honour and Ritual Pollution in Early Modern Germany* (Cambridge: CUP, 1999).

Syndram, Dirk, 'Princely Splendour: An Introduction', in Dirk Syndram and Antje Scherner (eds), *Princely Splendour: The Dresden Court 1580–1620*, exh. cat. (Milan: Electa, 2004).

Taatz-Jacobi, Marianne, *Erwünschte Harmonie: Die Gründung der Friedrichs-Universität Halle als Instrument brandenburg-preußicher Konfessionspolitik—Motive, Verfahren, Mythos (1680–1713)* (Berlin: De Gruyter, 2014).

Tacke, Andreas, *Der katholische Cranach: zu zwei Grossaufträgen von Lucas Cranach d. Ä., Simon Franck und der Cranach-Werkstatt (1520–1540)* (Mainz: von Zabern, 1992).

Terpstra, Nicholas, *Religious Refugees in the Early Modern World: An Alternative History of the Reformation* (Cambridge: CUP, 2015).

Thiel, Ulrich, *Stadt- und Bergbaumuseum Freiberg* (Chemnitz: Sächsiche Landesstelle für Museumswissen, 2005).

Thum, Veronika, *Die Zehn Gebote für die ungelehrten Leut'. Der Dekalog in der Graphik des späten Mittelalters und der frühen Neuzeit* (Munich and Berlin: Dt. Kunstverl., 2006).

Titze, Mario, *Das barocke Schneeberg: Kunst und städtische Kultur des 17. und 18. Jahrhunderts in Sachsen* (Dresden: Sandstein, 2002).

Titze, Mario, *Barockskulptur im Herzogtum Sachsen-Weissenfels* (Halle an der Saale: Landesamt für Denkmalpflege und Archäologie, 2007).

Titze, Mario, 'Der Altar von Valentin Otte und die Kanzel von Abraham Conrad Buchau in der Stadtkirche Unser Lieben Frauen in Mittweida', *Sächsische Heimatblätter: Zeitschrift für sächsische Geschichte, Denkmalpflege, Natur und Umwelt*, 55 (3) (2009), 222–36.

Titze, Mario, 'Vor 325 Jahren wurde der Grundstein zur Dreifaltigkeitkiche in Carlsfeld gelegt', *Erzgebirgische Heimatblätter*, 31 (4) (2009), 11–14.

Törmer-Balogh, W., 'Zur Entwicklung des protestantischen Altars in Sachsen während des 16. und beginnenden 17. Jahrhunderts. Versuch einer Typologie der Aufbaukonzepte', in Landesamt für Denkmalpflege Sachsen (ed.), *Denkmalpflege in Sachsen 1894–1994*, vol. 2 (Halle an der Saale: Stekovics, 1998), 411–36.

Troßbach, W., 'Volkskultur und Gewissensnot. Zum Bilderstreit in der "zweiten Reformation"', *Zeitschrift für Historische Forschung*, 23 (1988), 473–500.

Ulbrich, Claudia, 'Tränenspektakel. Die Lebensgeschichte der Luise Charlotte von Schwerin (1731) zwischen Frömmigkeitspraxis und Selbstinszenierung', in Mineke

Bosch, Hanna Hacker, and Ulrike Krampl (eds), *Spektakel (L'Homme. Europäische Zeitschrift für Feministische Geschichtswissenschaft)*, 23 (1) (2012), 27–42.

Ullmann, Klemans, *Katholische Hofkirche Dresden* (Dresden: Pellmann, [1993]).

Unger, C., *Barocke Emporenmalerei in Dorfkirchen des Herzogtums Sachsen-Gotha. Bedeutung, Entstehung und Gestaltung* (Weimar: Ges. für Thüringische Kirchengeschichte, 2006).

Verhoeven, Gerrit, 'Calvinist Pilgrimages and Popish Encounters: Religious Identity and Sacred Space on the Dutch Grand Tour (1598–1685)', *Journal of Social History*, 43 (3) (2010), 615–34.

Vierhaus, Rudolf, *Germany in the Age of Absolutism*, tr. Jonathan Knudsen (Cambridge: CUP, 1988).

Volz, Hans, *Martin Luthers deutsche Bibel* (Hamburg: Wittig, 1978).

Vötsch, Jochen, *Kursachsen, das Reich und der mitteldeutsche Raum zu Beginn des 18. Jahrhunderts* (Frankfurt am Main: Lang, 2003).

Wagemann, Julius August, 'Hilscher, Paul Christian', in *Allgemeine Deutsche Biographie* (Leipzig: Duncker und Humblot), vol. 12 (1980).

Wallmann, Johannes, 'Johann Arndt und die protestantische Frömmigkeit. Zur Rezeption der mittelalterliche Mystic im Luthertum', in Dieter Bauer (ed.), *Frömmigkeit in der frühen Neuzeit. Studien zur religiösen Literatur des 17. Jahrhunderts in Deutschland (Chloe. Beihefte zum Daphnis. Band 2)* (Amsterdam: Rodopi, 1984), 50–74.

Wallmann, Johannes, 'Philipp Jakob Spener in Berlin 1691–1705', *Zeitschrift für Theologie und Kirche*, 84 (1987), 58–85. Reprinted in ibid, *Theologie und Frömmigkeit im Zeitalter des Barock. Gesammelte Aufsätze* (Tübingen: Mohr Siebeck, 1995), 295–324.

Wallmann, Johannes, *Der Pietismus* (Göttingen: Vandenhoeck & Ruprecht, 1990).

Wallmann, Johannes, 'Johann Arndt (1555–1621)', in Carter Lindberg (ed.), *The Pietist Theologians* (Malden, MA: Blackwell, 2004).

Wallmann, Johannes, *Gesammelte Aufsätze,* part 2, *Pietismus-Studien* (Tübingen: Mohr Siebeck, 2008).

Wandel, Lee Palmer, *Voracious Idols and Violent Hands: Iconoclasm in Reformation Zurich, Strasbourg, and Basel* (Cambridge: CUP, 1995).

Wandel, Lee Palmer, *Reading Catechisms, Teaching Religion* (Leiden: Brill, 2016).

Wangsgaard, Martin Jürgensen, *Ritual and Art across the Danish Reformation: Changing Interiors of Village Churches, 1450–1600* (Turnhout: Brepols, 2013).

Wartenberg, Günther, 'Bilder in den Kirchen der Wittenberger Reformation', in Johann Michael Fritz (ed.), *Die bewahrende Kraft des Luthertums. Mittelalterliche Kunstwerke in evangelischen Kirchen* (Regensburg: Schnell & Steiner, 1997), 19–33.

Warwick, Genevieve, *Bernini: Art as Theatre* (New Haven and London: Yale University Press, 2012).

Watanabe-O'Kelly, Helen, *Court Culture in Early Modern Dresden* (Basingstoke: Palgrave Macmillan, 2002).

Watson, Róisín, 'Lutheran Piety and Visual Culture in the Duchy of Württemberg, 1534 – *c.*1700' (unpublished PhD, University of St Andrews, 2015).

Wenzel, Kai, 'Die Bautzener Taucherkirche und das Görlitzer heilige Grab. Räumliche Reorganisationen zweier Orte spätmittelalterlicher Frömmigkeit im konfessionellen Zeitalter', in Evelin Wetter (ed.), *Formierung des konfessionellen Raumes in Ostmitteleuropa* (Stuttgart: Steiner, 2008), 167–92.

Wetter, Evelin, 'Der Kronstädter Paramentenschatz. Altkirchliche Messgewänder in nach-reformatorischer Nutzung', *Acta Historiae Artium*, 45 (2004), 257–315.

Wetzel, C., 'Das kirchliche Leben an der Frauenkirche zu Dresden von ihrer Weihe bis zu ihrer Zerstörung 1945. 1. Teil', *Die Dresdner Frauenkirche*, 7 (2001), 113–35.

Whaley, Joachim, *Germany and the Holy Roman Empire,* vol. 1, *Maximilian I to the Peace of Westphalia 1493–1648* (Oxford: OUP, 2012).

Whaley, Joachim, *Germany and the Holy Roman Empire,* vol. 2, *The Peace of Westphalia to the Dissolution of the Reich 1648–1806* (Oxford: OUP, 2013).

Wieland, Christian, 'Spielräume und Grenzen religiöser Selbstbestimmung der Fürstin im konfessionellen Zeitalter: Renée de France und Anna von Preußen', in Irene Dingel and Ute Lotz-Heumann (eds), *Entfaltung und zeitgenössische Wirkung der Reformation im europäischen Kontext* (Gütersloh: Gütersloher Verl.-Haus, 2015), 233–48.

Wilsdorf, Helmut, *Zur Geschichte der Erzgebirgischen Bergbrüderschaften und Bergknappschaften* (Schneeberg: Folklorezentrum Erzgebirge/Vogtland, 1986).

Wilsdorf, Helmut, *Die letzte Schicht: Bergmännische Grabgebräuche* (Schneeberg-Chemnitz: Verl. Heimatland Sachsen, 1994).

Wimböck, Gabriele, '"Durch die Augen in das Gemüt kommen": Sehen und Glauben—Grenzen und Reservate', in Gabriele Wimböck, Karin Leonhard, and Markus Friedrich (eds), *Evidentia. Reichweiten visueller Wahrnehmung in der Frühen Neuzeit* (Berlin: Lit-Verl., 2007), 427–52.

Wimböck, Gabriele, 'Wort für Wort, Punkt für Punkt. Darstellung der Kreuzigung im 16. Jahrhundert in Deutschland', in Johann Anselm Steiger and Ulrich Heinen (eds), *Golgatha in den Konfession und Medien der Frühen Neuzeit* (Berlin and New York: De Gruyter, 2010), 161–85.

Wimböck, Gabriele, Karin Leonhard, and Markus Friedrich (eds), *Evidentia. Reichweiten visueller Wahrnehmung in der Frühen Neuzeit* (Berlin: Lit-Verl., 2007).

Winzeler, Marius, 'Burgkapelle, Patronatskirche, Familiengrablege – Tradition und Wandel der Adelsfrömmigkeit und ihres künstlerischen Ausdrucks im 16. und 17. Jahrhundert. Das Beispiel der Familie von Einsiedel', in Katrin Keller and Josepf Matzerath (eds), *Geschichte des sächsischen Adels* (Cologne etc.: Böhlau, 1997), 207–24.

Winzeler, Marius (ed.), *Dresdner Totentanz. Das Relief in der Dreikönigskirche Dresden* (Halle an der Saale: Stekovics, 2001).

Winzeler, Marius and Janos Stekovics, *Burg und Kirche. Christliche Kunst in Gnandstein* (Halle an der Saale: Stekovics, 1994).

Wischhöfer, Bettina, 'Kirche als Ort von Disziplinierung und Verweigerung. Die Einführung der 'Zweiten Reformation' in Hessen-Kassel 1605', in Andrea Bendlage, Andreas Priever, and Peter Schuster (eds), *Recht und Verhalten in vormodernen Gesellschaften. Festschrift für Neithard Bulst* (Bielefeld: Verl. für Regionalgeschichte, 2008), 223–31.

Wood, Christopher, *Forgery, Replica, Fiction: Temporalities of German Renaissance Art* (Chicago: University of Chicago Press, 2008).

Wood, Christopher, 'Iconoclasm and Iconophobia', in Michael Kelly (ed.), *Encyclopedia of Aesthetics* (Oxford: OUP, 2014).

Wunder, Heide, '>Gewirkte Geschichte<: Gedenken und >Handarbeit<. Überlegungen zum Tradieren von Geschichte im Mittelalter und zu seinem Wandel am Beginn der Neuzeit' in Joachim Heinzle (ed.), *Modernes Mittelalter. Neue Bilder einer populären Epoche* (Frankfurt am Main and Leipzig: Insel-Verl., 1994), 324–54.

Wustmann, Gustav, 'Das Tagebuch einer Leipziger Bürgerfamilie aus dem 16. und 17. Jahrhundert', *Schriften des Vereins für die Geschichte Leipzigs,* 2 (1878), 62–81.

Wustmann, Gustav, *Beiträge zur Geschichte der Malerei in Leipzig vom 15. bis zum 17. Jahhundert* (Leipzig: Seemann, 1879).

Wustmann, Gustav, 'Geschichte der Heimlichen Calvinisten (Kryptocalvinisten) in Leipzig. 1574 bis 1593', *Neujahrsblätter der Bibliothek und des Archivs der Stadt Leipzig,* 1 (1905), 1–94.

Wüthrich, Lucas Heinrich, *Matthaeus Merian d. Ä. Eine Biographie* (Hamburg, 2007).

Yates, Frances, *The Art of Memory* (Chicago: University of Chicago Press, 1966).

Zaugg, Roberto, '"bey den Italiern recht sinnreiche Gedancken […] gespürt". Joseph Furttenbach als kultureller Vermittler', in Joseph Furttenbach, *Lebenslauff 1652–1664*, eds Kaspar von Greyerz, Kim Siebenhüner, and Roberto Zaugg (Cologne etc.: Böhlau, 2013), 25–43.

Zaunstöck, Holger (ed.), *Gebaute Utopien. Franckes Schulstadt in der Geschichte europäische Stadtentwürfe* (Halle an der Saale: Verlag der Franckeschen Stiftung, 2010).

Zeller, Winfried, 'Protestantische Frömmigkeit im 17. Jahrhundert', in ibid, *Theologie und Frömmigkeit. Gesammelte Aufsätze*, vol. 1, ed. Bernd Jaspert (Marburg: Elwert, 1971), 85–116.

Zerbe, Doreen, 'Memorialkunst im Wandel. Die Ausbildung eines lutherischen Typus des Grab- und Gedächtnismals im 16. Jahrhundert', in Carola Jäggi and Jörn Staecker (eds), *Archäologie der Reformation. Studien zu den Auswirkungen des Konfessionswechsels auf die materielle Kultur* (Berlin: De Gruyter, 2007), 117–63.

Zobel, Alfred, *Die Anfänge der Reformation in Görlitz und der Preußischen Oberlausitz*, 2nd ed. (Görlitz: Hoffmann und Reiber, 1925).

Zobel, Alfred, 'Beiträge zur Geschichte der Peterskirche in Görlitz in den Jahren 1498–1624', *Neues Lausitzisches Magazin*, 108 (1932), 1–86.

Zobel, Alfred, 'Beiträge zur Geschichte der Peterskirche in Görlitz in den Jahren 1498–1624', *Neues Lausitzisches Magazin*, 109 (1933), 98–141.

Zorn, Günter, *Die Schlosskirche zu Zwickau—Planitz* (Altenburg: Beier und Beran, 2003).

Index